Early Mississippi Records

Volume #3

Washington County

- 1827-1880 -

Compiled by:
Katherine Clements Branton
and Alice Clements Wade

Southern Historical Press, inc.
Greenville, South Carolina

This volume was reproduced
from a personal copy located in
the Publishers private library

Please direct all correspondence and book orders to:
SOUTHERN HISTORICAL PRESS, Inc.
1071 Park West Blvd.
Greenville, SC   29611

Originally printed Leland, MS 1984
ISBN #978-1-63914-325-2
Printed in the United States of America

TABLE OF CONTENTS
EMR
WASHINGTON COUNTY
VOL.III

MAP-Mississippi River Plantations--1860---------------ii
MAP-Washington Co.Plantations------------------------iii
MAP-Choctaw Cessions--1822-1830----------------------iv-v
Original Townships--1827-1830------------------------vi-viii
Deed Books "A" thru "T"--1828-1868-------------------1-139
"New" Greenville--1865-1866--------------------------131a-131b
      Ben Roach Addition--1866--------------------131-c
      Blantonia--1865-----------------------------131-d
Probate Court Minutes, Bk."I"--1827-1839-------------140-147
Inventory of Dr.Benj.Moyler--1831--------------------147a-147f
Packet Gleanings:156 Packets Abstracted
      1841-1896-----------------------------------148-176
Random Census-Washington Co.-1880--------------------177-181
Bibliography---182
SURNAME INDEX--183-194

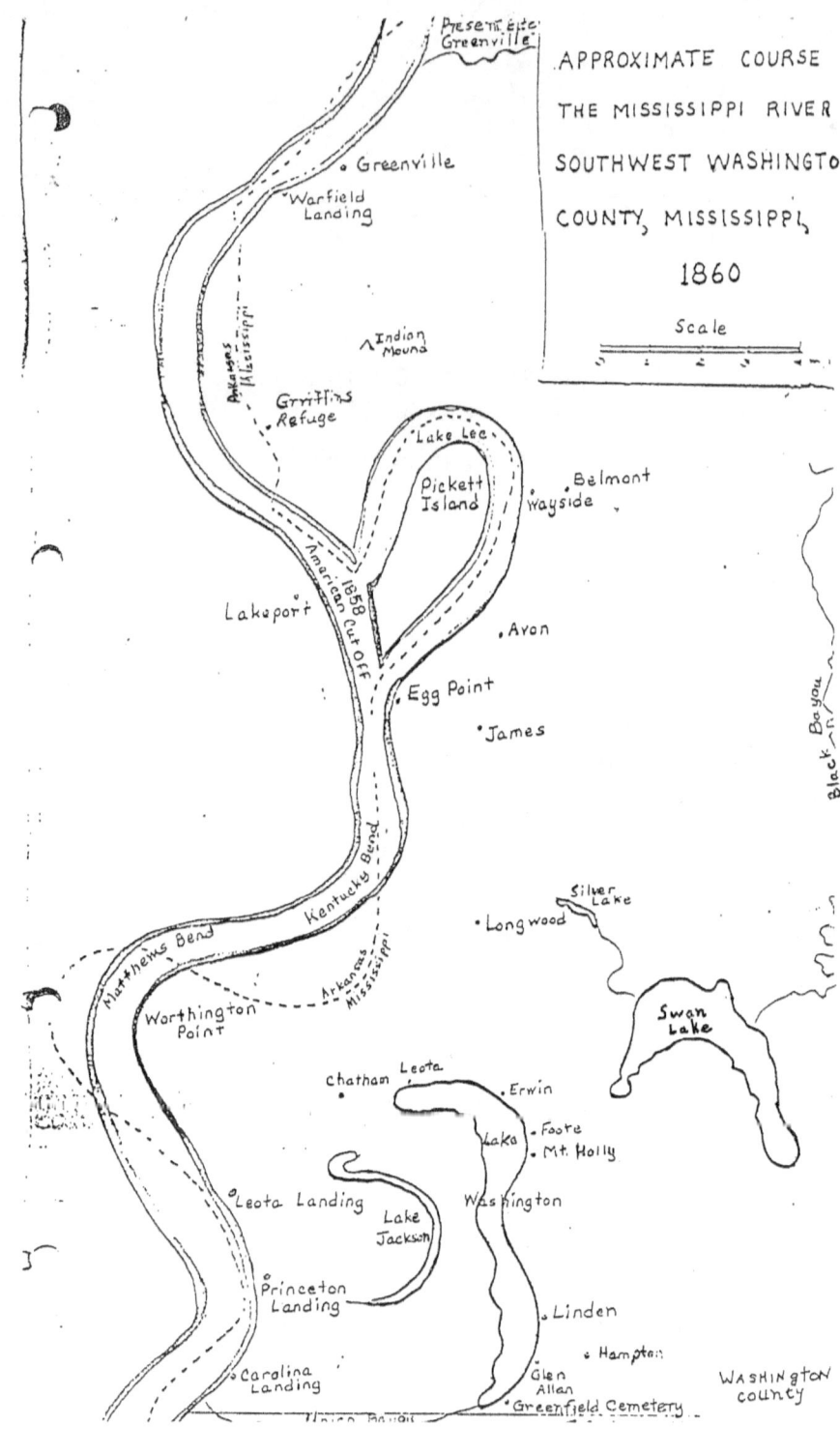

WASHINGTON COUNTY

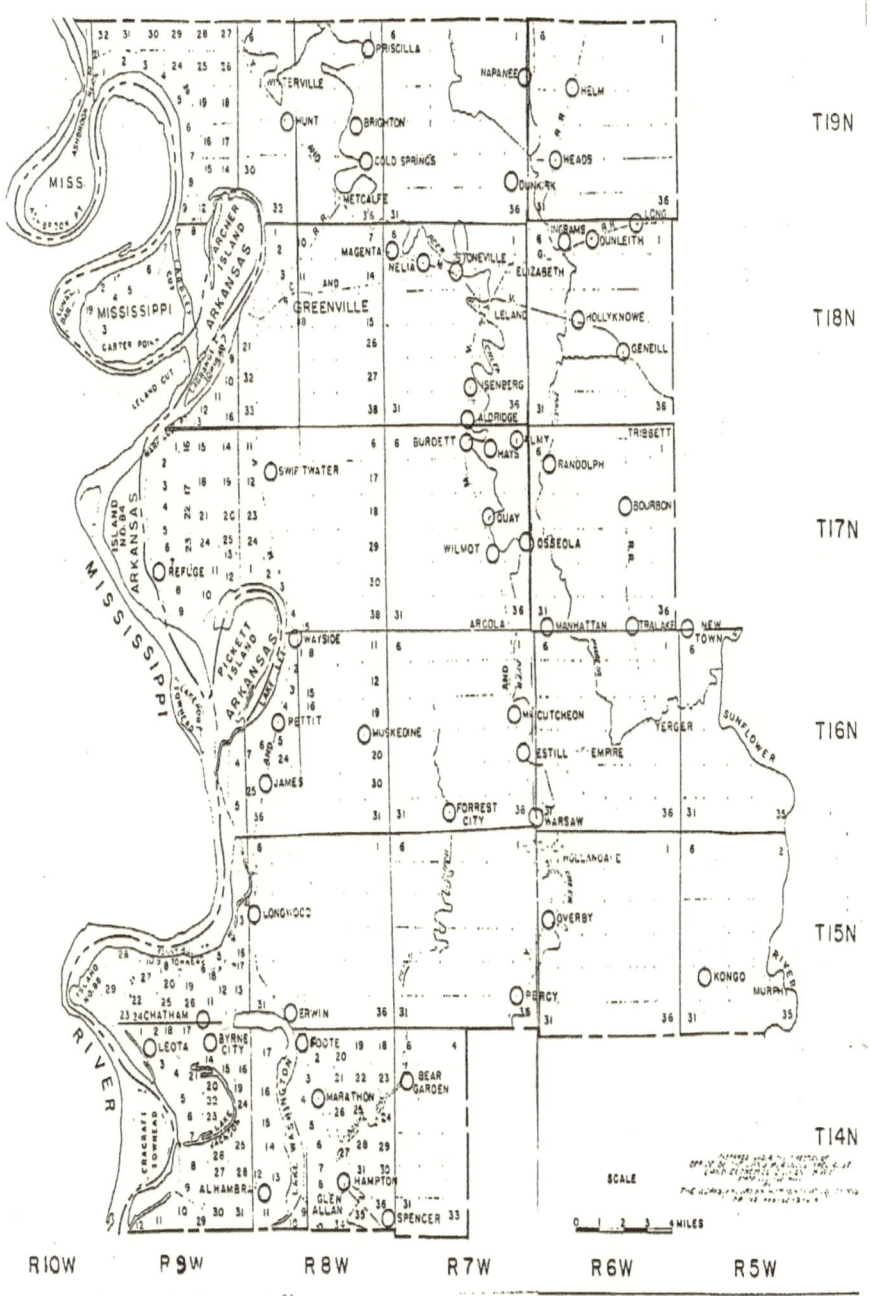

Prepared under the direction of Office of the Land Planning Specialist, Land Economics Div. B.A.E., State College, Ms.—by Works Progress Administration of Miss. O.P. 465-62-3-254

The Plats of Townships marked thus ⊞ have been recorded a second time.

The red shade marks the Townships yet to be surveyed, designated thus ▬

The green shade, marks the Townships for which there are no field notes on file, or on record, designated thus ▬

The Yellow shade, marks the Township boundaries for which there are no field notes on file, or on record, designated thus ▬

The field notes of Townships, marked thus, + have been transcribed.

The field notes of Townships marked thus, ○ have been recorded.

The Plats of Townships marked thus, ☐ have been recorded.

Surveyors office, Oct 1st 1840. } Volney E. Howard
Jackson, Mississippi.

DIAGRAM OF THE SURVEYING DISTRICT SOUTH OF TENNESSEE

WASHINGTON CO.MS.
ORIGINAL TOWNSHIP MAPS, CHOCTAW DISTRICT.

This is a large, flat volume, photo-lithograph of the Original Townships as issued in the Original Patent Offices...these were issued at Mt.Salus(Clinton,Ms.). The Surveyors were authorized by the United States Government and used the title "Surveyor of Public Lands South of Tenn."In the Choctaw District, early Patents were cleared at Washington, Ms. Later ones, at Jackson, Ms. All maps are hand drawn, some showing lakes,rivers,etc-if so, they are so noted. There were field surveyors, and a superior who examined and approved each map. T-is Township;R-Range.

T16N;R2W: Surveyed by Jas.P.Turner,and approved 24 Sept. 1828- contains BAYOU LOUCESH, YAZOO RIVER.

T16N;R2W: Surveyed by R.M.Williamson,Angus McPhail,Joshua P. McDonald--Dated 27 Aug.1834

T15N;R3W: Surveyed by A.Downing in fall of 1826-North Boundry; Seth McCleary-Dec.1827-S.Bdry;A.Easley-1827 E.Bdry.;Henry Hamblin 1827 W.Bdry. Exam.and Apprd. 18 June 1829 by Jas.P.Turner.

T15N;R-W:Seth McCleary- 1827-S.Bdry.; Rest by Archilles Easley in 1827: Ex.and app. by Jas.P.Turner 25 Sept.1828

T16N;R3W: Surveyed by Alexander Downing & Charles Brackin in Jan.& Feb.1827. Ex.& App. 17 Apr. 1827 by G.Davis. A notation of "Sky Lake".

T15N;R4W: Surveyed by H.Hamblin 1827. Ex.& App. 20 June 1842 by B.A.Ludlow.

T16N;R4W: Surveyed by Brackin & Downing 1827. Ex.& App. by James P.Turner 24 Sept.1828

T15N;R5W:Surveyed by Henry Hamblin Jan. & Feb.1827. Ex.& App. by G.Davis-8 June 1827.This Twp.contains a portion of the SUNFLOWER RIVER.

T16N;R5W:Surveyed by Brackin & Downing-winter of 1827/28, except for S.Bdry.,which was done by Henry Hamblin Jan.1827. Ex. & Appr.2 Oct.1828 by James P.Turner. Along the SUNFLOWER RIVER.

T16N;R6W: Surveyed by Alexander Downing-N.Bdry. 1828/29;Henry M.Bowling 1828 W.Bdry;A.Easley 1827-S.&.E.Bdry;Interior by H.Hamblin. Ex.& Appr.19 Oct.1831. Land along DEER CREEK. A note added,"the field notes of this Twp. were examined and approved by Joseph Dunbar,Esq.,late surveyor of U.S.Lands S.Of Tenn. as will be seen by his certificate of the 29 March 1831." Signed by Gideon Fitz.

T16N;R6W:S.&.W.Bdry. by A.Downing Dec.1828,Jan.1829. Ex.& Appr. 4 May 1829 by Turner. Along DEER CREEK & BOGUE PHALAIA.

T17N;R6W:N.&.W.&S.Bdry.by A.Downing Nov.& Dec.1828. Ex.& Appr. 4 May 1829 by Jas.P.Turner. Along the BOGUE PHALAIA.

T.16N;R8W:N.Bdry. by McCleary 1828;S.Bdry.by Bowling 1828;W. Bdry.by Henry T.Williams 1829;E.Bdry. by Hamblin Oct. & Nov. 1830. Had been approved by Dunbar, now deceased. Signed by Gideon Fitz 19 Oct.1831. Map shows MISS.RIVER with lots perpendicular to the water.

WASHINGTON CO.MS.
ORIGINAL TWPS. MAPS, CHOCTAW DISTRICT

T 17N;R9W: Surveyed by Henry T.Williams Jan.1829. Ex.& Appr.
by Turner 15 July 1829. Land on MISS. RIVER, shows ISLAND #84,
SAWGRASS LAKE, another Lake with no name. Note written across
the Island "see comm.letters Hon.W.Barksdale/June 23/56 relating
to this Island. See opposite 16 S.1W and 1E.-Ark." Same ink,
and same writing as rest of the document.

T18N;R9 & 10W:Henry Hamblin Jan.1830;Castleman-Jan.18--. Ex.&
Appr.by Jos.Dunbar 31 May 1830. MISS.RIVER-in lots-top corner
a section denoting "BEN ROACH".[According to Joe Reilly,Abst.
for the Corps of Eng., this section was a "floater", so designated as a piece of land chosen by a member of the Choctaw
Nation, unsettled, as their 1 square mile of land. Ben Roach
purchased it from the Original Patentee.]

T19N;R9W:by Henry Hamblin in Jan.1830. Ex.& Appr.by Jos.Dunbar
31 May 1830. Map shows MISS. RIVER ISLAND #82, and BLACK BAYOU.

T19N;R10W:Map shows MISS.RIVER, ISLAND #80, ISLAND #81. "Quality
of land- the whole of this fractional twp. is subject to overflow from 1-4 feet,excluding Sec.3, a part of which is good
cane land, timber principally cypress, ash, cottonwood, hack-
berry,etc." Surveyed by Stephen Castleman in Jan.1830. Ex.&
Appr. by Joseph Dunbar 31 May '30.

T18N;R8W: Map shows MISS.RIVER, ISLAND #83,and marked off in
blue ink on lower end of this twp.is "BENJ.ROACH", appr.by
A.H.McKee. Written off to one side-Ex.& Appr.by C.A.Bradford,
Survey Office,Jackson,Ms.,8 July 1848. Surveyd by Stephen Castle-
man from Dec.1830 to Jan.1831;W.Bdry. by Hamblin in Jan.1830.
On S. By McCleary. Appr.by Jos.Dunbar 15 Feb.1831,Washington,Ms.

T19N;R8W:N.S.E.Bdry. by Castleman in fall & winter 1829/30.
On W. by Hamblin Jan.1830; Interior by Griffin,winter 1832.Ex.&
Appr..by Gideon Fitz 21 Mar.1832. Map shows DEER CREEK.

T14N;R9W:S.Bdry.by James Babbett 1827:Rest by Bowling 1828
& Williams 1828/29. Ex.& Appr.by James P.Turner 17 June 1829.
Shows MISS.RIVER, LAKE JACKSON, LAKE BRITTON, LAKE WASHINGTON-
at top right, and MINORCA NUTT LAKE off ISLAND # 89.

T15N;R9W:Surveyed by Bowling fall 1828;Williams Feb.1829; Ex.&
Appr.by Turner 15 Feb.1829. Contains a plot marked "POLLY BELL
ALIAS POLLY COLLINS" which is Sec.27, marked off next to ISLAND
#88-off Island chute. Note at top of page;"Island #88 in Ms.
River Surv.by D.W.Connelly in 4th quarter 1843-under instruc-
tions from Surv.South of Tenn.at $8 per mile. Double traverse
round the Isl.amt.to 14 mi.+ 23 Jan.1844"-signed by A.Downing.

T15N;R9W:Ms.River Overflow land,good timber. By Williams in
Jan.1829;Ex.& Appr.by Turner 10 June 1829.

T18N;R6W: all surveyed by Reuben McCarty 1828. Ex.& Appr.4
May 1829 by Jas.P.Turner. Along the BOGUE PHALAIA.

T19N;R6W:Surveyed by Benjamin Griffin Nov.1830-Apr.1831;and
R.McCarty in fall 1828. Ex.& Appr.by Gideon Fitz 16 Apr.1831.
On BOGUE PHALAIA and also shows "ROAD TO LAKE BOLIVAR".

T14N;R7W:A.Easley-E.Bdry.Feb.1827;S.Bdry.by Henry Hamblin Dec.
1827;and the rest by Seth McCleary in winter of 1828/29. Ex.&

DEED BOOK "A": WASHINGTON CO.,MS.*

P.1:Deed-4 Mar.1828:ALEX.G.PRINCE,Adm of ROBERT PRINCE,decd.to WM.TERRY (THOS.W.BECK,Trustee for WM.TERRY)Wit;Alex.Montgomery, J.P.

P.3:Deed-18 Mar.1828:ABRAHAM BLUE(BLEW,BLEU)of Wash.Co. to JOHN BLUE.(Mentions cattle now in possession of Jesse Blue) Wit: Allen Wynens,Joel Morse.

P.4:POA:A.BLUE TO JOHN BLUE: Abraham Blue state that"because of advanced age"he gives POA to son John of Wash.Co.17 Mar.1828 Wit:Allen Wynens.

P.5:Deed-16 July 1828:ALEX.G.PRINCE of Wash.Co. to THOS.SHELBY of Jeff.Co.Ms.:(draft drawn on John K.Ferguson, and another made payable to John L.Irvin of Jeff.Co.Ms.) Wit:John Shelby: Peter H.Burnet, J.P.

P.7:WM.PENRICE of Chicot Co.Ark.& ALEX.G.PRINCE enter into an agreement:States that Robert Prince of Adams Co. Ms. decd.,Sept. 1827. Wm.Prenrice in the right of his wife Elizabeth A.Prince, the sister of the said Robert Prince,decd. is entitled to 1/9th of Est. of Robert Prince,decd. Dated 3June 1828:Wit:J.M.Maury

P.8:WM.BRITTON of Wash.Co. gives his POA to ALLEN WYNENS to procure 2 slaves,James & Louisa(abt.30 yrs.old & dark complected)who"eloped from me 10th of May". He thinks they may be found in Hardin Co.Tn.18 Nov.1828:Wm.B.Cook,Pres. Judge of Co.Court.

P.9:Mort.-1 Sept.1828:CHARLES McGLOTHLIN(McSTOTHLIN)* to ABRAHAM DEHART: Wit. John Morrison

P.10:Indenture:Mort:-5 Feb.1829:LOMAX BRASHER of Wash.Co.1st pt-to WM.B.COOK Trustee of Wash.Co.2nd pt. &JOS.HOUGH 3rd pt. Wit:Wm.Brittan,Seborn Brazer; F.G.Turnbull, Clerk of Court.

P.13:WM.B.KEENE(KEINE)Wash.Co.,purchased land for HARTWELL COCK of same Co. on 14 June 1828 at Public Sale(Mount Salus)#3476. Located on E.Bank of Ms.River(79ac) and now turns title over to Cock. 13 Feb.1829.N.R.Selser,J.P.

P.14:Mort.-27 Mar.1829:JAS.C.HAWLEY of Wash.Co.Ms. gives notes to RICH.BLAIR. Signed by Hugh R.Gordon, Notary Public for Parish of New Orleans,La. Hawley states that he has slaves working on his plantation in Ms. called "Washington Pltn."

P.15:Deed-28 Feb.1829:JAS.S.CLAYTON of Wash.Co.Ms.sells property he bought from Thos.H.Garner,toARTHUR DANNER & JOHN DANNER. Land is on E.Bank of Lake Bolivar & borders on Barnett Dempsey on N.& John Clark on S. Wit:Thos.C.Jones.

P.17;Bond-10 Mar.1829: Bond for Tax Assessor appointeeJOHN LOVE. Bdsmen-FREDERICK G.TURNBULL,P.A.GILBERT to GOV.GERARD BRANDON.

P.19:Mort-9 Apr.1829:NIMROD R.SELSER of Wash.Co 1st pt:JOHN D.VERTNER of Claib.Co.Ms.2nd pt. Wit:Jas.R.Boice

---

*Deed Bk."A" has been transcribed in long hand. We could not ascertain the availability of the original.

DEED BOOK "A" WASHINGTON CO. MS.

P.21:Gift-29 Apr.1829:From JOHN D.VERTNER of Claib.Co.Ms."for friendship, love,and affection"for daus. of NIMROD R.SELSER - MARY RUSK,INDIANA SELSER,RACHEL SELSER,SUSANNAH SELSER, gifts of land and slaves-Nimrod and his wife Martha are to have the use of this prop. during their lifetime and at their demise the property is to be divided equally at such time that Susannah should become of age.Wit:S.Rusk,Jas.R.Boice($10pd by S.Rusk)

P.23:Deed-17 Nov.1829:N.R.SELSER states that on 16 Sept.1828 he entered a "lot of land"at Mt.Salus for WM.B.KEENE located in Wash.Co.Ms. Selser relinq. title in favor of Keene.("lot of land"denoting around 80-90 ac,& land sold in"lots".)

P.24:Indenture:5 Apr.1829:Gift:JOSEPH LAIRD*of Wash.Co. 1st pt.:R.H.HOLMES of Jeff.Co.Ms.the other part. For love and affection Jos.Laird bears his wife MARY T.LAIRD,gives a negro woman and child to Holmes to hold in trust for the welfare of his wife Mary T.

P.26:Deed-10 Dec.1829:HENRY W.VICK of Yazoo Co.Ms.toSAML.WORTH-INGTON of Wash.Co.(land on the river)Wit:J.LANE CALDWELL,JNO.A QUITMAN,Chancellor of State of Ms.

P.27:Release-3 Feb.1830:City of New Orleans Notary P.,J.R.KRIN-GER states that THOS.BARRETT acting for the firm of John Hagen & Co. of N.O.,granted a release to JAS.C.HAWLEY of Mort.as pd.

P.28:Deed-26 Mar.1830:FREDERICK G.TURNBULL of Wash.Co.Ms. 1st pt:Wm.R.CAMPBELL OF Warren Co.Ms.2nd pt:JAS.M.REYNOLDS,JOHN B.BYME,Wm.FERRIDAY-trading under the names"Reynolds Ferriday & Co" in Natchez and"Reynolds Byme"in N.O. for 3rd pt.(Mort. pd in full 17 Mar.1838) Wit:Mark Leod(?),Rich.Nugent.

P.32:Mort.:4 May 1830:WM.PENRICE of Wash.Co.Ms. 1st pt:PHILIP A.GILBERT & FRANCIS PENRICE of same,2nd pt:HARBIRD HOOD of Ouachita P.La.3rd pt. Wit:Andrew Knox,Wm.Brittain,Jno.Thornbury

P.34:Mort.-20 May 1830:JOEL MORSE & SAML.ODLE of Wash.Co.Ms. 1st pt;F.G.TURNBULL 2nd pt;ALLEN WYNENS 3rd pt.

P.37:POA-3 May 1830:SALLY S. PRINCE of Wash.Co.Ms. gives her POA to ALFRED COX of same, to attend to matters of EST.OF W.B. PRINCE,decd.

P.37:POA-3 May 1830:CATHARINE L.PRINCE of Wash.Co. to ALFRED COX of same in matters of Est.ofBayless Prince.Wit:Wm.H.Collins

P.38:Mort:27 May 1830:PHILIP A.GILBERT 1st pt;Wm.BLANKS 2nd pt:both of Wash.Co.Ms.Wit:Wm.W.Collins, Thos.Stephens.

P.40:Deed-26 June 1830:WM.RUSSELL of Wash.Co. sells to WM.W. BLANTON of same. Delivered to Blanton 19 Oct.1830. Wit:A.W.Mc-allister,Chas.Thomas. Peter Wilkerson Clk. of Court.

P.41:Deed-3 Jan.1831:JOHN R.LUCAS 1st pt:MILES FLEETWOOD 2nd pt:BENJ.RUSK WALLACE 3rd pt.Lucas sells slaves & land to Fleetwood & Wallace,some lots had been purchased by Bernard Dempsey &Obedience Bankston,J.Brown & Benj.Moore. Wit:Edward Matthews, Natl.H.Pegram, both of Hds.Co. & Jas.Cobb.

---

*Marr.Rec.Jeff.Co.Ms.Bk."B":Jos.Laird to Mary Walton 17 Aug.1827

DEED BOOK "A" WASHINGTON CO. MS.

P.47:Bond-20 Jan.1831:WM.J.PENRICE,FRANCIS PENRICE,WM.PENRICE post bd. to GOV.GERARD C.BRANDON($5,000) Wm.J.Penrice appointed County Clerk.

P.48:Mort.-27 Nov.1830:JOHN G.COCKS 1st pt;A.FISK & CO.of N.O. La. 2nd pt;Wit:F.P.Smith,Wm.W.Collins. Pd.1831.

P.50:Mort.-1 Jan.1831:ISAAC WORTHINGTON & MARGARET his wife of Wash.Co.Ms. 1st pt;THOS.G.PERCY of Ala.other pt.(land between Lake Wash. and Ms.River)

P.51:Deed-18 Jan.1831:BENJ.MOORE sells JACOB YOIST 10 negroes. Wit;Miles Fleetwood, Wm.C.Cross.

P.52:Mort.25 Jan.1831:SAML.WORTHINGTON of Wash.Co.1st pt;THOS. G.PERCY of Ala. other pt. (Orig.Pat.)

P.53:Mort.25 Jan.1831:ISAAC WORTHINGTON & wife MARGARET to THOS.G.PERCY.

P.56:Deed-21 Jan.1831:SAML.WORTHINGTON of 1st pt;THOS.G.PERCY & JAMES BROWN,Trustees under the Will of SAML.BROWN,decd. of other pt. Percy acting on behalf of SUSAN C.BROWN &JAMES BROWN who hold an"undivided 3rd part".[Saml.Brown m.Catherine Percy-Adams Co.9/27/1808]

P.58:Deed-21 Jan.1831:ISAAC WORTHINGTON & wife MARG. 1st pt.; & JAMES BROWN & THOS.G.PERCY under the Will of Saml.Brown,decd. for benefit of Susan C.Brown,Jas.Brown, heirs of Saml.Brown.

P.60:Mort. 1Jan.1831:SAML.WORTHINGTON to THOS.G.PERCY.

P.62:Bond-9 Dec.1830:EZEKIEL HYDE,SR. of Wash.Co.Ms.bound to Wm.P.Montgomery of same for $1500.Wit;Alfred Cox.Robt.Cocks.

P.63:Mort.9 Dec.1830:EZEKIEL HYDE,SR. & THOS.MORRIS HYDE of Wash.Co.Ms.1st pt;WM.P.MONTGOMERY 2nd pt.

P.67:POA-23 May 1830:J.H.BOWLING gives POA to ALFRED COX,Esq. both of Wash.Co.,to handle all of his business. Wit:A.G.Creath

P.67:Deed-22 July 1830:SAML.McJENKIN sells to Wm.B.COOK(land on Wms.Bayou) Wit: Wm.Brittain.

P.68:Deed-20 July 1830:JOHN MAY of Wash.Co. sells to AUGUSTUS W.McALLISTER.(Orig.Patent)

P.69:Deed-28 Oct.1830:EDMUND P.BASS of Wash.Co. to JOHN FOSTER of Jeff.Co.Ms. Wit:John Briscoe,Jr.,B.H.Maylee, John G.Cocks.

P.71; Agreement*:8 Dec.1830:WM.HUNT,1st pt;THOS.LACY of other pt. Wit:C.Gibson,Thos.Ward,Theodorick M.Dabney,W.W.Blanton.

P.72:Deed-2 Feb.1831:GEORGE SHANKS & ELIZABETH his wife of Wash.Co.Ms. 1st pt;JOHN G.COCKS 2nd pt. Wit:S.E.Jones

*A HISTORY OF MS.by Mc Lemore:p.274:"Since 1807, it had been illegal to settle on public lands before it opened for sale. There was an effort to make it possible for these settlers to buy land on which they had squatted at the minimum price without competitive bidding". Miles, Jacksonian Democ.

DEED BOOK "A" WASHINGTON CO. MS.

P.74:EST. OF JOS.LAIRD:2 Nov.1830:Wm.Carnes, legal representative of Mary Laird,admx. of Jos.Laird,decd.,appoints Wm.W.Worthington lawful Atty. Mary Laird is now Mary Carnes. Wit;Jno. G.Cocks.

P.75:Deed of Trust-12 Jan.1831:Smith Minton of Wash.Co.Ms. 1st pt;WM.W.MCKEE of same, the other part;Minton sells tract of land to McKee to be kept in trust for use of Bennett M.Hines of Warren Co.Ms.Wit:Benj.E.Phillips,J.E.Aullson.

P.76:Deed-24 June 1830:CHARLES LILES sells"land I now live on" to WM.RIFE.He received a note from Wm.W.Blanton(Orig.Pat)¶Wit; Wm.W.Blanton

P.78:Deed-16 Feb.1831:WM.A.DROMGOOLE & F.G.TURNBULL of Wash.Co. 1st pt;A.F.SHEPARD & SIDNEY BURBRIDGE of same, other part.

P.79:Article of Agreement*-¶11 Feb.1831:WM.HUNT loaned money to WM.FRAZER to buy lot, then buys it from him

P.80:Deed-14 Feb.1831:ENOCH ROSE of Wash.Co.Ms. unto THOS.B. WARFIELD & NICHOLAS W.FORD of Vicksburg,Ms. Wit;C.Gibson, Jonathan Ballard.

P.82:Art.of Agreement*¶-11Feb.1831:WM.HUNT & ARCHIBALD HESTER (ORIG.PAT) Wit:C.Gibson, W.P.Montgomery, Signed by A.H.Estes.

P.83:Art. of Agree.*¶-19 Jan.1831:PETER W.WILLIAMS of Wash.Co. Ms. and CLAUDIUS GIBSON of same.(Orig. Pat.)

P.85:Art.of Agree.*¶;JOS.STRINGER of Wash.Co.Ms. applies for Patent on land on which he now dwells, if granted he will turn over the land to CLAUDIUS GIBSON.

P.86:Art. of Agree.-14 Feb.1831:WM.TAYLOR of Wash.Co. and HOWEL HINDS of Jeff.Co.Ms. Wit:W.P.Montgomery, Henry Murphy.

P.88:Mort.-3 Feb.1831:JOHN G.COCK of Wash.Co. 1st pt; CHARLES R.CAMPBELL, Trustee of 2nd pt;JAS.STEWART of Yazoo Co. 3rd pt.

P.90:Deed-Dec.1820:EDMUND P.BASS sells to THOS.TUNSTALL both of Wash.Co.Ms.

P.92:Deed-14 Feb.1831:PETER WILKERSON of Wash.Co. sells to THOS. B.WARFIELD & NICHOLAS W.FORD of V'burg.Wit:C.Gibson,Jona.Ballard

P.93:Deed-27 Dec.1830:JOHN MCJENKIN of Wash.Co. sells to WM.B. COOK,"place I now live on".Wit:Wm.Williams, Saml.McGunkin(?)

P.94:Deed-27 Dec.1830:JACOB TALLEY sells Orig.Pat. to WM.B.COOK land below Wm. Bayou. Wit:Jos.McGuire,James H. Fisk.

P.95:Deed-24 Dec.1830:SAML.MCGUNKIN(?) of Wash.Co. sells to WM.B.COOK.

P.96:Deed-18 Dec.1830:JOCOB B.RICE OF Wash.Co. sells to WM.B. COOK. Wit: Wm.Williams, S. Castleman.

---

*See Footnote bottom page 3.
¶A HISTORY OF MS.by Mc.Lemore:p.289:"These(Original Patent) lands were sold under the provisions of the Act of 1820-cash, $1.25 per acre, 80 acre minimum. Money was scarce, but credit was easy to obtain under Jackson's changed banking policy".

DEED BOOK "A" WASHINGTON CO. MS.

P.97:Deed-18 Mar.1831:HUGH McDANIEL sells to WM.B.COOK & JOS. HOUGH.

P.98:Deed-18 Mar.1831:BENJ.MOORE to WM.B.COOK.

P.98:Deed-2Mar.1831:THOS.WARD splits an Orig.Pat.with CLAUDIUS GIBSON.

P.100:Relinquishment-8 May 1828:A.G.PRINCE of Wash.Co.Ms. relinq. right to cattle sold as property of J.J.Pfully(?),conveying it to Saml.Odle.

P.100:Deed-2 Apr.1831:WALTER TRIMBLE to EDM.P.BASS all of Wash. Co.Ms.

P. 102:Deed-8 Dec.1830:WM.TUNSTALL1st pt:ANDREW KNOX 2nd pt. Wit:Francis Penrice,John Snow,Paul Ginet.

P.103:Deed-19 Feb.1831:ELIHU KILPATRICK to ISAAC WORTHINGTON. Wit:C.R.Campbell,Wm.J.Penrice.

P.104:Deed-11 Mar.1831:ANDREW KNOX of Wash.Co. to ROBT.H.BUCKNER of Adams Co. & Jas.M.Reynolds,John Bymes,Wm.Ferriday.

P.108:Art.of Agree:-15 Feb,1831:MARY STEPHENSON of Wash.Co. toW.W.BLANTON of same:Wit:Hiram D.Miller,Wm.Miller.(Land she had been living on, Orig.Pat.)

P.109:Art.of Agree.-15 May 1831:HIRAM D.MILLER & WM.W.BLANTON OF Wash.Co. Wit:Wm.Miller,John Stephenson.

P.111:Art.of Agree.:15 Feb.1831:WM.MILLER & WM.W.BLANTON.

P.114:Bond-16 Feb.1831:WmSTEPHENSON bound to MILES FLEETWOOD. Wit:Wm.W.Blanton,W.R.Campbell.

P.116:Art.of Agree.-15 Feb.1831:BENJ.JACKSON of Wash.Co. to WM. MILLER.

P.117:Bond-4 May 1831:WM.RUSSELL to HARBIRD HOOD.

P.119:Bond-20 May 1831:Orig.Pat. WM.RIFE of Wash.Co. to JOHN F.ANDERSON of same. Wit:Wm.W.Blanton,F.Marshall.

P.120:Bond-30 Apr.1831:MARTHA RANDAL & SAML.KENNAN of Wash. Co. to AUGUSTUS McALLISTER of same. Wit:Wm.P.Montgomery,Wm.W. Blanton.

P.122:Art. of Agree.-15 Feb.1831:ZACHARIAH JONES of Wash.Co. 1st pt:WM.W.BLANTON of same, 2nd pt. Wit:Hiram Miller,Larkin Bacon

P.124:Art.of Agree.-15 Feb.1831:LARKIN BACON of Wash.Co. 1st pt:WM.W.BLANTON 2nd pt: B.JONES & HIRAM MILLER 3rd pt.

P.126:Deed-14 May 1831:ISAAC WORTHINGTON & WM.W.WORTHINGTON of Wash.Co. to SAML.WORTHINGTON of same.

P.127:POA:9 Apr.1831:SARAH ROYSE & CHAS. ANDERSON & POLLY his wife;JOHN RAYBOURN & NANCY his wife;ANNA BENNETT-all of Madison Co.Ky. give their POA to Wm.Purcell of Daviess Co.Ky.,to act in their behalf in matter of Est.of Peter H.Bennett,decd. late of the State of Ms. Sarah,Polly,Nancy,Anna being sisters and heirs of said Peter Bennett,decd.

DEED BOOK "A" WASHINGTON CO.MS.

P.128:Deed-25 May 1831:HENRY HUGHS,SR. & HENRY HUGHS,JR. of Copiah Co.Ms. who have preemptive rights *(Squatters) borrow money from JOS.HOUGH,WM.B.COOK,WM.R.CAMPBELL to buy Orig.Pat. Wit:James C.Dickson, E.P.Bass.

P.133:Deed-27 May 1831:JOHN CAMMING & TOBIAS CAMMING of Warren Co. were too destitute to buy Orig.Pat., and were advanced the money by JOS.HOUGH,WM.B.COOK,WM.R.CAMPBELL (Preemptive rights)* They then conveyed the O.P. to Hough,Cook,Campbell.

P.138:Preemptive Rts*-7 June 1831:JOHN DIVINE & WASHINGTON S. DIVINE of Yazoo Co. Borrow from Hough,Cook,Reynolds.Wit: E.P. Bass, Will T.Robertson.

P.148:Lease:28 May 1831:WM.DUNN & BARTHOLOMEW DUNN of Yazoo Co.Ms. 1st pt:THOS.LAND 2nd pt.-who then transfers the lease to THOS.A.ARNOLD & WM.M.PINCARD of Warren Co. on 30 May 1831. Wit:Wm.R.Campbell,Wm.B.Cook.

P.151:Preemptive Rts.28 May 1831:PETER R.CABANISS & ELISHA MAYFIELD of Yazoo Co. 1st pt:THOS.LAND 2nd pt.,who again transfers 99yr.lease to Pincard & Arnold of Warren Co.Ms.

P.154:Preemptive Rts.30 May 1831:WM.DUNN & B.DUNN to THOS.LAND.

P.157:Mort.-11 June 1831:THOS.JAMES of Wash.Co. 1st pt:WM.J. PENRICE,Trustee of same Co. 2nd pt;CHAS R.CAMPBELL,same Co.3rd.

P.160:Lease-28 May 1831:RICH.TIDWELL & WM.TIDWELL of Yazoo Co. 1st pt:THOS LAND 2nd pt.

P.166:Preemptive Rts.28 May 1831:PETER CABANISS & ELISHA MAYFIELD of yazoo Co. to THOS.LAND.

P.168:Deed-17 May 1831:SAML.WORTHINGTON of Wash.Co. 1st pt. buys from ISAAC WORTHINGTON of same.

P.169:Deed-6 June 1831:STEPHEN DUNCAN of Adams Co.Ms. sells to ELIJAH ATCHISON.

P.170:Deed-6 June 1831:ROBT.M.CULLOUGH of Adams Co.Ms. sells to ELIJAH T.ATCHISON.

P.171:Rental Contract-May 1831:GEORGE BEAL 1st pt:WM.W.BLANTON 2nd pt.all of Wash. Co. Wit:Wm.Rife.

P.173:Deed-4 Apr.1831:WM.FOSTER$ late of the Choctaw Nation of Indians 1st pt; sells to JOS.MCGUIRE of Wash.Co.land on bank of Ms. River below the mouth of the Ark.River. Wit:Jos.Stockton, Joel Huntington.

P.174:Bond-4 Mar.1831:SARAH MCCAMMAN of Wash.Co. bound to WM.W. BLANTON of same & WM.R.CAMPBELL of V'burg.Wit:A.B.Montgomery, R.A.Langley.

---

*Preemptive Rights gave the occupant of land the right to buy said land at a fixed price, unoccupied land was put up for auction.Minimum amt.of land-80ac.,$1.25 per.Act.Cong.29May 1830. Speculators advanced cash to purchase"lots",later owning by default,or by transference of title.
$HOMETOWN MISS.by Brieger:P.49:WM.FOSTER,HUGH FOSTER & JAMES FOSTER were half-breed Choctaws. Their father was Moses Foster, white, & their mother a Choctaw. They came originally from Claib.Co.Ms. & settled on Indian Point.

DEED BOOK "A" WASHINGTON CO. MS.

P.176:Bond-7 May 1831:GEORGE BEAL unto WM.W.BLANTON.Wit:Wm.Rife

P.178:Bond-7 June 1831:RUEBEN MARSHALL unto WM.W.BLANTON

P.179:Bond-16 June 1831:JOSLIN MILLER,Wash.Co. unto WM.W.BLANTON Wit:Zachariah Jones,Robt.A.Langley

P.181:Bond-30 May 1831:BENJ.JACKSON of Wash.Co. unto WM.W.BLANTON Wit:Wm.Rife,Hiram D.Miller.

P.182:Lease-7 June 1831:GEO.MARSHALL,SR.1st pt;WM.W.BLANTON 2nd pt;both of Wash. Co. Wit:Wm.Rife.

P.184:Lease-May 1831:RUEBEN MARSHALL 1st pt;WM.W.BLANTON 2nd Wit:Wm.Rife.

P.186:Bond-7 June 1831:GEO.MARSHALL,SR. Wash.Co.unto WM.W.BLANTON

P.188:Lease(until Jan.1840)17 May 1831:THOS.WARD,natural guardian and father to JEREMIAH S.WARD unto WM.HUNT all of Wash.Co.Ms.

P.189:Agreement-10 May 1831:WM.HUNT buys from Wm.Johnson who had Preemptive Rts. Wit:C.Gibson

P.191:Bond-30 Apr.1831:THOS.ROSS & HUGH ROSS of Rankin Co.Ms. unto WM.HUNT.Wit: Wm.W.Blanton,W.Montgomery.

P.193:Bond-30 Apr.1831:MICHAEL Wolforth of Hds.Co. to WM.HUNT of Wash.Co.Wit:Wm.W.Blanton,Wm.Rife,W.P.Montgomery.

P.195:Bond-16 May 1831:JOHN PERVIS of Wash.Co. unto CLAUDIUS GIBSON of same.Wit:WM.Hunt,Edw.W.Ross

P.196:Bond-30 Apr.1831:FREEMAN LACEY & CHAS.C.SMITH of Rankin Co.Ms. to HOWELL HINDS & WM.P.MONTGOMERY of Wash.Co. Wit;WM. Hunt, A.W.McAllister,W.W.Blanton.

P.198:Bond-30 Apr.1831:DAVID ROSS & ALVIN TAYLOR of Rankin Co. to HOWELL HINDS of Jeff.Co. Wit:W.P.Montgomery,A.W.McAllister.

P.200:Conveyance-May 1831:CHAS.WELCH(WELSH)of Wash.Co. to THOS. B.WARFIELD.Wit:W.T.Bodley,Jefferson Wilkerson.

P.201:Bond-May 1831:ENOCH ROSE to THOS.B.WARFIELD:Enoch names his children-Rebecca Rose, Elizabeth Rose,John Rose,(name also spelled Ross in this same document)

P.202:Bond-30 Apr.1831:DAVID ROSS & ALVIN TAYLOR of Rankin Co. to WM.P.MONTGOMERY.

P.204:Bond-7June 1831:EPHRAIM G.LUNCY(LUNEY) Wash.Co. unto Wm.P.Montgomery

P.206:Lease-7 June 1831:EZEKIEL HYDE,SR.father & natural Guardian of ANDREW JACKSON HYDE of Wash.Co., 1st pt.:WM.P.MONTGOMERY 2nd pt. Wit:Thos.M.Hyde,Andrew Jackson Hyde.

P.208:Petition for Partition-16 June 1831:SAML.KINNAN 1st pt: MARTHA RANDALL other part,both of Wash.Co. They hold land in common,and agree to divide it.

P.211:Petition for Partition-3 June 1831:HIRAM D.MILLER 1st pt;WM.STEPHENSON other pt.,Wash.Co.Hold land in common and want division. Wit:W.W.Blanton, WM.Miller.

P.214:Bond-7 June 1831:RUEBEN MARSHALL unto GEO.BEAL.

DEED BOOK "A" WASHINGTON CO. MS.

P.215:Bond-16 May 1831:THOS.M.HYDE & EZEKEIL HYDE of Wash.Co. unto JOS. H.NEWMAN of Claiborne Co. Ms.

P.219:Deed-28 July 1831:JOHN E.FERGUESON,owner of Preemptive rt. land borrowed from Thos.Y.Chaney of Wash.Co.,John sells out to Chaney.

P.221:Bond-5 Aug.1831:WM.W.COLLINS, WM.A.DROMGOOLE & F.G.TURNBULL under bond to GOV.GERARD C.BRANDON,for Wm.W.Collins to become Sheriff(he had been elected,but the bond allowed him to collect fines).

P.222:Relinquishment-10 Aug.1831:THOS.TUNSTALL to ROBT.COCKS, (former partners in trade) Tunstall sells out.

P.223:Bond-9 Aug.1831:JOHN M.MERIWETHER,THOS.JAMES,WM.TERHUIME, SEBORN BRASHER all of Wash.Co. under bond to GOV.GERARD C.BRANDON($2000).Meriwether has been appointed Coroner.

P.225:Deed-24 Aug.1831:JOS.COULTER of Wash.Co.Ms. to JOSEPH EGG.

P.226:Lease-22 June 1831:REASON HARBIN of 1st pt:WM.WILLIAMS of 2nd pt; both of Wash.Co. Wit:Wm.C.Cook, Thos.Dark.

P.229:Agreement-23 May 1831:EDWARD SELLERS of the 1st pt;JOS. EGG,2nd pt; Edward Sellers binds his son David Sellers unto Jos.Egg until he is 21 yrs.old, being now in his 13th yr.Egg agrees to give him 9 mos.schooling a yr, and at the end of his "bondedness"give David a horse,saddle,bridle,two suits of"comfortable clothes".Wit:E.Block,Sr.,Wm.Block.

P.230:Bond-25 May 1831:JABEZ BOWMAN of Wash.Co. to HARBIRD HOOD of Ouachita P.,La. Wit:Washinton Ford, Jas.B.Rusk.

P.232:Deed-24 Aug.1831:OWEN HILL of Wash.Co. to Wm.W.Worthington & Elisha Worthington.

P.233:Deed 23 Aug.1831:PARLEY HILL & CALEB HILL to WM.W. & ELISHA WORTHINGTON.

P.235:Deed 13 Sept.1831:ANDREW KNOX & MYRA JANE his wife of Wash.Co.,1st pt;GIDEON FITZ of Hinds, 2ndpt.

P.237:4 Dec.1831:Receivers Office, Mt.Salus,Ms.:Received from BENJ.F.WEST of Jeff.Co.Ms.,$750.80 for lots.Signed by H.G. RUNNELS.West drew a loan from Alvarez Fisk of New Orleans, 11June 1831. Original Patent #5662

P.P.239:10 Jan.1831:ANDREW G.HOLLAND of the 1st pt;JAS.COBB of the other pt.,both of Hinds Co.Ms. Cobb assumes responsibility for a note to John Elliott.

P.240:17 May 1831:CHAS.WELLS, WM.POOL of Rankin Co.Ms., sign over preemptive rights to Jas.C.Dickson.

P.243:17 May 1831:Same ones as on p.240

P.247:16 May 1831:EDMUND HESTER, THOS.OUSLEY of Hds.Co. have preemptive rts.,and borrow from JAS.C.DICKSON.(also on p.249)

P.253:17 May 1831:JAMES McDANIEL, Wm.McDANIEL of Hds.Co. preemptive rts.,borrow from JAS.C.DICKSON.(also P.256)

DEED BOOK "A" WASHINGTON CO. MS.

P.259:Deed-20 Sept.1831:Frederick G.Turnbull to JOS.EGG,both of Wash.Co.

P.261:Deed-11 Oct.1831:JOHN G.COCKS of Wash.Co. to WM.P.WALKER of same(land in Princeton, bounded by lot of Robt.P.Shelby)

P.262:11 Oct.1831-Schedule for payment of notes:WM.P.WALKER of Wash.Co. 1st pt;WM.W.COLLINS,Trustee of 2nd pt;JOHN G.COCKS 3rd.pt.

P.265:Deed-16 June 1831:A.G.HOLLAND of Hds.Co. to JAS.C.DICKSON. Wit:Daniel Fore, Milton Alexander.

P.268:Deed-22 Oct.1831:WM.FRAZIER of Wash.Co. to WM.HUNT.

P.269:Lease-20 Sept 1831:HENRY COFFETT, SARAH COFFETT formerly Sarah McCanawan(sp?) of 1st pt;WM.W.BLANTON & WM.R.CAMPBELL other pt. Wit:Robt.A.Langely,Saml.Carson. *

P.272:.18 July 1831:JOHN W.JENKINS,SR.,SAML.W.JENKINS of Wash.Co.hold preemptive rts.,and borrow from W.B.COOK.Wit;Wm.Williams,John McGunkin,Jr.(sp.?)

P.274:18 June 1831:JACOB B.RICE,Wash.Co. preemptive rts., borrows from WM.B.COOK. Lease on P.281

P.276:Deed-20 July 1831:WM.B.COOK 1st pt;JOHN W.JENKINS & SAML. W.JENKINS other pt. P.278-same.

P.283:29 May 1830:JOHN McJUNKIN,Jr.*from WM.B.COOK(preem.rts.)

P.285:Mort.24 Nov.1831:JOHN G.COCKS, JOHN WATT,Trustee for City of Natchez, and ALVAREZ FISK of New Orleans. P.289-same

P.292:Deed-19 Oct.1831:JOHN DODD & BENAJAH DODD of Hds.Co. 1st pt;JOHN L.MARTIN & JOHN F.ANDERSON of KY. other pt.

P.297:Bond-16 Mar.1831:BENJAMIN R.BOOKOUT of Wash.Co. to REDDING B.HERRING of same.

P.298:Mort.-Nov.1831;LOMAX BRASHER of Wash.Co.1st part;WM.J. PENRICE,Trustee of Wash.Co. 2nd pt;CHAS.R.CAMPBELL of Wash. 3rd pt.

P.301:Deed-21 Dec.1831:HENRY JOHNSON of Ky.& JUNIUS WARD of same.Wit:John C.Miller.

P.302:Deed-17Dec.1831:JOHN C.MILLER to JUNIUS R.WARD.

P.303:Deed-17 Dec.1831:JOHN C.MILLER toJUNIUS WARD. Wit:Henry Johnson,Jas.Miller.

P.304:Deed 7 Jan.1831:THOS.TUNSTALL of Wash.Co. to WM.PENRICE & FRANCIS PENRICE of same.

P.306:Deed-10 Jan.1832:WM.A.DROMGOOLE of Wash.Co. 1st pt;THOS. JAMES of same, other part.

P.308:Deed-15 Dec.1829:E.P.BASS toJOS.WALLACE.

P.309:Mortg.20 Nov.1831:FRANCIS GRIFFIN of Wash.Co.to BERNARD & McNUTT of Natchez.

---

*DBK."A"has been transcribed,& these abstracts were taken from that transcription.The name spelling is very questionable.

DEED BOOK "A" WASHINGTON CO. MS.

P.311:Deed-19 Jan.1832:JOEL HIGGINS of Wash.Co. to JOHN C.MILLER

P.312:Deed-23 Jan.1832:JEFFERSON WILKERSON of Wash.Co. to ELISHA WARFIELD & THOS.B.WARFIELD of Fayette Co. Ky.

P.314:Deed-20 Dec.1831:BENJ.F.WEST & PAULINA M.WEST,his wife of 1st part;H.R.MOSS & A.F.McMURTRY of other.

P.318:Deed-9 Jan.1832:WM.A.DROMGOOLE,Adm.of PHILLIP A. GILBERT decd. of Wash.Co., of the 1st part;ALLEN WYNENS of same, the other part. Wit:THOS.STEPHENS,C.R.BASS.

P.323:Deed-23 Dec.1831:ALFRED COX,Wash.Co;to WALTER C. LOFTON & wife MARGARET of same.

P.326:Deed-16 Jan.1832:THOS.CLARY of Wash.Co.; to JOS.PURVIS of same.

P.327:Jan.1832:F.G.TURNBULL turns over a note signed with N.R. SELSER to JOS.H.NEWMAN.

P.329:Deed-31 Jan.1832:THOS.WARD & ELVIRA,his wife of Wash.Co. to CLAUDIUS GIBSON, of same.

P.330:Deed-5 Jan.1832:ENOCH ROSE*& MARY ROSE,his wife of Wash. Co. to ELISHA WARFIELD, THOS.B.WARFIELD of Fayette Co. Ky.

P.333:Deed-17 Feb.1831:REBECCA ROSE, ELIZABETH ROSE of the 1st pt;ELISHA WARFIELD, THOS.B.WARFIELD of Fayette Co.Ky.other pt.

P.335:Deed-16 Jan.1832:PETER WILKERSON &wife REBECCA,of Wash. Co.;to ELIZHA & THOS B.WARFIELD.

P.337:Deed-16 Jan.1832:JOS.PURVIS & LATTICE(sp?)his wife of Wash.Co;to ELISHA & THOS.B.WARFIELD.

P.339:Deed-2 Jan.1832:THOS.CLARY of Wash.Co. of 1st pt;ELISHA & THOS.B.WARFIELD of other.

P.340:Deed-19 Jan.1832:CHAS.WELSH(WELCH) of Wash.Co. to ELISHA & THOS.B.WARFIELD.

P.342:Deed-16 Feb.1832:JOS.STRINGER & wife DRUCILLA of Wash. Co;to CLAUDIUS GIBSON.

P.344:Deed-13 Feb.1832:JOHN ROSE of Wash.Co. to ELISHA & THOS.B.WARFIELD of Ky.

P.345:Deed-30 Jan.1832:JOHN PURVIS & wife ELIZABETH of Wash. Co. to C.GIBSON.

P.349:Deed-9 Jan.1832:WM.A.DROMGOOLE,Adm.of Est. of PHILLIP A.GILBERT,decd.of Wash.Co. to ORREN(ORIN)JONES of same.

P.351:Deed-16 Feb.1832:SIDNEY BURBRIDGE to JOHN A.BARNES.

P.353:Relinq.of Dower-15 Feb.1832:SUSAN BURBRIDGE,wife of SIDNEY BURBRIDGE,relinzuishes her claim to dower in the Deed above(P.351--Burbridge to Barnes)

---

*MS.COURT REC.by King:Adams Co. Ms.Adms.Co.Will Bk.
WILL OF ENOCH ROSE:Written Oct.1810-Prob.21 Nov.1812,wife Mary Rose;Sons-Enoch,Phillip.Daus.Polly Rose,Abr---?,Betty Herryman,Jemina Slater.
Ibid;Marriage Rec;Rose,Enoch to Margaret Wade 3-24-1810
Rose,Phillip to Patsey Hogg,8-13-1813,Rose,Polly to Alexander Owen, 1813

DEED BOOK "A" WASHINGTON CO. MS.

P.354:Mortg.16 Feb.1832:JOHN A.BARNES of Claib.Co.Ms. to SIDNEY BURBRIDGE.

P.357:Deed-19 Jan.1832:EDM.P.BASS of Wash.Co. to COUNCIL R. BASS of same.

P.359:Judgement-20 Sept.1831:WM.W.COLLINS,Sheriff of Wash.Co. 1st part;JEFFERSON WILKERSON,2nd pt;Document states that a judgement was found in Jeff.Co. Ms.Circuit Court on 24 Sept. 1823 in favor of F.Gibson,survivor, against Phillip A.Gilbert. Land was advertised for sale and Wilkerson was the purchaser.

P.361:Bond-30 May 1831:SELBY SHEPHARD of Wash.Co. to THOS.RIGBY & JOHN M.HENDERSON.Wit:Abijah Downs of Warren Co.Ms.

P.365:Bond-30 May 1831:WM.McKEE of Wash.Co. to THOS.RIGBY & JOHN HENDERSON.

P.369:Deed-9 Dec.1830:EZEKIEL HYDE,SR.,of Wash.Co.to WM.P. MONTGOMERY.

THE END OF DEED BOOK "A"
SUPPLEMENTARY INFORMATION:

Nimrod Selser,son of George Selser and his wife Rachel Newman, the founders of Selsertown-12 miles north of Natchez, married Martha R.Stampley,dau. of Jacob Stampley and his first wife- Mary Cole.
Nimrod Selser & Martha R.(Stampley) marr.13 Oct.1808 Jefferson Co.Ms. and had the following Children:
    1. Isaac M.Selser b1809 died age 3
    2. Mary N.Selser b 7 Feb..1811-d 4 July 1833 marr.24 Feb. 1828 to Wm.Rusk
    3. India T.Selser b 10 Dec.1812 marr.2 Aug.1832 to James A.Bass
    4. Rachel Selser b 1815 marr. John Henry Harmonson 4 Feb. 1833
    5. Susannah N.Selser b 9 May 1817 marr. 9 May 1833 Edward Harmonson who died Apr.1834,age 26
Taken from "Stampley Family" by Gordon M.Wells-Fayette Chronicle; and the "Stampley Family Bible" Cem. and Bible Rec.Vol.X
==

GREENWOOD CEMETERY,JACKSON,MS.
Guion,John I. b 18 Nov.1802 - d 6 June 1858
McNutt,A.G. b 3 Jan.1802 - d 22 Oct.1848
Poindexter,George d 5 Sept. age 75
Scott,Abram M. b S.C. d 12 June 1833 - age 48
[All former Governors]

ODGEN CEMETERY,ADAMS CO.,MS.
Ferriday,Mrs. Helen Catherine 1805 - d New Orleans 1857

ROUTH CEMETERY - ADAMS CO.MS.
Dorsey,Sarah Ann Ellis 1829/1879
Ellis,Thomas George Percy b 1 May 1805 - d 25 Jan.1838
Ellis,Thomas LaRoach (CSA) 1836/1862

DEED BOOK "B" WASHINGTON CO. MS.

Deed Book"B"-dated 1832-signed by Clerk, Wm.J.Penrice, is the original: dog-eared, but has been laminated. 414 pages, indexed in Master Index, also in back of this book. The new Territory called Washington Co. was still in the throes of dealing with Original Patents, Preemptive Rights, and aggressive land speculators. Deed Dk."B" picks up immediately after DBK."A", and the names are repetitive. For this reason, only genealogical information has been copied-i.e.-family relationships, Estate information not previously given in Early Miss.Records Vol.I, Vol.II of this series.

P.5:Deed-4 Feb.1832:WM.P. MONTGOMERY & wife CATHARAINE of Wash. Co. to ELISHA & THOS.B.WARFIELD of Fayette Co. Ky.[Note:Wm. Pinkney Montgomery marr.Catherine Cameron 24 Dec.1831. Catherine decd.1848, and W.P. marr.2nd Evelyn C.Bacon in 1850]

P.9:Deed-12 Feb.1832:WM.JOHNSON & wifeNANCY to WM.HUNT.

P.10:Deed-3 Mar.1832:JOSEPH HOUGH of Butler Co.Ohio;to SEBORN BRASHER of Wash.Co.Ms.
A Mortg. follows this, with WM.W.COLLINS,Trustee relinq. all rts. to DT granted to him as Sherf. of Wash.Co.date 5 July 1838

P.17:Deed-12--1832:AUGUSTUS W.McALLISTER & wife ANN E.(Original Patent)to WM.W.BLANTON.[Papers of Wash.Co.Hist.Society: p.339:"Augustus Wm.McAllister-first wife was a Miss Longley". Wm.W.Blanton was marr. to A.W.McAllister's sister-Harriet.]

P.18:Deed-10 Jan.1832:GEO.MARSHALL & wife REBECCA(X),Orig. Pat. to WM.W.BLANTON.

P.20:Deed-13--183-(Corners torn off page);HIRAM D.MILLER & wife SARAH(X)to WM.W.BLANTON.

P.21:Deed-14 Jan.1832:GEORGE BEAL & wife ELVIRA,Orig.Pat. to WM.W.BLANTON.

P.22:Deed-10 Jan.1832:REUBEN MARSHALL & wife BETSEY(X) to WM. W.BLANTON.[Claib.Co.Ms.Deeds,1823-Reuben Marshall and wife RACHEL,heir-at-law of ABEL EASTMAN,decd.--Marr.Rec. Claib.Co. Ms.:Reuben Marshall to Rachel Eastman-1816:Wm.Marshall to Caroline M.Eastman-1829]

P.24:Deed-12 Jan.1832:ZACHARIAH JANES[Sp.Jones in Bk."A" but carefully spelled Janes, here] & wife MARTHA to WM.W.BLANTON.

P.27:Deed-12 Jan.1832:WM.(X)MILLER & wife EDITH(X) to WM.W. BLANTON.

P.32:Deed-11 Feb.1832:WM.W.BLANTON & wife HARRIET B.McALLISTER to JOSEPH NEWMAN,both of Wash.Co[Jos.Newman is marr. to Harriet's sister CHARLOTTE]

P.38:Deed-4 Feb.1832:EZEKIEL HYDE & wife MARY(X) to WM.P. & ALEXANDER MONTGOMERY.

P.46:Deed 10 Jan.1832:MARTHA JANES(X)formerly Martha Randal, now wife of ZACHARIAH JANES(Jones?),land she bought as joint tenant with Samuel Kinnan;to Aug.W.McAllister.

P.55:Deed-14 Feb.1832:ELIZABETH V.POWELL,RODERICK POWELL & wife CATHARINE(X)all of Warren Co.Ms;to BENJ.ROACH,Adms.Co.Ms.

DEED BOOK "B" WASHINGTON CO. MS.

P.57:Deed-14 Feb.1832:RICHARD(X)PARKER & wife SARAH(X)of Wash. Co.;(Orig.Pat.)to Benj.Roach of Adams Co.

P.64:Deed-24 Jan.1832:SAML.SCOTT & wife ANNA of Jeff.Co.Ms. for $12,400,sell land entered as Public Lands by Henry Fake (Wash.Co.)who is decd. and the land then descended to Anna, as only heir and representative(867ac.)Bought by John Foster, 25 Jan.1832-Saml. & Anna Scott transfer title. Orig.Pat.s obtained by Henry Fake are listed:#4687,#4104,#4688,#4689- at Mt.Salus(now Clinton,Ms.) 15 Dec.1829

P.77:Deed 24 Mar.1832:ALFRED GALLOWAY & wife ELIZA of Wash.Co. to FURNEY HERALD.

From this point, the original investors and land holders begin to sell to each other, presumably to square-up holdings, bought in small"lots"from squatters or occupants with preemptive rights. Larger acreages were bought at Mt.Salus at Public Auction, Jackson's banking changes making credit very easy to get. Even though the Original Patents continued to be sold through the early'50's, the most desirable lands were sold, early, along the waterways, for transportation would remain a problem for years to come. Some speculators start to sell their holdings. ED.K.B.

P.86:Deed-19May 1832:ALFRED COX & wife ANN of Wash.Co. to JOHN A.BARNES of Claib.Co.Ms.(John A.Barnes marr.Sarah Humphreys Claib.Co.1826;Will of John A.Barnes,Claib.Co.Ms.WBK"A",p.262 dated 9 Dec.1832)[Jno.A.Barnes m.Harriett Willis-1823,Claib.Co.]

P.89:Agreement-(5 yr.partnership)ROBT.McCULLOUGH & STEPHEN DUNCAN-copartners in Plantation on left bank of Ms.River in Wash.Co.lands entered by Duncan and purchsed by McCullough: Orig.Pat.#5450(Mt.Salus)25 Oct.1830 by HARBIRD(X)HOOD and transferred to Duncan & McCullough;#5505 also by Harbird Hood and transferred to the same.

P.97-105:The team of JOHN L.MARTIN & JOHN F.ANDERSON, known later as Martin and Anderson,make many land deals:WM.HYDE: WM.H.LANE:JEREMIAH HILL:DAVID T.SHOAT & ANDREW C.SHOAT OF Madison Co.Ms.;CHAS.(X)ROBERTS & JOHN(X)of Mad.Co.,ARTHUR & Benj. FORTNER;and others.

P. 106:Deed-26 May 1832:WM.FOSTER & STEPHEN VAN RENSSELARN RYAN.

P.107:HUGH ALLEN FOSTER TO RYAN(above-same date)

P.122:Deed-21 Apr.1832:JAMES LEARD(sp.?)and wife Agnes(X)to MARTIN & ANDERSON of Ky.

P.124:Deed-9 Apr.1832:Recorded 26 June 1832;WM.RIFE & wife MARTHA, of Wash.Co. to JOHN F.ANDERSON of KY.($400 for Orig. Pat.granted to Rife on 30 Apr.1831-156ac.)[Note:Wm.Rife,son ofMary(Rutledge)Rife Chambliss,marr.28 Oct.1819 Jeff.Co.Ms. to Martha J.Collins and they came to Wash.Co. sometime prior to 1830. When Wm.died in the early 1840's, Martha went to live in Carroll Parish,La.(Lake Providence) where she had relatives. The oldest son Thos.C.Rife had gone to Texas and joined the Rangers;the oldest dau.Mary Jane Rife had marr.(cont.)

DEED BOOK "B" WASHINGTON CO. MS.

(cont.from p.13)Lawrence T.Wade in 1842 and they had several children;Martha A.Rife m W.L.Sibley, but she lived only a short time after their marr.,leaving one child,Rife Sibley;and the youngest son Wm.W.Rife settled in Bolivar Co.Ms. and had extensive holdings there. Yellow fever wiped out the children of Lawrence T.Wade and Mary Jane(Rife), and they moved across the river to Issa.Co.,started a new family, later winding up in Bolivar Co. with WM.W.Rife. They left many descendants in this area.]

P.129:Deed-21 Apr.1832: 323 ac.Orig.Pat.ISAAC S.WILKERSON(X) & wife JANE of Wash.Co. to ELISHA & THOS.B. WARFIELD of KY.

P.12-:HARTWELL COCKE-Orig.Pat.#5571-95.25ac; + #5560-96 ac; transferred title to STEPHEN ARRINGTON.

P.138:Bond-26 Mar.1831:($1800)-ANTHONY A.WYCHE of Warren Co. Ms.to ANDREW TURNBULL of Wash.Co.

P.144:Deed-7 Dec.1831:E.F.ATCHINSON(also sp. Atcherson)and wife KIZIA(HARMAN)of Wash.Co.to STEPHEN DUNCAN of Natchez. [Note;Jeff.Co.Ms.Marr.Rec.Bk."B":E.F.Atchinson to K.Taylor-20 Sept.1828-lisc.ret.22 Sept.]

P.151:Deed-18 June 1832:JACOB RICE & wife REBECCA(X)to WM. COOK.

P.154:Mort.-26 Sept.1832:BENJAMIN HASHBARGER & MARY ROSS- 1st pt;A.G.McNUTT & JOS.P McNUTT-2nd pt;JAS.J.CHEWNING 3rd pt.

P.157:Deed-19 Aug.1832:FREEMAN LACEY & wife REBECCA(X),CHAS. SMITH & wife MANAH(X):to HOWELL HINDS of Jeff.Co.

P.158:Deed 19 Aug.1832:JOHN(X)GATES & JOHN B.GATES of Rankin Co.,REBECCA(X)GATES (wife of one of them, but not clear which one);toHOWELL HINDS of Jeff.Co.Ms.

P.161:Deed-18 Aug.1832:ALVIN TAYLOR and wife LYDIA(X):DAVID ROSS and wife ELIZABETH(X) to HOWELL HINDS.

P.163:WILL OF JOHN FOSTER:Written-Lexington,Ky.22 July 1832 States,"being in bad health and weak..".John names his brother Cato Jas.Foster of Adams Co.Ms.and friendJoseph Dunbar of Jeff. Co.Ms.co-executors of his Est.and Guardian of his children, and asks that they keep his Est.together, if possible, for the benefit of his wife(unnamed)and family. Further states that he has 2 children by 2nd wife;1.James Daniel Foster,2.Mary Eveline Foster. They are to get $500 more than the other children since he(John)received more from their mother than"any of my other wives". Bequeaths gold watch to oldest son, James Daniel Foster;Names his mother Mary Foster-$50 per yr.;Will Wit.byThos.Bodly(age about 60) and Littleberry Hawkins. Later David Megowan wit. a correction. Recorded Fayette Co.Ky.14 Aug.1832.No record date in Wash.Co.Ms.[Ed.Note:Noncupative Will of Wm.Brooks;dated 3 Dec.1826;Will Bk."A"Jeff.Co.Ms.; Names brother-in-law JohnFoster;& 3bros.Robt.Brooks,George Brooks,Saml.Brooks.WILL OF GEO.BROOKS,11 June 1829;W.Bk."A" Jeff.Co.Ms.Names Martha Ann Foster;Neices Helen Jane &Mary Eliza Foster;Nephew James Daniel Foster;to Mrs.Mary Foster-wife of John Foster.(Abst. by Gordon Wells)

DEED BOOK "B" WASHINGTON CO. MS.

P. 175:Deed 16 Oct. 1832:WM.TAYLOR & JAMES TAYLOR,heirs of WINDSOR TAYLOR of Wash.Co. to HOWELL HINDS & JOHN D.HARDING of Jeff.Co.Ms.

P.177:Deed-25 Oct.1832:JOHN G. COCKS,Adm.to EST.OF JOHN McFADDEN (widow still living) toJOS.WALLACE, all of Wash.Co.(land on Lake Jackson(

P.183:Deed-23 Oct.1832:GEO.BEAL & wife ELVIRA(X) & REUBEN MARSHALL & wife BETSEY of 1st part;WM.FRAZIER of the other part. All of Wash.Co.

P.188:Marriage contract:12 Nov.1832:MARY ROSS & BENJ.HASHBERGer have become married and she has property in her own name and right and will retain full control of it after they are married. Wit:Rich.Armstrong,J.H.Robertson.(Orig.Pat.-E½ of SE 1/4,Sec.2,Twp.12,R7W to Mary Ross.)

P.190:Deed-27 Jan.1832:JOHN FOSTER & MARY M.his wife of Adams Co.Ms.;and SAML.SCOTT of Jeff.Co.Ms. other part.

P.194:POA-21 Jan.1833:WM.P.WALKER to act for ANDREW KNOX in receiving a negro girl named Gracy, now in jail at Padducah at the mouth of the Tenn.River. She was stolen last Nov. by a man namedPaul A.Gines,who died in neighborhood of Golconda, Ill. The girl was taken to Padducah.

P.196:Deed:CHAS.SCOTT & wife ELIZABETH of Choctaw Nation to WM.MONTGOMERY.

P.198:Deed-15 Jan.1833JOS.WALLACE & wife RUTH(X)(widow of Isreal Matthews) sell to Wm.E.Hall.

P.202:Deed 26 Jan.1833:WM.B.COOK & wife ELIZABETH D.W. to Andrew Knox,all of Wash.Co.

P.204:Deed 9 Nov.1832:JOHN(X)DEHART of 1st part;GEOR.MOONEY, Co.Trustee, 2nd pt. both of Wash.Co.;ABRAHAM DEHART of 3rd pt. (John owed Abraham $39-pd.in full 4/24/34

P.208:Deed-7 Dec.1833:JOSEPH R.NEWMAN & CHARLOTTE A.E.(McALLISTER)NEWMAN his wife-1st pt;JAS.FERGUSON of Natchez other part.Wit;WM.Hunt,Jonathon Ballard,Benj.Miller.

P.210:Mortg.7 Dec.1832:EDWARD SWANSON of 1st part;JAS.J.CHEWNING & HENRY S.DAWSON of 2nd pt;JOHN F.BUKENBOROUGH(also sp. Brokenborough)3rd pt; Wit:Wm.H.Paxton,A.G.McNutt.[Ed.note; Will of Edward Swanson;Warren Co.Ms. 30 Mar.1833. Names-wife Margaret;Exec.Joshiah C.Smith,Robt.Garland."Ms.Court Rec" by McBee; p.51-"Edward Swanson was buried 4thMar.1833 & Joshiah C.Smith, his exec.,died 3 Apr.1833, both of cholera. Margaret Swanson died 21 June of that same year in Ky.,where she went after her husband's death. Her brother A.D.S.Dillingham, having died earlier in June-same year." From Claib.Co.Ms.Court records we know that Alfred D.S.Dillingham marr.Nancy Thomson 20 June 1820, with the consent (of her father)John Thomson. Also from Claib.Co.Ms. Edward Swanson marr. Margaret E.Dillingham 23 Dec.1828, and Saml.Rusk marr. Myra Thomson 1 Oct. 1834. A.D.S.Dillingham & wife Nancy(Thomson)had 2 daus.Mary Eliza & Margaret. Apparently the Swanson"s had no issue for the 2 girls,neices, inherited Swanson"s Est.as well as their

DEED BOOK "B" WASHINGTON CO. MS.

(cont.from p.15)fathers! MARY ELIZA DILLINGHAM marr. THOS.LAND In Holmes Co.Ms.,Bk.Q.p.450-Release-by Nancy Rhodes & Margaret Dillingham to Mary E.Land,"the following slaves", in Ests.of Edw.Swanson & A.D.S.Dillingham- 2 Jan.1841. The Wash.Co.Ms. Plantation(now in the Co. of Sharkey)was heavily mort.to W.R. Campbell.]

P.215:Deed: 9 Feb.1833:THOS.G.PERCY of Madison Co.Ala;JAS.P. BROWN,for himself and as the Trustee under the will of Dr.Saml. Brown,decd. for the benefit of Susan C.Brown,now Susan C.Ingersoll,of the other part.[Saml.Brown marr. Thos.G.Percy"s sister Catherine Percy]

P.218:Will of JOHN COWDON:Written 21 Jan.1832 "on the eve of my starting to New Orleans". Names wife-Elizabeth Cowdon, children-unnamed: Wit; to signature Eli Henly, Sarah H.Cowdon who say they are familiar with John"s signature. Will probated 30 Apr.1833.(Adams Co. Marr.-Jas. Cowdon to Sarah Ker.1 Apr.1821)

P.221:Deed-,20 Oct.1832:MANUEL FERRENO & wife NANCY(X)to CLAUDIUS GIBSON.

P.222:Deed-28 Oct.1832:JOHN MAY & wife ELIZABETH of Wash.Co. to CLAUDIUS GIBSON.

P.224:Deed 7 Mar.1833:FELIX HUSTON & wife MARY E. of Adams Co.Ms. to Thos.Barnard of same.(Adams Co.Marr. Felix Huston to Mary Elizabeth Dangerfield 10 Feb.1829)

P.225:Deed-25 Mar.1833:THOS.WARD,proclaimed natural Guardian of "his son"JEREMIAH SANDERS WARD,by a special Act of the Assembly of the State of Ms.,passed Jan.1833 and approved 24 Jan. 1833 of the 1st part; to WM.HUNT of the 2nd part.

P.234:Deed 23 Mar.1833:Orig.Pat to GEO.W.WARD of Wash.Co. of the 1st pt;THOS.T.TUNSTALL & wife SARAH, & THOS.TUNSTALL OF the other part.

P.245:Deed-10 Apr.1833:HENRY K.MOSS* & wife NARCISSA ANN*of Natchez & ALEXANDER T.McMurtry* & wife Rebecca M.* of Natchez of the 1st part; to Elijah Atchinson & wife KIZIAH H.(TAYLOR) OF Wash.Co.,other part.
[MS.COURT RECORDS by King:Adams Co. Marriages;]
    *Moss.Thos.K.? to Narcissa Ann Ross 3-4-1824
    *McMurtry, Alex to Rebecca M.Moss 11-5-1829
    *McMurtry, Alex. to Eliza A.Miller 1-13-1848

P.248:Deed 10 Apr.1833:JOSEPH NEIBERT & wife SARAH of the 1st pt.;DR.STEPHEN DUNCAN & ROBT.McCULLOUGH of the other. The J.P. is Covington Rawlings.[Marr.rec.of Adams Co.;Jos.Neibert to Sarah Prewitt-12-2-1824]

P.250:Deed-24 May 1831:ISAAC CALDWELL bought Orig.Pat. obtained by James & Wm.H.Condray as Preemptive Rights.

P.251:Deed-9 Apr.1831:ANNA(X)GREGORY & RUFFIN(X)GREGORY sell Orig.Pat. obtained by Preemptive Rts. to Isaac Caldwell.

P.256:Deed-16 Jan.1831:(large acreage)HENRY W.VICK of Yazoo Co.Ms.,sells,for $10-toMARTHA P.WILLIS of Madi.Co.Ms.Wit; Guston Kearney,J.G.Vick.[E.N;Henry W.Vick had a sister, Martha, who marr. Wm.Willis-Warren Co.]

DEED BOOK "B" WASHINGTON CO. MS.

P.259:Deed-8 Feb.1833:BENJ.HUGHES & wife NANCY of Claib.Co.Ms. ANDREW KNOX & MYRA JANE(Prince, dau. of Robt.Prince;WBK.A.p. 26,Jeff.Co.Ms.:ed] of Wash.Co. of the 1st pat;HENRY W.BARNES & WM.P.RUSSUM both of Claib.Co.Ms. of 2nd.

P.261:Deed 8 Jan.1833:MARTHA CLARK & GEO.W.REYNOLDS of Claib. Co.Ms.-1st pt;PASMORE HOOPES of same,Security;Jas.L. & Geo. Douglass of 3rd Pt.

P.264:Deed-16 Mar.1833:Orig.Pat. secured by JOHN G.COCKS & SARAH D.(SHELBY)his wife of Wash.Co.Ms. to Geo.M.Smith of Claib. Co..Ms. the other.

P.266:Deed-20 Apr.1833:GEO.M.SMITH of Port Gibson,Ms. to HORACE & JOHN M.CARPENTER.

P.275:Deed-21 May 1833:HORACE CARPENTER & wife MARTHA M.of Port Gibson,Claib.Co.Ms; to GEO.SMITH of same.[Note;Newspaper notices of Ms.1820-1860:"Mrs.Mary Hassan Green,wife of Abram A.Green, decd.11 Dec.1844. The only dau. of Orville & Ann Carpenter,she was ophaned at an early age, and was adopted by her Uncle, Horace Carpenter...Mrs. Green was born 5 Sept.1822 at Charleston, Maryland."]

P.279:Mortg.:1 Jan.1833:Hds.Co.,Clinton:WM.B.DAMERON of the 1st pt;JAS.McLARAN,surviving partner of Jas.McLaran & Co.,late merchants in Clinton,2nd pt; all of Clinton. Dameron owes McLaran, & CO. notes co-signed by Senaca Pratt,made payable to Geo,B.Dameron, all dated 1 Jan.1833;1st for $4,636;2nd $4, 820;3rd $5,006. Wm.B.Dameron mortg. several tracts of land. 480 ac. near Leaf River(S.Ms.)where Military Rd.(Jackson's) crosses and generally known as"the place whereon Jos.Fisher lived at the time of the Treaty of Dancing Rabbit Creek"... another tract,480 ac.known as the"place whereon Tickbohoma, an Indian Captain,lived at the time of the same Treaty"... Schedule of payments included.

P.282:POA-4 July 1833:GEO.W.WARD of Wash.Co. appoints TURNER JOYNER his Atty.and representative to return a runaway slave named Bob,believed to be held in jail in Jeff.Co.,Territory of Ark.

P.284:Mortg.-18 June 1833:U.S.A.Territory of Ark. JAS.DOZWELL of Wash.Co.Ms. of the 1st pt;JAS.BLAIN 2nd;JOHN & LEVI MITCHELL & ANTHONY H.DAVIS(John Mitchell & Co.) 3rd pt.

P.290:Deed-11 May 1833:ISAAC CALDWELL* & wife ELIZABETH H., THOS.D.DOWNS* & wife LUCY of 1st pt; to STEPHEN CASTLEMAN* of 2nd pt.--Finders Fee.

*Wills of Hinds.Co.Ms.taken from MS.COURT REC.by King.
WILL OF ISAAC CALDWELL:written 27 Feb.1829,Rec.Feb.1836
    Wife-Elizabeth;Son-Raymond
    Exec;wife and James B.Robinson, a friend.
WILL OF RAYMOND ROBINSON:Written 13 Feb.1836;Rec.May 1836
    Est.left to his 2 daus.Elizabeth Caldwell & Lucy Downs.
    Also names his nephew James B.Robinson
    Wit;E.W.Haring,James B.Robinson,Henry G.Johnston
Marriage Rec.Hinds Co.Ms.
    Castleman,Stephen to Elvira Harvey(1833-35)

DEED BOOK "B" WASHINGTON CO. MS.

P.292:Deed-3 Apr.1833:ALLEN WYNENS & MRS.ELIZABETH A.PENRICE of Wash.Co.[Note; She was the former Elizabeth A.Prince] sell to Jos.Wallace-120 ac.

P,295:Deed-21 June 1833:DAVID HUMPHREY, BENJ.G.HUMPHREYS & SARAH L.BARNES(formerly Sarah Humphreys), exec. of Last will and Test. of John A.Barnes,decd. of the 1st part; Albert Dunbar of 2nd;Orig.Pat awarded to Wm.A.Dromgoole +other land + slaves.($27,000)

P.298:Deed-11 Feb.1833:MICHAEL CLOY & wife JANE OF Wash.Co.; ALLEN WYNENS of 2nd part.

P.299:Deed-11Feb.1832:SAML.KINNAN & wife MARY(X) to ZACHARIAH JANES of 2nd part;(carefully sp.Janes not Jones)

P.302:Deed 12 apr.1833:BLUFORD MITCHELL & wife SALLY(X) of Hinds Co.Ms; to GEO.H.JONES OF Petersburg,Va.(Carefully sp. Jones)Bluford Mitchell marr.Sally Evans in Claib.Co.Ms.-4 Dec. 1819)

P.303:Deed-15 Oct.1832:PHINEAS F.MERRICK & wife MARIA (she signed H.M.MERRICK)of Natchez;WM.HARRIS of same.(From Goodspeed's;HANNAH M.born 1802,N.J.d 1841-marr. in NewYork City, 1822, to Phineas P.Merrick b 1796 Mass. d 13 May 1833. A dau. Helen M.Merrick marr.Jas.H.Rowan of Natchez. Hannah M.Merrick marr. 2nd Judge Wm.A.Stone.)(Wm.Harris marr.Caroline Harrison 1827,Adams Co.)

P.315:Deed 4 Apr.1833:HEZEKIAH BILLINGSLY & wife JERUSHA of Wash.Co., & ANDREW G.HOLLAND & wife PRICILLA of Hinds Co.Ms. of the 1st pt; ISAAC CALDWELL of Hds. the other.

P.318:Deed 8 Feb.,1833:HARBIRD(X)HOOD & wife NANCY to ZENAS PRESTON, all of Carroll P.La.

P.325:Deed 26 Nov.1833:WM.M.BOICE & wife NANCY ANN of Wash. Co.;to GEO.R.REYNOLDS & MARTHA CLARK 2nd pt.

P.326:Deed-22 Apr.1833:JAMES S.DOUGLASS & wife EMELINE & GEO. DOUGLASS of Claib.Co.Ms. of the 1st part;TO GEO.R.REYNOLDS & MARTHA CLARK of Wash.Co.

P.328:Deed-30 Oct.1833:ZENAS PRESTON & wife MARTHA of Wash. Co. to STEPHEN DUNCAN of Natchez. They later entered into a 5 yr.contract for a partnership in the operation of a plantation.[Note;Brieger in"Hometown Miss"'states that Zenas, Robert McCullough & E.F.Atchinson were bro-in-law and Stephen Duncan was kin."Zenas Preston marr. Martha Harmon,5 July 1831, Adams. Co.;McCullough marr. twice-1st to Maria Harmon 29 Dec.1824, 2nd to Elizabeth C.Perkins 22 Aug.1839. Atchinson marr.Kiziah Taylor, widow of Sheperd Taylor,decd.1826.Stephen Duncan marr. 1st Marg.Ellis and at her death marr.2nd Catharine Bingamon in 1819. All the above marr.in Adams Co.except Atchinson's. which was in Jeff.Co.Ms.]

P. 336:Deed-21 Sept.1833:EZEKIEL HARLAND & wife ELIZABETH(X) of the 1st pt; to FRANCIS Patterson,Jr.2nd pt.,all of Wash.Co.

P.340:POA:THEODORICK J.JAMES & wife FRANCIVA BARB JAMES of Wash. Co.appoints G.C.BEDFORD of Lafouche P.,La. to collect their share from the Est.of Mary Madeline Burwar(sp?)decd.OfLaf.Par. La.

DEED BOOK "B" WASHINGTON CO. MS.

P.347:WILL OF JOSEPH WALLACE:decd. of Wash.Co.Ms.[This will was abst. in Vol.II of this series,Packet sec. p.143]Wallace asks that the property brought to him by his present wife Ruth,widow of Isreal Matthews,be left to her children, and (Wallace's)property go to his children. A small bequeath to Frances McFadden,and asks that Robt.McCullough be exec.and Guard. of both sets of children. Spoken 17 Aug.1833;Rec.28 Oct.1834.(Joseph Wallace marr. Polly Dowells in Adams Co.10 May 1805.)

P.348:WILL OF JAMES BARR:½ of his Est.to go to his only child MARGARET ANN GILMORE, dau.of Nancy Gilmore, an unmarried woman; If child decd.,Est. to be divided between"my Mother"Katharine Barr* and only living bro. John Barr. States that his relatives listed above are in Ireland.Exec;John C.Swan of Wash.Co.Ms. Written-4 Oct.1833;Prob.28 Oct.1833.*& only sis.Marg.Barr. Wit:Wm.P.Walker, Stephen Warren.

P.349:Deed-11Dec.1833:JOS.C.(X)ESTES & wifeRACHEL(X)ROWAN of Wash.Co. to THEODORE D.ELLIOTT of Adams Co.Ms.

P.351:EST.OF JOSEPH WALLACE:by Adm.Robt.McCullough of Wash.Co. Ms.-25 Dec.1833 sells to Wm.E.Hall of same, 68 ac. on Lake Jackson,+120ac.,+80ac.,+78ac. Wallace stated in his Will,1833, that he wanted his property sold. Wm.E.Hall bought for$10,000.

P.353:Deed-28 Dec.1833:HENRY JOHNSON & wife ELIZABETH JULIA JOHNSON* of the 1st part;to John C.Miller,land on Lake Washington.$16,000.(*She was dau.ofMatthew Flournoy)

P.354:Deed-28 Dec.1833:JOHN C.MILLER & wife JANE of 1st pt; Henry Johnson buys land acquired from Junius R.Ward;also on Lake Washington.

P.356:Deed 28 Dec.1833:WM.M.ROBINSON sells to ANDREW TURNBULL. Robinson is from Tenn.

P.359:Release-29 Aug.1833:MARY TURNBULL states that her husband,FREDERICK G.TURNBULL became owner of several tracts of land and he sold 340ac.to Jos.H.Newman of Claib.Co.Ms.,7 Feb. 1832. Mary releases all claim of Dower and any other rights to the property.[Frederick Guerin Turnbulls' wife was Mary Fitzpatrick]

P.360:Deed-12Nov.1833:EDMOND HESTER & wife EDITH of Hds.Co.Ms. to JOS.H.NEWMAN of Claib.

P.363:Deed-13 Nov.1833:JAS.McDANIEL & wife LUCY(X),& WM.McDANIELS of Hds.Co. to JOS.H.NEWMAN of Claib.Co.Ms.

P.364:Deed 18 Nov.1833:Rankin Co.Ms.THOS.(X)OUSLEY & wife PRICILLA(X) to JOS.H.NEWMAN.

P366:Deed-14 Nov.1833:CHAS.WELLS & wife MARY(X),&WM.(X)POOL & wife BITSEY(X) all of Rankin Co.to Jos.H.Newman.

P.375:EST OF JOHN FOSTER:by surviving exec.JOS.DUNBAR of the 1st pt.-1 Jan.1834;and Jos.Neibert of Natchez,2ndpt. Dunbar, as Adm. of Foster's Est.,sold to Neibert for $116,000, land near Lake Wash.,abt.2,724ac.-569ac. of which land Foster bought from Saml.Scott & wife ANNA-26 Jan.1832. Also land bought from Edmond P.Bass on 28 Oct.1830;also Orig.Pat.issued to John Foster +slaves,stock,household furnishings,etc.

DEED BOOK "B" WASHINGTON CO. MS.

P.378;Release-1 Jan.1834:MARY M.FOSTER,widow of JOHN FOSTER, decd. releases all claim to Dower share,and claim to land for $1.She appeared in Adams Co.Ms.

P.379:POA-26 Nov.1833:GRACE W.STEELE gives P.O.A. to bro.Nathaniel Steele,both of Giles Co.Tenn.,for the purpose of selling a parcel of land originally entered in name of Bluford Mitchell-133ac. It was bought by McCullough & Duncan for $670.

P.380:Deed-13 Feb.1834:JOHN MILLIKEN of Carroll Parish La.of the 1st part;JOS.D.PEEBLES ofHds.Co.Ms. of the other part.

P.388:Mort.-1 Jan.1834:$96,000-JOS.NEIBERT of Natchez and wife SARAH(PREWITT)mortg.to Jos.Dunbar,exec.of Est.of John Foster, decd.for sum of $1...2,724 ac.

P.392:Deed 13 Feb.1834:SMITH MINTON & wife EMALINE of Cape Girardeau,Mo. to BENNETT M.HINDS OF Wash.Co.

P.394:Deed-11Feb.1834:WM.McKEE & wife PHEBE of Union Co. Ill. toB.M.Hines & Thos.Rigley of Wash.Co.

P.396:POA-26 Mar.1834:Natchez-RENE LA ROCHE & wife MARY,formerly Mary Ellis,by their Atty.Nathaniel A.Ware;&THO.G.ELLIS of Natchez, sole heirs of late Col.John Ellis,decd. of the 1st pt.;Thos.G.Percy of Huntsville,Ala.2ndpt.Orig.Pat.issued to John Ellis is sold.*

*Adams Co.Ms.WILL OF JOHN ELLIS:Written 7 Nov.1808,Prob.Dec.1808 Wit;Sam Brown,Ann Percy,Thos.Rodney.
    Wife-Sarah;Children;Thos.,Mary Ellis,father,Rich.Ellis;
    bro.Abraham Ellis.Exec.:Wife,Abraham Ellis,Thos.Percy.
Adams Co.Marr:John Ellis marr.Sarah Percy 22Feb.1800
   "   "   ":Nathaniel A.Ware to Sarah Ellis 1 Sept.1814
   "   "   ":Thos.G.Ellis to Mary N.Routh 14 May 1828
Sarah Percy Ellis Ware was the sister of Thos.G.Percy,& Catherine Percy(who marr. Saml.Brown.)& Ann, Susanna,Luke,& Wm.,all being the issue of Charles Percy & wife Susanna Collins.See McBee's"Natchez Court Rec.1767-1805".

Adams Co.WILL OF RICHARD ELLIS:Oct.17,1792:names w.Mary;dau.'s Jane(marr.Geo.Rapalje);Mary (marr.Benj.Farrar);Martha(marr. Stephen Minor and they had twins Mary & Martha)and sons Wm. Cocke Ellis,decd.;John;Rich;Abraham. No probate date.

P.405:Deed Apr.1834:ALFRED COX.Adm. of Est. of Wm.Penrice, decd. of Wash.Co.Ms. to Allens Wynens of same.

P.406:Deed 4 May 1833:JOS.DUNBAR & OLIVIA his wife of Jeff.Co. Ms. of the 1st Part;WM.SHIPP of Natchez & DAVID HUNT of Jeff.-Co.Ms. the other part.[Jos.Dunbar marr.Olivia Magruder,Adams Co.1808;Wm.Shipp marr.Lucy Barnard 12 Apr.1810,Adams Co.]

P.412:Deed-4 May 1832:POA:GEO.H.JONES of Petersburg,Va. gives P.O.A.to John W.Jones of Raymond,Ms. to act in all ways for him in Ms.,especially in Warren Co.Ms.

END OF DEED BOOK "B"

DEED BOOK "C":WASHINGTON CO.,MS.
DATED:1 Oct.1834-9 July 1835

P.1-24:Documents all deal with fund raising for Jefferson College at Washington,Ms.permissable through an Act of the State Legislature. For the rest of this DBk."C" only documents giving genealogical information have been included - i.e.names of spouse,Est.Notices,Family relationships,etc. This is the Original Deed Book,Indexed in Deed Index Bk.1, and on microfilm.

P.33:2 May 1834-Deed:Stephen Howard and wife Mary to J.C.Lobdell. Delivered 4 Jan.1840.[Note:Stephen Howard was a Government Engineer & Surveyor]

P.37:27 Mar.1834-Deed:Council R.Bass and Jesse Bass, Adms. of Est. of Edmond P.Bass,decd. of Wash.Co. - 1st pt;Thos.James of same - the other part.[Note:See Vol.II of this series for Est. of E.P.Bass.Pkt.#78,p.144.]

P.74:12 July 1833-D:Hiram Coffee and wife Elizabeth Ann of Hds. Co.,Ms.;to Alfred Cox.[Hiram's Obit.Hds.Co.1836 states he was 41 yrs. old, and died 30 Jan.1836]

P.78:10 Dec.1833-D:John T.P.Yerger and wife Martha A.of Wash.Co. to Alfred Cox.

P.70:July 1834-D:Thos.J.Chambliss of Wash.Co.,Adm.of Est.of Jenkins W.Shelby, decd. to Wm.A.Dromgoole.

P.78:6 Mar.1832-D:Thos.Ferguson and wife Caroline M.,Thos.Downs and wife Lucy, all of War.Co. to Alvarez Fisk of Natchez.

P.103:31 May 1834-D:Henry T.Irish of Claib.Co.Ms. to Horace Carpenter and John M.Carpenter of same.

P.105:6 Nov.1834-D:Wm.M.Boice and wife Nancy Ann ofWash.Co.to Wm.M.Gwin of Adams.

P.126:21 May 1834-D:Hiram G.Runnels and wife Obedience A.and Isaac Caldwell and wife Elizabeth (Robinson) of 1st pt;Hugh R.Austen of the other pt:all of Hds.Co.[Note: According to "Goodspeed","the wife of Gov.Runnels was Obedience Smith,dau. of Capt.David Smith,and the ½ sister of Sarah, who marr.Geo. Wilson Humprheys."Gov.Runnels' father was Col.Harmon Runnels who died Lawrence Co.Ms.20 July 1839,at age 80.]

P.142:3 Nov.1834-Mortgage:Jilson P.Harrison of the 1st pt;and his wife Sidney Ann Harrison of Warr.Co.Ms. and the Ms.Insurance Co. at Vicksburg,2nd pt;[Note:Jilson P.Harrison marr. Sidney Ann Norton - Jan.14,1834, Adams Co.Ms.]

P.147:3Nov.1834-Mort:Samuel Mason and wife Polly(X) of Warr.Co. 1st pt;and Ms.Insr.Co. - 2nd.

P.151:26 Nov.1834-D:Jos.Stringer and wife Drucilla; Andrew Knox of Wash.Co.,2nd pt.

P.153:12 Feb.1834-D:Francis Griffin and wife Lenora to Andrew Knox.

DEED BOOK "C":WASHINGTON CO.,MS.
DATED:1 Oct.1834-9 July 1835

P.161:19 Aug.1834-Deed:Land sold at Public Auction.Isaac Caldwell Adm. and Lucy (Robinson)Downs,widow of and Admx.of Est. ofThos.D.Downs,decd.of Hds.Co.Ms.of the 1st pt;Jilson P.Harrison of Vicksburg,other pt; Isaac and Lucy sell him "undivided 1/4th portion" of a large tract of land,containing 2,593 ac.in all.

P.164:14 Aug.1834-Release:Power of Atty.to Isaac Caldwell from Lucy (Robinson) Downs,widow,relinq.all rights to property named above,part of the Est. ofThos.D.Downs,decd.of Hds.Co.Ms.

P.170:6 Jan.1834-Bill/Sale:W.Hunt sells a slave to Thos.Ward, Guardian of son J.S.Ward. Wm.F.Jeffries,dep.clerk.

P.171:16 Aug.1834-Bill/Sale & Mortg:Albert W.Dunbar of Adams Co. - 1st pt;Isaac Franklin of Sumner Co.Tn. and Jos.Alsop of Spotsylvania Co.Va. of 2nd - security; and Saml.Alsop, also of Spots.Co.Va.,3rd pt; Saml. has sold slaves to Dunbar for $12,000.

P.176:Probate Court-Mar.Term,1834 - Gibson Co.Ind. Court held at Princeton,Ind.12 May 1834:Robt.Frazier appointed Guardian to Julya and Jeneza Frazier,minor ch. of Wm.Frazier,late of Ms.decd. Filed - 13 Aug.1834.

P.180:Circuit Court of Appeal-Wash.Co.Ms.Bill/Sale:F.G.Turnbull, Adm.of John Love,decd.vs Wm.A.Dromgoole,Adm.of P.A.Gilbert,decd. A slave Gilbert bought is sold to Jesse Blue,6 Jan 1835.Thos.T. Stephens is the dep.Sheriff.

P.181:23 Dec.1834-D:Stephen Howard and wife Mary E. of Warr.Co. 1st pt;Robt.P.Shelby of Wash.Co. other pt.

P.192:4 Dec.1834-D:Hugh Foster and wife Winney (X),by preemptive rights-1200 acrs.to F.E.Plummer and Egbert Harris; Jos.R.Plummer asignee for F.E.Plummer.[Hugh was of the Choctaw Nation[

P.201:3 Feb.1835-Deed:Cornelius Haring (also sp.Hering) forhimself and Eleazar W.Haring,Clarissa A.Haring,Chas.W.Vantine and his wife Rhoda - heirs and distributees of Est.of Aaron Haring, decd.by Cornelius Haring of the 1st part;Preston Frazier,Frances A.Newcombe,Daniel G.Benbrooke of Natchez of the other part: $105,000 for D/T on land joining Princeton* and fronting on the Ms.River,the Original Patent issued to Matthew Flournoy at Mt.Salus;another O.P. issued to Geo.Irish & Council R.Bass; Haring heirs sell slaves,real est.,etc. Cornelius Haring appearing before Clerk in Adams Co.Ms. Document filed Wash.Co.Ms. 13 Feb.1835.

P.204:20 Jan.1834-Gift:Recorded 16 Feb.1835:M.Flournoy gives to his son,out of love and affection, for $1, "a tract of land where he now lives",around 1,000 acrs.near Princeton* on Ms.River The son's name is N.M.Flournoy.
==

*The town of Princeton was once the County seat of early Wash.Co. The Ms.River eroded the banks so badly, that Princeton finally sluffed off into the River,taking huge chunks of the banks along with it. The County seat had been moved to "Old Greenville" prior to this.

DEED BOOK "C":WASHINGTON CO.,MS.
DATED: 1 Oct.1834-9 July 1835

P.205: Jan.1835-D:Joel Higgins and wife Ann L. of Wash.Co. to John C.Miller of Scott Co.Ky.

P.209:1 Jan.1835-D: Zachariah C.Offutts of Scott Co.Ky.1st pt; John G.Cocks of Wash.Co.2nd pt.

P.211: 5 Feb.1835-D: John Read and wife Rebecca,Phillip Gice(?) and wife Sarah of La.of 1st part; Benj.B.Ford,Wm.Davenport,Wm. R.Lewis of Ms.2nd pt;[Writing very difficult to read]

P.233: 27 Oct.1834-D:Louisanna Brasher,widow of & Admx. to Est. of Seborn Brasher (also sp.Seaborn) decd.of Wash.Co.Ms.of 1st part;Alfred Cox 2nd; Wit:Wm.T.Breckenridge,Wm.W.Collins.

P.236:Release - Louisanna Brasher signs a relinq.to all rights pertaining to lands belonging to her late husband Seborn Brasher.

P.243: 3 Feb.1835-Mortg:Preston Frazier,Francis A.Newcombe,Danl. G.Benbrook of Natchez,1st part;Pasmore Hoopes of Port Gibson, 2nd pt;Cornelius Haring for himself and Eliza,Clarissa Haring, and Chas. and Rhoda Vantine - heirs of Est. of Aaron Haring,decd. Signed by Preston Frazier,D.G.Benbrook,Margaret Benbrook,Eliza L.Newcomb. [Note: Francis A.Newcomb marr. Eliza L.Morehead May 1830 - Adams Co.Ms.

P.248:26 Jan.1835-D: Richard H.May and wife Elizabeth of Tn. of 1st part;Wm.Harris of Natchez, of the other.

Between pgs.248 - 266 are many land transactions between Wm. Shipp of Natchez and David Hunt.

P.266:18 Nov.1834-D:Wm.Mills & Claborn Steel and his wife Eliza Steele of Warr.Co.Ms. of 1st part;Thos.Rigby of same,other pt.

P.269:18 Feb.1835-D:John A.Lane and Nancy P.Lane,his wife, to Thos.Rigby,all of Warr.Co.

P.272: 18 Mar.1834-Mortg:Wm.R.Campbell and wife Margaret of Warr.Co.,1st pt;Thos.Rigby,Wm.Mills,Claborn Steel of other.[Note: Wm.R.Campbell,son of Chas.and Susan (Reynolds)Campbell of Bowling Green,Ky. was 1 of 7 brothers.One bro. Dr.Jas.Campbell,lived New Orleans,another had a large sugar plantation in La. Wm.R. Campbell marr.,Vicksburg,Ms.Margaret Teideman,(she was 18) only child of Rebecca and Nicholas Teideman of Philadelphia. Nicholas was a sea Capt. and died in Calcutta of yellow fever. Mrs.Teideman was apopular artist. Wm.R.and Marg.Campbell had 7 ch. Lula,Caroline,Martha,Wm.Jr.,Stella,Richard,Margaret... Taken from P.W.C.H.S.,Court Rec.,Census,etc.]

P.275:11 Jan.1835-D:Thos.L.Thomby of Mayson Co.Ky. of the 1st pt: to James Noe of Warr.Co.Ms.2nd pt:

P.290:31 Dec.1834-D:Catharine L.Prince of 1st part; to John A.Miller of other,both of Wash.Co.Ms.

P.310: 13 Apr.1834-D:Andrew Carson and wife Elizabeth of Wash.Co. to Saml.Carson of same.

DEED BOOK"C" ; WASHINGTON CO.MS.
DATED: 1 Oct.1834 - 9 July 1835

P.312:--- 1835 - Deed and Release: Andrew Turnbull of Wash.Co. to John Turnbull,Jr. and Thomas Aston Coffin of S.C. Gracia M.Turnbull,wife of Andrew Turnbull, signs release to all claims, including dower rights,to the land.Recorded - 15 May 1835.[For Est. of Andrew Turnbull,decd.1870,see Vol.II of this series. Pkts.Issa.Co.Ms - p.58,59.]

P.322:13 Feb.1826-Power of Atty:Wm.Trahern(Frahern?) gives his P.O.A. to Jas.C.Dickson,Esq. to sell 1 sq.mile (640 ac.) bought of Alex.McKee an Orig.Pat.

P.323:21 Mar.1835-D:Henry(X)Crow and wife Ann(X) to Joseph Egg.

P.325: 20 Mar.1835-Quit Claim:Jacob Coulter "only heir" of Jos. Coulter,decd. and also apparently the only survivor of 4 bros. - Joseph,Hamilton,Matthew,Jacob - and Jacob wants possession of tracts of land in Ms.& La.to be declared his as survivor.Jos. Egg has agreed to investigate the claims.Jacob,then quit claims all lands to Joseph Egg for $150.

[The page numbers skip from 326 to 337]

P.337:30 Apr.1835-Power of Atty:Benjamin M.Steadman and wife Belinda Ann of Jeff.Co.Ms.,give their P.O.A. to Christopher Dart of Natchez for purpose of selling,conveying,mortg.,etc. any lands they hold in Ms.,La,Terr. of Ark,owned jointly with Dart.[Note:They had large holdings around Fitler,Hays Landing in Issa.Co.Ms. Benjamin M.Steadman marr. Belinda A.Clapp,Adams Co.Ms. 18 Jan.1835]

P.340:9 May 1835-D/T: Christopher Dart and his wife Catherine B.Dart of 1st pt;Thos.Henderson of 2nd, all of Natchez.Dart owes the Bank of the U.S.at Natchez - $118,000. Dart and Steadman own Orig.Pat. and land descriptions run to p.349.

P.365:18 Jan.1835-D:Jas.J.Chewning and wife Sarah M. of 1st part with Henry L.Dawson - all of Warr.Co.; John Stamps,Geo.A. Summers,Hugh Watts - all of Claib.Co.Ms. - the 2ndpart.

P.368:1 Jan.1835-Deed:Wm.Bacon and wife S. of Warr.Co.- 1st; Elihu Kilpatrick of Wash.Co. - 2nd.

P.370:11 May 1835-D:Horace Carpenter,Exec. for George M.Smith, decd. of Claib.Co.Ms.(Port Gibson) of the 1st part;John M.Carpenter of same,2nd.[Will of Geo.M.Smith recorded Claib.Co.Ms. WBk."A", 3 July 1833]Smith owned land at foot of Lake Washington + slaves,having bought it for $24,000 at Public Auction. Henry T.Irish loaned John the money,p.374. Some of the Orig.Pats held in name of Peter C.Chambliss.

P.380:20 Jan.1835-D:Walter C.Loftin and wife Margaret of Wash. Co.,1st part;John Stamps,Geo.W.Summers,Hugh Watt of Claib.Co.,2nd.

P.382:11 Apr.1835-D:Soloman(X)Kirby and wife Mary Ann(X) of 1st part;David W.Comaly (Connelly) and Andrew S.Wilson of 2nd.

P.389:1 Mar.1835-Mortg:Robert J.Walker and wife Mary B. of Adams Co.Ms;to John C.Potts of Wash.Co.Potts mortg. about 400 ac., the whole tract containing 1170 ac.+ slaves.

DEED BOOK "C": WASHINGTON CO.,MS.
DATED:1 Oct.1834 - 9 July 1835

P.403: 2 Feb.1835-D:Cowles Mead and Ulyssis W.Moffet and wife Mary C.Moffet of 1st part;Gideon Fitz of 2nd;Names signed to document - Dowly Mead,Ulyses W.Moffett,Mary E.Moffett.

P.405:26 Dec.1834-D:Daniel Lindle and Jane (X)Middleton of Frank. Co.Ms to Gideon Fitz of HD.Co.2nd.

P.408:26 Dec.1834-D: Daniel Huffman and Delilah(X) Huffman of Copiah Co.Ms. to Gideon Fitz,Hds.

P.411:26 Dec.1834-D:Benj.(X)Vickers and wife Elenore(X) of Copiah Co.,Ms.to Gideon Fitz.

[Many more deed follow,all to Gideon Fitz of Hds.Co.Ms.]

P.420: 8Dec.1834-D:Isaac R.Nicholson and wife America of Hds. Co. of 1st part;to Nathaniel A.Ware of Penn. 2nd pt.

P.422: 24 Dec.1834-D:John Tatum and Wm.C.Tatum of Copiah to Gideon Fitz.

P.425:3 Mar.1835-Mortg:$84,500 - Zenas Preston and wife Martha (Harmon) to Stephen Duncan.

P.428: 2 May 1835-D: John Stamps and wife Henrietta of Claib.Co. Ms.to Walter C.Loftin of Wash.Co.Ms.

P.430: 7 Apr.1835-Deed and Release:Alexander G.McNutt and wife Elizabeth A. of Warren Co.,1st part;to Walter C.Loftin.[Note: PWCHS.P.380 - A.G.McNutt marr. the former Elizabeth Lewis,widow of Joel Cameron. Gov.McNutt decd.1848. Eliz.marr. 3rd George A.Fall. Gov.McNutt was the Uncle of Col.A.J.Paxton.]

P.438:27 Feb.1834-D:Wm.H.Taylor and wife Mary E. of Adams Co. to Jefferson J.Hughes.

END OF BOOK "C" - INDEX IN REAR

SUPPLEMENTARY INFORMATION:
Marriage Records - Claib.Co.,Ms.
Dart,Christopher to Elizabeth Price - 1823
Ellis,Thos.Leroche to Appoline H.Ingraham - 1859
Ellis,Thos.P. to Ann Colgate McCaleb 1876
Haring,Cornelius to Mary E.Hughes 1821
Haring,Cornelius to Susan Abercrombie 1830
Marshall,Levin to Sarah Ross 1834
Rusk,Wm.L. to Louisa Nugent 1834
Stamps,Volney to Jane Stowers 1832
Sutton,James M. to Eliza Vanorman 1829
Sutton,James M. to Laura Cross 1846

Marriage Records - Hinds Co.Ms.
Caldwell,Isaac to Elizabeth H.Robertson (Robinson) her father
          Raymond Robertson consents 19 July 1827
Downs,Thos.D. to Lucy Robinson - Alfred C.Downs,Bdsm. her father
          Raymond Robinson,consents 1 Oct.1829
Kearney,Thos.L. to Mrs.E.H.Caldwell 20 June 1837.

Marriage Records - Warren Co.Ms.
Griffith,Francis to Patsy Downs - 20 Aug.1817

DEED BOOK "D": WASHINGTON CO.,MS.
DATED:29 July - 7 Jan.1836

This is the Original Book. Page numbers are hard to read as the edges of the pages have been reinforced with tape.294 pages Index in rear. Also Indexed in Master Deed Index Bk.1. Damaged but repaired.Dep.Clk. - N.Lambe. On microfilm.
==

P.1:4 Mar.1835-D:Wm.Gilbert and Webster Gilbert of Copiah Co.Ms. of 1st part;Ephraim Peyton of same,2nd part.

P.11:22 Feb.1833-D:Evans Moore,Margaret Newman,Amos(X)Moore, Patterson Moore,Hiram Moore of Wash.Co.,1st pt;to Isaac Caldwell of Hds.Co.Ms.- other.This document signed by all the above + Hiram P. Newman.

P.16:21 May 1835-D:Cathraine (X)Dickens and Nancy(X)Graves of Copiah Co.Ms. to Robert H.Buckner and David W.Connely.

P.22:20 May 1835-D:Wm.W.Bailey and Elijah Bailey of Copiah Co. to Robert H.Buckner and David W.Connely.

P.26:15 Apr.1835-D:Zenas R.Fulton,Isaac W.Arthur and wife Margaret M.Arthur of Natchez of 1st part;to Jefferson Wilkerson of Wash.Co.,2nd pt.

P.29:21 Mar.1835-D:Wm.Rife and wife Martha(Collins)Rife of 1st pt;to Wm.R.Campbell of the other. Campbell pd.$4,000 for 320 acrs.an Orig.Pat.issued to Wm.Rife.

P.34:1 Mar.1835-D:Joseph Callender and wife Sally to Lawrence P.Maxwell,all of Claib.Co.Ms.

P.38:2 Jan.1835-D:Wm.Harris and wife Caroline of Adams Co. to Richard H.May of same.[Note:Wm.Harris marr.Caroline Harrison in Adms.Co. 1827]

P.40:28 Feb.1835-D:JosephD.Peebles of 1st pt;and Henry W.Peebles of the other.

P.42:17Dec.1834-D:Angus McNeill and wife Rebecca J.of ADMS.Co. to Jesse Perkins.[Note:Angus McNeill marr. Rebecca Jane Adams, Adams Co.Ms. 4 Feb.1829]

P.46:3 Apr.1834-Petition for Partition:Angus McNeill,Jesse Perkins,Malcolm McNeill,Hector McNeill own land jointly in Wash. Co. and want it divided.[Note:Hector McNeill marr. Lucy Crane in Claib.Co.Ms.27 Mar.1817]

P.48:Article of Agreement-21 Aug.1834:A note written on margin states the original article is recorded 20 Dec.1841,and signed by Wm.Bodley.This agreement is between Wm.Foster of the 1st pt;Jos.A.M.Raven,Hiram Coffee, Franklin E.Plummer of other pt; Wm.Foster[half-Choctaw Indian]is entitled to 1½Sec.of land by Treaty of Dancing Rabbitt Creek - entered 27 Sept.1830 by U.S. and Choctaws. Foster sells,for $7,000 - retaining 80 ac.that enclose "his present residence."Sec.21,Twp.22R8W to be divided between Jos.A.M.Raven &H.Coffee ½/½,and Plummer getting the other ½.Attys.are Jos.R.Plummer,Thos.J.Coffee,Stuart M.Raven to secure title.

DEED BOOK "D":WASHINGTON CO.,MS.
DATED: 29 July 1835 - 7 Jan.1836

P.51: 11 May 1835-D: Isaac Caldwell and wife Elizabeth H.(Robinson) of Hds.Co.to Lucy Caniel(Carriel)land on Deer Creek in the area around Wilmot.S24(part of);S23,T17,R7W.

P.53: 31 Mar.1834-D: Daniel W.Connely of 1st.pt,sells to Malcolm McNeill and Hector McNeill - $120,000.

P.64: 15 Dec.1832-D:David Yarbrough and Joseph Yarbrough to Wm.B.Cook, all of Wash.Co. Wit:Wyett R.Boice,Jos.Milan,Wm.(X) Yarbrough.

P.65: 9 Dec.1834-D:Joseph Castleman and wife Leney of Warr.Co. to Jilson P.Harrison of same.

P.72:9 May 1835-D:Biddy Bankston sold 130 ac.for$10 to Bennet M.Hines.

P.74:9 May 1835-D:George L.Crane,Nancy Crane and Joseph Bankston of 1st pt;to Bennet M.Hines of 2nd.

P.89:27 Jan.1834-D:Jos.D.Abney,Adm. of Est. of Aron Laville, decd.of Hds.Co.,sells to Wm.H.Sims of Warren.

P.90:24 Nov.1834-D:Wm.E.Hall and wife Lucinda,Elijah F.Atchison and wife Kiziah(Taylor),all of Wash.Co.to John G.Cocks,Wm.L.Scott of same.$27,000.

P.92:3 Mar.1835-D:Stephen Duncan and wife Catharine(Bingamon) Duncan,sell for $5, a Plantation opposite Lake Providence,La. on E.side of the River to Zenas Preston + slaves. They had a co-partnership.

P.94:2 Mar.1835-D:For $1,Stephen Duncan sells to Robert McCullough and wife Maria M. of Wash.Co. Duncan is in Adams Co.,and they have a co-partnership.[Note:Robt.McCullough marr.Maria Harmon - Adms.Co.29 Dec.1824; He marr. Elizabeth C.Perkins Adms.Co.22 Aug.1839]

P.105:25 May 1834-D:Wm.Russell and Sherwood Russell of Rankin Co.Ms,to David W.Connely and Andrew L.Wilson.

P.109:20 May 1835-Declaration of a Witness:"I last left Natchez which was on the 28th day of Feb.last to come to Princeton that a proposition was made on the part of Doct.D.B.Benbrook and Francis Newcomb of that place to Doct.Preston Frazier to erase some words in a article that existed - them in relation to a farm thatthey bought at this place,of Genrl.C.Haring - the sd. Frazier was bonded in sd.article to pay $5,000 and Benbrook & Newcomb were to place so many slaves on this place and couldn't comply - so a new article was signed." This document was signed A.W.Samuel, who was the wit.to the "erase"part.[A.W.Samuel was overseer to Preston Frazier at this time]

P.114:3 Sept.1835-Mortg:$40,000 on 1,160 ac.in Hds.Co.Nathaniel A.Ware of Ms.,1st pt;andChas.I.Ingersoll of Penn.the other pt. 10,000 + ac.in Wash.Co.Ms.,land description runs 4 ppgs.Wit: Henry Baldwin,John Ingersoll.

P123:21 June 1835-P.O.A.: David McAllister of Hds.Co.gives P.O.A. to Thomas James to sell land.Thos. then sells it to John James p.124. Wit:R.S.Foote.

DEED BOOK "D": Washington Co.Ms.
DATED:29 July 1835 - 7 Jan.1836

P.125:27 Mar.1834-D:Council R.Bass and Jesse Bass,Adms. of Est.of Edmond P.Bass,decd.of Wash.Co.to Thomas Grimes of same. (See Vol.II of this series.)

P.127:15 Dec.1834-D:David Hunt and Ann F. his wife,Jos.Dunbar and wife Olivia of 1st pt;to Zenas Preston and Benjamin Harmon of Wash.Co.,2nd/ Orig.Pat.issued to S.M.Dickson(also sp.Dickinson)[Note:"Hometown Ms."by Brieger,states that Zenas Preston, Robt.McCullough and E.F.Atchinson were brothers-in-law, and that Stephen Duncan was kin.][Jos.Dunbar marr.Olivia Magruder 1808 in Claib.Co.,Ms.]

P.134 17 Dec.1831-D:Henry Prout to Richard Armstrong.Wit:T.Y. Chaney.

P.136:26 Nov.1835-D:$34,000 - Preston Frazier of Wash.Co.to Granville H.Frazier of Bedford Co.Tn.Land Preston Frazier,D.G. Benbrook,F.A.Newcomb bought from C.Haring in Jan.,known to be former property of Matthew Flournoy - and lands bought from Edmond P.Bass...below Princeton.Wit:Jesse Grant,Jas.Evans.

P.153:--Mar.1835-Mortg:Henry T.Irish and H(Hannah)Mary Irish of Claib.Co.Ms.1st pt;Passmore Hoopes,2nd.

P.162:2 Jan.1835-Quit Claim:Mary Fleetwood ,wife of Miles Fleetwood of Wash.Co.1st pt;to Wm.Vick of Warr.Co.Bennet M.Hines is now J.P. for Wash.Co.

P.164:6 Mar.1835-D:Parish of E.Baton Rouge,La.:Elijah Selser sells to Mordecai Powell of St.Helena P.,La. and Morgan Morgan of Hempstead Co.,Ark.Terr...the undivided Est. of "my brother Elisha Selser,decd".of Wash.Co.[Note:Hist. of Sharkey Co.as compiled by the W.P.A. states that"Elisha Sulsor died of Cholera in 1831"- Sharkey was made from part of Wash.Co.+ others.]

P.165:6 Oct.1835-D:Mary Wilkins and David(X)Wilkins to Mordecai Powell and Samuel Folks.

P.167:4 July 1835-D:Oliver B.Cobb to Saml.Folkes and Miles C. Folks all of Warr.Co.Ms.

P170: 13 July 1835-D:Morgan Morgan and wife Elizabeth of Vicksburg, to Saml. and Miles C.Folks

P.191:10 Nov.1835-D:Wm.Lewis Sharkey and wife Minerva of V'burg to Jas.J.Chewning and John S.Gooch.Wit:Edw.Yager,Ferdinand Sims.

P.198:28 Nov.1835-D:Robert McCay and wife Eliza of Hds.Co.to Alexander G.McNutt of Warr.

P.203:8 June 1835-Mortg: A.B.Reading and wife Sophia E. of 1st pt;J.W.Walker,2nd;Edw.Ford & Co.,3rd.

[Note: Many pages of Mortgages follow for the next 45 pages, giving no genealogical information.]

P.240:1 July 1835-D:Henry Rufus William Hill and wife Margretta E.(McAllister) of Nashville,Davidson Co.Tn.to Wm.M.Gwin of --Co.Ms.[Note: see Vol.II of this series for Hill information.]

DEED BOOK "D": WASHINGTON CO.,MS.
DATED:29 July 1835 - 7Jna.1836

P.243: 7 Dec.1835-D:A.G.McNutt and wife Eliza A.(Lewis) to Thos.S.Sumerall.

P.244: 7 May 1835-D:Roland M.Whitman and wife S.A. of Wash.Co. to Martha Clarke of same.

P.250:22 Dec.1835-D:Elijah Bennett to John Morrison, both of Carroll P.La.

P.252:4 Jan.1836-D:Alexander Montgomery and Matilda B.his wife of 1st part;H.B.Austin of 2nd, all of Hds.Co.

P.253: 2 Jan.1836-D:John Wesley Vick of Warr.Co. to Hugh R.Austin of Hds.[Note:John Wesley Vick was the youngest son of Rev.Newitt Vick and Elizabeth (Clarke) Vick of Vicksburg.]

P.255:22 Dec.1835-Mortg: Hugh R.Austin of Hds.Co.1st prt;John Ingersoll of New Orleans,2nd pt;Theodoric Thompson of Philadelphia,Pa. 3rd pt.

[Note:Next followed a series of small acreage tracts,Original Patents, around $400,being sold to Robert H.Buckner.]

P.274: 8 Dec.1834-D:John Lane and wife Sarah C. and John Allen Lane and wife Nancy P. all of Warr,Co.1st pt; to Joseph Neibert and James C.Wilkins of Adms.Co. [Note:From the J.W.Vick Bible: John Lane marr.Sarah Clarke Vick 27 Oct.1819,dau. of Rev.Newitt Vick and his wife Elizabeth (Clarke) Vick, for whom Vicksburg is named. The Bible is available at the "Old Courthouse Museum" in Vicksburg,Ms.]

P.276:16 Jan.1836-Petition for Partition: Samuel and Amanda Worthington of Wash.Co.Ms.of the 1st part; James Rucks and wife Louisa V. - the former Louisa V.Brown, Wm.B.Reese and wife Henrietta M. - formerly Henrietta M.Brown, Orlanda Brown and wife Mary W.Brown, Robert W.Scott and wife Elizabeth W.- formerly Elizabeth W.Brown,John P.W.Brown all of the 2nd part.
The late Preston W.Brown of Ky. entered an agreement with Saml. Worthington,9 Sept.1825,to co-partner a farm in Ms. This agreement was modified by Saml.Worthington and John Brown and Elizabeth Brown,widow and relict - acting asExec.of sd.P.W.Brown, decd.- document bearing date - 18 Mar.1828. Worthington bought land in 1830, and distributed ½ to the heirs of partner Brown. The whole is around 1563+ ac.near Ms.River. Both groups seek partition of these lands. One reference is to Indian lands known as the Polly Collins Tract, at "the chute and Island,now owned by Thos.G.Percy."On P.280: 16 Jan.1836 - Deed of Partition: Saml.Worthington to Elizabeth Brown of Frankfort,Ky - land around Lake Washington,Wash.Co.Ms.

P.282: 16 Jan.1836-Relinq:Elizabeth Brown of 1st part; Samuel Worthington, James and Louisa Rucks,Wm.B.Reese and Henrietta, Orlando and Mary Brown,Robert and Elizabeth Scott,John P.WBrown of the other pt. Concerns partnership between Worthington and Preston Brown,decd. Even though the heirs sought to protect Elizabeth's dower rights,she elects to relinquish all rights in their favor.

DEED BOOK "D": WASHINGTON CO.,MS
DATED: 29 July 1835 - 7 Jan.1836

P.286:26 Dec.1833-D:Joseph K.Newman and wife Charlotte A.E. of Natchez to James Ferguson of Natchez.[Note:Charlotte A.E.(Mc-Allister)Newman was the dau. of Capt.John McAllister,and the sister to Augustus W.McAllister, and Harriet (McAllister)Blanton both of whom came early to Wash.Co.]
                End of DBk."D": Partial Index in Rear
===

SUPPLEMENTARY INFORMATION
Marriage Records - Adams Co.,Ms.
Butler,Thos. to Ann Ellis   15 Aug.1813
Crane,Wm.to Elizabeth Walbert   7 July 1825
Crane,Wm.C. to Caroline M.Brooks   11 Mar.1836
Dameron,George C. to Mary T.Gwin   2 Feb.1838
Quitman,John A. to Elizabeth Turner 20 Dec.1824
Rawlings,Covington to Caroline Grayson   30 May 1833
Taylor,Shepherd to Keziah Harman   1 June 1823

Marriage Records - Wilkinson Co.,Ms.
Christmas,Richard to Mary W.Sims   11 June 1833
Gwin,James to Delilah Lea,Zachariah Lea sec. 6 Nov.1806
Philbrook,John to Susan Scott   27 Aug.1834

Marriage Records - Madison Co.,Ms.
Balfour,Charles R. to Catherine Hudnall 7 Jan.1839
Gwin,Alexander M. to Elizabeth Caroline Lowry   13 Sept.1843

Newspaper Notices of Mississippians 1820 - 1860
Goodman (Giddeon) Bass died at the residence of his brother,
        Jesse Bass   15 Sept.1837 - age 22. Jackson,Ms.

Will book "A" - Claib.Co.Ms.
P.149:Will of Waterman Crane,formerly of Nova Scotia
        Dated 5 Feb.1826
        Wife:Catherine (formerly Brashears)
        Daus:Lucy McNeil and Clarissa Young
        Gr.Sons:Wm.Crane and Robert Mitchell
        Son:James Crane
        Gr.Dau:Caroline Christian and Catherine Quinn

Calviton Cemetary - Church Hill - Jeff.Co.,Ms.
Hunt,David b 1779,N.J. decd.1861 - marr.Mary Calvit who decd.
        1810,age 17;marr.3rd Ann Ferguson,who decd.1874.(From
        Ms.Cem.& Biblr Rec.Vol.III)

Marriage Records Jeff.Co.Ms - Bk."A"
Prince,Wm.B. to Sally S.Jefferies   Dec.1819
Terry,Wm. to Martha Ker   28 Feb.1818

MARRIAGES,DEATH & LEGAL NOTICES FROM EARLY ALA.NEWSP.,1819-1893
by Gandrud.P.474:Marr.Thurs.evening,24th Nov.by Rev.Dr.Delaney, Charles Ingersoll to Susan Catharine, only dau.of the late Dr. Samuel Brown of Ala.(Dec.10,1831)

DEED BOOK "E": WASHINGTON CO.,MS.
DATED: 16 Jan.1836 - 14 Nov.1836

This is the original book. The edges have been taped to keep
them from wearing off,making page numbers difficult to read.
721 pages - writing varies from passable to horrible. A partial
index is in the rear of this volumn,which has been included,
since only documents showing genealogical information have been
abstracted. Indexed in Master Deed Index,Bk.1. On microfilm
in Ms.Archives,Jackson,Ms.

Partial index:1st 162 pages,only.

Austin to Ingersoll 117	McCay to Ferguson 59
Bookout to Herring 3	McNeill to Hughes 70
Black,E. to D.Montgomery 22	" " Paxton 125
Butler,N. to Buckner 39	" Dawson 127
Barrow,G.W. to Connely,et al 47	Moore to Wilkinson 143
Byrd,et al to " , 62	Overton to Lewis 146
Bullen & Co. to Kilpatrick 87	Montroy,F.S. to Trice 158
Bowling,R.E. to J.G.Parham 123	Powell to Hart 95
Barnard to Offutt 120	Peyton to Traseman 105
Baley to Hood 138	Paxton to Dawson 130
Cox,A. to C.Turnbull 2	Patton,M.D. to Foote 151
Cunningham,B.C. to Arthur 16	Powell,M. to Folks 136
" . to D.W.Connely 29	Shirley to Lane 8
Crockett,L. to R.H.Buckner 41	Steen,Robt. to D.Montgomery 29
Campbell,Polly et al to Fitz 75	Skinner,H. to Connely 34
Cadwid(?),et al to Fitz 77	Spell,J. to Connely 34
Cox & Co. to Fisher 90	Stuart & Co. " 63
Campbell to Ware 113	_____ to Grimes 96
Claiborne to Offutt 115	Stephens to Chapman 97
Campbell to Smith,B. 122	Spikes to Martin 155
Chewning to Sharkey 132	Tunstall,J. to Arthur 14
Carter to Lambeth 144	" " " Connely 31
Dixon,Robt. to P.T.Williams 37	Touchstone,D. to Buckner 42
Denham,S. to Connely 49	Tunstall to Connely 67
" " " 67	Tunlow & Co. to Fitz 73
Downing to Fitz 71	Turnbull,C. to Lamb 141
Davis,Labon to Fitz 82	Van Cleave,T to Fulsom 20
Dawson,W.B. to Dawson,G.C. 148	Vick,J.W. to Vick,G.J. 131
Evans to Reynolds 7	Vanclive to Wilson 139
Everette to Conley 55	Wilkinson,P. to Wilkinson,J.1
Fisk,A.to W.H.Sims 162	Witmire to Connely & Wilson 51
Godin to Morris,E. 11	Whiclin to Conely * Wilson 53,57
Garland to Ford 99	Williams to Dickson 67
Helburn to Fitz 79	Whitman to Paxton 108
Howell to Fitz 86	Worthington,W. to F.P.Plant 150
Holland to McCuddy 102	" ," " Blackburn 157
Henly to Mason 130	
Hinds,B.M. to Ball 158	
Jasper,A. to Arthur,J. 13	
Johnson,E. to D.Montgomery 24	
" ,W. to Arthur,L.M. 25	
Lastley,A & C. to G.W.Arthur	-- Lobdell,L. to Lobdell,G.C. 135
Laird,A. to D.W.Connely 33	Muir to Robt.Garland 4
Lee,J.D. to R.H.Buckner 44	Monge to Arthur,G.& C. 10

DEED BOOK "E": WASHINGTON CO.,MS.
DATED: 16 Jan.1836 - 14 Nov.1836

"Mississippi had three land offices in 1832 - Washington,Augusta, and Mt.Salus (Clinton). Two more were added in 1833 - Columbus and Chocchuma. Between 1833 and 1837, seven million acres of land were sold in the state. In one year alone - 1835-land sales in the state accounted for 2,931,181.15 acres. Mt. Salus was the busiest in 1834 and 1835. These lands were sold ...cash,$1.25 per acre,80 ac.minimum." Taken from "A HISTORY OF MISSISSIPPI", Vol.I,Ed. by McLemore;p.289.
==

[Note: The first 40 - 50 ppgs. deal with small "lots" of land:]

P.8: 4 Feb.1835D:Adam Shirley and wife Elenda(X) to John Allen Lane.

P.11: 19 Oct.1835-D:Wm.F.Godin and wife Amanda, and John Stamps and wife Henrietta of 1st pt; to Edmund Morris of 2nd part.

P.13:D:Archibald (X)Jasper and wife Emily S.(X) of Hds.Co. 1stpart; to Isaac W.Arthur and Zenas K.Fulton of Adms.Co.(160ac)

P.16:18 Aug.1835-D:Belinda B.Cunningham wife of Calvin Cunningham Wash.Co.,1st pt; to Isaac W.Arthur and Z.K.Fulton other part of Adms.Co.

P.18:29 Aug.1835-D:Alexander Lasley and wife Catharine of Wash. Co.1st pt; to Arthur & Fulton of Adms.Co. Wit:John Fulton,H.C. Brown.

P.22: 12 May 1834-D:Ezekiel Black,Adm. of Est. of Ezekiel Black, Sen.,decd. of Wash.Co. to Davis Montgomery.

P.23:27 July 1835-D:Winn Johnson and wife Elizabeth (X) of Hds. ;Davis Montgomery of other part.

P.25:27 July 1835-D:Wm.Johnson and wife Leanna of Hds. to Arthur & Fulton.

P.47:25 July 1835-D:George W.Barlow and wife Lydia of Simpson Co.,Ms.for $450 to David E.Connely and Andrew L.Wilson.

[Note: Many more small transactions follow, many to Connely & Wilson; many to Robert H.Buckner.]

P.115:13 Nov.1835-D:John F.N.Claiborne and wife Martha D. of Madison Co.,Ms. to Z.C.Offutt; an Orig.Pat.issued to Claiborne and Thomas Barnard.

P.120:8 Nov.1835-D:Thos.Barnard and wife Eliza Jane of Adms.Co. to Z.C.Offutt of Wash.Co.

P.122:5 Jan.1836-D:Jos.O.Campbell and wife Narcissa, and John Campbell of 1st pt; to Benj.Smith of Scott Co.Ky,2nd pt;

P.123:2 Dec.1835-Mort:Robt.Bolling [He signs document - Richard E.]sells for $10 to John G.Parham,land jointly owned with John F.Brodnax.Land descriptions show the property lying in present Sunflower Co.,on East side of Sunflower River,opposite Darlove @1500 ac.+ several more hundred ac. in present Sharkey Co.

DEED BOOK "E": WASHINGTON CO.,MS.
DATED: 16 Jan.1836 - 14 Nov.1836

P.131:16 Jan.1831-D:Henry W.Vick of Yazoo Co.,sells for $10,to Grey P.Vick of same.[Note:Brothers - sons of Burwell Vick] Filed 6 Jan.1836.

P.136:21 Mar.1835-D:Nevi(X) Henley,Adm. of Est. of Eli Henley, decd. of Warr.Co. to Saml.Mason.

P.138:13 Jan.1836-D:Elizabeth (X) Bailey of Helena,Ter. of Ark. Adm. of Est. of Thos.Bailey,late of sd.Terr.,decd.to Goved(Gary?) Hood of Carroll P.,La.Elizabeth is also Guard. of her infant children - Christiana Bailey and Jas.Thos.Bailey.

P.143: 3 July 1832-P.O.A.:Benj.Moore gives P.O.A. to Peter Wilkerson,both of Wash.Co.,to tend to land sold as Preemptive rights on Public lands in 1830, and entered jointly with John McJenkins.Benj.says that Miles Fleetwood deposited the full amount of money and Wm.B.Cook said he obtained the receipt for same. Moore then agreed to swap his Orig.Pat.for one obtained by a "man named Price" - but nothing had been settled.

P.148:26 Oct.1835-D:Wm.B.Dameron of the 1st pt;Geo.C.Dameron of 2nd - both of Hds.Co.

P.151:12 Jan.1836-D:Matthew D.Patten and wife Susan B. of Hds. Co. - 1st pt; to Henry S.Foote of same,2nd.Ingersoll & Co.of New Orleans (merchantile) 3rd.

P.153:23 Dec.1835-D:Wm.Spikes and wife Lacissa(X) and John Ragland,all of Simpson Co.,Ms.to Joshua C.Martin of other pt.

P.162:30 May 1834-Petition for Partition:Alvarez Fisk of Natcz. and Wm.H.Sims of V'burg, purchased in 1831,divers tracts of land with the intent of holding such as partners.Some transactions in Fisk's name and some in Sim's.An agreement was reached that Fisk deed ½ of what he holds to Sims and for Sims to do likewise.P.164: is the release of Dower Rights by the two wives Sarah Jane Sims,wife of Wm.H.Sims, and Eliza W.Fisk - wife of Alvarez Fisk. This release was signed - 30 May 1834.

P.165:12 Jan.1835-D;Susan Philbrick of Wilk.Co.Ms.,sells,for $5,500 to her son Benj.Franklin Scott of same Co.,thereby releasing all claim she,Susan,may have had in the real estate of the late Abram M.Scott,"my late husband"...1 undivided 4th of@ 6,000 ac.Wit:S.Harriet Scott,W.Howard West,B.K.Mabrey.

P.168:16 Jan.1834-D:Benj.F.Scott of Wilk.Co.Ms.,sells,for $2,750 to his brother John A.Scott of same,½ of above tract,received from their mother.Wit:J.Joor,Wm.H.Eggleston.

P.170:29 Jan.1835-D:Wm.R.Campbell and wife Margaret of Warr.Co. sell to Nathl.A.Ware,land around Wilmot for $4,827.Orig.Pat. had been issued to Campbell.

P.188:Andrew Knox and wife Myra Jane [Prince] of Wash.Co.sell to Thos.T.Theobald and Patterson L.Bains of Frank.Co.Ky.Orig. Pat. for $24,000.

P.192:18 Feb.1834-D:Rich.Armstrong and wife Sarah (X) of Warr. Co. to Wm.Rushing of 2nd pt.

DEED BOOK "D":WASHINGTON CO.,MS.
DATED: 29 July 1835-7 Jan.1836

P.196:Jan.1836: Passmore Hoopes and wife Eliza T. to Jos.H.Moore
of Port Gibson;$175,000 to J.Waldo Putnam,Mortg.Large amt. of
land described,located in Wash.Co.,Claib.Co,Copiah Co. Documents
entered in 3 different handwritings. Dates of purchase listed.
Last date entered - 1 Jan.1839.

P.205:5 Feb.1836-P.O.A.:Passmore Hoopes gives P.O.A.to Jas.Derrah
to take possession of land deeded to him by D.G.Bainbrook,F.A.
Newcomb.P.Frazier.

P.209:12 Dec.1835-D:Abraham Dehart,Geo.Mooney and wife Margaret
of Wash.Co.,1st part;to Wm.E.Bain and John H.Robb of Fayette
Co.Ky - Orig.Pat. - 504+ ac.

P.221:29 Feb.1836-D:John T.Brodnax and wife Mary E. to Alexander
T.B.Merritt and Wm.H.E.Merritt.[Note:John T.Brodnax marr.Mary
Elizabeth Vick,dau. of Hartwell Vick and his wife Slyvia(Cook)
Vick.Alex.T.B.Merritt and his bro.,Wm.H.E.Merritt were the bros.
of the 1st wife of John Greenway Parham,M.D. ,who marr.in Greens-
ville Co.Va.Rebecca F.M.Merritt. In 1829, the Parhams came to
Warr.Co.The parents of Rebecca F.M.,Alexander T.B.,Wm.H.E. were
Rev.Henry Merritt and Elizabeth (Walker)Merritt. There is no
indication that the Merritt brothers ever came to Ms. to live.
Rebecca (Merritt)Parham died in 1844 and Dr.Parham marr.,2nd,Eliza
Hulda Morse,gr.dau.of Newitt and Elizabeth(Clarke)Vick. Mary
E.(Vick)Brodnax was also the gr.dau. of Newitt Vick.]

P.223:6 Nov.1835-Petition forPartition:Isaac Caldwell,Alfred C.
Downs,Jilson P.Harrison desire a partition of their holdings.
Isaac and Alf.C. own ½, and Jilson the other undivided ½,land
originally entered by Isaac Caldwell and Thos.D.Downs.[Note:
Alf.C.Downs marr. Mary Jane Robinson; a son- Jas.Robinson Downs
marr. 1859 Letticia F.B.Vick - dau. of Letticia Frances Booker
of Ky and John Wesley Vick of Warr.Co.Ms.Lettie (Vick)Downs
was also, a gr.dau.of Newitt and Elizabeth(Clarke)Vick. Isaac
Caldwell marr.Elizabeth Robinson, and Thos.D.Downs marr. Lucy
Robinson.See "The Journal of Lettie Vick Downs in the Yr.1863"
in Archives,Jackson,Ms.]

P.228:18 Feb.1836- The State of La.,New Orleans; Wm.Ley and
Wm.H.Taylor bought,in partnership,various lands.Wm.Ley sells
out to Taylor for $15,000 - Orig.Pat.received at Mt.Salus.[See
Vol.I,II of this series for Est. of Wm.Ley.]

P.245:19 Jan.1836-D:Orig.Pat.issued to Ezekiel Courtney and
wife Elizabeth (X) of Wash.Co/1st pt;to Egbert Harris of Mad.
Co.Ala.

P.246:5 Mar.1836-Release:Rebecca Wilkerson,wife of Peter Wilkerson of Wash.Co.,for $1,releases all claims of dower rights,etc.
to Jefferson Wilkerson of same.

P.248:2 Jan.1834-D:Joslin(X)Miller and wife Hester Ann(X) sell
land obtained by Preemptive rights,to Wm.W.Blanton...all of
Wash.Co.Ms.

P.255:2 Jan.1834-D:Hiram D.Miller and wife Sarah (X);Wm.Steph-
enson and wife Mary;[In margin is written John (X)Stephenson].Wm.
Johnson and wife Nancy; Wm.Miller and wife Edith;Joslin Miller
and wife Hester Ann(X) - all of the 1st pt; to Alfred G.Carter

DEED BOOK "E": WASHINGTON CO.,MS.
DATED: 16 Jan.1836 - 14 Nov.1836

P.255: cont. from last page: of the 2nd pt;All of the 1st part sign,including John Stephenson, except Nancy Johnson.

P.260:15 Dec.1835-D:Thos.B.Haralson and wife Isabella Ann[she signed Isabella M.]of Wash.Co. to Jas.P.Parker of Claib.Co.Ms a tract of land entered at Chocchuma (Land Sales Office)by Robt.J.Walker of Adams Co.Ms.

[Note:The next pages are taken up with many land transactions as Chas.R.Campbell makes his holdings in the new land extensive. Also,Wm.R.Campbell & Jos.Hough of Butler Co.Ohio buy - buy - buy.]

P324:14 Mar.1836-Power of Atty.report:Jas.Derrah,atty. for Passmore Hoopes,finds Newcomb,Benbrook,Frazier unable to make payments to C.Haring;so Hoopes buys land in question directly from C.Haring,et al...heirs of A.Haring.

P.353:3 Jan.1836-D:John McCaughan and wife Susan T. of Hds.Co. to Jos.W.Robertson of Wash.Co.,2nd pt;

P.372:10 May 1835-D:Thos.G.Ellis to wife Mary N.(Routh) who signed in Adms.Co. to Thos.Barnard and Robt.J.Walker.

P.386:13 Apr.1836-D:David Vertner and wife Elizabeth, and Vans M.Sullivan of 1st pt;to John D.Vertner of other...all of Claib. Co.Ms.,for $2,000.

P.392:4 Dec.1834-D:Cassandra Selser",surviving widow of John Whitten,late of Parish of E.Baton Rouge,decd"of the 1st pt;to Mordecai Powell of same of the other pt;She sells her interest in her "brother Elisha Selser's Est." who lately died in Ms. Wit:Elisha S.Whitten and Wm.Whitten.

P.393:23 Mar.1835-D:Chas.S.Abercrombie and wife Mary Caroline of Adms.Co;to Wm.H.Bryan and Wm.S.Ellis of Bourban Co.Ky.Orig.Pat. held by Abercrombie.Wit:C.Haring

P.395:29 Dec.1835-D:Saml.Saxon and wife Milly of Wash.Co. of 1st pt;to John Turnbull of 2nd.Briggs Lacoste & Co. -3rd.

P.400:1 Feb.1836D:Gideon Gibson and wife Adeline,Jeremiah Ellexson,Benj.Hughes and wife Nancy,Passmore Hoopes and wife Eliza T.of 1st pt - the Gibsons and Ellexsons are from Warr.Co. and the Hughes and Hoopes from Claib.Co.;to Ambrose Gibson of Warr. Co.of the 2nd pt;Land fronting on the River(Ms.)and near Steeles Bayou,entered at Mt.Salus 27 Nov.1834 by Hoopes,Gibson,Ellexson, Hughes. Around 5,000 ac.in t12,R8W - #25,000.

P.402:30 May 1834-D:Hiram G.Runnels and wife Obedience (Smith), Isaac Caldwell and wife Elizabeth H.(Robinson) of 1st pt;to Alvarez Fisk of Natchez,the other. In 1830-31,Fisk,Runnels,Caldwell were partners in purchasing land - large portions are in the name of Caldwell.This document is an agreement to equalize the holdings.Caldwell and Runnels sell their 2/3rds to Fisk,at $5 per ac...$8,780 - 2,611 ac. on Deer Creek(T13N,R6W) now in present Sharkey Co. Furthermore Caldwell had entered an agreement with R.B.Herring to swap some small pieces. Runnels and wife,and Caldwell signHds.Co.[Runnels was Gov.Nov.1833-Nov.1835]

DEED BOOK "E": WASHINGTON CO.,MS.
DATED: 16 Jan.1836 - 14 Nov.1836

P.404:9 June 1835-D:Wm.H.Hamer and wife Amazon J.of Warr.Co.to A.Fisk of Natchez,$2,090 for Orig.Pat.issued to G.B.Dameron May 1832. P.406:D: Same people,deals with an Orig.Pat. by Hamer & Fisk.

P.409:26 Mar.1832-D:Thomas Ferguson and wife Caroline M.,Thos.D. Downs and wife Lucy Downs of Warr.Co. of 1st pt;to Alvarez Fisk of Natchez. Land near a "newly discovered lake" near Manchester [now Yazoo City]adjoining land of Benjamin Roucks (Rucks?)

P.416:18 Feb.1836-D:Ezekiel Black and wife Mary (X),Chicot Co., Ark.Terr. and Andrew J.Black of 1st pt; to Isaac W.Arthur and Zenas K.Fulton of Adms.Co.

P.420:26 Apr.1835-D:Carroll P.,La. - Judge Felix Bosworth,Parish Judge,presiding;Robt.Jas.Chambliss and wife Lucinda L.Hood and Gary (Grey?)Hood and wife Nancy C.Phillips sole heirs and representatives of late Harbird Hood of sd. Parish,decd. All above majority age,and reside in same Parish...heirs sell to Robt. McCullough of Wash.Co.Ms.Orig.Pat.issued to Harbird in 1830, another Orig.Pat.#5451 issued to John S.Hood of the U.S. in 1830 at Mt.Salus,also,#5505 Orig.Pat.issued to Harbird. The heirs further state they are also the only heirs of John S.Hood, decd. Wives sign release to all rights,including dower. Wit: Charles H.Webb, Eli Harris.[Note:Robt.J.Chambliss,the son of Peter Chambliss and his 2nd or 3rd wife - Mary (Rutledge)Rife, widow,of Jeff. Co.Ms.,marr.,as his 2nd wife,Lucinda (Hood) Everette,widow of Abner Everette, of Carroll P.,La. Lucinda and her brother Gary,or Grey,Govan as sometimes spelled,Hood,were the children of Harbird Hood and his wife Nancy Stanford.Gary marr.Nancy Catherine Phillips. Lucinda (Hood) Chambliss decd. New Orleans by 1847,her Succession - Drw.11,Carroll P.,La.R.J. Chambliss decd.1850,Carroll P.,leaving a hugh Est.]

P.431:16 Feb.1836-D:Bill of Sale - Chas.Clark,Robt.Dixon,B.M. Markham,Adm.of Putnam T.Williams,decd. of Jeff.Co.Ms. - intestate...offer land at Public sale. Sold to John V.Newman and Wm. F.Markham.Est.contained 1,117 ac.+ slaves in Wash.Co.

P.433:14 Jan.1836-D:Jas.J.Chaney,West Feliciana P.La.of 1st pt;John J.McCaughan of Hds.Co.Land on Deer Creek,lot 5,6,,S25, T15,R7W - 140 ac.Orig.Pat.#5312.for $1400.

P.434:2 June 1836-D:Robt.F.Moore and wife Celeste A. of Claib. Co.of 1st pt;to Jos.H.Moore of Port Gibson of other;Robt.sells his portion of partnership MOORE & MOORE...land on Lake Wash.+ slaves.The land was formerly owned by Benj. and Nancy Hughes, Andrew and Myra Jane Knox,who sold it to Henry W.Barnes and W.P.Russum on 8 Feb.1833.[See page 18,this Vol.]

P.436:11 May 1836-D:Geo.W.Summers and wife Maria Jane of 1st pt;to Hugh Wall of 2nd..all of Grand Gulf.

P.442:1 Feb.1836-D:Wiley Davis and wife Mary Jane of Holmes Co.1st pt;to Levin R.Marshall of Natchez.

DEED BOOK "E": WASHINGTON CO.,MS.
DATED: 16 Jan.1836 - 14 Nov.1836

P.444:30 May 1836-Transfer of D:Wm.W.Collins,Trustee,appointed by Wm.P.Walker in Deed dated 11 Oct.1831,to collect payment from Walker to John G.Cocks of Wash.Co.of $2,000 of 1st pt; and Chas.Turnbull of 2ndof Wash.Land @ Princeton.

P.445:3 Jan.1836-D:Jesse M.Hooker and wife Cinderella of Warr. Co. of 1st pt;to Jas.Noe of 2nd.

P.449:10 Mar.1836-D:Wm.Henderson and wife Louisa of Warr.Co. 1st pt;to Jas.Noe - 2nd.

P.452:10 Mar.1836-D:Thos.S.Thomley and wife Angelina and Jas. Noe of 1st pt; to John A.Porter - 2nd.

P.454:6 Apr.1836-D:Robt.M.Spicer of Carroll Co.Ms. - 1st pt; to Theodorick B.Skinner of Baltimore,Md. - 2nd.

P.457:14 Mar.1836-D:Wiley Newberry of Chambers Co.,Ala - 1st pt;Wm.L.Davidson of Hds.Co - 2nd;Orig.Pat.obtained at Mt.Salus for $31,000 - whole of Sec.26,23,25, all in T14N,R4W + much more scattered about.

P.459:24 May 1836-Mortg:Henry S.Dawson and John Templeton,Jr. of 1st pt; to Jilson Harrison and Jas.O.Harrison,Trustees of 2nd;Wm.H.Taylor of 3rd. 1st part owes 3rd part.

P.461:4 June 1836-D:Alfred Cox of 1st pt;to Lake Wash.& Deer Creek Railroad and Banking Co.of 2nd.Land in town of Princeton.

P.469:Deed:Jacob Oates of Warr.Co. and Wm.H.Sims obtained lands and Oates sells his undivided share to Sims. Lands "situate... on Yazoo River...and known and designated in the U.S.Survey... as Sec.28,T18N,R1W,being the section of land on which was located the "floating reservation reserved jointly to Robt.M.Jones and Jas.M.McDonald under...Treaty of Dancing Rabbitt Creek on 27 Sept.1829..."Releasefollows,signed by Temperance(X) Oates, relinq.all claims to the property.2 Jan.1836.

P.471:5 May 1836-D:Gideon Gibson sells to John P.Overton for $100,000 - 1280 ac. on Bachelor's Bend - fronting on the Ms. River. Land Gideon bought from Claudius Gibson that Claudius "still lives on for the past 4 or 5 yrs.",bounded on N. by Jas.McCutcheon,on S.by the plantation of Wm.Hunt.

P.473:31 Mar.1836-D:Wm.H.Tegarden and wife Margaret of Hopkinsville,Ky.to Wm.H.Pope of Louisville,Ky.

P.477:D:Josiah(X)Loflin and wife Hetty(X) of 1st pt;Matthew D.Patton and Jas.McG.Cuddy of 2nd.$8,000 - 28 May 1836.

P.482:13 Feb.1835-D:Frederick G.Turnbull of Wash.Co.to Harvey Miller and Geo.W.Ward of same.Signed by F.G. and Mary Turnbull.

P.486:10 Oct.1832-D:Wm.R.Campbell sells to Wm.Bacon for $1. Wit:J.P.McNutt.Many transactions follow as Wm.Bacon of Warr.Co. buys land from Jas.Reilly & wife Ellen H.;from Stephen Howard, 1832;Burwell Ederington,1835;Elihu Kilpatrick and wife M.H., 1834;Archibald and John McAllister,1831;Dixon and Geo.W.Jelks, 1831;John and Arthur Ragland,1830 - recorded 22 June 1836.

DEED BOOK "E": WASHINGTON CO.,MS.
DATED: 16 Jan.1836 - 14 Nov.1836

P.506:20 June 1836-D:Jos.Marlow and wife Matilda of Wash.Co.to Andrew and Samuel Carson of 2nd pt;

P.509:15 Apr.1836-D:Nathl.A.Ware of Louisville,Ky of 1st pt; and Thos.Lyne,Chas.S.Hyatt,Chas.Sims all of Wilk.Co.Ms.

P.510:6 Dec.1834-D:George Irish and wife Ann E. to Passmore Hoopes of Claib.Co.Ms.

P.512:7 May 1836-D:Passmore Hoopes and wife Eliza of Claib.Co. to Cornelius Haring of Natchez.[Haring was a partner in the firm ROOD WELLS & CO.,with Harvey L.Rood and Eleazer H.Wells.]

P.514:16 June 1836-D:Cornelius Haring and wife Susan of Adms.Co. to Jas.H.Claiborne and Thos.Kershaw of same.$95,000 - land Cornelius bought from Matthew Flournoy.

P.517:12 Oct.1835-D:Francis (X)Cunningham and wife Jane(X) to Joel H.Willis.

P.524:3 Mar.1835-D:Benj.Franklin Scott of Wilk.Co.Ms.,sells undivided 1/4th for $15,000 - part of which lies in Hds.Co. and the rest in Wash.Co...he inherited from his late father, Abram M.Scott,decd.,+ undivided 1/8th he bought from his mother, Susan Philbrick in 1835;B.F.Scott sells to Thos.Lyne. Wit:E.H. Waills,John A.Scott.[Note:"Abram Scott was elected Gov. of Ms. 1831, and served from 9 Jan.1832 til his death on 12 June 1833." FromHIST.OF MS.By McLemore.Abram M.and Susan Scott had at least 2 ch. - Benj.Franklin,and John A.Scott who came to live in Wash.Co. and was the father of Guignard and Calhoun who were killed in the Civil War,John,Sarah- who marr.Harry Percy Lee,Car-oline - who marr.a Gibbs and lived in Columbia,S.C. and Fannie. From PWCHS.]

P.548:18 July 1836-D:Jas.McCutcheon and wife Susan of Wash.Co. 1st pt;to Thos.E.Helm of Adms.Co.the 2nd.[Note:Susan Mosby marr. 22 Dec.1835 in Oldham Co.Ky.to Jas.McCutcheon of Ms. and she marr.2nd Dr.Taylor.Jas.and Susan(Mosby)McCutcheon had a son, John McCutcheon; and by Susan's marr. to Dr.Taylor,she had a dau.Bettie Taylor who marr.Henry T.Ireys(Irish).From the MONT_ GOMERY PAPERS.]

P.596:9 Sept.1836D:Plantation named "Holly Ridge",sold by Step-hen Duncan and wife Catherine A.(Bingamon)Duncan to Ambrose and Gideon Gibson.T14N,R9W - bound by Moss & McMurtry on N. and on Duncan & McCullough on S.,by Ms.River on W. and vacant lands on E. Land conveyed by Jos.Neibert and wife Sarah (Prewitt) to Atchinson & Duncan by deed in 1833.(DBk."C"-30,31,32)

P.600:19 Sept.1836-D:Ambrose Gibson and wife Margaret,Gideon Gibson and wife Adeline,all of Warr.Co.of 1st pt; to Stephen Duncan of Adms.Co.

P.611:22 June 1836-D:Hugh W.Dunlap and wife Susannah of Hds.Co. of 1st pt;sell to Thos.J.Harper of other for $130,000.Many pgs. of land descriptions.

DEED BOOK "E": WASHINGTON CO.,MS.
DATED: 16 Jan.1826 - 14 Nov.1836

P.620:9 Nov.1835-D:John Hebron,Geo.Smith and wife Mary Y.G. Smith of Warr.Co. to A.M.Austin.On P.623:30 Nov.1835 - Julia G.Hebron,wife of John Hebron,releases all claims to sd.land.

P.627:23 Sept.1836:A.M.Paxton,Wm.H.Paxton to A.M.Austin - all sign + H.R.Austin,by "his lawful Atty."

P.629:13 July 1835-D:Mordecai Powell,now of Wash.Co. - to Morgan Morgan of Warr.Co.

P.631:29 Feb.1836-D:Bailey D.Chaney of E.Felic.P.La.to Morgan Morgan.P.632:Martha D.Chaney,wife of Bailey D.Chaney signs release to all claims to sd. land. 20 May 1836

P.633:24 Mar.1836-D:Morgan Morgan and wife Elizabeth of E.Felic. P.,La.to Samuel and Miles C.Folkes and Mordecai Powell.

P.651:6 Oct.1836-D:Rolin(also sp.Rowland,Rowlan)M.Whitman and wife Sarah A. of Wash.Co.of 1st pt;to John H.Cocks and Jas.Cocks of same(Name sp.Cox,Coke).Whitman sells undivided 1/5th land fronting on Ms.River that Hartwell Cocke,late of sd.Co.bought, and alsoall claim they - Rowland and Sarah A.-may have to dower of the present Mrs.Elizabeth Walker,formerly Mrs.Cocke,their parent, in the property of her decd.husband,Hartwell Cocke. [Note:Hartwell Cocke and wife Elizabeth had 5 ch.-Jas.Cocke, John H.Cocke,Mary Jane Cocke who marr.Wm.W.Collins in 1840, Louisianna Cocke, and Sarah A. who marr.Rowland M.Whitman.]

P.661:29 Feb.1836-D:R.J.Meigs of Nashville, of 1st pt;Jas. and Louisa V.Rucks - for $1, 1 undivided 1/5th of 8,787 ac.near Lake Wash.,which Louisa V.inherited from Preston W.Brown,decd... subjected to dower of Elizabeth Brown,widow. Jas.and Louisa V.Rucks are also from Nashville,Tn.

P.669:26 Nov.1834-D:Volney Stamps and wife Jane of Claib.Co. to Horatio N.Spencer of same.

P.671:1 Oct.1835-D:Saml.T.McAllister and wife Elizabeth of Natchez to Edward Sparrow and wife Minerva of Concordia P.La.

P.681:23 Mar.1836-D:Wm.Henry Taylor of Montg.Co.Ala.to Henry Dawson and John Templeton of Warr.Co. Land adjoining Wm.Ley,G.W. and Wm.H.Taylor,except some sold to Henry Brawner. Mary E.Taylor, wife of Wm.H.Taylor,releases all claims.Sold for $34,000.

P.686:7 July 1835-D:Jane (X)Hough,wife of Jos.Hough of Butler Co.Ohio quit claims a deed to Thos.Marsten Green,Saml.Templeton of Warr.Co.

P.691:26 Oct.1835Mortg:John Ingersoll,Atty.for Thos.G.Percy of Huntsville,Ala.to Henry Bechett of Philadelphia,Pa.

P.715:5 Oct.1836-D:Isaac Worthington of 1st pt;Jas.P.Brown of Bolivar Co.Ms and Thos.G.Percy of Mad.Co.Ala - trustees under the Will of Dr.Saml.Brown,decd.late of Mad.Co.Ala.Land descrp. includes the Polly Collins,alias Polly Bell, tract.

P.720:17 Sept.1834-D:Preemtive Rights of Henry Crow - 1/4th Sec. near Ms.River.He borrowed the money from Jos.Egg.

End of Deed Book "E"

DEED BOOK "F": WASHINGTON CO.,MS.
DATED: 17 Nov.1836 - 30 Dec.1837

Deed Bk."F" is the original book,512 pages,patched with darkening tape. Readable most of the time. Indexed in Master Index to Deeds - Bk.1;on microfilm. Only deeds showing family connections, or the first mention of persons to be found later in Wash.Co.documents, have been abstracted.
==

P.9: 5 Oct.1836-D:Thos.G.Percy and wife Maria of Mad.Co.Ala, and Jas.P.Brown,trustees by Will of Dr.Saml.Brown of 1st pt;to Isaac Worthington. Brown is now "of Bolivar Co.,Ms."

P.14: 8 Nov.1836-D:Thos.Lyne,John A.Scott and wife Sarah Slann Scott,Preston W.Farrar and wife Eliza Judith all of Wilk.Co.Ms. of the 1st pt;to George Joor of same - 2nd pt.

P.18:8 Nov.1836D:Wm.L.Rusk of Wash.Co.of1st pt;BIER & STEEVER of New Orleans,2nd.[Note:Wm.Rusk was marr.to the former Mary N.Selser,who decd.4 July 1833 leaving 3 ch. - Elan Selser Rusk b1829,Martha Eleanor Rusk b 1830,Wm.Jeff.Rusk b 1832.]

P.21:11 Nov.1836-Mortg:Robt.Jas.Turnbull,Physcian and his wife Anne of Westchester,N.Y.of 1st pt;to Gouverneur Morris Wilkins of N.Y.,N.Y;R.J.owes Wilkins $34,000,for which he puts up 1/5th of "Walnut Grove Plantation" in Wash.Co.,Ms. R.J.Turnbull and Wilkins entered into an agreement about certain slaves,9 Feb.1836 in Charleston,S.C.The slaves are listed under 2 headings - "by purchase of Trust of Est.of Mary C.Allan" and the other "by inheritance",apparently all of the slaves are on "Riverside Plantation".

P.26:10 Nov.1836-D:The State of S.C.;Anna B.Turnbull of Charleston,S.C.,widow,is pd.$3,000 by Dr.R.J.Turnbull - land in Ms.in Deed of partition between heirs of Robert J.Turnbull,decd. - called "the Wyche Tract."960 ac.in Sec.14,15,T13N,R9W.[Note:Land below Lake Wash.and now in present Issaquena Co.]Anna B.Turnbull received 1/5th of this tract as heir of Robt.J.Turnbull,decd.

P.28:11Nov.1836-Bond:Dr.Robt.J.Turnbull and wife Anne of Westchester,N.Y.submit bond of @$6,000 to Mrs.Anna B.Turnbull of Charleston,S.C.

P.32:2 Jan.1835-Agreement:An agreement between Andrew Turnbull of Wash.Co.Ms. and Dr.Robert James Turnbull of the state of N.Y. By last Will and Testament of Robert James Turnbull of S.C.,decd Dr.R.J.Turnbull is entitled to 1/5th portion of "Walnut Grove Plantation".Andrew Turnbull is fully entitled by inheritance and purchase made from remaining heirs - viz - Anna B.Turnbull-Robert M.Allan and wife Mary,Wm.Izard Bull and wife - Gracia,to 4/5ths of tract. All agree to partition "Walnut Grove Plt."into 5 parts and Dr.R.J.gets 1/5th...All heirs equal under the Will o Robert J.Turnbull,decd.of S.C.The heirs are:1.Anna B.(widow of) 2.Mary Allan,wife of Robt.M.Allan;3.Gracia Bull,wife of Wm.Izard Bull;4.Dr.R.J.Turnbull of N.Y.:5.Andrew Turnbull of Wash.Co.Ms. The land was divided into 1/5ths and lots were drawn - #1 to R.J., #2 to the Bulls,#3 Andrew,#4 the Allans,#5 Mrs. Turnbull.Andrew acts as the Atty.of the heirs and all agree to settlement terms.

DEED BOOK "F": WASHINGTON CO.,MS.
Dated: 17 Nov.1836 - 30 Dec.1837

P.34:1 Nov.1834 -D:Wm.Izard Bull and wife Gracia(Turnbull),sell their 1/5th portion to (her brother)Dr.R.J.Turnbull.Deed recorded Wash.Co.Ms.20 Dec.1836,and wit.by Andrew Turnbull.

P.36:1 Mar.1835-D:Frederick G.Turnbull and wife Mary of 1st pt; to Dr.R.J.Turnbull of Westchester,N.Y. - for $8,000.
[Note:Robert J.Turnbull,decd.,Charleston,S.C.sometime between Feb.1833 and July 1833. His Will is filed in Issa.Co.Ms.1910.For abstracts of the Wills of R.J.Turnbull#1;Dr.R.J.of N.Y.;Andrew's Est.;Est. of Chas.Turnbull;and others,see Vol.I,II of this series. Robert J.Turnbull who decd.Charleston,S.C.1833,left a wife Anna B. and 4 ch. - Andrew,Dr.R.J.,Mary and Gracia. Also in this area and active at the time were John Turnbull - described as a "merchant of Savannah" who had sons John Turnbull,Frederick Guerin Turnbull,Charles Turnbull by one wife, and Wm.B.Turnbull and Robert J.Turnbull by another. The two groups are obviously kin as they use the same names,and are in close contact.Robert J. Turnbull,the first one,was the largest absentee owner in Ms., supposedly sending John down to look after it all]

P.77:7 June 1836-D:Nicholas Gray and wife Ellen N. of Warr.Co. of 1st pt:and Jas.E.Sharkey & Thos.Rigby of 2nd.

P.82:2 Dec.1836-D:Mathias Overman and wife Ellen of Wash.Co.of 1st part;to John S.Penrice of same.Mrs.Overman signs - Sarah E.

P.91:12 Dec.1836-D:Albert G.Creath and wife Mary B.(Barnard) of Warr.Co.Ms.;to Horace B.Hill and Wm.Prather of Louisville,Ky.

P.127:10 Dec.1836-D:Jordan R.Bass of Mad.Co.Ms.to Thos.James of Wash.Co..

P.131:14 Nov.1836-D:Alexander B.Montgomery and wife Davidella of Wash.Co.,for $5 to Wm.Pinkney Montgomery.[Note:From THE MONTGOMERY PAPERS:Wm.Pinkney Montgomery was the brother of Alexander Barkley Montgomery. Alex.marr.25 Aug.1831 Davidella Flournoy dau.of David Flournoy of Fayette,Ky. Only 3 of 9 ch.lived to maturity.]

P.133:10 Jan.1835-D:Henry T.Irish and wife H.Mary of Claib.Co. Ms.to Peter C.Chambliss of Jeff.Co.Ms.

P.134:13 Jan.1837-D:Wm.Mann and wife Elizabeth of Hds.Co.1st pt; to Duncan G.Campbell and Cornelius Campbell of 2nd.

P.149:25 Jan.1836-D:George Poindexter and wife Ann of Wilk.Co. Ms.;to Boanerges Roberts of Ky.,Jacob Morgan of Hds.Co.,Ms. Philip Thornton of Va.2nd pt.The parties of the 2nd pt.buy land for $270,650...the land descriptions run to p.157.

P.165:--Feb.1837-Mortg:James Glass and wife Judith, and Geo.W. Reynolds of War.Co.of 1st pt;Wm.W.Wilkins of 2nd; and John G. Parham and Thos.C.Randolph of 3rd.

P.200:10 May 1836:Jas.J.Chewing and wife Sarah M., and Henry Dawson; to John Mitchum...all of Warr.Co.

DEED BOOK "F": WASHINGTON CO.,MS.
DATED: 17 Nov.1836 - 30 Dec.1837

P.209:9 Jan.1837-Mort:Henry S.Foote and wife Elizabeth, and Robt.H.Davidson of 1st part;Leroy Faulkner of 2nd;Saml.C.Faulkner of 3rd.[Note:Henry Stuart Foote,son of Richard Helm Foote and Jane (Stuart)Foote,was b.Fauquier Co.Va.28 Feb.1804,came to Jackson,Ms.1826,was Gov.of Ms.1852.He d.Nashville,Tn.19 May 1880 where he had settled.He was elected as a Unionist to the U.S.Senate from Ms. - 1852-54.He supported the Republican ticket 1876; marr.1st Elizabeth Winters,dau. of Thos.Winters and Catherine Storke Washington.From THE FOOTE FAMILY as compiled by Rupert Watson.]

P.230:1 Mar.1837-D:Wyle Bohanon and wife Ann; to W.H. and A.M. Paxton.

P.231:13 Apr.1837-Power of Atty:Emily Fisher of Wash.Co.,Admx.of Est. of Sidney S.Fisher,decd. of same - gives P.O.A. to John Fisher,"because of her great faith in him."

P.243:30 Dec.1836-D:Simon J.Strong and wife Martha H. of Warr.Co. of 1st pt;to Luke C.Standefer

P.251:8 Feb.1837-D:Nathl.Wilson and wife Margaret of Warr.Co. to Claudius and Gideon Gibson of same Co.

P.254:9 Feb.1837-D:Wm.A.Dromgoole and wife Sally of Wash.Co. 1st pt;Jesse M.Hooker,Archibald Nailor,Addison B.Carter - merchants and partners under firm name of HOOKER NAILOR & CO.

P.258:10 Jan.1837-D:Philip Augustus Haxall of Wilk.Co.Ms.to David W.Haxall of same.

P.267:18 Jan.1837-Agreement: Entered into 10 Jan.1835 between Ley and Taylor of 1st pt;Henry Brawner and Saml.Dent of 2nd. Wm.H.Taylor of Montgomery,Ala.sells 1,040 ac. of land on Silver Creek. This document filed in New Orleans.P.268:20 Jan.1837 - Mary E.Taylor signs a release to all rights in sd. land.

P.271:5 Mar.1836-Power of Atty:Henry Brawner of Chas.Co.Md., but "at present of Vicksburg"gives P.O.A.to Wm.A.Lake,Esq. of V'burg to take care of all matters pertaining to the land he bought frm Taylor(P.267 - above).Lake has instructions to deliver deed to Wm.M.Pinckard and Johnathon Karsner.

P.275:24 Jan.1837-D:Andrew L.Wilson and wife Ann Eliza and David W.Connely of Natchez - 1st pt;to John Overton of Warr.Co.

P.281:3 Jan.1837-D,Release:New Orleans - Before Felix Grima, Notary Pub. of N.O.,came Robt.Livingston Decoin of N.O.,who sells to Frederick Wm.Schmidt,also of N.O.,land bought in Wash. Co.Ms. Wife of Decoin is "Madam Jane Elizabeth Righton"- of full age - who signs release to all future claims to sd.land.

P.286:4 Mar.1837-D:John M.Scanlon sells to Eleazar H.Wells both of Ms.Said Scanlon and Cornelius Haring,and Harvey S.Rood do business as merch.in firm ROOD SCANLON & CO. in Princeton(Wash. Co.) and Rood Scanlon owned the building upon which lot the store is on,along with several other lots in towns of Princeton and Columbia.Scanlon sells his share of the store and partnership to Wells.

DEED BOOK "F": WASHINGTON CO.,MS.
DATED: 17 Nov.1836 - 30 Dec.1837

P.300:1 Apr.1836-D:Richard H.May and wife Elizabeth of Sumner Co.Tn.to Felix Chenault. Land inWash.Co.Ms.

P.304:1 Nov.1836-D:Manilus V.Thomason and wife Mary Ann of Scott Co.,Ky - 1st pt; to John L.Chapman of same.Land on Lake Wash. @ 940 ac. for $48,000.

P.316:15 Feb.1836-D:Morgan McAfee and wife Salina W. of Talla.Co. Ms. to Jefferson J.Hughes and Sargent Prentiss of Ms. - 1320 ac. for $17,000.

P.322:9 May 1837-Est. of Henry Crow,decd.Ann Crow(X),admx;to Geo.W.Ward.Document states that the late Henry Crow entered bond to Ward and Thos.Stephens for titles to land and died before he had paid for them.They pay Ann Crow,widow,$1, and retain title to the land.

P.323:24 Apr.1837:Est. of John DeHart,decd.Mildred(X)DeHart, Admx;John borrowed from Geo.W.Ward and Thos.Stephens to buy land,but died before he could make the payments.She,Mildred, relinq.all claim to the land.

P.325:20 Apr.1837-Mortg:Alexander T.McMurtry and wife Rebecca M.(Moss) of Natchez,mortg.to Wm.Ferriday of same and Henry L. Bennett of New Orleans...The plantation "Andalusia" + slaves. Ferriday and Bennett operate under the firm name SHIPP FERRIDAY. The mortg.was paid off in Sept.1838 and signed by Ferriday as "only surviving partner",by his atty.A.W.Samuels.

P.337:24 Mar.1837-D:Wm.Mills and wife Minerva G. of Warr.,Wm.S. Bodley and wife Ellen, also of Warr.;to Alfred T.Moore of Wilk. Co.Ms. and Isaac N.Glidwell of Warr.

P.338:13 Mar.1837-D:Julius J.Heite and David Fitzpatrick and wife Clementine of 1st pt;Isaac N.Glidwell and Cyrus Griffin.

P.339:30 Mar.1837-D:Sidney Fisher,late of Wash.Co.decd. was indebted to Thos.James of Wash.Co...Fisher signed notes,30 Dec. 1836 giving Council R.Bass,counsel for James,a D/T - land on the Ms.River,about 2 miles N.of Princeton,where Thos.James "Now resides"+slaves.If Fisher should default on one payment,Bass can then sell land,slaves,etc.at Public Auction, and since Sidney Fisher is "now decd" Bass sells the land in question,and James buys it for $15,000.

P.342:4 Apr.1837-Power of Atty:Andrew Carson of Wash.Co.gives P.O.A.to F.G.Turnbull of same Co.for Turnbull to sell hisrights to certain lands to Anderson Miller.

P.343:8 Mar.1837-Diss.of Partnership:Elijah Atchinson and wife Keziah H.(Harmon-Taylor) of Jeff.Co.Ky.of 1st pt;to Stephen Duncan of Natchez the other.The Atchinsons sell to Duncan "all their undivided ½ of land bound by MOSS & MCMURTRY on the N. by MCCULLOUGH on S.;by Ms.River on W.;vacant on E.[Note:T12,R9W area roughly in the Mayersville,Issa.Co.locale]Land bought from Jos.Neibert and wife Sarah (Prewitt) 15 Oct.1834 by ATCHISON & DUNCAN,named "Holly Ridge Plantation"containing 1700 ac.+ another piece of land and slaves.Wit:Robt.McCullough,Maria (Harmon)McCullough,John McCullough.

DEED BOOK "F": WASHINGTON CO.,MS.
DATED: 17 Nov.1836 - 30 Dec.1837

P.364:27 Sept.1836 - State of S.C.,recorded in Ms.:Andrew Turnbull is bound unto Alexander W.Campbell,Trustee under Marr.settlement of Thos.O.Elliott and Irwinia A.Elliott,his wife,for $34,800 - $17,000 of which is pd. by Turnbull's sale of 37 negroes and by Mortg. P.366:Andrew Turnbull and (his brother-in-law) Robert M.Allan borrow from the Trustee - Campbell. They give a mortg.on a plantation named "Penford",that belongs to Turnbull.[Note:Documents do not explain the location of "Penford.]

P.378:27 June 1837-D:Christopher Davidson to Wm.S.Dawson,both of Hds.Co."1 equal undivided moity" - all containing 382 + ac.

P.388:10 Mar.1836-D:Robert J.Walker and wife Mary B. and Thos. Barnard and wife Eliza J.,all of Adams Co. and signed for by their atty.Thos.Barnard - of 1st part;to Abram M.Feltus of Wilk.Co.Ms.

P.390:24 Apr.1837-Mortg:Chas.G.Walker of Wash.Co.1st pt;Thos.A. Walker of New York City - 2nd;Isaac Walker of N.Y.C. 3rd.

P.395:25 Mar.1837-Mortg:Aaron Alexander and wife Sarah A.and Wm.Moore and wife Margaret - all of Warr.Co.1st pt;Montford Jones and Wm.F.Ritchie of Warr.- 2nd;Sterling Neblett of Va. 3rd pt;In list of signatures - E.H.Moore also signed.

P.399:[Note:This document has been xxxx out,but was still readable]25 Apr.1837-"I,Emily Fisher,Admx.of Sidney Fisher,decd. give my P.O.A.to Thos.W.Endecott" to see to her interests as Admx.for Est. of Sidney Fisher.She revokes a former P.O.A. given to John Fisher.[This document is repeated on P.401]

P.400:29 Apr.1837-D:Theodorick J.James and wife Frances(X) of Wash.Co.to Frederick P.Plant of same.

PPgs.403,404 missing from book

P.407:25 Dec.1836-P.O.A.:John L.Chapman gives his P.O.A.to McLin Evans incase his present atty - Wm.F.Jeffries can't act.

P.409:25 --D:[Note: Edge of paper taped heavily]James E.Sharkey and wife Lavinia to Robt.Riddle.

P.412:15 Jan.1837-D:Thos.J.Harper and wife Mary Jane of 1st pt;Hugh W.Dunlap and wife Susannah of Hds.

P.426:6 Dec.1836-Mortg:Jas.E.Sharkey,Robt.H.Crump,Geo.Crump, James Crump - all of Warr.Co.1st pt;H.R.Austin of Hds.2nd;Jesse B.Ragan and Wm.H.Hunt of Warr. - 3rd.

P.428:13 Jan.1837-D:Daniel Comfort of1st pt;E.H.Cladwell(should be Caldwell)of Hds.2nd pt;Comfort buys,for $10,000 - Elizabeth's undivided 1/4th part of 2,571 + ac.entered in the name of Isaac Cladwell(sp.Caldwell) and Thos.D.Downs in Wash.Co.T18N,R8W, adjoining land of Augustus W.McAllister and Wm.Blanton[In general vicinity of present Greenville]See P.51,this Volumn.

P.429:12 Jan.1837:Est.of Isaac Caldwell,James B.Robinson,Exec. with E.H.Caldwell,execx of Will of Isaac Cladwell,decd.of 1st pt;to Danl.Comfort of other.

DEED BOOK "F: WASHINGTON CO.,MS.
DATED: 17 Nov.1836 - 30 Dec.1837

P.484:10 June 18--:Recorded 28 July 1836:Petition of Wm.Harris of Natchez:Harris states that he and Phineas F.Merrick were owners of some land in Wash.Co. - around 2,000 ac. Merrick is now decd.,leaving his widow Mrs.Merrick M.Merrick [copied as it is written] Admx., who has taken out Guardianship papers on persons and Est. of Charles Merrick and Delen(Helen?)Merrick only ch.and heirs of Phineas F.Merrick,decd. That sd.Hannah M. Merrick and the 2 ch.are the only heirs. Harris seeks partition of property - land on "Bunches Bend Island".

P.503:15 Aug.1837-Mortg:Wm.Barr and wife E.June,Geo.M.Pinckard and wife Sarah Ann,James McCutcheon and wife Susan P. - all of Louisville,Ky of 1st part;Wm.Richardson,Trustee for President Director & Co.of Northern Bank of Ky. - 2nd pt.

P.506:1 Apr.1837-D:John A.Scott and wife Sarah S. of Wilk.Co. of 1st pt; to Claudius F.Legrand of Warr.-2nd pt.

P.508:9 Sept.1837-D:David Suggett and wife Polly; to Asa Smith.
=====================================

THE FOLLOWING HUSBANDS AND WIVES NAMED IN SIMPLE DEEDS IN DBk. "F",WITH DATE OF DOCUMENT,AND THEIR PLACE OF RESIDENCE.

Faulkner,Saml.C. - Mary Ann Virginia Hds.Co. 1837
Hall,Wm.E. - Lucinda Wash.Co.Ms. 1837
Hanson,--- Pamala 1836
Leflore,Greenwood - Pricilla Carroll Co.,Ms.
McMurtry,Vincent W. - Eliza A. Wash.Co. 1836
Martin,Joseph - Matilday Ky. 1836
Moss,Henry K. - Narcissa Ann Hds.Co. 1835
Powell,John - Margaret Warr.
Puckett,Walter R. - Ann Matilda Warr.1836
Shirley,Adam - Ellender 1835
Slocum,Wm - Sobrina Yazoo Co.,Ms. 1836
Spencer,Horatio N. - Sarah A. Claib.Co.Ms. 1837
Taylor,Wm. - Maria. Wilk.Co.Ms.
              End of Deed Book "F"
==

SUPPLEMENTARY MATERIAL

¶[Note:The financial "bubble"burst in 1837. The current loose banking policies had caused severe shortages of reliable currencies on hand. The Specie Circular of 1836 that required the payment of gold and silver be made for the sale of Public Lands, left many of the banks floundering. The Specie Circular caused a general run on many banks and resentment in Ms. was strong against the U.S.Government.Naturally this hatred showed up in the political machinations of the State.]

Gov.McNutt was Gov. 1838 - 42, and tried to establish a firm foundation for the State's financial base."Gov.Runnels became so incensed over the remarks of the editor of the MISSISIPIAN (Published,Jackson,Ms.),Volney Howard,that he fought a duel with him in 1840.Because Gov.McNutt reputedly wished Howard "good Luck",Runnels caned McNutt in the streets of the State Capitol."HISTORY OF MS. by McLemore.

DEED BOOK "G": WASHINGTON CO.,MS.
DATED: 30 Dec.1837 - 23 Nov.1839

This volumn has been repaired with tape,then laminated. 545 pages - Indexed in Master Index 1 - on microfilm in Jackson.

The era of "loose credit"has taken its toll of the banking system that evolved out of President Jackson's policies.The Panic of 1837 was the end of flush times, and depression naturally followed. By 1840,many Mississippians had moved to the Republic of Texas...many stealing away in the night,taking everything that was moveable. Texas was,at this time,a "foreign country". A scramble ensues for the next few years, as land holders seek every means to hold on to their investments.

P.15:9 Dec.1837-Gift:Francis Penrice ofWash.Co.gives his gr.dau. Marian Auroria Collins,for $5 pd.by her father,Wm.W.Collins - 6 negroes:Winney - 35 yrs.old,Lucy- 35,1 boy named Beverly-17, Washington-16,Venus - 25, and her child Ophelia - 9 mo. Wit: John L.Penrice,Parker B.Long.

P.24:Robt.H.Buckner and wife Sarah F. and David W.Connely of 1st pt. of Hds.Co.;Wm.P.Stone of same - 2nd.

P.25: 20 June 1835-D:Jas.A.(X)Thack and wife Elizabeth and Reason Whitehead and wife Nancy of 1st pt;to Hiram G.Runnels, Jas.B.Davis,Wiley Davis - 2nd.

P.28:[Corners worn off] 28 Sept.1834:Jas.Gwin of David.Co.,Tn. and Saml.Gwin of Ms.of 1st part;to Wm.Gwin of Adams Co.,Ms A note signed by L.A.Plummer and endorsed by Wm.Gwin to Jas.Gwin dated 27 Aug.1834 - for benefit of Mary Gwin,widow and relict of late Thos.W.Gwin,decd. and his 2 daus. - to wit:Caroline J. and Sarah E.Gwin. James and Saml. sell out to Wm.[Note:Wm.M. Gwin was a U.S.Marshall - a supporter of Robt.J.Walker in 1834. George Poindexter, candidate for 1836 Senatorial election,had a former law partner - Isaac Caldwell,who challenged Saml.Gwin to a duel for alledgedly hissing a Poindexter speech against Pres.Jackson."Four hundred people witnessed the duel at Clinton, Ms.,in which Caldwell was killed instantly and Gwin,severly wounded. Gwin died 2½ yrs.later".HIST. OF MS. by McLemore. Robt. J.Walker came to Ms. from Pa.in 1826, and dominated the political scene from 1835-45. He resigned his Senatorial seat to serve in Pres.Polk's cabinet as Sec.of Treasury. He later became the first Gov. of the Terr. of Kansas.]

P.30:20 Mar.1837-D:James J.Moreland and wife Sarah H. of 1st ptof Philips Co.Ark;Wm.M.Gwin of Adms. - 2nd;In 1832 Jas.J.Moreland sold to Gwin,land in Wash.Co.,that he,Moreland,had entered as Orig.Pat.at Mt.Salus in the name of his son - Columbus Moreland,who has since decd.Deed just now being recorded.

P.42:2 Dec.1837-D:Larkin Bacon and wife Juliana of Bolivar Co.Ms.of 1st part;to Zachariah James.

P.44:2 Dec.1837-Mortg:Henry W.Vick of Warr.Co.of1st pt;Wm.L.Bodley,exec.of Est. of Wm.Pescod,decd.of 2nd;Will of Pescod states that Bodley is to invest certain funds for benefit of infant ch.of Malinda Taylor - $4,000 - which amt.is loaned to Vick @10%. Vick puts up land near Deer Creek - T14N,R6W 640 ac.+.

DEED BOOK "G": WASHINGTON CO.,MS.
DATED: 30 Dec.1837 - 23 Nov.1839

P.54:3Jan.1837-Mortg:Mordecai Powell and wifeEmily M.[formerly Johnson,widow of Thomas Y.Chaney] of 1st;Saml. and Miles Folkes of V'burg of 2nd;Archibald McLauren and Robt.T.Rogers of 3rd.

P.65:-- Jan.1838-D:Wm.S.Scott and wife Martha S.of Wash.Co.to John G.Cocks.

P.83:3 Jan.1838-Mortg:Nicholas H.Rapplye (Rapalje?)and wife Matilda of Warr.Co.-1st;John Guion,Thos.M.Green,Walter R.Puckett of Warr. - 2nd;Walter B.Green and Wm.Flaherty of 3rd.

[Page after page of Mortgages follow:Money borrowed from N.Y., Louisville,Ky,New Orleans,ect.]

P.112: 7 Feb.1838:Lake Providence,La.(Carroll P.)Martha Harrison (Harmon) wife of Zenas Preston of Wash.Co.signs release to all rights,including dower,to lands Zenas sold to Wm.Meredith Lambeth in Wash.Co. + slaves - for $42,000.Lambeth is in N.O.

P.126:18 Jan.1838-D:Arthur M.McCracken and wife Mary Ann of Mad. Co.Ms.to John Peevis Cunningham of Yazoo.[See John Peavy Cunningham's Will - Vol.I of this series.]

P.140:24 Mar.1838-D:Wm.Ley of Wash.Co.of 1st;Henry R.W.Hill of David.Co.Tn. - for $50,000,sells land on Silver Creek,@ 1,040 ac. plus Leys undivided ½ of the slaves.

P.143:2 Mar.1838-P.O.A.:Russell Montgomery of Adms.Co.givesP.O.A. to Philip Riley to receive from B.R. and Edwd.Garland,Adms. of Est. of Danl.B.Garland,decd. - unsettled accounts.

P.147:15 Mar.1838-D:Levin Marshall and wife Sarah E.(Elliott)of Adms.Co of 1st;to Thos.Lyne of Wash.Co. of the other part.

P.179:9 May 1838-D:Thos.A.Walker,Trustee of City of N.Y. of 1st pt;Isaac Walker of same city - 2nd;Thos.A.Walker forecloses on Chas.G.Walker - Thos.was appointed Trustee by D/T from Chas.G. for the use of $12,000, and since Chas.G. couldn't repay,the land was sold at Public Auction. Isaac waspurchaser at $4,374.

P.184:20 Mar.1837-D:Thos.G.Ellis and wife Mary M.[Routh]of Adms. Co. and Wiley Davis and wife (Unnamed) of Holmes Co. of 1st pt; to Abram M.Feltus of Wilk.Co. - T28N,R6W - Orig.Pat.

P.213:6 Feb.1837-P.O.A.Geo.Potts of City of N.Y. gives POA to John Ker of Adms.Co. to conduct all business. On 25 May 1838, John Ker of Adms. substitutes Geo.S.Manderville for the POA - business in Wash.Co.,specifically a deed by John C.Potts,exec. 15 Dec.1835.

P.254:2 Apr.1838-D:Felix Chenault and wife Ann of Rep. of Tx., Harrisburg Co. of North America;to Richard H.May of Sumn.Co.Tn.

P.271:18 Jan.1836-D:Henry Hagan and wife Elizabeth(X) of Yaz.Co. Hiram (X)Hagan and wife Martha (X), and Soloman Hagan all of Yaz.Co.of 1st pt;to Jas.B.White,late of Richland Dist.of S.C. and now of Wash.Co.Ms. - $40,000.

P.342:2 July 1838-D:Benj.Wiltshire,Adm. of Peter Arnold,decd.of Holmes Co.,Ms;to Saml.Barret of same.Wiltshire finds it necessary to sell the undivided 1/8th part of land owned by Arnold,in order to pay Arnold's debts...land in T16N,R4W...it sold for $663.

DEED BOOK "G": WASHINGTON CO., MS.
DATED: 30 Dec.1837 - 23 Nov.1839

P.366:-- Apr.1838-D:Council Bass and Jesse Bass,Adms.of Edmund P.Bass,decd.of Wash.Co. of1st pt;to Francis Penrice of same. Edm.Bass and Penrice had an agreement concerning a "lot" of land and the two Adms.honor it, and convey the title.

P.374:6 Mar.1838-D:Amos Alexander and wife Lavinia of Adms.Co.; to Elizabeth Newsom,Joshiah Montgomery,Mary Allison,Jos.Carroll, Saml.Carroll,Elizabeth Davy - heirs at law of the late Hugh Montgomery,decd.of La.P.376:A.B.Montgomery is the Adm.of Hugh Montgomery's est. - 13 Mar.1838 and sells to Robt. Allison of Pike Co.,Mo. and John Harrison of Phillip Co.,Ark.[Note:From THE MONTGOMERY PAPERS - Hugh Montgomery b 1792 S.C.d.1836 - marr. Mary Chaney - 1821 and was the brother of A.B.Montgomery.]

P.415:20 Dec.1838-D/T:Nathaniel Ware of 1st pt;to Thos.B.Warfield of Lexington,Ky of the other. A relinquishment made by Elisha Warfield and wife Catharine Ann to sd.Ware to any rights to certain notes executed by Wm.S.Wells and John D.Craven - and put into the hands of Charles Ingersoll of Philadelphia,Pa. in trust for Catharine Ann to secure her inheritance from "her mother's Est.".The mother and Nathaniel Ware made a promise in writing,4 Sept.1814 to secure to such ch.as sd.Ware might have by her.Ware turns the land over to Elisha Warfield,as husband of Catharine Ann,as promised. 1 undivided ½ of "Utopia Plantation" in Wash.Co.on E.bank of Ms.River - containing 880 ac. - +lots in S2,3;T19N;R10W, and a fractional portion of Sec.21,T19N,R9W + ½ of all boats,guns,mills,provisions,carts,crops,etc.on sd. place +½ int.in slaves + other land in Black Bayou,also a Plantation in Ark.+ slaves"to Catharine Ann Warfield and her ch."Elisha is to manage the property and submit accounts,but Elisha cannot sell anything. After 10 yrs.,if he proves worthy,he will have conveyed to him a portion not to exceed 1/4th.After Catharine Ann's death,land goes to her ch. If her father,Nathl.Ware dies,he asks that Col.Thos.G.Percy see that the above conditions are met.[Note:Nathl.'s wife was the sister of Col.Percy]

P.423:31 Jan.1838-Relinq:Thos.S.Thomley of Wash.Co. of 1st pt; Louisa Noe,wife of James Noe of Pt.Coupe P.La. Louisa relinq. all claims.

P.470:30 June 1835-D:Wm.P.Gadberry,by last Will and Test. instructed his exec.to sell whatever he deems necessary of his Est. The Exec.Milton Pyles and Execx.Juliet G.Gadberry - (has since marr. with Thomas Caldwell)sell to Henry Hagan to pay Wm.P.'s debts - land on W.bank of Yazoo River,adjoining HAGAN & BROTHERS 142 ac. Pyle and Juliet appear in Yaz.Co.

P.540:6 Feb.1839-D:Zenas Preston vs [Note:The following names had no punctuation between them]Andrew M.R. Theador E.Martha Ann Julia Ann and Frederick S.Harman,minor heirs of Benjamin Harman, decd. by their Guardian - Frederick Stanton,Comm.appointed 1839.

===
End of Deed Book "G"
===

SUPPLEMENTARY INFORMATION:
"Couples" named in DBK."G"-and date of the document:
ADAMS,JOHN S.& wife NANCY E.of Texas-May 1838
ARRINGTON, STEPHEN & wife MARY of Wash.Co.-1838
BEATY,WM.marr.Claib.Co.Ms. to CATHERINE R.MURPHY in 1834
BREL(BEIL)GEORGE & wife ALMIRA of Wash.Co. 1838
DeHART,MARGARET is wife of GEO.MOONEY-1839
DICKEY,MILES W.& wife ISABELLA-Scott Co.Ky. 1837
GLASS,JAMES & wife JULIET of Warren Co. -1838
MORGAN,JACOB B. &wife MINERVA of Hinds Co.Ms.-1839
NUTT,RITTENHOUSE & wife ELLEN-1838
OWEN,MILLS & wife MARTHA of Adams Eo. 1838
PATRICK,ISHAM T. & wife JANE of Claib.Co.Ms.1837
PIERSON,JOSEPH & wifeSARAH S. of Claib.Co.Ms. 1837
POINDEXTER,GEORGE & wife ANN-1836
POTTS,JOHN C. & wife SARAH E. of Wash.Co.Ms. 1838
   (Note: GOV. POINDEXTER was a very bombastic character.
   In 1828, he separated from his wife LYDIA,dau. of JESSE
   CARTER...Their son, ALBERT GEO.POINDEXTER filed suit- in
   Wilkinson Co.Ms. for non-support, then dropped the suit
   settling out of court in Natchez. In 1833-Marr.Rec.BK."A"
   Wilk.Co.Ms. GEOR.POINDEXTER marr. VIRGINIA POINDEXTER,
   F.DAVIS security. His Will, probated Hds.Co. Ms. 2 Mar.
   1854,names his wife ANN and Ann's brother WM.G.HUGHES of
   New Orleans. He left large land holdings in Wash.,Bolivar,
   Issa.,Sunfl.,Scott,Mad.,counties Ms.+ 1300 ac.on Red River
   in La. + 2,000 ac. in Todd Co.Ky.)

CONT. FROM PAGE 55 DBK"I" listing husbands & wives
WILKINS,JAMES C. & wife CATHARINE L. ,Adams 1839
WILKINSON,NATHANIEL W. & wife ANGELA LAURIE, N.O.La.1836
WILLIAMSON,RUSSEL M. & wife ELIZABETH A.,Madison Co.Ms.1838
WILSON,JOHN R. & wife ELIZABETH PITTS WILSON. David.Co.Tn.1837
WITMIN,JESSE & wife MARY(X), Rank.1839
WITMIN,JOHN & wife ELIZABETH (X(, Rank.1839

SUPPLEMENTARY INFORMATION:WARREN CO.MS.,WILL BOOK"A":
P.100;Will of William Bacon:Written 14 Sept.1839-Prob.Oct.1839.
Wife-Sophia Bacon,Mother-Lydia Fellows to receive her inheritance
in N.Y.along with his 2 sisters-Charity Harmon(Hannon)and Laura
Warren..Names Daniel Messinger in Egremont,Mass:Neph.Danl.Bacon
Messinger;2 sisters-Mary Messinger and Lydia Ann Eliza Messinger-
their payments to be made N.Y.City.:Exec.wife and Danl.Bacon
Messinger with no bond.Wit:E.D.Walcott,Franklin White,S.W.Perkins
Ignatius Flowers.(Owned large tract of land in Warr.Co.on Big
Black River,+ another Pltn.in Warr.Co. Called "Baconham".
Buried in "Baconham"Cemetery on Old Messinger Ferry Rd.Warr.Co.
Wm.Bacon,decd.19 Sept.1839 in 56th yr.
Sophia Bacon Messinger decd.1 Oct.1864
George Messinger b 28 Apr.1818,d 13 Dec.1866
"Our Mother"Mrs. Lucinda Vaughan d 10 Oct.1859-87 yrs.
Janette,dau.of Wm.& Sophia Bacon d.1 yr.
Wm. son of Wm.& Sophia Bacon d. 1 yr.
Saml.G.Messinger d.May 22,1844-21 yrs.
George Wm.Bacon Messinger d 25 Sept.1862-26 yrs.
Daniel Bacon Messinger d 8 Feb. 1841-age 26 yrs.

DEED BOOK "H": WASHINGTON CO.,MS.
DATED:23 Mar.1839 - 27 June 1839

DBk."H" is in delicate condition.608 pages,the Original,has been rebound,and has a few loose pages.This book overlaps time with DBk."G", and the most plausible explanation for this can be found in the banking laws of Ms. The Panic of 1837 resulted in the formation of another bank,called "The Union Bank",which was the Legislatures' answer to hard times. It permitted the sale of bonds on the credit of the State. Not long after,it was noted that "The Union Bank" was not altering the depression, and many turned against it,declaring "mismanagement".But for 1839-'40,it opened a source for money to those desperate for backing.
===

P.2:25 May 1838-Mortg:Levin Marshall and wife Sarah E.Marshall ofAdms.Co.[Note:She was the former Sarah E.Ross]The Marshalls mortg.their considerable holdings to the "Incorporated Banking Institutions of New Orleans". The membership for this banking Institute covered nearly all of La.'s Banks.The land descriptions for the mortg.cover the next 23 pages.This document is signed by L.R.Marshall,Sarah E.Marshall;Thos.Henderson;J.T.McMurran; Sam J.Peters;Jos.Barthel;Edw.J.Forstell;H.Lavergne;M.Mintown; Jas.Hopkins;A.Hodge,Jr.;Y.B.Milligan;Ed.York-Pres;J.Burthe;Benj. Story;J.W.Brudlorck;Thos.C.Magoffin;Wm.Y.Hughes-Pres.

P.26:14 Feb.1839-Perfection of Title:Robert J.Chambliss and wife Lucinda L.Hood,dau. of Harbird Hood,decd.;and Govy (Gary, Grey)Hood and wife Nancy C.Philips - Gary is Harbird's son - all of Carroll P.La. of the 1st pt;to Zenas Preston of 2nd.
 Robt.J. and Lucinda Chambliss,Gary and Nancy Hood show that Harbird sold land to Zenas 23 Apr.1833...land that Harbird received as Orig.Pat.,but that the dower rights to this tract of land had never been relinquished. Since Harbird's wife, and the mother of the 2 heirs - Lucinda and Gary - Nancy Hood,is decd.Lucinda Chambliss and Nancy,wife of Gary Hood,sign release to any rights they might have to sd.land.634 ac.T11N,R9W, on the Ms.River.

P.47:30 Mar.1839-Perfection of Title:[Note:Ms.Law required that the wife sign a release of all rights - dower,etc.to property sold by her husband.Since he had full control over all property she brought into the marr. - unless a marr. contract to the contrary, had been signed - she must sign a relinq.of all property he sold] Elizabeth Miller of Wash.Co. signs relinq.to land sold by her husband Anderson Miller on 10 Apr.1837 to Nathan B.Graham of N.Y.State...land on Lake Jackson.

P.51:1 Nov.1838-D:Wm.Izard Bull and wife Gracia Caroline (Turnbull)Bull of Charleston,S.C. of the 1st pt:to Andrew Turnbull of Wash.Co.,2nd: The Bulls(she is Andrew's sister)sell to Andrew for $2,000 all rights' to property due them by the Will of Robert J.Turnbull,late of Charleston,S.C.,decd. S27;Twp.13;R9W-640ac.Lot 2,S12;Twp.13N;R9W-96 ac.

P.72:25 Oct.1838-Deed;Anna Bensford Turnbull, widow of Robert J.Turnbull,decd.of Charleston,S.C. sells to Andrew Turnbull of Wash.Co...for $2,000 her claim to Sec.27,Twp.13N,R9W,Choct. Land Dist.640ac.L.2,Sec.2,Twp.13,R9W 96 +ac.

DEED BOOK "H":WASHINGTON CO. MS.
Dated:23 Mar.1839-27 June 1839

P.78:State of S.C.24 Oct.1838:Robert M.Allan of Charleston,S.
C.sells to Andrew Turnbull,for $5,a Plantation called"Glen
Allen-500 ac.fronting on Lake Wash.,on N.by F.G.Turnbull, E.by
F.G. & Chas.Turnbull, S.by Jonathon McCaleb-+ slaves "now on
Glen Allan".Robt. states he has given bond to A.W.Campbell,R.T.
Allston, Mary Allston Exec.of Est. of Jos.Allston-1 Feb.1837
for $20,000;Also given bd. to R.W.Rosser,assigneeof E.R.Lawrens.
23 Mar.1836-$3,335:also bd. to Ed.Blake & Geo.Huig,Trustees,
for $30,000. Andrew Turnbull acts as sec.for these loans.

P.183:4 May 1839-Mortgage:Stephen M. Jackson and wife Ann D.
of Wash.Co. on 25 July 1838 subscribed for 800 shares of 100
each($80,000) of stock in the Union Bank-created by Legislature
21 Jan.1837, and reapproved 5 Feb.1838.Stephen further states
that he is a citizen of Ms.and owns real estate inthe said State
The following land is Mort:Sec.11;Twp.18N;R9W-639ac. Lots 3,4
5,8;Sec.10,Twp.18;R9W 314 ac.W½of Sec.32,Twp.18;R8W-316 ac+

P.190:10 Oct.1838-Deed:Harrison Taylor and wifeSarah(X)Jane
of Hds.Co. and Wm.Taylor and wife Milly(X)of Claib.Co.Ms. heirs
of Jackson Taylor,decd.sell to Davis Montgomery of Wash.Co.
(for $400)

P. 195;22 Apr.1838-Deed:Harrison Taylor & wife Elizabeth(X)
and Wm.L.Parker all of Newton Co.Ms. to Davis Montgomery.
==========================
Note:There follows many mortg.to the Union Bank of Miss. with
lengthy details of land descpt.and slaves,+ other holdings,
not all neccessarily in Wash.Co. There being no family relationships given except forthe husband and wife, I have listed these
at the end of DBk."H".
==========================
P.283:19Apr.1839-Deed:Johnathon Karsoner and wifeJunnettah V.
(?)M. of Woodford Co. Ky. of 1st part;to Albert G(allatin)
Creath of Warren Co.Ms. andGeo.W.F.McConnell of Woodford Co.
Ky. of the 2nd.

P.309:21 Mar.1839-Deed:Alexander H.Peck and wife Julia A.Peck
of Claib.Co.Ms. to Gilmon M.Peck.

P.389:2. Jan.1834-Deed;Hiram D.Miller & wife Sarah, Wm.Stephen-
son,John & Mary Stephenson, Wm.Johnson & Nancy his wife,Wm.Mill-
er and wife Edith, Joslin Miller and wife Hester Annn...of the
1st part; to Alfred G.Carter of other;Lots 1,2,3,4,5,6,7,8,;
Sec.2;Twp.18N;R9W;Choct.Dist. All signed Wash.Co. except John
and Wm.Stephenson who signed inBoliver Co.Ms.

P.367:(OUT OF SEQUENCE)28 Jan.1837-DeedJohn P.Guien and wife
Mary Ann of La. to Wm.L.Rusk of Wash.Co.Ms.

P.392:10 May 1839-Mort:Wm.Johnson & wife Louisa(X) of Chicot
Co.Ark.and Benj.(X)Jackson & wife Zanna(X) of Bolivar Co.Ms.
of the 1st part;to Alfrd G.Carter of the other part.

P.507:2 Feb..1839-Mort:(Descpt.covers 30 pages)John Bligh Byrne
& wife Azemia Kinny, Louis Florider Herman & wife Adele Longer,
Charles Briggs & wife Louisa Wood, Charles A.Lacoste, all of
New Orleans except Lacoste who is of Natchez, of the 1st part;
to Thomas Henderson of Natchez of the 2nd part.

DEED BOOK "H": WASHINGTON CO. MS.
Dated: 23 Mar. 1839-27 June 1839

P.569:3 May 1839-Deed: Francis Penrice & wife Elizabeth(X) to Alfred Cox all of Wash. Co.

---

*Husbands and their wives named in DBk. "H", not before mentioned, or if so, given to show the date of document.
AUSTIN, ALEX. M. and wife MARY L. of Augus. Co. Va.
BOICE, Wm. and wife MARY E. H. Adams Co. Ms. 1839
BOOKOUT, BENJ. K. and wife SOPHIA H. of Wash. Co. Ms. 1839
CHAPMAN, JOHN L. and wife CATHARINE REBECCA of Wash. Co. Ms. 1839
COFFIN, THOMAS ASTON and wife HARRIET B. of S.C.
COOPER, WM. and wife ANNA MARIA(X) of Copiah Co. Ms. 1839
CRAIN, CHAS. and wife MARY, Rank. Co. Ms. 1839
FERGUSON, JAS. J. and wife PERMELIA(X) of Wash. Co. Ms. 1839
HALEY, WM. and wife ELIZABETH(X) of Newton Co. Ms. 1839
HARDEMAN, D. and wife SARAH ANN of Wash. Co. Ms. 1839
HARRIS, EZEKIEL and wife ANN of Adams, Co. Ms. 1839
HELLMS, THOS. E. and wife MARY of Adams. Co. Ms. 1837
HERRING, GEO. W. and wife SARAH BOHANNON of New Orleans-1839
HUNT, WM. and wife PRUDENCE B. of Wash. Co. Ms. 1839
JAMES, JOSHUA and wife MARY K. of Adams Co. Ms. 1839
KILPATRICK, ELIHU and wife MISSOURI of Hds. Co. Ms. 1839
LAIRD, ARCHIBALD and wife MARGARET, Rankin Co. Ms. 1839
LOFTIN, WALTER C. and wife MARGARET(X) of Wash. Co. Ms. 1839
McCALEB, JAMES F. and wife SOPHIA W. of Adams Co. Ms. 1839
McINTYRE, DUNCAN and wife DICA(X) of Rank. Co. Ms. 1839
McINTYRE, HUGH and wife JANE(X) Rankin Co. Ms. 1839
McINTYRE, MALCOLM and wife MARGARET of Rank. Co. Ms. 1839
McCUTCHEON, JAMES and wife SUSANP. of Wash. Co. Ms. 1839
McMURTRY, VINCENT W. and wife E. A. of Natchez. 1839
MONTGOMERY, DAVIS and wife ELIZABETH L. of Wash. Co. Ms. 1839
MOORE, MICHAEL M. and NANCY GORDAN are issued O.P., Hds. Co. Ms.
RUNES, JESSE(X) and PEGGY, his wife of Copiah (Premp. Rts.)
STOKES, ROBT. E. (X) and wife RACHAIL(x) of Copiah Co. Ms. 1839
STONE, WM. P. and wife AMANDA S. of Hds. Co. Ms. 1839
TERRY,--- and wife SUSANNAH(X) of Wash. Co. Ms. 1839
THOMSON, MANILUS V. and wife MARY ANN of Scott Co. Ky. 1839
TOUCHSTONE, WM. H. and wife JANE(X) Rankin Co. Ms. 1839
TRADWELL, REUBEN H. and wife PENNY(X) Copiah 1839
TURNBULL, JOHN and wife MARY ANN of Wash. Co. Ms. 1839
WROTEN, WYLIE and wife MARGARET(X) of Simpson Co. Ms. 1839
*The following nine lines show wives signing releases to land already bought by BUCKNER & CONNELLY:
ARNOLD, THOS. L and wife ELIZA-Warren Co. Ms. 1839
BURKE, ELIHU P. and wife ELIZA(X) 1839 Rank. Co. Ms.
DEFORE, JAMES and wife ANDERMEDA, Copiah Co. Ms. 1839
DYASS, DUMPSEY and wife MARTHA(X) Rank. Co. Mx. 1839
FORSYTH, WM. and wife MARGARET(X) Rank. Co. Ms. 1839
HILBURN, FREDERICK and wife ANNA(X) Copiah Co. Ms. 1839
LEE, JAS. D. and wife SARAH(X) Rank. Co. Ms. 1839
TOUCHSTONE, DUMPSEY and wife SARAH(X) Rankin Co. Ms. 1839
WHITE, JOHN and wife MARY(X) Rank. Co. Ms. 1839

END OF DEED BOOK "H"""

DEED BOOK "I": WASHINGTON CO. MS.
Dated;29 June 1939-22 Feb.1840
471 pages-handwriting very bad;

P.7;11 June 1839-P.O.A.:Henry S.Foot to A.W.Samuels; Foot wants Samuels to execute a release on a D/T executed to Hugh R.Austin on22 Jan.1836"to me as Trustee for that purpose of securing the punctual payment of $40.000 to John Ingersoll & Co.of New Orleans".Doc.signed in Hds.Co.Ms.

P.8;8Apr.1830-Deed:Isaac W. Arthur and wife Margaret of New York City and Zenas K.Fulton,who all appeared in Adams Co.Ms. ofthe 1st part;Jas.Hamilton Cowper of Ga.of the other part.

P.39:15 Oct.1838-D/T:Minor W. O'Bannon of Shelby Co.Ky. of 1st part:John C.Richardson Jr. of Mercer Co.Ky. the other.O'Bannon-for love and affection to his 2dau.-Mary A.& Jane R.O'Bannon-land in Twp.14,R3W,Choc.Dist.638 ac. John C.Richardson to use profits from this land for benefit of O'Bannon's daus. until they come of the age of 21, at which time the land will be turn-ed over to the girls.

P.42:3 June 1839-Deed:Elihu Kilpatrick of Wash.Co. and wife Missouri H.of 1st part;Ebenezer Kilpatrick of Marshall Co.Ms.2nd

P.43:--Jan.1837-Deed:E.M.Daingerfield of Adams Co.Ms.1st part; Hannah M.Merrick,Adm.of P.F.Merrick,decd.and Guard.of minor heirs of P.F.Merrick,decd.of same Co.

P.47:14 May 1838-Release:Jas.Allison & wife Mary of Pike Co. Mo. of 1st part:Sidney R.Smith of Scott Co.Ky. the other part; The Allisons release claim to lots conveyed by Amos Alexander & wife,Mary Newsome,Joshia Montgomery,Mary Allison,Jos.Carroll, Saml.Carroll & Elizabeth Davis by deed dated 6 Mar.1838, which they bought from Geo.B.Crutchen,an O.P.

P.49:27 Nov.1838-Release:Jos.Carroll & wife Martha of Henderson Co.Tenn. of 1st part:Sidney R.Smith of Scott Co.Ky.the other; O.P.of Geo.B.Crutchen to Amos Alexander on July 18,1831 + O.P. #6628 + many others.

P.52:22Nov.1837-P.O.A:John Harrison & wife Olive J. of Philips Co.Ark.appoint Robert Allison of Pike Co.Mo. their lawful Atty., to sell any lands owned by Harrison in Wash.Co.Ms.

P.54:13 Mar.1838-Deed:Robert Allison & wife Elizabeth of Pike Co.Mo.,and John Harrison & wife Oliveof Philips Co.Ark.of the 1st part;Sidney R.Smith of Scott Co.KY. the other:Smith buys land in Wash.Co.Ms.(Olivia(sp.)in signature).

P.56:28 July 1838-Release:John Davey & wife Elizabeth(X),Samuel Carroll & wife Huldah(X)all from Hardin Co.Tn. and Jos.Carroll & wife Martha of Henderson Co.Tn.of 1st pt:toSidney R. Smith ofScott Co.Ky.Wit:Bowen Davey,Thos.Davey.

P.64:6 May 1839-P.O.A.:Horace Anderson give P.O.A.to Kinan(Hi-ram?)O.Anderson to act in all issues for him. Wit:Geo.W.Sharp, Hiram E.Metcalf. Filed in Claib.Co.Ms.

P.66:7 May 1839-Release:Horace Anderson & Kinan(Hiram)O.Anderson late co-partners in firm in Claib.Co.Ms. of the 1st pt:Hiram R.Metcalf of same Co.,Acting as trustee for some of the prop-erty inPort Gibson,conveyed by Horace Carpenter,Martha M.Car-penter,John M.Carpenter, & Virginia C.Carpenter on 25 Nov.1835 to said Horace Anderson & Kinan(Hiram)Anderson.Also Land in

DEED BOOK "I": WASHINGTON CO.MS.
29 June 1839--22 Feb.1840

Cont.P.66:-in Wash.Co.,Rankin Co. + slaves...to protect Parmenas Briscoe from the responsibility of the debt. Other co-signers were Alexander Towney,Guilford G.Towney,Lewis Williams,Mabin Cooper,Stephen F.K.Albay,Johnson B.Thrasher,Henry W.Barnes, Volney Stamps,Seth Rundell,Eliza Rundell,Simon Rundell,Wm.R.Buck, Saml.Dorsey,Jos.Newman,Abram K.Shaifer,Francis Patton,Jas.Cuard, Fletcher Creighten,Alexander H.Peck,Miles Luster-all of Claib. Co.Ms.and Peter C.Chambliss,Isaac R.Wade,Evan S.Jefferies,Robert H.Bagley all of Jeff.Co.Ms.

P.72:7 Feb.1839-P.O.A.:John Mitchum of Woodford Co.KY. gives P.A.to Wm.B.Mitchum to attend to his business with Wm.H.Taylor of Ala...Land lying on Silver Creek,Wash.Co.Ms.known as the Plantation of Mitchum Creath & Pinckard-1220 ac. J.Mitchum sold out to A.G.Creath & Pinckard 1837 and other land sold to Benj. F.Hall + slaves.

P.108:10 Aug.1839-Relinq:Frances wife of Robert Steen,relinq. her dower,ect.,in land sold by her husband to Davis Montgomery. She signed- Frances(X)Boothe.

P.109:10 Aug.1839-Relinq;Mary(x)Blue,wife of Jesse Blue relinq. dower,etc.to land sold to Davis Montgomery.

P.116:5 Aug.-Deed;Belinda B. Cunningham of Scott Co.Ms.to Zena K.Fulton of Wash.Co.Ms.

P.143:27 Aug.1839-Mort:Mary(x)Stephenson,Benj.(x)Jackson &wife Zana(X)..all of Bolivar Co.Ms. to Alfred G.Carter of Wash.Co.Ms.

P.166:--day of001839-Deed:Robert H.Crump,George P.Crump,Selina M.Crump,Fanny Crump,James E.Sharkey &---Sharkey to H.R.Austin.

P.186:9--1835:Isaac Caldwell & Archibald S.Kennedy as Adms. ofEst. of Robert E.Menefee,decd.of 1st part:Burr Garland of Hds.Co. the other part:Menefee had an O.P.which Adms.sold to Garland.

P.206:19 Apr.1839-Mort.:Alexander R. Depew of Vicksburg of 1st part:John D.Woolfolk of Ms.,Dudley Woolfolk of Woodford Co.Ky. the 2nd:Col.Jos.Woolfolk of Woodford Co.Ky. the 3rd.

P.218:--May 1839-Deed:Wm J.Smith of Hds.Co. 1st part:John E.Smith Andrew Smith of same-2nd part.

P.263:23 Aug.1839-Deed:Stephen Arrington & wife Polly, Wm.Arrington-of 1st part:Henry K.Moss & wife Narcissa Ann,Alexander McMurtry & wife Rebecca M. all of Natchez, of the 2nd part.

P.279:14 May 1839-Gift-D/T:Adam Shirley of Wash.Co. gives a deed of Trust to D.Hardeman of same to act as Trustee for benefit of Ellender Shirley-wife of said Adam,Andrew J.Shirley, Martha Shirley,& Missouri Shirley,children of said Adam & Ellender Shirley and all other children of Ellender by Adam.."for love and affection" he(Adam) gave them tracts of land in Wash. Co.Ms. + slaves.

P.307:13 Aug.1839-Gift:George W.Adams of Wash.Co.Ms.gives to his children-Robert Wood Adams & Betsy Malvina Adams of KY... 1,090 ac.in Wash.Co.Ms.Land in Twp.19,R8W

DEED BOOK "I": WASHINGTON CO.MS.
29 June-22 Feb.1840

P.327:7 Aug.1839-Quit Claim:<u>Andrew</u> <u>Haynes</u> & <u>wife</u> <u>Charlotte B.</u>
<u>(Downs)Haynes</u> of the 1st part, of Warr.Co.Ms. give to their
son <u>Andrew Ferguson Haynes</u> for love and affection, land in
Wash.Co.Ms. on Silver Creek-Twp.14N,R4W,Choc.,an O.P.issued
to <u>Andrew</u> <u>Haynes</u> & <u>Thomas</u> <u>Ferguson</u> at the Clinton(now)Jackson
Dist. of lands. Also Twp.12N,R3W + other O.P's

P.382:19June 1837-Deed:<u>John W.Faulkner</u> & <u>wife</u> <u>Martin</u> <u>Louisa</u>
of Hds.Co.1st part:<u>Saml.C.Faulkner</u> of the other.

P.394:1Aug.1839-Deed:<u>John</u> <u>James</u>,Wash.Co.,1st part:<u>Theodorick</u>
<u>J.James</u> of other..for$1 John sells 168 ac.NW1/4,S26,Twp.16,R8W

P.395:1 Aug.1839-Gift:<u>Thos.J.James</u> & <u>wife</u> <u>Frances(X)</u>of Wash.Co.
to their son <u>Thos.James</u> of same.220ac.Wit:<u>Green</u> <u>McCarroll</u> &
<u>Duncan</u> <u>G.Campbell.</u>

P.403:4 May 1831-Gift:Jefferson Co.Ms.with love and affection
to brother <u>Samuel</u> <u>Collins</u> and my 4 sisters-<u>Mary</u> <u>Jane</u> <u>Susan</u>
<u>Louisana</u> <u>Collins</u>,with <u>Octavia</u> written in above the line. A gift
of slaves..signed by <u>H.F.Carradine</u>. Recorded Jeff.Co.,Yazoo
Co.17 Nov.1838,Wash.Co.18 Jan.1840[Note:there was no punctuation between the girl's names]The slaves were Rachel & Peggy
and all their increase.

P.446:27 May 1839-Deed:"I,<u>James</u> <u>Stewart</u>, of Yazoo-only son and
representative of <u>James</u> <u>Stewart,</u>decd.of Yazoo,"sell to <u>Soloman</u>
<u>Wolfe</u> of Wash.Co.Ms.

END OF DEED BOOK "I"

*Husband and wives listed in Deed Bk."I",+date of document
ALLEN,WM.S. & wife ELSEY BLUES Mason Co.Ky.1839
BOSTICK,FERD.& wife MARTHA C. Yazoo 1840
CARTER,ALF.G. & wife ELIZABETH S. Wash. 1839
DAVENPORT,WM.V. & wife HENRIETTA V. Warr.1840
DAWSON,DAVID W. & wife SARAH E. Jeff.Co.Ms.1837
GIBSON,WM.W. & wife ELLA Warr.1839
HAMMEDIEN,WM.A.L. & wife CATHERINE A.L. Warr.1839
HUNTER, MILLFORD & wife SUSAN Claib.Co.Ms. 1838
HASHBERGER,BENJ. & wife MARY, Warr. 1839
JOHNSON,GEORGE B. & wife ANN ELIZABETH Scott Co.Ky.1838
JOHNSON,GEORGE W. & wife ANN E.,Scott Co.Ky. 1837
KAVANAUGH,NELSON & wife MARY E.,Hds.Co.1836
LILES,CHARLES & wife FRANCES(X) Hds. 1839
McCLOUD, WM. & wife MARIA, Warr.1839
MILLER,JOHN & wife SARAH,Warr.1840
MILLER, JOHN C. & wife JANE, Fayette Co.Ky. 1839
RAGAN,JESSE B. & wife SARAH K.,Wash. 1839
SCOTT,JOHN F. & wife FRANCES, Warr.1838 (Prem.Rts.)
SHEPHARD,A.F. & wife CASSANDRA, Scott Co. Ky.1839
SMITH,BENJ. & wife IRENE, Scott Co.Ky. 1840
SPELL,JOS.G. & wife ELIZA(X), Rank.1839
SUGGETT,DAVID & wife POLLY, Scott Co.Ky.1837
SURGET,JAMES & wife CATHERINE, Adams 1837
TAYLOR,BEN & wife ELIZABETH, Louisville,Ky. 1839
TUSSELL,WM. & wife MARY(X) Rank.1839
TUSSELL,SHERWOOD & wife CHARLOTTE(X) ,Rank.1839
<u>SEE PAGE 49 FOR CONT.LISTINGS.</u>

DEED BOOK "J": WASHINGTON CO.MS.
22 Feb.1840-16 Mar.1841

This Deed Bk."J" is badly watermarked;is the Original;636 pages. Only information adding to family relationships has been abstracted. Will Bk."1"began with 1839, so most of the Estates are covered in that Vol.(See EMR Vol.I for Abst's)

P.16:5 Feb.1840-Deed:Archibald Dunbar of Adams Co.Ms. sells to Alexander C.Dunbar, for $170,000 (1) a Plantation in Wash. Co.Ms.on Ms.River @2300 ac.bought from Saml.A.Plummer,who had bought it from Wm.M.Gwin; (2) a "lot of land" below the hill in Natchez on Ms.River on which is "the lower cotton press", bounded by lands of Andrew Brown,Mrs.Sentor,James Densmore and the River..bought from Saml.A.Plummer; (3) a Tract of land in W.Feliciana Parish La.upon the waters of Bayou Sara @100 ac. "originally being my undivided interest as one of the heirs of Wm.Dunbar,decd. and interest conveyed to me from Alexander Dunbar,also one of the heirs":(4) 400 ac.in Wilkinson Co.Ms. on Buffaloe River;(5) lands in Natchez, + slaves on above named plantation.

P.50:21 Jan.1839-Mor;Ambrose Gibson & wife Margaret C.M. of the 1st part;George Selser of 2ndpart;Jos.Templeton & Artemesia Blunt,Adm. & Admx. for Est. of James R.Blunt,decd.-of the 3rd pt. of Warren Co.Ms.

P.71:3 Mar.1840-Deed:John G.Parham & wife Rebecca F.M. of Warren Co. sell to A.T.B.Merritt & W.H.E.Merritt of Va.-for $7,000 "his ½ of certain tracts..Twp.16,R5W,+380 ac.Twp.13, R6W..plus much more land described as land he owned jointly with his brothers-in-law."[Dr.Parham's wife Rebecca F.M.(Merritt)Parham was a sister to the two Merritts named above.]

P.74:1 Jan.1840-Est.Sale:Wm.Bacon,decd.,his Adm. is D.Bacon Messinger & Sophia Bacon; Wm.Bacon's Est.owes a note for $6,000 to Alexander M. Paxton & Robert Garland,and the land is ordered sold at court house in Vicksburg on 13 Dec.1839. D.Bacon Messinger was the highest bidder. Land descriptions hard to decipher- but seems to be 750+ac. in Tpw.15,R6W(Choctaw Div.)parts of Sec.19,17,

P.78:27 Mar.1835-Mort.:Daniel Wilkins of Wash.Co. owes Wm.Bacon & Daniel B. Messinger both of Warren Co.Ms.

P.104:8 Oct.1839-Gift:Caroline M. Ferguson of the 1st part; to her nephew, for his education-Andrew Ferguson Haynes of the 2nd part. Land on Silver Creek, formerly belonging to Andrew Haynes & Thomas Ferguson as Orig.Pat. The land is in Sec.14, 15,Twp.14,R4W;(Note:Andrew Ferguson Haynes b.20 May 1834 on ST.Peters Plantation, Warren Co.Ms. was the son of Dr.Andrew Haynes & wife Charlotte B.Downs who were married in Vicksburg-2 Jan.1825. Dr.Haynes died between 20 Apr. & 3 Nov.1840. From B.B.Parham Family by Myrtis Hyde)

P.107:10 Jan.1840-Deed:Hugh Montgomery & wife Mary M. of Perry Co. Tn.,Elizabeth Montgomery & Hugh S.Newsom of Fayette Co. Tn.,heirs-at-law of late Mary Newsom of 1st part-sell to Sidney R.Smith of Scott Co.Ky. their share of land conveyed by Amos Alexander & wife to Mary Newsom,Josiah Montgomery, Mary Allison, Joseph Carroll, Samuel Carroll & Elizabeth Davy by deed dated 6 Mar.1838

DEED BOOK"J": WASHINGTON CO.MS.
22 Feb.1840-16 Mar.1841

P.116:1Mar.1840-Deed:Daniel Downing of Warren Co.of the 1st part:John C.Downing of New York City of the 2nd.

P.135:5Apr.1839-Deed:Wm.M.Newsom & Elizabeth Montgomery of Fayette Co.Tn.,Josiah Newsom of Parish of Catahoula,La.Robert J.Newsom of Baton Rouge,La.Hugh S. Newsom of Marshall Co.Ms. of the 1st part;to Sidney R. Smith of Scott Co.Ky. Same land descriptions as in document above-p.107.

P.172:Will of Henry Brawner,Charles Co.Md.Writ.7 Aug.1830.Leaves his plantation and dwelling called"Ellerslee"to his wife Maria Campbell Brawner. Plantation located on west side of Port Tobacco Creek,bought from the trust of the "Daniel of St.Thomas Jenefer...by whatsoever name be known to her and her heirs" in payment for lands that Maria brought to their marriage that he sold with her permission, promising that he would leave her a replacement. Ellerslee"is the only block of land"he owns, and he leaves her everything on it except the slaves. (2)Everything else is left in Trust with Maria, for education of "my children", for Maria to use as she sees fit.(3)Wife is his executrix without bond..unless she should remarry and her husband mismanage the property, she is to have full control of it all. Wit:B.J.Semmes,John R.Fergulson,Wm.Fergulson(Ferguson?)Geo.W. Barnes.Annexed-8 Oct.1838 came Maria Campbell Brawner,exect.,of Charles Co.Md.Court: Will Rec.Bk.of Orphans-Chas.Co. Feb.1839- Warren Co.Courts Probate Henry Brawner's Will and Maria relinquishes exec.in favor of Wm.A.Lake. Lakes' securities are Eilbeck Mason, John A. Frost..bond $40,000. 25 Apr.1840--Will of Henry Brawner is rec. in Wash.Co.Ms.
Wash.Co.Ms.Deed Bk."F":p.267:10 Jan.1835-Deed:Wm.H.Taylor of Mont.Co.Ala.sells to Henry Brawner for $8,220,land on East side of Silver Creek-Sec.17,18;Twp.12;R4W..Ley & Taylor to Henry Brawner & Samuel Dent.[The will seems to be carelessly composed, and the handwriting of the transcriber is very bad.]
¶ See Supplementary material for follow-up,on page 147

P.194:Aug.1839-Deed:Alfred O.Eggleston & wife Anne Maria of Amelia Co.Va.;Jane R.Irvin, George William Johnson & wife Martha T.of Chesterfield Co.Va.;James May & wife Charlotte T.of Petersburg,Va.all of the 1st part;sell to Soloman Woolfe of Ms..land belonging to the late Edward M.Eggleston,decd...land lying in Wash.Co.Ms.Judge of the Court in Va.is John Young Mason

P.196:21 Oct.1838:Gift:Matthew Flournoy of Fayette Co.Ky. gives to his son-for "love and affection"-Victor M.Flournoy of Wash. Co.Ms.,for the sum of $1...land on Ms.River near Princeton "he now lives on".@1100+ac.

P.200:5 May 1840:H.Carpenter & Co.'s surviving partner-John M.Carpenter of Claib.Co.Ms.liquidates the holdings of the co..

P.227:12Jan.1840-Deed:Thos.J.Tinnie of Adams Co.Ms.-for $6,100 by him paid to Wm.J.Carroll,Matilda Carroll, Isreal Carroll & George W.Carroll sell their land.

P.232:5 May 1840-Mort:Alfred C.Downs & wife Mary Jane(Robinson) of Warren Co.Ms.owes $16,000in notes to Roche(Rose?)H.Robinson (female).

DEED BOOK "J": WASHINGTON CO.MS.
22 Feb.1840-16 Mar.1841

P.235:12 May 1840-D/T;Peter C.Chambliss of Jeff.Co.Ms.sells toCortez Chambliss of same for $1,notes held by Peter C.Chambliss on Mort.s-several pages of land descpt. Some in Twp.6, R2E;some Twp.19,R10W;Some land is in Chochuma Dist.[Note:Gen. Peter Corbin Chambliss marr.Drucilla Harper & they had 7 children:Cortez was the eldest,born 1818 Jeff.Co.Ms. In 1847 Cortez Chambliss marr.Eliz.N.Bolls,Jeff.Co.]

P.243:11 May 1840-Est.Sale:Harriet B.Blanton,Adms. & Saml.R. Dunn,Adm.of Est.of Wm.B.Blanton,decd.intestate of Wash.Co.Ms. Adms.seek to sell land on Canal Bayou(Williams)in Wash.Co.for benefit of Orphans,+ some of the slaves. Samuel Burks of Jeff. Co.Ky.is the buyer. Children unnamed.

P.255:15 Apr.1840-Mort.:($175,000+)George N.Parks & wife Mary Ann of Wash.Co.Ms. of the 1st pt:Absolom Spielman-Adm. & Sarah Neibert-Admx.of Est. of Jos. Neibert,decd:Saml.J.McAllister Adm. & Ann P.Gemmill Admx. of Est. of Peter Gemmill,decd.;& James C.Walker-all of Natchez of the other part. The Parks pick up the mort. on "BenLomand Plantation",Wash.Co.-East Bank of Ms.River near foot of Slack(Stack)Island,Sec.15,16,Twp.11,R9W; also the "Bailey Tract"+ the "Lofton Tract"+ slaves.

P.271:13 Apr.1840-Mort;Joseph Jones of Warr.Co.Ms.of the 1st pt;to David Hay,Matthew Pickett,Thos.J.Mulhollen of Haywood Co.Tenn.

P.276:26 Feb.1840-Mort;Albert G.Creath of Warr.Co.Ms.of the 1st pt;WM.A.Lake,Adm.of Est.of Henry Brawner,decd.(Lake from Warr.Co.)of 2ndpt;Jacob S.Yerger of Warr.Co.,Johnathon Karsner & Wm.M.Pinckard are indebted to said Lake as Adm.of Brawner's Est.,and gave notes signed by Creath as sec.,and they are due.

P.332:23 July 1839-Deed:Joseph Ryions(Ryinis?)& wife Louisa J.of Simpson Co.Ms. & Abraham W.Harrelson of same,of the 1st part;toEdward P.Johnson of same.

P.333:6 May 1840-Deed;David W. Connelly of Wash.Co.Ms. of 1st part;Thos.H.Buckner & Bernard H.Buckner of same.(Thos.H.&Bernard H.are brothers)

P.344:23 Mar.1840-Mortg.;Andrew Haynes & wife Charlotte B. (Downs)of Warr.Co.Ms.of the 1st part;President and Directors & Co.of Planters Bank,of Ms..1600 ac.+slaves. Document signed by Andrew, Charlotte Haynes and Wm.Vick.

P.346:6 June 1840-Mort:$20,000 Thos.Kershaw of Wash.Co.Ms. of the 1st part;Frances R.Kershaw of S.C.(female)loans Thos.[Note; her son]money on 1632 ac.Twp.14,R6W-a Plantation below Princeton + slaves.

P.350-354;Johnathon Karsner & Wm.H.Taylor seek to clear the title to Plantation on Silver Creek,bought from Henry Brawner, now decd.WM.A.Lake,Adm.of Est.of Brawner.

P.354:20 Jan.1840-Pet.to clear Title;James J.Chewning,Adm.De bonis non of Est.ofThos.D.Downs,decd.of 1st part;Alfred C.Downs, J.B.Robinson of the 2nd part,state that on 15 May 1833 Isaac Caldwell & Thos.D.Downsexecuted a Bond to A.C.Downs and said

DEED BOOK "J": WASHINGTON CO. MS.
22 Feab.1840-16 Mar.1841

(Cont) P.354:Robinson for certain land. Chewning, Adm.agrees to petition and turns the land over to Alfred & Jas.B.(In Twp. 18,R8W-@2500 + Ac.) [Note: Isaac Caldwell was killed in a duel 1836. Thos.D.Downs & Caldwell married sisters,cousins of J.B. Robinson]

P.390:2 July 1840-Mort:Benjamin L.Tappan & wife Margaret M.B.;& Charles C.Hardy & wife Martha M. of the 1st part:to President Dir.& Co. of Union Bank of Tenn.in Nashville. Mortgage land Tappan & Hardy bought from Richard Christmas & his wife Mary E..The Atty. for the bank of Nashville is James H.Wilson.

P.395:P.O.A. 8 June 1840 at Louisville,Ky:Elijah J.Atchinson of Jeff.Co.Ky. gives his P.O.A to Zenas Preston of Wash.Co.Ms. to handle all his business.

P.397:28 Sept.1840-Mort.Adams Co.Ms.-Alexander C. Dunbar of Wilkinson Co.Ms. of the 1st part:John P.Walworth of Natchez of 2nd Part:Pres.Dir.& Co. of Planters Bank. Plantation called "Dunbarton"-2300 ac..Land originally conveyed by Wm.M.Gwin to Saml.A.Plummer..and from Plummer to Archibald Dunbar of Adams Co...and from Archibald to Alexander C..Land in Twp.10,R8W, Twp.9,R9W,+ slaves on said plantation.

P.405:7 Oct.1840-Deed:Charles Turnbull & wife Pricilla of the 1st part;to Frederick G.Turnbull of the 2nd[Note:Charles & Fred. G. are brothers.]

P.416:9 Nov.1840-D/T:Octavia Sulivan(also sp.Sulivane) of Claib. Co.Ms. sells land to Wm.H.Martin of same,for payment of her husbands'debts. Her husand was Vans M.Sulivan,decd.

P.435:3 Dec.1840-Mort:Stephen M.Jackson of Wash.Co.Ms. of the 1st part; Commercial Bank of Natchez of the other part.$9,534 + note co-signed by Herbert W.Hill [Note:his brother-in-law], Wm.Mills & W.R.Campbell as securities. Dated 17 Nov.1840,Payment schedule follows.Land in Twp.18,R8W.

P.   :9 Jan.1835-Mort.;Gideon Fitz & wife Mary,Jacob B.Morgan & wife Minerva of the 1st part;Wm.M.Rives,Jesse Perkins,Mordecai Baldwin of the 2nd part;Geo.Rives of the 3rd Part.

P.457:8 Nov.1839-Mort;Samuel Mason of Warren Co.Ms. of the 1st part;Jacob Oats & Thos.S.Mason of Warren Co. & Wm.W.Kincheloe of Owensborough,Ky of the 2nd part;[Note;by Oct.1842,Kincheloe(w) & wife Roseannah are from Warren Co.Ms.Deed Bk."A"Issa.Co.Ms. P.3].Saml. owes $82,681-partly to Pres.Dir.& Co. of Commercial R.R.Bank of Vicksburg. Oats signes as his security, as did Alfred C.Downs to another note,also WM.M.Pinckard & WM.H.Sims. Saml.now living on tract of land called"Pleasant Hill Plantation" in Warren Co.-Pearl River Dist. There is also a Plantation on Deer Creek in Twp.11,R7W,Choctaw Dist. + much,much more.(Polly Mason did not sign.)

P.493;3 Nov.1840-Deed:Daniel Farrar & wife Eliza K.of Adams Co.Ms.sell to Isaac Sellers of same-for $95,000"Andalusia Plantation" on Ms.River Wash.Co.in Twp.11,R9W,Choctaw Dist.They sell "their share"in 1920 ac. according to a survey made by Benj.A.Ludlow,deputy Surveyor of U.S.for said Dist.-+ slaves, stock,equipment, etc.

DEED BOOK "J": WASHINGTON CO.MS.
22 Feb.1840-16 Mar.1841

P.495:23 Nov.1840-Deed:Vincent W.McMurtry of Wash.Co.Ms. sells his undivided 1/4 of "Andalusia Plantation"to Isaac Sellers of Adams Co.Ms.for $25,000 + slaves.

P.497:28,Nov.1840-Deed:Alexander T.McMurtry & wife Rebecca M. (Moss)of Natchez to Isaac Sellers of Adams Co. sell land for $15,000 in Twp.12,R8W,Choctaw Dist..stating that the deed to this land has either been lost or mislaid.

P.511:22 Sept.1840-Mort.:Ambrose Knox of Wash.Co.Ms. of the 1st part:Andrew Knox of same of the 2nd part:Wm.H.Davis of Pasquotank Co.,N.C.of 3rd.

P.519:9 Apr.1840-Gift:Ulysses W.Moffett & wife Mary C. of Hinds Co.Ms.of the 1st part;give to Martha Ann Mead-daughter of Cowles Mead"for love and affection"a gift of land.(lots 6,2;Sec.21) (lots 3,4;Sec.22)(lot 5;Sec.15)all in Twp.15;R3W-Choc.Dist.

P.520:9 Apr.1840-Gift:Cowles Mead and wifeMary of the 1st part give their moiety in a tract of land to Martha Ann Mead, daughter of Cowles Mead. Land description matches the one above(p.519) [Note:Cowles Mead Married Mary Ann Green dau.of Abner Green.]

P.543:27 Oct.1840-Mort:John Montgomery of Madison Co.Ms.Mortg. land and slaves to Isaac N.Selser of Hinds(Bro-in-law)

P.547:14 May 1840-Petition for Partition:Doc. states:"Whereas in month of June 1827 John M.Taylor who lived in Madison Co. Ala.applied for and obtained letters of Adm." with the Will annexed on the Estate of John Taylor,decd. from Orange Co.Va. He gave bond on 25 June for $36,000 with Gilbert D.Taylor as security..John Taylor owned land in Orange Co.Va.,Giles Co. Tenn.,& slaves in Va. John M. sold out the Va. holdings & removed the remainder of the slaves to Madison Co.Ala. and later to Chicot Co.Ark. The terms of the Will(John Taylor"s)beinghis whole Est. to be divided equally between Gilbert D.Taylor and such Children as John M.Taylor should have at the time of John M."s death.John M. claims that the distance between Orange Co.Va. & Madison Co.Ala.prevented his making regular reports as Adm.but in 1831, JohnM. made a settlement with Gilbert D. for his½ of Est. and paid Gilbert $14,628.16. In 1840 John M. Taylor is from Vicksburg, and Gilbert D.Taylor is living in Giles Co.Tenn. John M.sells to Gilbert D. some of the slaves and property in Chicot Co.Ark.to equalize the inheritance.

P.568:17 Mar.1840-Deed:Robert G.Fitz of Warren Co.pays $800 to Gideon Fitz & wife Mary of Hds.Co.[Note:See Probate Drw. Unnumbered;E-G,Issa.Co.Ms. Est. of Gideon Fitz. Abst. in EMR Vol.II,p.20,for follow up on this family]

P.583:20 Feb.1840-Mortg:George P.Crump & wife Frances of Warren Co.-1st part;Thos.N.Jackson & Wm.H.Paxton-2nd part;Thos.B.Ingram of 3rd Part.Land in Yazoo Co.and Wash.Co.

P.590:1 Dec.1840-Deed:John L.Penrice & wife Julia R.of Wash.Co. Ms.-1st part;Erastus Towsey of Boone Co.Ky.2nd part.

END OF DEED BOOK "J"

DEED BOOK "J":WASHINGTON CO.MS.

HUSBANDS AND WIVES NAMED IN DEED BOOK "J"

ARRINGTON Wm. & wife Elizabeth Wash.1840
BENNETT, HENRY L. & wife MATILDA -New Orleans 1839
BIGELOW,RICH. & wife MARTHA-Hartford Co.,Conn.1839
BRYAN,Wm.P. & wife VIOLA Yalob.Co.Ms. 1840
BUSH,DAVID & wife MARTHA-Port Gibson,Ms.1840
CAMPBELL,JNO.P. & wife SEMANZA W., Maury Co.,Tenn.1838
DAVIS,JNO.R. & wifeMARGRETTA Warren Co. 1836
GRAFTON,JOHN & wife MARIA ELLIS Adams 1836
GRUBBS,FRANCIS & wife MORNING
HATCH,BENJ. & wife ELVIRA Hinds.Co. 1840
McCAUGHAN,SUSAN T. & husband JOHN J. Hinds Co. 1839
MILLER,ANDERSON & wife ELIZABETH of Miss.1839
MURPHREE,JNO. & wife ELIZABETH -Claib.Co. 1839
PECK,ALEXANDER H. & wife JULIA ANN -Claib.Co.Ms.1840
PORTER,GEO.C. & wife HARRIET M. -Hinds Co. 1840
PORTER,JOHN A. & wife MARY-Orange Co.Va.1839
READING,ABRA. & wife SOPHIE E. Warren Co.Ms. 1840
ROBARDS,WM.H. & wife ANN ELIZA-Wash.Co. Ms.1840
SNODGRASS,JOHN & WIFE MARGARET -Claib.Co.Ms.1839
WASHINGTON,HENRY F. & wife CAROLINE M.--Warren Co. 1840
VERTNER,JOHN D. & wife JANE-Claib.Co. 1837
WHITFIELD,BENJ. & wife LUCY E.-Hinds Co. 1840
YERGER,JOCOB S. & wife MARY H.R. - Warren Co.Ms. 1840

Cont.listings from Deed Bk."L",p.71.Husbands & wives:
SUMMERS,GEO.W. and wife MARIA JANE, Claib.Co.Ms.1842
VICK,HENRY W. and wife SARAH, Warren Co. 1842
WILKINSON,EDWARD C. and wife ELIZA C., Yazoo Co.Ms.1843
WOOLFOLK,Jos.h. and wife MARTHA, Woodford Co.Ky. 1842
YERGER,GEORGE S. and wife SARAH M., Warren Co. 1842

SUPPLEMENTARY INFORMATION:WILL BOOK"A":WARREN CO.MS.
P.73:Will of Elizabeth Powell,decd.of Wash.Co.Ms.
Written 24 Dec.1836-Probated Feb.Term 1837
Names:Son,Roderick Powell-$10
   Dau.Serena Phillips-$10
   Son,Hugh Powell $10-Exec.
   Dau.Sarah Hilliard $10
   Son,Thomas Powell $10
   3 youngest children share the rest of the estate-
¶[NOTE.This Will is not recorded in Wash.Co.Ms.]

WILL BOOK "A":MADISON CO.MS.
P.21:Will of Wm.Balfour:Written 17(or19)Nov.1834-no probate date;
If his 3 ch.-Chas.R.Balfour,Eliza Ann Balfour,Emily Balfour should
have no issue, the prop.is to be divided between his son Wm.L.
Balfour & dau.Julia Gartley,wife of Wm.Gartley or their ch.;Exec.
Chas.R.Balfour. Wit:Robt.W.Davis,Wm.A.Echols.

P.60:Will of Norfleet,Wm.B.;Hinds Co.,Written 6 Sept.1840-prob.
25 Apr.1841:Names-Sis.Minerva Ann Norfleet;leaves prop. in trust
to Wm.Hardeman,now of Mad.Co.Ms. for the benefit of Mary E.Christ-
mas,wife of Rich.Christmas,now of Mad.Co.Ms.;a bequeath to Thos.
H.Christmas who is named exec.

DEED BOOK "K": WASHINGTON CO.MS.
16 Mar.1841--13 May 1842

Original Deed Book. Has been rebound, in good condition. Genealogical information only has been abstracted.

P.2:19 May 1840-Mort: to Wm.Ferriday & wife Helen C. of Natchez of the 1st part,for $10 to them paid by John Routh, Elias Ogden, Adms. and Mary M.(Routh)Ellis Admx.of Est.of the late Thos.G. Ellis"to save harmless the Est.of Thos.G.Ellis,decd"as herein provided:"Hollywood Plantation"-Wash.Co.Ms.@400 ac.in Twp.17, R8W,Choc.Dist.+ 143 ac.+ More in a lengthy description, in all 1322 ac. + slaves(57)on "Hollywood"+ stock,utensils,ect..Land under mortgage to A.& D.Demistones & Co.for $178,000, this a second Mort.:$38,486 to the Agri.Bank of Ms. for the 1st Mort. Thos.G.Ellis,now decd.,was Ferriday & John C.Potts' security in these matters.(This releases the Est.of Ellis from the financial responsibilities in these Mortgages.)

P.10:Jan.1841-Deed:Ambrose Knox of Wash.Co.Ms.of the 1st part: David F.Blackburn of same, for the 2nd part:Knox owes notes to Est.of late Wm.Shipp,decd.of Natchez, endorsed by Andrew Knox..another note held by Agri.Bank..and another to Wm.A.Davis of N.C.:Ambrose sells to Blackburn.
The next document deals with the same persons,additional information stating that Wm.W.Collins,who had been one of the securities has now removed to Ark.[WM.Shipp Marr. the dau.of Jos.L.Barnard, Lucy-1810 Adams Co.Ms.]

P.20:3 Feb.1841-Mortg:Archibald L.Kenney of Hinds.Co.Ms.of the 1st part;Wm.W.Frazier,Thos.E.Robins,Wm.S.Bodley assignees of the Pres.& Directors & Co. of the Comm.&R.R.Bank of Vicksburg.

P.23:9 Jan.1841-Deed:Wm.Barr & wife Eliza Jane of Woodford Co. Ky.,Geo.M.Pinckard & wife Sarah Ann of Wash.Co.Ms.Jas.McCutcheon & wife Susan of V'burg,Ms. all of the 1st part;Wm.Barr & John L.Barckley of Woodford Co.Ky.the 2nd part..land on Shirttail Bend-1611 ac.in Twp.17N,R8W-awarded as O.P. to Alex.G.McNutt and sold by him to Barr & Pinckard.

P.74:4 Mar.1841-Perfection of Title:Geo.Smith & wife Mary J.G. ofWarren Co.Ms.,John Hebron & wife Julia G.of Warren,Alex.M. Austin & wife----,by his Att.H.R.Austin of Warren,Wm.H.Paxton & A.M.Paxton,Jesse B.Ragan of Warren and wife Sarah K.Ragan, Wm.P.Stone & wife Amanda S. of Hinds.Co.all of the 1st part; Richard Christmas of the 2nd part:The Smiths and Hebrons sold by deed on 9 Nov.1835 to the Austins. The land description was in error in Original Deed. Land had passed from Austins to Paxtons, to Ragans, to Stones and now to Christmas, who wants a clear title.

P.94:16 Apr.1841-Deed:Mary Jane(Cocke) & Wm.W.Collins sell to George Yerger their undivided 1/5th portion of land which Hartwell Cocke died seized and possessed of. About 2900 ac. + stock. in Twp.10N,R9W and partly in R8W.¶Note:WM.W.Collins was marr.1st to a dau.of Francis Penrice and they had a dau.Marian Aurora Collins,who is given a gift of slaves by her grandfather Francis Penrice in Dec.1837.He(Collins)marr.2nd Mary Jane Cocke dau. of Hartwell Cocke,July 1840. The heirs of Hartwell Cocke-James, John H., Mary Jane, Louisana-whose Guard. was WM.W.Collins.
(Cont.next page)

DEED BOOK "K": WASHINGTON CO.MS.
16 Ma.1841-13 may 1842

(Cont.)Sarah A. who marr. Rowland Whitman. Hartwell's wife at
the time of his death was Elizabeth who later Marr. a Walker.
It is not clear whether or not she was the mother of the above
children. WM.W.Collins and his wife Mary Jane(Cocke)Collins
moved to Ark.and then on to Lake Providence, La.where in 1862
Mary Jane sued her husband, Wm.W.Collins, for mismanaging her
affairs,and said he owed her $24,000 compensation for "the em-
barrassments & mismanagements of her Husband".The court awarded
her $20,800 with 5% int.Pkt.#4464, Carroll Parish,La. The issue
of Mary Jane & Wm.W.Collins are as follows:George H.b1841 Ark:
Sallie b1848 Ark;Thomas J.b 1850 Ark.;John G.b 1851 Ark;Susan
b 1854 La.;Fannie b 1855 La.;Willie b 1859/60 La. Many connections of this family moved into Issa.Co.]

P.100:26 Apr.1841-P.O.A.:"I,Mary Ann Turnbull Executrix of the
Last Will and Testament of John Turnbull,decd.late of Wash.Co.,"
gives P.O.Ato Abram F.Smith of Wash.Co. to collect all debts
due the Est.and to attend to all Business.

P.111:27 Apr.1841-DeedGeorge N.Parks & wife Mary Ann Parks of
Wash.Co.,sell to Thos.Parks of Claib.Co.Ms. for $125,000 part
of "BenLomand Plantation"+ slaves.

P.125:19 Nov.1839-D/T:James B.White is Securing title to his
wife Rebecca S.White and to James's son Samuel Warren White
by his first wife. He leaves Rebecca S. in full control, but
seeks to unencumber Wm.Hardeman from any endebtedness. The Deed
is put in Trust to Isaac H.Hilliard & Wm.Ley.Notice of Public
sale is published in Yazoo"Whigg", where the land on which
White resided was sold to H.R.W.Hill.

P.134:9 Apr.1841-Deed:Lawrence Pike Maxwell of Claib.Co.Ms.
of 1st part;to James Anderson Maxwell,"son of John"Of Claib.Co.

P.221:--day of--1840-Deed:James B.Robinson and wife Lucy of
Hinds.Co. & Alfred C.Downs & wife Mary J.(Robinson)of Warren;
sell to Thos.Kearney their undivided 1/4th of tract of land
in Wash.Co.,entered in the name of Isaac Caldwell & Thos.Downs.
[Note:Thos.Kearney marr. the widow of Isaac Caldwell-Elizabeth
Robinson]

P.243:16 Jan.1840-Pet.for Partition:Felix Huston & wife Mary
E. & P.F.Merrick bought a tract of land in 1832. Merrick,now
decd.and his Adm.is Hannah M. Merrick who is now Hannah M.Stone
sold the undivided ½ of Est.of P.H.Merrick to Elizabeth McDan-
gerfield..and Eliz.McDangerfield wants a partition from Felix
Huston's part.

P.268:26 Oct.1841-Gift:Gideon Fitz of Hinds.Co.Ms.-for love
and affection to "my daughter Minerva Morgan"of Hinds Co..gives
her land that had been conveyed to him by Robt.J.Fitz on 22
Jan.1838, land in Twp.13N,R9W-with the understanding that Gideon can continue to use the Plantation along with Minerva as
longas he shall live and further exacting the promise that
should he(Gideon) or his wife(unnamed) ever need financial
assistance, Minerva will give them $500 per anum.(Note:Gideon
Fitz's Will, filed in Sunflower Co.Ms. 1859)

DEED BOOK "K": WASHINGTON CO.M.
16 Mar.1841-13 May 1842

P.276:1 Nov.1841-Quit Claim:Robert J.Fitz of the 1st part;Martha E.Fitz & A.F.Smith of 2nd..all of Wash.Co.Ms.Rob has intermarried with Martha E.When she was a citizen of La. and she being entitled to the following slaves..names 24: They want to bring the slaves to Ms. to work a Plantation without endangering her claim to them. So Robert J.Quit Claims them to Smith to keep in trust for Martha.Written in above this indenture: "Delivered to Robt.J.Fitz-16 Dec.1845."

P.277:4 Oct.1841-Deed:Wm.C.Richards buys land at Public Auction, sold by Sheriff Wm.W.Collins..lots in Twp.16,R5W,& Tpw.18,R6W 1988 ac.previously belonging to Thos.B.J.Hadley, John A.Grumball, Robt.A.Patrick,Henry R.Moss.

P.294:11 May 1838-Deed(Recorded 29 Nov.1841)Thos.B.P.Ingram and wife Maria & Corbin Baker & wife Dorcas G.all of Fauq.Co. Va.of the 1st part:James Payne of Jeff.Co.Ms.of the 2nd;Mort. for $51,000-land and slaves.

P.296:8 Jan.1841-Deed of Conveyance:Edward P.JOhnson of Lexington,Ky.of the 1st part;for $10 paid by Geo.Downing of Wash.Co. Ms..together with the love and affection he bears for his wife Betsy W.Johnson wife of said Edw.P.Johnson, gives land to Geo. Downing to hold in Trust for Betsy. Land on Ms.River in Twp. 16,R8W-570 ac.+ slaves (29).

P.304:31 Aug.1841-Gift:Micajah Terrell for love and affection to wife Martha E.Terrell, gives her land in Wash.Co.Ms.in Twp. 14,R4W-721 ac.for her sole use. Terrell's live in Warr.Co.Ms.

P.305:9 Nov.1841-Deed:Gideon Fitz & wife Mary Fitz of the 1st part,of Hds.Co.,sell to Jacob B.Morgan of HindsCo. Next document-Morgan mortg.the land bought from Gideon & Mary Fitz to Union Bk.,and the Mort.is signed by J.B.Morgan & his wife Minerva Morgan.

P.307:1 Dec.1841-Deed:Isaac Sellers sells to (his bro.)Wrenna B.Sellers, part of"Andalusia Plantation". Isaac signed in Adams Co.Ms.

P.311:24 Nov.1841-Sale:Wm.R.Jones,Adm.of Est.of Jas.B.Maulding, decd. Maulding had acquired @240 ac.in Wash.Co.,which Jones now proposes to sell at Pub.Auc.Wm.H.Gaines was the buyer.

P.317:17 May 1841-P.O.A.:FromEdward Sparrow to Wm.S.Scott of Claib.Co.to act in instance of D/T fromGeo.G.Gregory of Wash.Co. Sparrow is in Concordia Parish,La.

P.330:11 Dec.1841-Deed:Robert J.Chambliss & wife lucinda, Govey (Gary,Grey?)Hood & wife Nancy all of Carroll P.La..all legal heirs of Harbird Hood,decd. sell O.P.to John H.Farr and the heirs of Saml. W.Sullivan,decd. Farr buys 4/5ths and heirs of Sullivan buy 3/5th(?8/5ths?). Land on Ms.River Choctaw Dist. Twp.11,R9W-371 ac. O.P.#6250 dated 4 June 1833;another O.P. #11075-310 + ac.;another 682+. [For Est.of Saml.W.Sullivan, see EMR Vol.II,p.1]

P.341:26 Jan.1842-Deed:Gen.Warantee:Wm.J.Carroll for himself & as Atty.in fact for Isreal Carroll,Geo.Carroll-the heirs of John H.Carroll,decd.of Adams Co.Ms.of the 1st part;(cont.)

DEED BOOK "K": WASHINGTON CO.MS.
16 Mar.1841-13 May 1842

(Cont.)to Isaac Elmore of Carroll P.La.of the 2nd part.

¶Note;Several pages of lands being sold at Public Auction by the Sheriff,John R.Downing-Jan.1842. Also several sales by Tax Collector, Wm.W.Collins -Jan.1842

P.364:March Term 1841-Probate Court, Holmes Co.Ms.Joseph W. Miller,Adm.de bonis non of Est.of James C.Dickson,Decd.filed a petition stating the Est.is largely in debt, and asks permission to sell part of it to pay debts. Permission granted, Miller sells land at Pub.Auction, some of which was bought by Wm.Barnes of Hds.Co.Joseph W.Miller & his wife Martha Ann Miller, formerly Martha Ann Dickson, one of the heirs-at-law of said Dickson,decd. & Michael J.Dickson,son and minor heir.[Note: it is difficult to tell whether Martha Ann is widow of Jas. Dickson or one of his children.]

P.371:25 Dec.1841-Deed:Joseph W.Miller & wife Martha Ann(Dickson) Miller of Hinds Co.of the 1st part;& Wm.Burns of Hds.Co.2nd part;Document states that on 1 Feb.1838, by Circuit Court of Yazoo Co.Ms.,Hugh Dickson,Adm.of Est.of Jas.C.Dickson,decd. who died Intestate, recorded a judgment against David Temple and his security-Jas.Dox. Jas.C.Dickson & Temple purchased land together. This document deals with Jos.W.Miller buying ½ land, located on West bank of Yazoo River.

P.399:2 Mar.1840-Quit Claim:Andrew Wilkins;John B.Huff & wife Mariah,formerly Mariah Wilkins;Wm.Earnest & wife Polly,formerly Polly Wilkins;Jacob Earnest & his wife Zerelda,formerly Zerelda Wilkins:George B.Wilkins;Thomas Wilkins..all of Sullivan Co. Ind.and heirs-at-law of John Wilkins, late of Vicksburg,Warren Co.Ms.,decd. of the first part;quit claim to David Wilkins for $500 an O.P.-David is also from Sullivan Co.Ind. Wit:Chas.L. Thrasher,Saml.Myers,Margaret Myers.

P.400:15 Jan.1842-Deed:David Wilkins and wife Frances(X)Wilkins of Sullivan Co.Ind. by their Atty.-Benj.Wolfe of same Co.,sells the above O.P. to Elhannan W.Morris of Warren Co.Ms.

P.408:1 Nov.1841-P.O.A.:Wm.H.Gaines gives his P.O.A. to Edw. A.Meaney-both of Chicot Co.Ark. Wm.R.Jones wants a mortgage on some "lots".

P.412:29 Nov.1836-Deed:Quachita P.La.:John M.A.Hamblin & Martha E.Morehouse,both of said place, state she paid Hamblin $2500 for property due her by the partition of her father's estate. Hamblin passes on to her several slaves. Also appeared, Eliza W.,widow Richardson, wife of John M.A.Hamblen and mother of Martha E. & Widow of Saml.Richardson,decd.(Hamblin also spelled Hamblen)

P.414:Petition for Partition:John Hamblin states that Martha E. is now of age, and it is time to partition the Est.of Saml. Richardson. Hamblin has now married Martha E.'s mother, Eliza Williams, the widow of Saml.Richardson. Inventory follows of slaves. 17 Nov.1836. Martha E.Says she has seen the vouchers, and accepts the terms of the partition.

DEED BOOK "K": WASHINGTON CO.MS.
16 Mar.1841-13 May 1842

P.415:27 Dec.1837-D/Slaves:Quachita P.La.:R.J.Fitz & wife----,from John A.M.Hamblin:appearing before Parish Judge Lewis F.Laney, was Eliza Williams,widow of Saml.Richardson, and now wife of John M.A.Hamblin-testify to the partition of the Est. of Saml.Richardson and to see that the only heir Martha E.(Richardson)is now widow of Charles F.Morehouse, and now wife of Robt.J.Fitz...gets her share of her father's Est.

P.417:Partition of Est.of Saml. Richardson,decd.29 Nov.1836-Quach.P.La.:Heirs-Eliza W. Richardson,now wife of John M.A. Hamblin & Martha E.Richardson, the widow Morehouse...both- of the said Parish. Land is on Bayou de Liard(Quach.P.?).Recorded Wash.Co.Ms.28 Feb.1842.[Note:cannot find the reason for this Est. to be filed in Wash.Co.Ms.,at least not from these docu.]

P.437:21 Apr.1841-Deed:Richard Christmas and his wife Mary E. of Warren Co.Ms. to Rueben A.Gentry of Williamson Co.Tenn. Land in Will.Co.Tn.on the Little Harpeth-"which land was given to my wife and myself jointly by the father and mother of my wife-except for 100 ac. which I paid her father, which was about half what it was worth, the other half intended as a gift." In order to protect his wife's portion, Richard quit claims slaves to be held in Trust by Benj.D.Smith, for her use.

P.499:30 Mar.1842 D/T:George Joor of Wash.Co.Ms.of the 1st part; Wm.Rushing-2nd. George Joor signs a D/T to Rushing to hold for his infant daus. Caroline Amanda & Laura George Joor.

P.511:23 Dec.1834-D/T:Wilkinson Co.Ms.George Joor signs D/T to Peter H.Joor both of Wilkinson Co.Ms. for Peter to hold in trust. George Joor, for love and paternal love and affection unto his wife Laura Ann Joor and their children.[Note:George Joor marr.2nd Catherine P.Shelby and they had a son John Shelby Joor b.1845. Geo.Joor decd. 1848. See EMR Vol.I,II:From the
* COLUMBIA HIVE(S.C.)1831-1832"On this Thurs.evening,20th,by Rev. Dr.Goulding,Mr.Peter Henry Ioor(Joor)of Woodville,Ms. (marr.) to Charlotte Withers Herron of this place.Oct.29,1831..name also spelled Peter Horry Ioor.]

Husbands & wives named in Deed Bk."K":
BARKLEY,JOHN S.and wife LUCY Versailles,Ky.1841
COLEMAN,NICHOLAS D. and wife LUCY A. Warren Co.Ms.1842
DEMPSEY,SOLOMAN and wife ROSAMOND(X) Coahoma Co.Ms. 1841
HILL,H.R.W. and wife MARGARETTA E.Wash.Co.Ms.1839
HOLLAND,ANDREW G.and wife PRICILLA ,Wash.Co.Ms. 1835
LEWIS,WM(X) and wife LEANA(X),Pope Co.Ark. 1841
PARRISH, THOMPSON M. and wife MARY PRUDENCE, Woodford Co.Ky.1840
PATTERSON,ANDREW and wife MARTHA, Yazoo City,Ms.(Manchester,Ms.'39)
PAYNE,ANDREW M.and wife HENRIETTA M.Vicksburg,Ms.1842
PORTER,GEO.C.and wife HARRIET M. Hds.Co. 1842
WALL,JAS.M.and wife MARTHA H. Hinds Co. 1839
WILLIAMS,JOHN and wife ELIZABETH, David.Co.Tenn.1841
WOODFORK,JOSIAH and wife CAROLINE, Wash.Co.Ms. 1841

END OF DEED BOOK "K"

*"MARRIAGE & DEATH NOTICES FROM COLUMBIA S.C.NEWSPAPERS-1792-1839" by Holcomb.

DEED BOOK "L": WASHINGTON CO.MS.
19 Apr.1842-26 Feb.1844
500 pages-writing very difficult to decipher.

P.1:19 Apr.1842-Est.Settlement:Jas.A.McAlister and "other unknown heirs of David L.McAlister,decd"..are involved in a suit-Apr.1842-with Theodorick J.James.
¶[Note:Anderson Miller is now the Marshall of Southern District]

P.11:28 Dec.1840-Deed:Saml.R.Moss of Robertson Co.,Republic of Texas of the 1st part: Wiley Newberry of same of the 2nd: Moss sells to Newberry ½ of Moiety of lands in Wash.Co.Ms.Wit: Harrison Owen,Robert Henry. The following documents were signed in Texas by officials----Joseph Love,Clerk;Robert E.B.Baylor, Dist.Judge of 3rd Judicial Dist.;J.S.Mayfield,Sec.of State of Rep.of Tex.:Geo.A.Flood-charge d'affairs-from Legation of U.S.

P.14:24 Nov.1834-Deed:Wm.E.Hall and wife Lucinda,Elijah F.Atchinson and wife Kesiah all of Wash.Co.Ms.of the 1st part:John G.Cock & Wm.S.Scott of same the other part. Wit:Jas.D.Hall & JOhn Cocke. Recorded:17 May 1842.

P.19:23 May 1842-Deed:Thos.J.Finney is indebted to Thos.J.Harper for $11,500 by note dated 4 Aug.1836-Clinton. Payment schedule follows. Harper owes Jos.Peebles,also Andrew Ritchey--Adm. of Jas.Ritchey, decd.,also to Christopher C.Porter. Finney makes notes to secure the above debt. C.C.Porter transfers his part to R.F.G.Porter. The land had been bought at a Sheriff's sale in Wash.Co. and known as the Nathaniel K.Killem prop.@800 ac.

P.35:23 May 1842-Deed:Wm.White and wife Henrietta E.of Wash. Co. of the 1st part;Abram M.Feltus of Wilk.Co.Ms.-other: The sec.'s for White;Mordecai Powell,George Joor,Wm.Rushing.

¶[Note:Many transactions follow as Jas.R.Downing,Sheriff of Wash. Co. sells land at Pub.Auction,for default of payments.]

P.89:1 June 1842-Deed:Robert H.Buckner and wife Sarah F.sell to Stephen M.Jackson of Wash.Co...Sarah F.signed giving the stipulation that Robt.H.give her a life interest in the place "he now occupies called "Edge Hill"near Clinton,in return for her signing the above release of dower,in this Wash.Co.land. Lands in Twp.18N,R7W-824 ac.

P.129:21 Mar.1842-Deed:John R.Downing,Sherf.,sells at Pub.Auction, and Mary Allen is the buyer for $60.73-@2080 ac. Circuit Court of Madison Co.Ms.returned 2 writs of"Fieri Facias"against the goods and chattels and tenements of Thos.Saunders,Chas.W. Allen & Wm.Henry,defendants against Pres.Dir.& Co.of Commerce & R.R.Bank of V'burg. May 1838-debt of $4,373.32 + interest. Lands entered by Chas.Allen,Chas.W.Clifton,Richard Christmas, Jas.A.McAlister.

P.133:Lands sold at Pub.Auction:Mary Allen is the buyer:Wm. H.Fleming,surviving partner of late firm of Fleming & Bennett, Chas.W.Clifton & Alexander Allen partners in trade under the name Clifton & Allen-in suit against the Pres.Dir.etc.Bank of V'burg. 21 Mar.1842

P.146:18 Apr.1842-Deed:John H.Woolfolk of Wash.Co.Ms.sells to John Munn,Adm.of Est.of Jos.Meek,decd.Woolfolk signed in Yazoo Co.Ms.

DEED BOOK "L": WASHINGTON CO.MS.

P.147:21 June 1842-Deed:Jas.A.Stevens of Yazoo, sells,for $25 to Joab R.Richards in Wash.Co.-Land on Yazoo River in Twp.11N, R3W.Stevens bought it for taxes from WM.W.Collins,Tax Collector, 11oct.1841.1year was allowed for its redemption.

P.163:2May 1842-Deed:George Joor of Wash.Co.Ms.of 1st part:Wm. White of same-for $20 per ac.buys Joors'undiv.½ of a plantation, owned jointly(by White & Joor)and bought from Josiah P.Woolfolk, usually known as the'Rolling Fork Place-situate & lying on both sides of Rolling Fork of Deer Creek in Wash.Co.Ms.6,195 ac. Lengthy descpt.-mostly in Twp.12,R7W-Twp.12,R6W.

P.205:3 Jan.1843-Deed of Slaves:Charles Turnbull of Wash.Co. of the 1st part;Andrew Turnbull of 2nd;Andrew paid Chas. $1 for slaves(5)+ all his homestead equipment-furniture,stock,etc. with the understanding that Chas.owes money with Andrew as security and Chas.wants to keep Andrew "harmless".

P.205:6 June 1842-Partition of Est.:Ellen Bodley wife of Wm.S. Bodley, is owner of Estate conveyed to her by her father,James A.Pearer(very difficult to read),now decd. Partition made in deed of John W.Tyler,Commissioner of Jeff.Co.Court,Ky. On 13 Dec.1833 Bodley and wife Ellen, living in V'burg,Ms...want to either sell or swap her inheritance. Harry J.Bodley of Lexington,Ky.pays them $1 for land lying in City of Louisville,Ky.- to be handled or sold and the interest to be sent to Ellen should she need it and then it is to be passed on to her children(and Wms.)

P.212:12 Jan.1842-Mort:Abram Autex of Louisville,Ky. of the 1st part;John Bull in his own right and John Bull & Jacob Cordwell,Exec. of last Will and Testament of Robt.Bull,decd. of Shelby Co.Ky.of the 2nd.;480 ac.John C.Bull & Robt.T.Black are co-partners under firm name John C.Bull & Co.

P.238:24 Jan.1843-Sale of slaves:Gideon Fitz & wife Mary. & Jacob B.Morgan & wife Minerva all of Hds.Co.;John S.Harris of Nelson Co.Va.2nd part;George Rives of Albermarle Co.Va.3rd; a contract between Fitz & Morgan & Wm.M.Rives of 1 part & Geo. Rives of other-1843-sale of slaves.

P.249:18 Jan.1843:Wm.H.Taylor,Exec. of Will of Wm.Ley,decd. of 1st part;John A.Rowan of other:Wm.H.Taylor, as "Committee of the Est.of the said Ley," the said Ley being a Lunatic", sold to Rowan a Plantation of Ley's,owned jointly by Ley and Jos.H.Woolfolk..land in Twp.12,R4W + slaves..deed signed on 8 Mar.1842. Ley had a plantation that belonged solely to him, and since making bond for the sale, Ley died, leaving a Will written"during a lucid interval"which appointed Wm.H.Taylor & James H.Taylor exec.with full powers. Ley's Will filed in Wash.Co.[Note:see Vol.I,Vol.II of EMR series]Wm.H.Taylor signed in Warren Co.Ms.

P.266:22 Mar.1843-Deed:Henry R.W.Hill & Stephen Stafford pay $6,300 for land owned by Levi Mitchell(Mitchett?)."I have this day sold and delivered...on Plantation occupied by Mr.Unz.Ephraim,an old man, and his wife Sarah-and Elizabeth & Milly her 2 children..slaves,Nick-about 26 yrs.old and Washington 21 yrs. old and his wife Nancy" + others.

DEED BOOK "L": WASHINGTON CO.MS.

P.268:P.O.A.:Hiram Russell & Eliza Stow of Meigs Co.Ohio,Adm. of Est.ofJohn Stow,decd.late of same Co.,give their P.O.A.to Wm.H.Barton of same Co.to transact business in Princeton, Wash. Co.Ms. 28 Nov.1842.

P.269:24 Nov.1838-D/T:Wm.Ferriday and wife Helen- co-trustees, must sell land recorded Deed Bk."G",Wash.Co.p.418-422. Land for sale at the door of the courthouse at Natchez,3 Jan.1842. A foreclosure on $25,000note held by Z.C.Offutt, + 2 more for $2,000. A Plantation on East Bank of the Ms.River, between Anderson and Martin-Offutt & Warfield called "Liberia" about 1135 ac.(located in Twp.18,R10W, some in same Twp.,R9W)+ other land in Bolivar Co.Ms. + cattle. This document signed by Alexander Offutt & Thos.B.Warfield. The buyer at Natchez was Z.C Offutt for $10,000.

P.271:P.O.A.:28 Mar.1843:Robert J.Ward of Louisville, Ky.appoints brother George W.Ward of New Orleans, agent and attorney, to sign for mortgage on "my 1/3rd part of Plantation"on Lake Washington. A note to A.L.Addison,J.L.Addison,L.D.Addison & J.R. MacMurdo,merchants acting under the firm name of Addison & Co.; to Edward Heath & Robt.Heath ,merchants under the name of E.& R.Heath-Liverpool,England;cotton to be shipped to Liverpool. A later document concerning these same merchants adds the name of Junius R.Ward of Wash.Co.Ms.

P.276:1 Sept.1838-P.O.A.:Peter Swanson & Richard Swanson give their P.O.A.to James Swanson to sell or quit claim a deed to 2 tracts of land in Wash.Co.Ms."land granted"to Edward Swanson, Junior,decd."by the United States of America"..Document signed in Giles Co.Tenn.Rec.Wash.Co.Ms.13 Feb.1843.

P.279:1 Dec.1842-Deed:Williamson Co.Tn.George W. Pollard of the 1st part;James Swanson of same Co.,agent for Peter Swanson, land on both sides of Deer Creek, granted to Edward Swanson. (no land descpt.)Wit;James Swanson,Jr., W.W.Peace.

P.280:2 May 1840-Deed:Richard Christmas & wifeMary E.-Warren Co. of the 1st part;to David Horn(Harnd?)for $40,000, land on Yazoo River + slaves-1500 ac.

P.283:16 Mar.1843-Mort:Crop Loan-Stephen M.Jackson of Wash.Co. Ms.of the 1st part;Drury D.Boikin(Boykin) of same and Hubbard W.Hill of Warren of the 2nd part;land is mortgaged to Sterling Neblett,N.T.Williams,Wm.Mills & Thos.P.Hardaway in Mar.1839. [Note:Jackson married Hill's sister-Ann Dunn Hill]

P.288:14 Apr.1843-Bill of sale:Archibald Kinney of Wash.Co.Ms. of 1st part:Nicholas C.Kinney of Augusta Co.Va. of the 2ndpart; and O.P. is sold. 340 ac.+ slaves living on Place,+ houses etc.

P.291:20 Apr.1842-Deed:Henry W.Vick of Warren Co.receives Mortgage from Harry J.Bodley,trustee for Ellen Bodley,by virtue of a deed to him(Harry) from Wm.L.(S)Bodley and Wife-dated 6 June 1842 at Marshall's sale.Land near Deer Creek.Twp.15,R6W.

P.293:6 Mar.1843-Gift:Littleton Mundy of Franklin Co.Ms.to grandson Daniel Littleton Cameron,"son of my son-in-law John C.Cameron & Angeline M.Cameron,his wife".Daniel Littleton Cameron is about 1yr.-receives a slave Benjamin, who is about 9 mos. Should(Cont.)

DEED BOOK "L": WASHINGTON CO.MS.

(Cont.)Daniel die,the slave,and his increase, will then go to other children of his mother's side(Angeline's)

P.304:9 Feb.1843-Mortg:Saml.Osborne Jeffries,exec.of Est. of Wm.W.Osborne,decd.of Coahoma Co.Ms.of 1st part;Thomas Penny,2nd.

P.312:13 Mar.1843-Deed:Anderson Miller-Marshall of Southern Dist.of Ms.of the 1st part;James Wallace of Yazoo Co.Ms.of the other:By order of Circuit Court of U.S.against goods and chattels of James C.Dickson,decd. & Jos.W.Miller & Martha Ann Miller his wife,of Hinds Co.late Martha Dickson,David Dickson & Michael J.Dickson heirs of James C.Dickson. David and Michael are from Rankin Co.Ms.[Note:From"Ms.Records"by King;Nov.1835 James C. Dickson decd.,leaving large est.& Children-Michael,David & Martha Ann..Martha Ann marr.Joseph W.Miller 1835 or'36.]James Wallace was the purchaser.

P.355:Bankruptcy:Nov.1842:James A.Brooks declares bankruptcy under the Bankruptcy law passed by Congress Aug.19,1841-for uniformity of acts pertaining to bankruptcy.

P.376:Bankruptcy-Nov.1842:Robert L.Andrews declares Bankruptcy under the same law as above.

P.379:Relinq.-9 Oct.1843:Wm.J.Penrice,one of the Exec.of the Est.of Francis Penrice,late of Wash.Co.Cs.who states that he has"wasted,spent and used for" his own use funds or property belonging to Francis R.Penrice & Susan E.Penrice,legatee and heirs named in his said Will-recorded Wash.Co.-and worth $7,000. Wm.James Penrice makes recompense by selling his interest in the said Est.for $100.[Note:The children of Francis Penrice named in his Will, filed Mar.Term 1841 were-Susan E.,John L. (S),Wm.J.,Cordelia A.,Jos.H.,Francis R.and an unnamed Dau.who had marr. Wm.W.Collins. Francis's wife was Elizabeth. The other Exec.was Francis R.]

P.387:3 June 1842-Order of Sale:R.L.Dixon,Commissioner & Supervisor of Court of the Chancery of Ms. orders sale of land.Sarah C.W.Faust of Yazoo, Exec.of Augustus B.Faust, is involved in a law suit with James J.B.White, and the land is ordered sold at Benton,Ms. Courthouse.

P.389:17 July 1843-Gift:James Mays & wife Lucy of the 1st part; sell to Nimrod Selser of Avoyelles Par.La. land which Nimrod deeds to his grandsons Elam S.Rusk & Wm.J.Rusk,minor children of Wm.L.Rusk & Mary Selser, wife of Wm.L.Rusk,decd.Land in Wash. Co.Ms.

P.437:31 Oct.1843-Deed:Elisha Warfield & wife Maria of Fayette Co.Ky.,sold to Thos.D.Carneal of Cincinnatti,Oh.their undivided ½ of land in Wash.Co.Ms.for $14,000.Wm.P.Warfield guarantees the title. Wit:T.B.Flournoy,Thos.B.Warfield.

P.443:P.O.A-18 Sept.1843:Susan A.Rowanof Woodford Co.Ky.gives her P.O.A.to John H.Woolfolk of same Co. to handle business of Est.of her late husband,John A.Rowan.

P.446:Deed-1 May 1843:John Walker Percy of Wash.Co.Ms.& heir of Thos.G.Percy,decd.of 1st part;Chas.B.Percy of same,2nd part; Thos.G. owned property in Wash.Co.Ms.,Ala.,Texas.

DEED BOOK "L": WASHINGTON CO. MS.

P.453:Deed-13 Feb.1844:Joseph Peebles & wife Martha of Hinds Co.1st part;Henry W.Peebles & wife Ann W.of Christian Co.Ky. the 2nd;Partition of land owned jointly by Jos.and Henry W. that was bought from Jas.C.Dickson.

P.458:10 June 1843-Deed:Eastern Division of Virginia appoints John N.Garland of LYnchburg,Va. as special assignee of Est.of Peter Fitzpatrick. Peter Fitzpatrick had been declared bankrupt. Garland sold land Peter had bought from David Fitzpatrick, recorded in Wash.Co.21 Jan.1842-about 640 ac. Garland signed the document in Campbell Co. Va.

P.484:16 Mar.1844-Gift:George R.Dent and wife Pricy of Jeff. Co.Ms.of1st part; to Warren R.Dent of same Co.."for love and affection"all land divided by Put Williams & George R.Dent in Wash.Co.,George's undivided½.(Relationship unexplained)

P.491:11 Apr.1844-Deed:Thos.D.Condy of Charleston,S.C. the Adm. of Est.of Robert M.Allan,decd.sells to John L.Chapman of Wash. Co.Ms.,Plantation "Glen Allan"that John L.Chapman now lives on

P.493:12 May 1843-Deed:James Swanson of Williamson Co.Tn.& Peter Swanson of Harrison Co.Tx.buy Geo.W.Pollard & wife Martha E.'s interest in the"Edward Swanson land"on Deer Creek. Wit:Jas. Swanson,Jr.,Richard Swanson & wife Deborah who sign in Will.Co.Tn.

Husband & wives named in Deed Book "L":
BALL,GEO.W. and wife MARY JANE, Warr.L842
BANKS,SAMUEL and wife ANN M. Wash.Co. 1842
BOSTICK,ABSOLOM and wife MARY G. 1842
BRISCO,Parmenas and wife POLLY. Claib.Co.Ms.1842
BUCKNER THOS.H. and wife LOUISIANA, Wash.Co.1842
CARTER,ROBERT G. and wife Sophia of Lewis Co.Ky. 1843
COOK,JOHN F. and wife CAROLINE A.,Madison Co.Ms.1843
DEMOSS,WM.C. and wife MARY, Hinds Co. 1842
GAYLE,RICHARD C. and wife EVELINA E.(x) Chicot Co.Ark.1843
HATCH,NEEDHAM W. and wife MARY C. ,Warr.Co.1843
HILL,HARRY R.W. and wife MARGARETTA E.,New Orleans 1842
JANDON,SAMUEL and wife MARGURITA PEYTON, Philadelphia,Pa.
JEFFERSON,JOHN R. and wife ELIAS ANN hinds Co. 1842
KINCHELOW,WM.W. and wife ROSANNAH, Warren Co. 1841
McCULLOUGH,GEO. and wife LOUISA, Lincoln Co.Mo.1842
McDUFFIN, MURDOCK and wife AGNES M.,Copiah Co.Ms.1834
MORRISS,ELHANNON and wife MINERVA, Warren Co.Ms.1843
NUTT,HALLER and wife JULIA, Jeff.Co.Ms.1842
OATES,JACOB and wife TEMPERANCE(X), Warr.Co. 1843
PARISH,SAMUEL and wife MARY A. Wash.Co.1843
PIERCE, GRANVILLE S. and wife ELIZABETH V., Rutherford Co.Tn."42
PEEBLES,JAS.S. and wife MARY F., of La.1843
PINTARD,JOHN M. and wife CLARISSA H.,Jeff.Co.Ms.1844
PRENTISS,SARGENT S. and wife MARY JANE, Warren Co.Ms.1842
PURCELL,EDMUND and wife MARGARET A., Holmes Co.Ms.1842
RAWLINGS,JOHN H. and wife SARAH JANE, Madison Co. Tn.1842
RIVES,GEORGE and wife MARY E., Albermarle Co.Va. 1835
SKINNER,JOHN S. and wife ELIZABETH G., Baltimore,Md. 1841
SMITH,FRANCIS P. and wife SUSAN A., Wash.Co.Ms. 1843
STAFFORD,STEPHEN and wife MARIA, 1843
cont.listings on page 61

DEED BOOK "M": WASHINGTON CO. MS.

There are three copies of DBK."M". Alarge fat one which is the Original, and 2 smaller volumns marked"copy". The following abstracts have been taken from the 1st hand written copy,which goes to p.304,and checked against the original. The page numbers are worn off the original, and some of the information is tattered. Only info. pertinent to genealogy has been copied.

P.2:21 Oct.1843-Deed:Littleton Munday of Franklin Co.Ms.,to his daughter,"for love and affection",Angeline M.Cameron,wife of John C.Cameron of Wash.Co.Ms.,land on which the Cameron's now reside(located in Sec.9,Twp.17,R8W + land in another sec.,same Twp.,range.,in all 404+ac. Should Angeline survive her father, she is not to inherit any additional property from his est., but is to have this land evaluated and then if she is due more from the other heirs' shares, she shall have it. Document signed by Littleton Munday and his wife Lucinda.

In June 1841,J.H.Woods was agent and proprietor of the "Yazoo Whig and Political Register"-published in Yazoo City,Ms.

P.13:"Whereas Mrs.Rebekah J.Williams of North Carolina,the mother of my wife, has recently died in that state, leaving some property to be divided amongst her four children,"and "Whereas J.L.D.Smith of Ala.,by his Will bequeathed to my wife $1,000+, I,James J.B.White relinquish All rights to his wife's inheritance."His wife, Rebekah Jane White is to have the property turned over to her by Lewis Williams or is to invest same as she sees fit. Should Rebekah Jane White die without issue, the property is then to go to Lewis L.Williams & Melinda R.Williams wife of Joseph L.Williams.Doc.dated 23 Mar.1843-signed by James J.B.White of Hinds Co.Ms.

P.16:14 Nov.1843-Deed:Thomas Kershaw & wife Mary Jane of the 1st part;John P.Cunningham of the other. John P. is security on a bond for Mary Jane(his sister) for $35,000,dated 10 Nov. 1843..and payable to the Adm. of Frances K.Kershaw,decd. In and effort to protect John, they sell slaves on the plantation to him for $10. Thomas & Mary Jane Kershaw now live on this Plantation.

P.35:P.O.A.;Charleston,S.C.-John O.Sanders appoints T.W.Endecott of Princeton,Ms.to receive from Thomas Kershaw of Wash.Co.Ms. a certain debt.

P.36:1 Jan.1844-Deed:George G.Dromgoole of the 1st part:sells to Sarah M.Droomgoole-both of Wash.Co.,his portion of a plantation called"Long Island"on which the late Wm.A.Droomgoole lived,@500ac. George is one of the heirs of WM.A.[Note:Sarah Droomgoole was a Gilbert-sister to Philip A.Gilbert & Mildred Cox wife of Seth Cox]

P.41:9 Feb.1844-Deed:James Rucks and wife Louisa V.Rucks & Wm.Yerger all of Jackson,Ms.:the 1st part:John P.W.Brown of Marshall,Tn.the other. Parties of the 1st part sell undivided 1/5th of 783 ac.in Wash.Co. belonging to Louisa V.Rucks and described in deed from Samuel Worthington and wife dated 16 Jan.1836 to the Brown heirs-+1/5th of 279 ac. adjoining same which descended to said Louisa from her mother,Elizabeth Brown + undivided 1/5th of 64 slaves. Louisa buys John P.W.Browns' undivided 1/5th of land and slaves.

DEED BOOK "M": WASHINGTON CO.MS.

P.42:11June 1842-Marriage Contract:John S.Penrice relinquishes all claim to the property of Amelia E.Long. She owns property in Mo.& Ms.and some of the land is held in the name of Alton Long, Trustee. John S.& Amelia sign in St.Louis,Mo.

P.45:6 Apr.1843-P.O.A.:New Orleans-Andrew Erwin of Nashville, Tn.appoints James Erwin of Caddo.P.La. his atty.

P.48:30 Jan.1842:Wm.W.Littler of Wash.Co.of 1st part:Catharine Littler of same,the other-lot in Princeton,Ms.

P.49:10 Mar.1844-Agreement:Eilbeck Mason of Warr.Co.1st part; Geo.S.Yerger-2nd;Richard F.Anderson & Co.of Va.,3rd;John M. Chilton & Jane Magee,Adms.of Est of Eugene Magee-4th. Anderson & Co.had received judgement in a suit against Jane Magee,Chilton, Jacob Oates,& Alexander Brown on May 1841.Anderson sells to Mason and Yerger is security.

P.65:2 May 1844-Deed:Wm.Y.Brown of Jeff.Co.Ky.,sells to Shephard Brown & Joseph H.Johnson of Vicksburg, property he bought from the following:Saml.Herring and his wife Susan A.Herring of Point Coupee P.La.sold to Wm.Y.Brown an undivided portion of the Est.of Redding B.Herring decd.of Vicksburg, the father of said Samuel. The land is on Deer Creek. Also a deed made by George Washington Herring of New Orleans to Wm.Y.Brown. Geo.W.is alsoa son of Redding Herring.

P.72:29 Mar.1844-Release:Wm.A.Lake of Warr.Co.buys from James B.Lake of Dorchester Co.Md.,land and slaves. The wife of Wm.A. Lake is Ann E.Lake.

P.82:18 July 1843-Deed:John Martin & wife Clerinda of New Orleans,Hugh Wilson of New Orleans,James Bradley & Adeline Bradley, his wife of Madison Co.Ala.,James J.Pleasants & Emily J. Pleasants his wife of Madison Co.Ala., of the 1st part; to Thomas Bibb & Arthur M.Hopkins of ------Parish,La.

P.84:27 Dec.1843-Mort:Newit H.Vick of Warr.Co.-1st:Wm.Vick, Wm.Bibb,Edward M.Lane,T.B.Brabston of 2nd:J.W.Vick of the 3rd.

P.93:26 Apr.1842-Deed:Stuart W.Fisk buys at auction a Plantation known as "Belzoni"on Yazoo River, opposite Honey Island, belonging to A.T.McMurtry,et al-Jan.1842..allin Twp.16,R3W-2120 +ac.+slaves. Auction set up by Comissioner Wm.C.Harris.Wit: Stephen Castleman,Jas.H.Wren,Clara Pentecost,Alvarez Fisk.

P.98:17 Jan.1844-Deed:John C.Richardson & Adelaide his wife, of Claib.Co.Ms.buys from JohnC.Richardson,M.D. of Fayette Co. Ky.and Samuel B.Richardson,M.D.of Jeff.Co.Ky.

P.116:13 Jan.1844-Deed:Hugh W.Dunlap and wife Susannah W.of Madison P.La.to John H.Dunlap of Henry Co.Tn.[NOTEFrom"Marr. from Early Tn.Newspapers,1794-1851"Lucas; Hugh W.Dunlap of Paris,Tn.marr.Miss Susannah McKiernan, dau.of B.M'Kiernan,Esq. in Franklin Co.Ala.,9 Feb.1830]

P.138:25 Oct.1842-Eastern Dist.of La.:Zenas K.Fulton & Isaac W.Arthur declare bankruptcy.

P.151:23 Aug.1841-P.O.A.:WM.H.Roberds, then of Granville Co. N.C.and now of Ms.,conveyed to Robert B.Gilliam of Granville Co.,N.C.,slaves-in trust to secure harmless William P.Williams

DEED BOOK "M": WASHINGTON CO.MS.

(Cont.)and Joseph B.Littlejohn who were securities on 2 bonds to Robert Tugler-recorded Granville Co.N.C.BookX,p.463, and recorded Wash.Co.Ms.Book K.p.313. sale is requested so Gilliam appointed Carter B.Harrison late of Ms. but at present in Franklin,N.C.,to be his atty. Gilliam is at present in Franklin,N.C.

P.215:25 July 1839 Deed:At.Louis Co.Mo.,Parks B.Long of St.Louis sells to John S.Penrice of same,slaves for $700.

P.219:18 Mar.1844:Ambrose Gibson files bankruptcy.

P.229:5 Dec.1844-Deed:Pleasant Dearing of Tusca.Co.Ala.,of the 1st part;to James H.Dearing of same.

P.231:25 Dec.1844-Gift:Daniel R.Williams gives to his sister, for love and affection,Martha C.Crabtree,a gift of land.

P.233:15 May 1844-Gift:Davis Montgomery of Wash.Co.Ms."for love and affection"for his daughter Louise Buckner,land in Twp.16,R8W

P.233:15 May 1844-Gift:Davis Montgomery gives to daughter Martha Thomson,land in Twp.16,R8W.

P.258:20 Jan.1845-Deed:Felix G.Gamble,J.P.for Wash.Co. acting as Sheriff in place of Thos.J.Likens who cannot act in this instance because he has interest in this case, acts in suit styled Thomas Wallace Plaintiff against Rachel Day, Mary Elizabeth Day & Ann Carter Day,minor heirs at law of WM.T.Day,decd. in Warr.Co.,Property put up for sale & Thos.J.Likens was buyer.

P.265:--Dec.1842-Deed:Fayette Co.Ky.Richard Allen & Helen Jane Allen his wife of KY.acknowledge receiving from Joseph Dunbar, exec.of last Will and Testament of John Foster,decd.-$13,280 in "full subscription of our share of the Est.of John Foster, including in said sum our portion of purchase money received by said exec. from sale of land to Jos.Neibert",who bought the plantation"Walnut Hills" from Foster's Est. There must have been a dispute over whether or not Dunbar could sell the property under the terms of the Will.
Next Document:p.266-dated 15 Dec.1844,deals with Dunbar's sale of "Walnut Ridge"to Neibert..and states that Dunbar was also the Guard.of James D.Foster,minor heir of John Foster,decd. who has now reached his majority. James D.Foster approved the sale.
Next Document:p.267-4 Dec.1842-Wm.A.Warren & wife Mary of Fayette Co.Ky. acknowledge that they received their share of Est. of John Foster,decd.from Jos.Dunbar,Exec.-$12,000 as"our share". The whole Est.was sold for$116,000 in 1834.[NOTE;Will of John Foster,recorded in Wash.Co.DBk."B"p.163,abst.in this Vol.p.14]

P.282:-- --1844-Deed:Henry Johnson & wife Elizabeth J.of Lexington,Ky.,Louise E.Sanders of Scott Co.Ky;Claudius M.Flournoy & wife Polly(signs Mary A.)of Scott Co.Ky.,Victor F.Flournoy & wife Elizabeth J.of Fayette Co.Ky.,all legal heirs of Matthew Flournoy,decd.sell to Robert J.Ward of Louisville,Ky.,All sign in Wash.Co.Ms.except Polly,who signs in Scott Co.Ky.

P.297:Est.of George B.Crutcher,decd.:21Sept.1845:Adm.of Est. is Henry Smith of Hds.Co.Ms.who states that the amount of the Est.insufficient to pay debts. Sale ordered at Wash.Co.Courthouse and notice placed in"South Western Farmer"a newspaper published in town of Raymond Ms. Sale on 21 Apr.1845-Wm.B.Shearer

DEED BOOK "M": WASHINGTON CO.MS.

(Cont.)of Hinds Co.bought it for $75.

P.298:22 Apr.1845-Deed:Wm.Briscoe of Claib.Co.Ms.is indebted to his wards-Claiborne & Warren Briscoe for $14,292+ and sells land to James Andrews & Wm.J.Briscoe.

P.299:15 Apr.1845-Mortg.:John L.Chapman of Wash.Co.Ms.bought the Plantation Glen Allan from Thomas Condy of S.C.-Exec.of Est.of Robert Allan,decd.,Condy retained the mortgage.P.302-Chapman rents the land to George G.Skipwith of Issa.Co.Ms.

P.301:7 Apr.1845-Deed:Henry A.Morris of Wash.Co.for love and affection for Nephew Wilson T.Morris-"in consideration that I am childless and may die"for $1-all my real and personal property. Wit:Jane Blaine, Thos.H.Rives.

P.304:10 June 1844-Deed:Harvey Miller releases all claim to any portion of Sec.16,Twp.15,R9W in Choctaw Dist.unto heirs of John C.Miller-reserving to myself the cypress.

END OF IST HANDWRITTEN COPY OF DBK"M"

¶DEED BOOK"M",CONT.Feb.6,1844-Apr.7,1847-Wash.Co.Ms. The other volumn of "M"marked "copy"is typed, so these abstracts have been taken from the tattered original book, and checked against the typed one,which was copied in 1907 when T.H.Hood was clerk.

P.305:10May 1845-Mort: Thos.J.Read of Louisville,Ky.,John R. Read of New Orleans of 1st part;James F.Gay & Benj.Toomer-merchants of Mobile under the name of "Toomer,Gay & Co."; Horatio Newcomb & Warren Newcomb of Louisville,Ky.under the name"H.D.Newcomb & Co.";John W.Redd of Versailles KY.and Joshiah Lawrence-merchants of Cincinnati,Ohio,under the name of "Jos.Lawrence & Co.";"Tyler & Rutherford"merchants of Louisville;all creditorsofThos.J.Read & Son"of Louisville,Ky.&"Jas. J.Reed Son & Co"."of N.O.

P.310:23 Apr.1845-Mort:James Rucks & WM.Yerger of Jackson,Ms. 1st part;Return J.Meigs & Edwin H.Ewing of Nashville,Tn.2nd; On 15 Oct.1836,Rucks,for joint use of himself and George W. Gibbs & Wm.Owen,purchased 100 negroes of Robert Taylor of N.C. for $71,161-payment schedule follows for next 14 years. Purchase made Nashville,Tn.The personal securities for these bonds were-Anthony Debrill,James Walton,Jacob S.Yerger,Charles C.Trabue,Geo.C.Childress,Boyd McNairy,Bromfield Ridley,Archibald M.Overton,Lewis C.Taylor,Edmund Rucks. Wm.Yerger and Jas.Rucks have bought out Gibbs and Owens + the land they were settled on in Clark Co.Ark.- now Dallas Co.-+ stock on Plantation. Wm. Yerger and Jas.Rucks then sell a Pltn.on East bank of Deer Creek in Sec.14,15,Twp.18,R7W-Wash.Co.Ms.-640 ac.to R.J.Meigs and E.H.Ewing. Document signed by W.Yerger,Malvina H.Yerger, Jas.Rucks,Louisa V.Rucks.

P.320:3 July 1844-Deed:Sarah H.Evans,St.Charles Co.Mo.sells to James H.McCoy of Adams Co.Ms.1840ac.for $2310 in Wash.Co. Ms.-undivided portion of 6 Sections-31,32, in Twp.14 and 5,6, 7,8, in Twp.13 all R3W.Land conveyed by Hugh H.Dunlap and wife-to James Pepper,and then to Sarah.Wit:Geo.McCullough(signed in New Orleans)Jas.Pepper,W.C.Duncan.

DEED BOOK "M": WASHINGTON CO.MS.
Feb.6,1844-Apr.7,1847

P.324;17 Mar.1845-Deed:At Bachelor's Bend,Wash.Co.Ms. Commissioner Herbert W.Hill,by decree of Superior Ct.of the Chancery of Ms.-dated 11Feb.1845-suit titled Sterling Neblett vs Stephen M.Jackson-Advertised for Public sale on 7 Mar.1845"at the residence of said Jackson"on lands directed to be sold. Highest bidder was Sterling and Wm.J.Neblett for $7,016..Sec. 11,Twp.18,R9W-+ lots in Twp.18-this being land on which Jackson "Now resides" _ W½S32T18R8W.Herbert W.Hills'signature acknowledged by Miles C.Folkes,Mayor of Vicksburg.

P.325:30 Apr.1845-Deed;S.Theobald,Adm.in right of wife Harriet B.Theobald,late Harriet B.Blanton,who was Admx.of Est. of Wm. W.Blanton,decd. to W.R.Campbell.

P.329:Certificate #13300-O.P.;Andrew Knox,assignee of John Black. Patent received Mt.Salus 475 ac+ signed -- Pres.Andrew Jackson by A.J.Donelson,Secretary;Elijah Haywood was Commissioner of General Land office. 25 Jan.1835

P.330:Same people involved.Cert.#13299, & #13830.

P.333:22Feb.1845-Mort:Wm.H.Elliott & wife Frances E.Elliott, who sign in Mont.Co.Tn.,sell to Thos.J.Mulhollan of Union Co. Ark. John Elliott acts as agent of Wm.H.on 8 Feb.1845. They then sell to Jos.H.Johnston & Shepherd Brown for mort.on land bought by Jos.Jones & Mulhollan and sold by Sheriff sale to said Elliott. + land on Deer Creek jointly entered by John G. Parham & Wm.R.Pryor-being Pryor's undivided interest sold at Marshal's sale and bought by Jones-whose interest was sold and bought by Wm.H.Elliott. Johnson,Brown,Mortgagers, are given permission to sell.

P.347:9 Aug.1840:Bankruptcy of Wm.Ferriday.

P.349:4July 1845-Quit Claim:Andrew Carson & wife Jane, Saml. Carson & wife Phebe of Wash.Co.Ms.toHaller Nutt.

P.351:23 Oct.1845 Deed:John L.Penrice and wife Amelia of Wash. Co.Ms.,Hotel Keeper,situated"inthe Grove,Princeton"to Manlius V.Thomson,along with the following a/c of the tavern and bar bills:R.J.TURNBULL-$88.35;R.J.FITZ-$69;W.L.ROBARD-$21.54;J.B. PENRICE-$32.62;M.ENDECOTT-$49.35;W.W.COLLINS-$25.75;M.F.SHANNON -$53,25;E.W.SHELBY-$12.63;L.R.UPSERY-$16.37;M.V.THOMSON-$21.50 J.P.CUNNINGHAM-$12.62;CHAS.TURNBULL-$5.75;W.L.ELLIS-$25;--- Williams-$8.25;R.J.SHELBY-$85.11;J.H.GARRETT-$23.48;F.R.PENRICE $101.04;T.J.SHELBY-$50.51;JOHN MCKEE-$11.13;J.C.CLARK-$18.97 JOHN FULTON-$7.75;JAS.JOHNSON-$7.25;A.RYAN-$25.79;E.C.MARKHAM $.12;THOS.SHELBY-$.88;WM.A.DROMGOOLE-$15.12;JOHN G.COCKS-$6.75; AMBROSE KNOX-$9.88;MCLIN EVANS-$8.25;T.W.ENDECOTT-%15.25;PERU P1TN.-$30.25;JOSIAH BROOKS-$129.29;MRS.SARAH A.DROMGOOLE-$5.25; T.J.DORSEY-$15,38;W.M.WILLOUGHBY-$70.17;T.JOINER & CO.$6.50;P.H. CRABTREE $179.95;T.L.PENRICE $65.57;W.B.GUION $171,67;J.L.KNOX $72.25;A.W.GOODLOE $.00;W.W.WILLIAMS $59.42;WM.WOODS $56.76; A.RYAN $14.20;F.G.GAMBLE $49.25;THOS.S.PENRICE $118;J.C.PARKS $50;THOS.J.SHELBY $307;

P.353;6 May 1845-Gift;Mary Jackson of Hds.Co.Ms.for"love & affection"for G.sonJoseph Jackson,son of "my son Stephen Jackson of Wash.Co.Ms"a negro boy"Henry,24 yrs."Wit D H.Jackson,G.J.Rawlings

DEED BOOK "M":WASHINGTON CO.MS.

¶[NOTE:(cont.)Joseph Littleberry Jackson killed a freed negro in the turmoil following the Civil War, the following account is given in "ENCLAVE:VICKSBURG AND HER PLANTATIONS";"Quote: A case arose out of a killing which took place in Wash.Co.,in the Ms. Delta, on 4thof July 1865.Joseph L.Jackson shot and killed"indefence of my own life",stated his attorney,one of the freedmen on the plantation,a man who had formerly been his slave. Jackson was subsequently arrested by the military authorities and taken to Vicksburg for trial, for the court which had jurisdiction in Wash.Co.would not admit the testimony of freedmen.Unquote."Jos.L. was caught in a power play between the Military occupational government and the local Reconstruction Gov. As both groups battled for jurisdiction, the case made its way to U.S.Sec. of State Seward. What happened to Jos. is a mystery. Thereis no mention of the tragedy in Wash.Co. records. The date of death in the families' record of 1866-Erie,N.Y.suggests he was sent North by the Military in the name of martial law.]

P.353:2 May 1845-Deed:Elisha Warfield,Jr.,Nathl.A.Ware,Catherine A.Warfield,Thomas B.Warfield of the 1st part sell to Jefferson Wilkerson the undivided ½ of "Utopia"Plantation,+ slaves,+ all appurt.etc. Wilkerson is to pay Thos.B.Warfield, who is trustee of a trust made by Nathl.A.Ware for his dau-Catherine A.Warfield and her Children. The land is in Twp.19, R10W, with some in R9W. Elisha,Jrand Catherine sign in Hds.Co. Ms.Nathl.A.Ware signs in Hamilton Co.,Ohio.

P.360:3 Nov.1845-Mort:Zachariah C.Offutt of Wash.Co.Ms.sells for $1 to Ezra N.Offutt,Ben B.Ford,Henry C.Offutt,Wm.C.Offutt, Bartlett Hall of KY.his undivided ½ of "Utopia"Plantation + slaves,household furn.,etc.of Zachariah"s. E.N.Offutt had acted as Zach.C."s bondsman in Scott Co.Ky. when Zach.was declared Guard. of Verlinda Ann Offutt 16 Oct.1837-for $8,000. Also in the deal are notes owed by Zack to the Counting House of Ward Jones & Co. of N.O. +other notes.[NOTE:Benj.B.Ford is Zack's father-in-law]

P.363:8 Nov.1845-Deed:John C.Berry & wife Polly(X)of Wash.Co.Ms. to WYLEY JAMES ELIZABETH DINWIDDIE ALBERT JOSEPH WILLIAM & HENRY JAMES-heirs of ZACHARIAH JAMES,decd.of same co.(No punctuation marks between names).

P.364:10 July 1845-Dissolution of Partnership:Ann Eliza Wilson and her husband Andrew L.Wilson & D.W.Connely of 1st pt;Thos. H.Bucknerof 2nd,(and his bro.)Bernard H.Buckner of 3rd;All parties own,jointly a plantation known as"PLantation of Buckner Wilson & Co."Wilsons'sign in AdamsCo.Ms.,all others sign in Wash.Co.Ms.

P.376:2 Nov.1844-Deed(Gift);Wm.E.Branham of KY.-for love and affection to my wife Elizabeth F.Branham-to insure a decent support in case of his death,sells 8 slaves to David Flournoy Blackburn of Wash.Co.Ms. to be held in trust for Eliz. + stock and household furnishings. At Eliz.'s death David is to hold the trust for "her"ch. Wm.Branham and David F.Blackburn sign in Wash.Co.

DEED BOOK "M":WASHINGTON CO.MS.

P.377:9 Jan.1845-Deed:On 15 Nov.1842,Alexander M.Austin files bankruptcy at Staunton,Va. 1300 ac.in Wash.Co.Ms. + 1house,+a lot in Vernon,Ms. The Commissioner Chesley Kinney sells the assets to James Points of Augusta Co.Va.,Deed rec. Wash.Co.Ms. on First date above;Clerk of Court in Aug.Co.Va.was Jeff.Kinney.

P.381:22 Jan.1845-Deed:John Payne,Exec.of Est.of George Downing.late of Wash.Co.decd.to Edw.P.Johnson of same

P.384:23 Dec.1845-Deed:Elizabeth Ann Dunn,wife of Saml.R.Dunn and trustee for Wm.Blanton Dunn,infant son of Saml.R.Dunn of Issa.Co.Ms.sells all her rights as trustee to lands received from James McCutcheon and wife-to her as trustee, except that sold to Thomas Dunn,S.-buyer is Thomas J.Likens.

P.388:20 Nov.1845-Deed:Robert James Turnbull & wife Mary Jane of Wash.Co.Ms.,sell all rights and Interest which they acquired as heirs at law of Wm.A.Dromgoole,Sr.,late of Wash.Co.Ms. decd.-an undivided 1/6th. The land lies on the Plantation on which Wm.A.Dromgoole was residing at the time of his death, on Lake Wash.and known as "Long Island Pltn." @400ac.+all land added before or since his death, also 1/6th interest in 42 negroes. All of which is the interest of Mary Jane Turnbull, formerly Mary Jane Dromgoole,dau of said WM.A.,Sr.,decd. they sell to Thos.J.Liken, and all sign in Wash.Co.

P.389:1 Jan.1846-Deed:Robert Jas.Turnbull & wife Mary Jane of Wash.Co.sell to Emily Long,wife of Parks B.Long of same,-one house and lot"being the same at present occupied by Parks B.Long as a grocery in front and by H.E.Davison in the rear as a warehouse-for $146. The said lot and house being situate in upper end of Bass Grove..and running backto the line of Council R. Bass.The Turnbull's then sell adjacent house, used as Clerk's Office, to Abram Barnett. Location-Princeton,Ms.

P.397:7 Apr.1845-Deed:Wiley Newberry of Chambers Co.Ala.,files for Bankruptcy in Mobile,Ala.P.T.Harris is his assignee. Land located in Wash.Co.Ms.-T14N,R4W-to be sold in front of Mansion House,Mobile;and advertised in"Register & Journal"of Mobile. Sold to Robert M.Livingston.

P.404:27 Jan.1845-Deed:Wade Hampton,Jr.buys land belonging to F.G.Turnbull & Thos.W.Endecott for settlement of suit-J.H.Moore vs Turnbull & Endecott. 1350 ac.more or less.

¶[Note;Many bankruptcies follow,not abstracted because they have no genealogical significance]

P.410:26 Jan.1846-Lease:Harvey Miller,and his wife Betty A.Miller,late Betty A.Adams of Wash.Co.Ms.,leases slave to George W.Ward of La. The negroe belonged to Betty before her Marr. to Miller, and according to Ms.law-still belongs to her.

P.411:23 Jan.1846-Deed:Thomas Shelby, one of the heirs of his father,Thomas Shelby,decd.and Mary B.Shelby of Wash.Co.Ms.sell to Catherine A.Blackburn wife of David F.Blackburn,land bought by Mary B.Shelby(Written in ink above this;"and the heirs of Thos.Shelby")at Mt.Salus-394+ac.+all parcels of land bought fromJohn A.Miller & wife Sarah S.Miller.

DEED BOOK "M":WASHINGTON CO.MS.

P.419:14 Jan.1846-Deed:John Martin & wife---of New Orleans sell to Saml.Garland of Lynchburg,Va.,land in Wash.Co.Ms. fronting on the Ms.River called"Menafee Tract",described at Mt.Salus as Lots,1,2,3,10;S2;T19N;R9W-387 + ac.Choctaw District.

P.427:19 Mar.1846-Deed:Parkes B.Longsells out to Robert A.Johnson of Wash.Co.Ms."all my property-all my liquors wherever in boxes,demijohns,bottle,barrels -also furniture,24 chairs,2 card tables,kitchen furniture,3 beds,carpets,window curtains, stair carpet,2 large boxes of Queen's Ware,1 horse,1dbl.barrel gun...in Princeton.

P.424:16 Mar.1846-Deed:David W.Connelly,Sheriff of Wash.Co.Ms. sells to Shepherd Brown,Jos.Johnson of Warr.Co.-May Term 1846 Circuit Court..against goods,etc.of Saml.Herring,Washington Herring,Mary Coons-heirs at law of Redding B.Herring,decd.V'burg

P.432:.6 Mar.1846-Deed:John G.Cocks,Guardian of Philip A.Cocks, Jr. of 1st pt;Philip A.Cocks,Sr.of 2nd. Land ordered sold at public sale. Redeemed by Philip A.Cocks,Sr.

P.445:6 Apr.1846-P.O.A.:Thomas J.Clarke & Ignatius K.Newton and wife Eleanor D.Newton,late Eleanor D.Clarke-part of the heirs at law of Geo.W.Clarke,decd.of Frank. Co.Ky.-appoint Junius R.Ward,Esq.of Wash.Co.Ms.their P.O.A.to attend to matters concerning Est.of"our brother",Geo.W.Clarke who died in Ms.

P.446:22 Jan.1846-DeedHenry T.Irish & wife H.Mary of New Port, R.I.to Geo.W.Summers of Warr.Co.Ms. The Irish's sign in Warr.Co.

P.448:5 Apr.1846-Deed:Sally Dromgoole of Wash.Co.Ms.appoints Mary Jane Turnbull as trustee for Martha Juliet(also sp.Julia) Turnbull,who is the infant dau.of Mary Jane & Robert James Turnbull. For love and affection for her gr.child, the said Martha Juliet Turnbull- Sally Dromgoole gives her her share of a conveyance from Geo.F.Dromgoole,from Est.of Wm.A.Dromgoole, decd. Mary Jane & Robert James Turnbull are to be the trustee for Martha J.Turnbull.On 25 Apr.1846:George G.Dromgoole gives a gift of land to Martha Julia,appointing her mother-MARY JANE TURNBULL AS Trustee.[Note:MARY JANE TURNBULL & GEO.G.DROMGOOLE are the children of SALLY & WM.A.DROMGOOLE]

P.464:4 June 1846-P.O.A.:Montague Endecott appoints his bro. Thos.W.Endecott his atty.

P.464:Seth C.Cocks of Natchez,sells a slave to Ann Alexander Penrice,wife of Thos.S.Penrice of Wash.Co.Ms.

P.466:13 Mar 1838-DeedJohn D.Carroll & wife Julia B.Carroll, in"consideration of discharge of Benj.M.Steadman from the prison bonds of Adams Co.Ms.,Chas.Gardiner & Roman Watson on the execution of GARDINER & WATSON against B.M.STEADMAN & CO." from Cir.Court of Adams,Co.Ms.Apr.term 1837 for $4,647.30 + int.+court Cost in Jeff.Co.Ms.,do sell to GARDINER & WATSON,land in Marshall Co.Ms.,near HOlly Springs. Land that John Carroll bought as an Orig.Pat.at Pontotoc 1836+ land in Wash.Co.entered at Chochuma in name of CARROLL ANDERSON & VINSON. Terms-If Gardiner fails to gain relief in case now in court, before mentioned, this land will be appraised and used as collateral against the judgement of STEADMAN & CO.

DEED BOOK "M":WASHINGTON CO.MS.

P.485:24 Aug.1846-Mort:Alexander H.Peck of Claib.Co.Ms. Adm. of Est.of John M. Marable,decd.-owes Georgiana M.Marable of Lexington,Ky. Peck offers her more security & Mortg.land issued to Alex.H.Peck & GILMAN M.PECK-O.P.'s#18740,#18742,#18743-entered at Mt.Salus-21 Mar.1839.

P.489:24 Sept.1846-Partition:Wm.Grimes(X)of Ohio Co.Va.(note: Now Ohio Co. W.Va.)sells to Sarah Berthoff,late Sarah Grimes, of state of Ohio(as written),to act as his Trustee,provided that she give him a suitable living out of the proceeds. The property is part of the Est. of Thomas Grimes,lately decd.of Wash.Co.Ms.in March1846,possessing a very large & valuable estate, and leaving the said Wm.Grimes,Said Sarah Berthoff & Jane Baker,late Jane Grimes-his heirs at law. Wm.Grimes signs in Wash.Co.Ms.

P.509:21 Oct.1845 Deed:James B.Chaplain;Charles S.Chaplain & Frances his wife:Anna M.C.Chaplain;Geo.H.Chaplain-all of Dorchester Co.Md.and Edward K.Chaplain & Amanda C.his wife of Adams Co.Ms.-heirs-at-law of Wm.R.T.Chaplain,late of Claib. Co.Ms.,decd.of 1st pt;Sell to Wm.D.Sayer of Claib.Co.Ms.

P.511:15 Sept.1846-Deed:Matilda Slemmons,Admx.of Est.of Wm. McB.Slemmons,decd.of Wash.Co.Ms.of 1st part:Charles L.Chamberlain,Jeff.Co.Ms.,by his agent Joshua James,Jr.,at Term of Probate Court in Claib.Co.Ms.in Port Gibson-on 4th Mon.Apr.1846. Matilda was ordered to sell parcels of land belonging to WM. McB.Slemmons, fronting on Ms.River-1239 +ac. Chamberlain bought the property for $150.

P.513:Sept.1846-Deed:Robert James Turnbull,Sheriff of Wash.Co. sells,at Public Auction,property belonging to Wm.J.Penrice. Buyer Thos.J.Likens.

P.514:4 Dec.1846-Deed:Gideon & Mary Fitz of Issa.Co.Ms.sell 320 ac.in Wash.Co., to Saml.Carson.

P.515:4 Dec.1846-Deed:Robert James Turnbull & Mary Jane(Dromgoole)Turnbull,his wife,sell to Thos.J.Likens of same. the - dwelling house and lot in which R.J.Turnbull is now living-for $600=being the same that Likens and wife sold to Mary Jane 20 Nov.1845, and the one the Likens bought from MONTAGUE ENDECOTT. ABRAM K.SMEDES is Judge of Probate,Wash.Co.Ms.

P.517:23 Oct.1846-Deed:Jesse O.Rundell and wife Martha Ann of Madison P.La.sell to Martha Rundell of same"for $5-880 ac.in Wash.Co.Ms";Wit Wm.S.Rundell,Jno.R.Marble of Madison P.La.

P.518:8 Dec.1846-Deed:Geo.W.Johnson and wife Ann Eliza of Chicot Co.Ark.,and Victor M.Flournoy and wife Elizabeth J.of 1st pt;Robt.W.Adams,Bettie A.Miller,heirs of Geo.W.Adams decd.and Harvey Miller of 2nd;For $16,500, Johnson & Flournoy sold land to Geo.W.Adams,14 June 1839-and the deed has been lost, and it was not recorded..2060.26 ac.on Deer Creek. For $1,another deed is given. All of 1st part sign in Wash.Co.Ms.

P.524:23 Dec.1846-Deed:Edward B.Church and wife Maria J. of Wash.Co.of 1st pt:Green S.McCarroll of same-2nd pt:"a certain lot..lying near or adjoining the town of Greenville."[Note; This is the first mention of Greenville]to wit:beginning on the line between said CHURCH & LEWIS K.GISH & JAS.MITCHELL(Cont.)

DEED BOOK "M":WASHINGTON CO.MS.

(Cont)at or near corner of the fence of said Church's stable lot,thence on said line between said Church and Gish & Mitchell to the Ms.River,then begining again at the corner of said fence, then in southerly direction 145 ft.on a line parallel with the levee..lot holding buildings occupied by Church and wife-leaving a 15 ft.strip between for road way.

P.526:1 Dec.1846-Deed:Wm.H.Lee and wife Eleanor P.(Ware) of hinds Co.-1st part;buy from Geo.Poindexter 1258+.ac. on Deer Creek-in T18,R7W-Orig.Pat.was entered by Gideon Fitz.[Note: Present day-"Ditcheley Plantation"]

P.527:23 Dec.1846-Deed:Robert W.Adams of New Orleans to Bernard H.Buckner of Wash.Co.Ms.,land lying along Deer Creek that had been purchased earlier by Geo.W.Adams,decd.

P.529:21 Oct.1846-Deed:Manlius V.Thomson & wife Mary Ann of Scott Co.Ky.,are deep in debt,and put the plantation they had occupied for sometime in trust to Geo.C.Gwathmey of Louisville, Ky.,as 1st mortg.under the conditions that said Manlius and wife can occupy said plantation part of the yr. and oversee its management. Wm.Z.Thomson and wife Ann Eliza of Fayette Co.Ky., hold the 2nd mortg. Plantation is in Wash. Co.

P.535:5 Jan.1847-Deed:Saml.Theobald and wife Harriet B.,Orville M.Blanton,& Wm.C.Blanton all of Wash.Co.to Charles B.Percy of same.

P.536:4 Jan.1847-Deed:Harriet B.Theobald,Admx.& Saml.Theobald in right of his wife(Harriet B.)Adm. of Wm.W.Blanton,late of Wash.Co.to Charles B.Percy of same. The Theobald's are ordered by the court to sell certain lots. Advertised in the V'burg "WHIG"and on 4 Jan.1847,did sell at the "late residence of Wm.W.Blanton known as "Blantonia"." Percy was the buyer. Joint security for Adm.are Jas.B.Jackson,&Augustus W.McAllister.

P.541:1 Jan.1847-Deed:Sarah Dromgoole,Admx.of Wm.A.Dromgoole, Sr.decd.-sells at public auction,decreed by Probate Court,to Thos.J.Likens"Long Island PLtn."where Wm.A. lived. This Propery was conveyed 1832 from Robt.P.Shelby to heirs of Philip A.Gilbert-DBk."B"p.84,85. Posted copies of sale at court house, house of T.J.James,Tavern of Isaac B.Beall.

¶[Note: the Sheriff was also the acting Tax Collector. If a person was in arrears for his Taxes, a public sale of property could be announced. If the said property was not redeemed before the announced time of sale, it went to the highest bidder-often at a fraction of its worth.]

Sheriff & Tax Collector Sales:

Owner	Buyer
G.W.BALL	SHEPHERD BROWN & JAS.H.JOHNSON
G.W.DENTON	" " " "
W.R.PUCKETT	" " " "
BROWN & JOHNSON	JAS.M. AIKEN
" ,RUTHERFORD & BLAIR	" "
E.HARRIS	JAS.M.BRABSTON
STEPHEN DUNCAN	" "

DEED BOOK"M":WASHINGTON CO.MS.

P.568:10 Dec.1846-Deed:Maria Percy,wife and execx.of Est.of Thos.G.Percy of Madison Co.Ala.,for herself and their children Chas.B.Percy & Leroy P.Percy,heirs of Thos.G.Percy. Sell to Isaac Worthington of Wash.Co.Ms. for $20,000 a Pltn. in Wash. Co.Ms. 970+ ac.,bounded on W. by Ms.River;on N.by pltn. of heirs of Preston Brown,decd.;on E.by pltn.of Wm.Worthington;on S.by Pltn.of Isaac Worthington. Maria & sons signed in New Orleans.

P.577:6 Jan.1847-Deed:D.Bacon Messinger,decd.,George Messinger Adm.of his Est.states:on 21 Mar.1840,D.Bacon Messinger entered into an agreement to convey to Sophia Bacon ½ of following tracts of land-some in Sec.17 & Sec.19 of Twp.15,R6W-740+ ac. in all. Since said conveyance was never recorded, Geo.Messinger now makes Sophia's ½ legal[Note;this was land inherited from Wm.Bacon,Uncle of D.Bacon Messinger.Wm.Bacon's widow-Sophia, marr.2nd the nephew of her late husband, and brother to D.Bacon-George Messinger. They are all buried in Baconham Cemetery in Warren Co.Ms. with Sophia buried between her 2 husbands.]

P.580:24 Feb.1847-Deed:Mortg.-Jane Baker of Wash.Co.Ms. sells to Mrs.Sarah Bertholf of Hamel Co.Ohio for herself and as Trustee of Wm.Grimes of Ohio Co.Va.(Present day Ohio Co.,W.Va.) $6,000 for 280+ac.Jane,Sarah,Wm.are the heirs of Thos.Grimes who decd.owning land on Lake Jackson. The 280 ac.represent Janes'and Wm's.share.

P.581:24 Feb.1847-Deed:Sarah Bertholf,heir at law of Thos.Grimes decd.late of Wash.Co.Ms.,Trustee of Wm.Grimes of Va.,on herown right and as Trustee,sells to Thos.J.Likens the land,slaves -all belongings of Thos.Grimes,except stock held in the Bank of Ms.& a note owed by W.G.Holmes of Carroll P.La.

P.600:[NOTE;Top of this page is torn off. The following is taken from the typed copy];4 Feb.1847-Deed:Benj.A.Ludlow & wife Martha A. of Harrison Co.Ms. to Harry J.Bodley of Lexington,Ky.-Trustee for Mrs.Ellen Bodley wife of Wm.S.Bodley of Vicksburg:Harry Bodley bought land on Deer Creek in T15,R6W-1740 ac.

P.607:31 Mar.1847-Deed:(Gift)"I,Nancy Hill of Warren Co.Ms... for love and affection I have for my dau.-Ann D.Jackson of Wash.Co.Ms."-give her a certain negroe girl named Lwiza and her 3 children-John,Len,Eliza-+ 1carriage,2 horses,and a lot of household furniture. Wit:Frances C.Jones,Thos.H.Hill. [Note:Will of Nancy Hill is in Warr.Co.Ms.Will Bk."A"p.313]

END OF DEED BOOK "M"

Husbands and wives mentioned in Deed Book "M"
ALLISON,ROBT. & ELIZABETH -Pike Co.Ms. -1841
BARRETT,THOS. & PALMIRA -New Orleans-1844
BARRETT,SAML. & SARAH--New Orleans -1842
BASS,COUNCIL R. & EUGENIA P. -Wash.Co.Ms. 1844
BUCKNER,BERNARD & FANNY --Wash.Co.Ms. 1846
BYRKS,SAML. & ANN M. -Wash.Co.Ms.-1846
CASON,CANADY & JANE--Yazoo Co.Ms. 1844
CRABTREE,PHILLIP H. & MARTHA CAROLINE--Wash.Co.Ms.-1844

*Husbands and wives in Deed Book"M"(cont.)
DANCY,DAVID M. & ELIZABETH-Hinds Co.Ms. 1843
DAY,RACHEL,widow of WM.T.DAY--Warren Co.Ms. 1846
DENTON,GABRIEL M. & ELIZ.M. --New Orleans -1845
DUNLAP,H.W. & SUSANNAH W. --Hinds Co.Ms. 1836
EFFINGER,FRANCIS A. & SUSAN E.-Rep. of Tex. Austin Co. 1845
HARRISON,JOHN & OLIVIA--Philip Co.Ark. 1841
HYDE,E.D. & ANNA MARGARET--New Orleans-1844
JACKSON,JAMES B. & BELINDA -Wash.Co.Ms. 1844
JOHNSON,EDW.P. & BETSY -Lexington,Ky. 1844
JOHNSON,JAS. & MARY REBECCA--Wash.Co. Ms.-1845
LEWIS,WM. & ELVIRA A. -Hinds Co.Ms. 1846
McALLISTER,A.W. & CAROLINE S. -Wash.Co.Ms. 1845
McCAUGHAN,JOHN T.------Harrison Co.Ms. 1845
McCAY,ROBT. & ELIZA-Pike Co.Ms. 1845
MOSELEY,SAML.F. & NANCY J.-Yazoo Co.Ms. 1844
PENRICE, THOS.S. & ANN A. -Wash.Co.Ms. 1846
PICKENS,JNO.O. & FRANCES--Wash.Co.Ms. 1846
RODES,CLIFTON &,AMANDA -Boyle Co.Ky. 1846
SELLERS,Wm. & CAROLINE--Calib.Co.Ms. 1845
SLATER,HENRY & MARY E.--Wash.Co.Ms. 1844
STRATTON,RICH.E. & ARABELLA M.--Hinds Co.Ms. 1846
SUMRALL,THOS.L. & MARG.---Hinds Co.Ms. 1844
TEAGARDEN,WM.H. & MARG.D.--Christian Co.Ky.----
THEOBALD,THOS.T. & SARAH W.--Frankford,Ky. 1844
THOMPSON,PHILLIP B. & MARTHA--Mercer Co.Ky. 1844
WARD,ROBT.J. & EMILY M. --Louisville,Ky. 1844
WILLCOX,JACOB & CATH.A.--New Orleans--1845
WINTER,JACKSON W. & SARAH A. ----,1845

===

WILLS OF MADISON CO.MS. WILL BK."A":
P.137;Will of James Dick of New Orleans;Prob.22 Mar.1849
Neice-Ann Jane Todd,wife of John B.Wallace of N.O.;Bro.-late
Nathaniel Dick;Mentions prop.in N.O.& on Ark.River in control
of Henry R.W.Hill,his business partner;Neice-Sarah D.Todd,wife
of Wm.B.Partee of N.O.,to get "NoMistake Pltn". at Sartartia,
Yazoo Co.Ms.;Miss Elizabeth Calhoun of Murray Co.Tn.,and to
Nathaniel Calhoun,& to Christopher Calhoun-his bro.$12,000 each;
To Children of Margaret Todd wife of Chas.Calhoun of Murray Co.
Tn.,;To Christopher Todd & wife Sarah-my sister;ToSusan K.Todd
wife of A.M.Looney to get land back of Helena,Ark.She is his
neice;To neice Mary R.Todd wife of Sterling H.Lester;To Amelia
Byrne;To Sally Atkinson of Louisville, Ky.;To Robt.N.Kelso living
in Va.;To Mrs.Geo.Dick living in Tyrene Co.,Ireland;To Mrs.Fulton
of Baltimore,Md.;To Mrs.Anna Atkinson of Louisville,Ky.;ToJane
Kemp McAllister living with H.R.W.Hill;To John Dick in Yaz.Co.Ms.;
To Elizabeth Calhoun and her 2 bros.in Murray Co.Tn.(named above)
To Mrs.Hill wife of H.R.W.Hill;H.R.W.Hill to be exec.

P.160:Noncupative Will of Ellen C.Comfort;15 Jan.1851:Pet.of
John Montgomery,Dorcas Parsons of Mad.Co.Ms.,state that on 7
Jan.(1851)at Ellen Comfort's,she decd.leaving a son Jos.Comfort,
a dau.Catharine,and 4 more ch.Danl.B.,David,John W.,Elizabeth.

DEED BOOK "N": WASHINGTON CO.MS.
DATED:Apr.1847-Oct.1850. Original Book-818 pages;

P.2:21 May 1846-Deed:Samuel Mason and wife Mary,Thos.S.Mason all of Harris Co.Tx.,sell out to Thomas Henderson of Natchez. Saml.signs for Thomas as his atty.in fact. Land on Silver Creek-2240 ac.

P.11:4 Feb.1847-Deed:Aaron Wickliffe & wife Mary of Wash.Co. Ms. 1st part;Saml.Worthington of same-2nd. Aaron buys land on "Schute"of Island #88.

P.13:25 Apr.1847-Deed:James B.Jackson & wife Mary I.of Wash.Co. Ms. to Bernard H.Buckner.

P.32:16 Dec.1846-Mortg:State of S.C.-James S.Guignard,Jr. & wife Elizabeth of Columbia,S.C.mortg.land to A.G.Carter of Wash.Co.Ms.409+ac. Guignard was Clerk of the Court of Common Pleas for Richland Dist.S.C.

Additional Public Sales of property by Sheriff and Tax collector-Thomas J.Likens:

OWNER	BUYER
I.Caldwell & T.D.DOWNS	JAMES ROACH(1844)
FOLKES & COBB	WM.S. BODLEY
C.W.ALLEN	BODLEY,ROBINS,WALKER(1844)
STEELE,GLASS,& JENKINS	" " "

¶[NOTE:This volumn has been rebound and the next 20 pages are in a scrambled order,mostly out of sequence]

There are 2 p.44's-15 pages apart:P.44(#1)-James L.Mayfield to Eugene Rouseau-17 Jan.1847;
P.44(2):Wm.S.Mayfield of Terrebonne P.La. to Eugene Rouseau.

P.91:2 Oct.1847-Debt:Nathan West owes S.Rose $44. He promises to pay by 1 Jan.1848,or A.F.Smith is to take his bay horse to pay the debt.[Note;In 1850 West is overseer for Thos.D.Carneal]

P.91:P.O.A.16 Sept.1847:J.Erastus Towsey of Wash.Co.Ms.gives his P.O.A.to A.K.Smedes to convey a mortg.to John G.Cocks.

P.101:28 Sept.1846-Deed:Andrew Wilson and wife AnnEliza to Thos.W.Wilson all of Adams Co.Ms.

P.107:16 Nov.1847-Gift:Alvarez Fisk gives to his 2 minor ch. Edward A.Fisk & Isabel Fisk-all of Natchez,Ms.for "love and affection" equal undivided parts of "Belzoni"Plantation. 2,102+ ac. Parts of Sec.14,27,23,26,35,22:T16N;R3W =365ac.in T15,R3W fronting on Yazoo River,running back to Wasp Lake, which A.Fisk bought from Stewart Fisk(his son)17 June 1845 + slaves.

P.136:12 Dec.1842-Mortg:Wm.H.Lee and wife Eleanor P.Lee, formerly Eleanor P.Ware of Hds.Co.Ms.and her father,Nathl.A.Ware of Adams Co.Ms.to Alex Dennistown,John Dennistown, Wm.Wood, Wm.Cross,Muny M.Thompson,Wm.C.Myline,A.J.Dennistown of New Orleans.Nathl.signed in V'burg, the Lees in Hinds Co.

P.174:10 Mar.1848-Gift:Rawley Hudson,for love and affection, to wife Mary,for her future security-household furniture, a lot, and undivided ½ of goods in grocery store co-owned with James S.Small,on the levee in town of Greenville.

DEED BOOK "N": WASHINGTON CO.MS.
Apr.1847-Oct.1850

P.185:31 Mar.1848-Deed:Wm.Rouse of Desha Co.Ark.& wife Martha Ann buy from Maria J.Church,widow, & Catherine,Wm.Edw.Church infant heirs of Edw.B.Church,decd. Land near the town of G'ville.

P.187:1848-Release:Eliza W.Fisk of Adams Co.Ms.signs a release to all rights, including dower to the land her husband Alvarez Fisk sold to Andrew J.Paxton.

P.195:26 Oct.1834-Deed:Hector Lasley and wife Frances & John Lasley of Wash.Co.sell to Allen Wynens of same

P.196:20 Oct.1834-Deed:Alexander Lasley & wife Catherine of Wash. Co.Ms. to Allen Wynens.
[Note:In Apr.1848-DAVID W.CONNELLY is Sheriff & Tax Coll.Wash.Co.]

P.213:14 Mar.1848-Deed:District of Columbia,Wash.to wit:Saml. W.Adams,decd.Wash.Co.Ms.,intestate. Robert M.Carter,is Adm.ad collegendum. Document states:Saml.had neither mother or father living at the time of his death and George A.Adams of Mo.; Adelia(X)Tuttle wife of John T.(X)Tuttle of Md.;Susannah J. Perrie a widow-of D.C.,are brother & sisters of said intestate; and Catherine M.Berrien wife of Hobart Berrien of state of N.Y.; Mary Ellen Adams & Ann Adams of D.C.the children and heirs at law of John Adams,decd.a brother of said intestate-which ANN ADAMS is a minor being no more than 10-and JUDSON MITCHELL of said District as her Guard. are only heirs at law. Most of the property of Saml.'s was in slaves, and since most of the heirs live where the slaves cannot be sent,CARTER asks perm.to sell.
P.215:Heirs appoint JUDSON MITCHELL their Atty.to see to the matter-signed by the Berriens,Tuttles,Susannah,& Mary E.Adams.

P.221:22Jan.1847-Deed:Catherine L.Prince,Wm.B.Prince & wife Martha,W.G.Humphreys & wife Baylissa-all of Claib.Co.Ms.;to John A.Miller of Wash.Co.Ms.

P.239:24 Apr.1848-Deed:Thomas S.Theobald,Adm.of Est.of Patterson S.Bains,late of Wash.Co.Ms.,decd.sells Bains'Est.to Geo. W.Ward & Henry Johnson[Note;Funeral Notice-Lexington,Ky.- Paterson Bain,8 June 1846]

P.249:23 Apr.1847-Mortg:Wm.H.Pope takes out mortg;Andrew Erwin of 2nd part;SAML.STACKER, JAMES WOODS, JOHN BELL,JANE BELL, JAMES E.YEATMAN,JAMES WOODS AS EXEC.OF Est.of ROBERT WOODS,decd. in firm known as STUCKER WOODS & CO. of Nashville.

P.311:8 Sept.1848-Gift:"For the love and affection I have for my dau.Mary E.Offutt"-a gift of 5 slaves in addition to the several more she has already received. Mary E.is now allowed to take them to the plantation in Ms. +some others for her to hire out. Signed by Benj. B.Ford at Georgetown,Ky.

P.313:25 Oct.1848-Mortg:On 7 Oct.1844,Wm.S.Ellis executed a mortg.to Richard Ellis of New Orleans. It has been paid.

P.324:2 Dec.1848-Perfection of Title:Alex.Montgomery & wife Mary Eliza of one part;Benj.Roach,David Roach,Wilkins Roach, Eugene Roach & Mary Roach of 2nd part;Benj.Roach is exec.of last Will and Testament of Benj.Roach,decd.late of Adams Co. Ms.Said Mary Eliza Montgomery sells dower rights to all real estate of said Benj.Roach,decd.-except'homestead Woodland in (cont.)

DEED BOOK "N": WASHINGTON CO.MAS.
Apr.1847-Oct.1850

(Cont.)Adams Co."Mary Eliza also gives up all rights to Benj. Roach's personal est.to the parties of the 2nd part.

P.338:4 Dec.1848-Deed:Harris Co.Tex.:Joshua Hendy & wife Hetty O.Hendy,formerly HETTY O.FALL,whose maiden name was HETTY O. CRUTCHER of Houston,Tex.-formerly of Ms.;sells to Jeff.Wilkerson & Z.C.Offutt.

P.345:2 Dec.1846-Perf.of Title:Abram F.Smith and wife Myra; Philip A.Cocks and wife Anna C.all of Wash.Co.Ms.;Seth C.Cox and wife Sarah F.of Adams,Co.;Alexander Montgomery of Adams; John G.Cocks of New Orleans-all of the 1st part-releases all claim in order to insure a clear title to "Long Island PLtn"- a tract that was the property of Philip A.Gilbert. the parties of the 2nd part-Geo.G.Dromgoole;Wm.A.Dromgoole,Jr.;Robt. Jas. Turnbull & wife Mary Jane;Philip Gilbert Dromgoole;Alex.M.Dromgoole;John G.Dromgoole-heirs at law of Wm.A.Dromgoole,Sr.decd. late of Wash.Co.Ms.Sarah M.Dromgoole is the Adm.of the Est.of Wm.A.Dromgoole, as well as his widow,and acting on court order, sold the property named above.[NOTE:PHILIP A.GILBERT had the following sisters-SARAH who marr.WM.A.DROMGOOLE(his 2nd wife), and the Dromgooles named above as 2nd parties, are their Ch.; another sister JANE marr. ALEX.MONTGOMERY-another sister MILDRED, marr. SETH COX and her ch. are;MYRA SMITH,JOHN G.COCKS, PHILIP A.COCKS,SETH COX. Seth never adopted the COCKS Spelling. Supposedly another sister-FRANCES,MARR.JAS.MONTGOMERY and they moved to Tex.,but they are not named here. Jas.& Alex.Montgomery were Brothers.]

P.348:28 Dec.1848-Perfect.of Title:A case of a lost deed.Green S.McCarroll of Wash.Co.,sells to Ann E.Penrice,wife of Thos.S. Penrice,and to Jos.S.Smith-land that McCarroll had bought from Dr.Edw.B.Church,in 1846.

P.372:26 Feb.1849-Deed:Jeff.Co.Ms.-Peter C.Chambliss & wife Drucilla(Harper),for love and affection to their dau.Laconia S.Berry,wife of James M.Berry,residing in Carr.Par.,La. Land in S.20,T.19,R8W,Choc.Dist.637+ac.and O.P.entered in name of Wm.B.Blanton &Peter C.Chambliss #19085(Chambliss was assignee of Blanton).The J.P.in Jeff.Co.Ms. was Lawrence Wade,Esq. 26 Feb.1849.

P.382:26 Mar.1849-Agreement:David W.Connelly of 1st part;Sarah F.Buckner,widow of Robt.H.Buckner,decd,Thos.Freeland Buckner, Emily E.Buckner,Sarah Roberta Buckner,Robt.H.Buckner,Cath.D. Buckner,Ellen F.Buckner-ch.and heirs of said Robt.H.Buckner. On Mar.8,1841,Connelly & Buckner had entered an agreement for Connelly to convey interest in certain Prop.&slaves.Resolved.

P.393:28 Dec.1848-Deed:L.V.Dixon,city Comm. of Jackson,Ms.acts in regard to suit styled-James Martin & Mary Ann Aiken,et al vs John R.Aiken. Suit states that Mary Ann Aiken is the sole heir of John R.Aiken.

P.391:31 Mar.1849-Deed:J.M.& Laconia Berry of Carr.P.La.sell to Wm.H.Lawson & Wm.Hunt.

DEED BOOK "N":WASHINGTON CO.MS.
Apr.1847-Oct.1850

P.399:25 Nov.1848-Deed Alfred C.Downs & wife Mary Jane(Robinson) of 1st part sell to Roche H.Robinson(Mary Janes's sister)some land in Wash.Co.Ms.located in T.15,R6W-@794+ac.

P.409:23 Apr.1849-Deed:W.L.Robards sells 5 slaves to Ann Eliza Robards for $250.

P.410:24 Apr.1849-Deed:Horatio C.Eustis & wife Catherine C.sell to Murray Mengier Thomson a plantation of 1322 ac.named"Hollywood Pltn." + 60 slaves,stock,etc. Eustis bought the place at Public Auction of Wm.Ferriday's bankruptcy sale in 1845.

P.456:24 Nov.1848-Deed:Olivia Dunbar,Admx.of Est.of her husband Joseph Dunbar,late of Jeff.Co.Ms.,decd.to John G.Courtney of Wash.Co.Ms.

P.464:25 Sept.1849:Aschedule of real and personal property of Eugenia P.Bass,wife of Council R.Bass,Wash.Co.Ms. This property is held separate by her from her husband under the law passed by the Ms.State Legislature,28 Feb.1846,entitled"an act to amend and act for the protection and preservation of the right of Married women-approved 15 Feb.1839"schedule lists slaves,land, Household furnishings,etc.

P.465:Next document Eugenia appoints her husband,Council R. Bass as her agent to handle her affairs.

P.484:15 Sept.1845-Deed:John P.Darden,Adm.of Est.of David M. Darden,decd.,late of Jeff.Co.Ms.to Chas.T.Miles.

P.488:17 Nov.1849-Sale:John Simpson of Decalb Co.Ga.did on 7 July 1846 obtain letters of Patent of U.S.for a certain improved Band Pulley known as"Simpson's improved Drum & Band Pully" on 12 May 1849-M.A.Steele-agent forSimpson,sold the exclusive and sole right of the invention to Henry Starn of Yazoo Co.Ms. to be vended in Wash.& Issa.Co.J.P.Robinson desires an interest in said Pulley and Pd.$150 to Starn for his whole interest. Patent good for 14 yrs. from July 1846.

P.489:3 Dec.1849-Deed:Alexander Yerger of Wash.Co.Ms.bought from W.Percy of Nashville,Tn.12 negroes. Securities for Alex. were Jas.Rucks,Arthur Rucks,Jas.P.Rucks & Wm.Yerger.

P.490:8 Apr.1845-Deed:Jas.H.Maury & Volney Stamps-execs.for Est.of George Irish,decd.of Claib.Co.Ms.of 1st part:Wm.D.Layer atty.for John J.Rundberg & Phebe T.Layer of same. George's will authorizes Maury & Stamps & Wm.T.Irish to sell any part of property necessary. Wm.T.Irish is now decd. George's Will dated 17 June 1835,and proven 24 Oct.1836. The surviving execs.exercise a division of Est.for heirs. 1/3rd of a certain tract of land, of which 2/3rd is owned by John Murdock & WM.R.T. Chaplain,which was bought at Public sale.

P.494:13 Dec.1842-Relinq.:Thomas Kearney of 1st part:toRaymond R.Caldwell,Jane E.Caldwell,Hannah H.Caldwell-the children & heirs of Isaac Caldwell who decd.1836:Some of Isaac's property was sold to Daniel Comfort by Jas.B.Robinson,exec.and Elizabeth H.Caldwell,widow & Execx.of Isaac's Est.,in 1837. 1/4 portion of a plantation-2520 ac. with Thos.D.Downs-in Wash.Co.+ residence of said Isaac in Hds.Co.,Clinton-conveyed by Col.Raymond

DEED BOOK "N":WASHINGTON CO.MS.
Apr.1847-Oct.1850

(Cont.)Robinson to Isaac,30 Apr.1830, + a portion of a pltn. of Isaac's @4 mi.from Jackson,Ms.in Hds.Co.-1400 ac. Comfort sells the property back to Elizabeth,and She purchases additional land-1837-from Jas.B.Robinson & Alfred C.Downs + negroes. KEARNEY states that he has intermarried with the widow ELIZ. H.CALDWELL,and out of love and affection he holds for her and her children by ISAAC CALDWELL,Kearney relinquishes all rights to the property Eliz.brought into their marr.in favor of RAYMOND R.,JANE E.,HANNAH H.CALDWELL.

P.500:5 Dec.1849-P.O.A.:John L.Harmon(X) & his wife Jeniza(X), late Jeniza Frazer;Levi J.Embry(X) & wife Juliza(X),late Juliza Frazer all of Gibson Co.Ind.,appoint John J.Frazer of same to collect their money from sale of 2 lots to Littleton L.Taylor and wife Susan P.,former Susan P.McCutcheon.

P.503:5Dec.1849-Deed:Andrew J.Paxton & wife Hannah M.,& Eliza. A.McNutt sell"Walnut Hill Plantation"in Warr.Co.Ms. to Stephen Barefield.

P.504:25 Oct.1849-Deed:Jane N.Simms of New Orleans,widow of Wm.Sims,lately decd.received $200 from A.J.Paxton to release dower rights to land located in T.17,R7W-213½ ac.Wit:Sarah Alstonecraft & Jacob Oates.

P.508:27 Nov.1849-Deed:D.L.Pattison & wife Jane E.,Hannah H. Caldwell,now of age,all of Claib.Co.Ms. & Raymond R.Caldwell of La.-the heirs of Isaac Caldwell,decd.sell to Harriet B.Theobald,Orville M.Blanton,Wm.C.Blanton of Wash.Co.by S.Theobald,Adm. J.P.wasOrville C.Rives.

P.525:21 Jan.1850-Deed:Bayliss P.Shelby,one of the heirs of his father,Thomas Shelby,decd.+ Mary B.Shelby of 1st part;Catherine A.Blackburn,wife of David F.Blackburn; Mary B.Shelby & the heirs of Thomas Shelby-she was his widow-bought land at Mt.Salus + some other land from John A.Miller and his wife Sarah A.Miller.The 1st part sells to Catherine A.Blackburn. [Note;THOMAS SHELBY and his wife MARY BERRY(PRINCE)SHELBY had the following children;BAYLISS P.:CATHERINE A. who marr. D.F. BLACKBURN:EVAN W. who marr.MARY L.CHANEY:MARY B.who marr. WM. B.KNOX 1st and then marr.DR.JOHN BUTTS:THOMAS who marr. BETTIE McALLISTER.]

P.551:20 Feb.1850-Deed:Elizabeth A.McNutt of Hinds.Co.appoints A.M.Paxton as her agent and atty.to act in her behalf in buying a number of negroe slaves from the N.O.Canal & Banking Co. She has hired these slaves for several years.

P.551:16 Feb.1850-Deed:Roche H.Brabston,wife of James M.Brabston buys from Alfred C.Downs & Mary Jane his wife @260 ac.located in T.15,R6W.[Note;ROCHE is MARY JANES' sister]

P.562:24 Oct.1849-Deed:Mary Pescod,spinster,heretofore of Stanwix Co.of Cumberland in Kingdom of Great Britain and now of the Borough of Carlisle in said Country, and Jane Murray & Catharine Murray,spinsters,both heretofore of Stanwix-all devisees of Will of Wm.Pescod,decd.late of Vicksburg,Ms. sell to Alex.Montgomery of Natchez,for $6,388,land in Wash.Co.Ms. 1277 ac.@$5 per ac. Land located in T14,R3W-Mt.Salus-Wit:(Cont.)

DEED BOOK "N": WASHINGTON CO.MS.
Apr.1847-Oct.1850

(cont.)G.G.Murray,----Carlisle,J.Morley.Doc.signed by Geo.Dixon, Esq.,Mayor of Borough of Carlisle in U.K.called Ireland. The Adm.of the Est.of Wm.PESCOD was Wm.S.Bodley of Warr.Co.Ms.

P.571:4 Mar.1850-Deed:New Orleans-Eliza Creswell of N.O.sells slaves to Eugenia P.Bate,wife of Council R.Bass,of Wash.Co.Ms.

P.593:28 Mar.1850-Deed:Wm.M.Pinckard and wife Susan S.of Parish of Plaq.La.sell to David F.Blackburn of Wash.Co.Ms.-land on which Robt.P.Shelby now resides, situated on Deer Creek,+ land on Shirttail Bend(Wash.Co.)

P.609:24 Apr.1850-Relinq.:Sarah Vick,wife of Henry W.Vick,reached an agreement with the heirs of Wm.Pescod,decd.,Wm.S.Bodley,Adm. & Catherine Elizabeth Pescod & her heirs,as heirs of Wm.Pescod, decd. Concerning a judgement against Sarah's Hus. Henry W. Vick.

P.701:20 Mar.1850-Deed:Mary B.Shelby;David F.Blackburn & wife Catherine A.;Evan W.Shelby & wife Mary L.;Wm.B.Knox & wife Mary B.;all of the 1st part-sell to Wm.B.Prince land conveyed to MARY B.SHELBY and the heirs of THOMAS SHELBY,decd. The land is on Lake Jackson,Wash.Co.Ms.

P.706:29 Apr.1850-P.O.A."I,J.Walker Percy of Davidson Co.Tn. as Guardian to minor heirs of Thos.G.Percy,decd."-appoints Chas.B.Percy his attorney in Wash.Co.Ms.

P.741:1 Apr.1850-Deed:Catherine Egg(X) of Wash.Co.Ms.1st part; Phillip A.Cocks & wife Ann;Seth Cox & wife Sarah F.of same-2nd part;Catherine deeds plnt.on which she now resides to her dau.'s ANN COCKS & SARAH F.COX. Written on side of document in ink "Sent by Boy Ned to PHILLIP A.COCKS Dec.21st 1850".[Note:From the Cox(Cocks) paper in the Carter Room-Greenville,Ms.Library-the spelling of the family name was changed from COCKS to COX about 1840. PHILLIP & SETH-named above were brothers.]
P.742:Phillip & Ann;Seth & Sarah have sold land conveyed to Joseph Egg by Thos.Stephens,Adm.of Allen Winings(sp.Wynens) decd.500 ac.according to a deed dated 7 Oct.1849. They sold it to Marcus F.Johnson and his wife Mary.

P.765 to 788:Many pages of land being sold by Thomas Shelby, Tax Collector and Sheriff of Wash.Co.Ms.

P.877:24 June 1850:Clarinda Martin,widow of John Martin,decd. late of New Orleans-1st part;George Wm.Martin of St.Tam.Parish, La.buys land that Clarinda has been ordered by the court to sell. Property belonging to the Est.of JOHN MARTIN,decd.lying in Wash.Co.Ms.Notice of sale posted on Davidson's Store in Princeton,at the Post Office at Worthington's Point and the front door of the Courthouse at Greenville on 29 Apr.1850.

P.791:18 Oct.1849-P.O.A.:"I,Harry J.Bodley & wife Sarah G.of St.Louis,appoint Wm.S.Bodley of Louisville,Ky."his attorney to act in all matters in Ms.-even in matters pertaining to his,Harry's,Trusteeship of Mrs.Ellen Bodley,wife of Wm.S. who conveyed the Trusteeship under certain deeds executed in 1842,1844.

P.797:23 Feb.1842-D/T:Anne Hardeman;Wm.Maney both of Williamson Co.Tn.& Oscar J.E.Stuart and wife Sarah J.E. of Franklin (Cont).

DEED BOOK "N":WASHINGTON CO.MS.
Apr.1847-Oct.1850

(Cont.)Co.Ms. Deed states that Sarah is"at present"in Wmson. Co.Tn. and her mother,ANN HARDEMAN gives her(in trust to WM. MANEY)a slave named MARY,whom Wm.Maney is to hold in trust for Sarah & her children-James Hardeman Stuart & Oscar Ewing--Stuart and any future children she may have by OSCAR STUART. Oscar, Sarah's hus.,will have no control over the slave Mary or her increase. Signed by W.Maney,Oscar J.E.Stuart,Sarah J.E. Stuart-and Wit;ANNA L.HARDEMAN, LAVINIA E.HARDEMAN.

END OF DEED BOOK "N"

Husbands and wives mentioned in DBk."N"
BAKER,CORBEN & DORCAS C. -1838
BARNETT,JAS.W. & MARY T.-1847
BRADFORD,Thos.H. & SARAH C. -Scott Co.Ky.-1847
BRISCOE,Wm.T. & EMILY M.--Copiah Co.Ms.-1848
FARRAH,PRESTON W. & ELIZA JUDITH-North Carolina -1847
GAY,JOS & SARAH E.C.-Lowndes Co.Ms. 1847
HADLEY,Wm. & SARAH-Clermont,Ohio--1847
HALLIDAY,THOS.& EMILY M.--Copiah Co.Ms. -1848
HILL,OREN W. & ELIZA JANE-Wash.Co.Ms. 1847
HUMPHREYS,WILSON G. & BAYLISSA- Claib.Co.Ms. -1847
HUNT,FIDELICO L. & NANCY -Hinds Co.Ms. 1848
INGRAHAM,THOS.B. & MARIA--- 1832
JOHNSON,MARCUS F. & MARY -Wash.Co.Ms. -1848
MORGAN,THOS.T. & SARAH(X)-1848
NYE,NATHL.G. & LUCY ANN-Yazoo Co.Ms.-1847
PATTON,Wm.Y. & CARESE M. -Copiah Co.Ms. 1848
PAYNE,JAS. & JANE C. -Jeff.Ms.-1847
PENRICE,THOS.S. & ANN A. -Wash.Co.ms.-1847
SHACKLEFORD,THOS. & SARAH T.-1846
TARPLEY,CONICA S. & ELIZA W. -Hinds Co.Ms. 1844
THEOBALD,THOS.S. & SARAH W. -Franklin Co.Ky.
WARD,GEO.W. & JOSEPHINE -New Orleans--1847

SUPPLEMENTARY INFORMATION:WARREN CO.MS.WILL BOOK "A":
P.212;Will of Alvarez Fisk;dictated at"Avaly Pltn". 31 Oct.1853 La. Prob.Feb.Term 1854 in Warr.Co.Ms.;State of La.,2nd Dist.Court of New Orleans-1st Dec.1853-Madison P.La.
Wife-Eliza Wilkins Fisk,who already has a fortune in Mad.P.La.
4 children- 1.Stewart Wilkins Fisk-gets "Avaly Pltn."in Mad.P.La. 2.Mrs.Alice M.Urguhart-gets prop.in Plaq.P.La.;3.Edw.Alvarez Fisk and 4.Isabel Fisk received "yrs.ago"a pltn.called "Belzoni" on Yazoo River,Wash.Co.Ms.;Neph.Fisk Postlewaite;Martha A.Wilkins relationship unexplained;Mrs.Eliza Ellison;Exec.son S.W.Fisk, and Wm.Perkins-both of Mad.P.,La.

MARR.,DEATH & LEGAL NOTICES FROM EARLY ALA.NEWSP.1819-1893 by Gandrud;
P.353;Died 3rd May at her res.in Chicot(not there in 1850)Co. Ark.,in her 60th yr.,Mrs.Nancy Taylor,wife of Judge John M.Taylor & dau.of the late Wm.Foote of Fauquier Co.Va.(May 26,1847)

DEED BOOK "O":WASHINGTON CO.MS.
DATED 1 Oct.1850-28 Mar.1853
787 pages-Original

P.5:2 Nov.1850-Deed:Wm.B.Bate of Sumner Co.Tn.sells two slaves to Mrs.Eugenia P.Bate,wife of Council R.Bass.

P.6:4 Nov.1850-Deed:John F.Dickinson & wife Ellen;John Goodwin and wife Sarah;Henry B.Lewis and wife Ellen;Wm.H.Dickinson-all heirs of John Dickinson,late of Caroline Co.,Va.,decd.,and all by their agent A.K.Smedes sell to Samuel Worthington. The signatures signed to the bottom of this document, and the next document giving P.O.A.to Smedes are as follows;

JOHN F.DICKINSON   HENRY B.LEWIS
VIRGINIA G.DICKINSON *   ELLEN C.LEWIS
JAMES E.DICKINSON *   WM.H.DICKINSON
ELLEN C.DICKINSON
JOHN GOODWIN   ALL BY A.K.SMEDES
SARAH A.GOODWIN
*Not named in the document above.

P.14:4 Feb.1850-Deed:Jane Baker sells to Thos.J.Likens,both of Wash.Co.her inheritance from Thos.Grimes.Land on Lake Jackson. Written on side of book,"delivered to Mrs.Browning 14th Dec.1850."

P.15:24 Feb.1850-Mort:Sarah Bertholf of Cincinnati,Ohio hold the Mort.of the property above, BAKER sold to LIKENS.

P.17:15 Jan.1846-Decree from Chancery Court at Jackson-case John T.McMurran,et al vs heirs of Cornelius Haring,decd.for 1 undivided 3rd of lands, which were ordered sold in 1847.

P.38:14 Nov.1850-Deed:Mary Ann Thomson,widow and survivor of M.V.Thomson,decd.sells land and slaves to P.S.Cable-all of Georgetown,Ky.

P.65:Nov.1859-Deed:Wm.Blanton & Orville W.Blanton,heirs at law of Wm.W.Blanton,decd.,quit claim to Elizabeth Ann Dunn,wife of Saml.R.Dunn-lot #4;Sec.11;T19;R8W-for love and affection. (She is their 1st cousin)

P.65:Nov.1850:Harriet B.Theobald,wife of Saml.Theobald,formerly widow of Wm.Blanton,decd, for love and affection she holds for Elizabeth Ann Dunn,relinq.all dower rights to L4;S11;T19;R8W. [NOTE;ELIZABETH ANN(MCALLISTER)DUNN was the dau.of THOMAS KEITH MCALLISTER,and neice of HARRIET BYRON(MCALLISTER)BLANTON THEObald.]

P.78:27 Apr.1830-Marriage Contract:Amelia Georgia Ann Bernard (also sp.Barnard) of Wilmington Island,Chatham Co.Ga.;Murdock Chisholm of Macon,Bibb Co.Ga.;John Y.Roland, Isaac B.Roland,of Macon and Timothy G.Bernard of Chatham Co.Ga. of 3rd part;Amelia and Murdock are to be married and Murdock agrees not to "intermeddle"with her said property. She puts her prop.in trust to parties of 3rd part,but if she dies, Murdock gets use for his natural life + her children's. But in default of such issue living at her death, it goes to Ann Matthews Wash John Brodley Bernard Timothy Guerard Barnard Caroline Barnard Solomon Barnard Marion Barnard Margaret Virginia Barnard-brothers and sisters of Amelia's.(Note;no punct.between the above names)(cont.)

DEED BOOK"O":WASHINGTON CO.MS.
1Oct.1850-28 Mar.1855

P.78:(cont.)Next document following the marriage contract between Amelia Barnard & Murdock Chisholm was dated 10 Feb.1851-Mortg:MURDOCK CHISHOLM of Wash.Co.Ms. of the 1st part;Willis L.Robard of same-2nd pt;John Y.Rowland & Isaac B.Rowland acting Trustees for Walter L.,Timothy B.,John B. & Wm.W.Chisholm-of Ga.-3rd part. Murdock Chisholm stated he entered the marriage contract with Amelia Barnard on 27 Apr.1830,and TIMOTHY G.BARNARD IS NOW DECD.-Amelia is also now decd.,leaving her lawful issue WALTER L.,TIMOTHY B.,JOHN B.,WM.W.CHISHOLM. Murdock owes the trustees $16,667, and wants to use his inheritance as collateral. The inheritance was slaves.

P.87:29 Jan.1851-Clarification of Title:June Ann Garmon of Brinham,Tex.(Wash.Co.Tex.)states that Oliver Gorman,decd.'s last Will and Testament gave his brother Felix Gormon 2,000 ac.of land. She further states that Starling Garmon,brother to the two above mentioned,departed this life before Oliver, and had left property to Felix,also. That Oliver had left land to Felix without knowing that Felix would inherit from Starling. She wants relief.[Note:Oliver Gormon decd.by 1850 leaving a widow ANN,no children. Also note interspelling of Ga(O)rmon]

P.115:22 Oct.1839-Deed:Thos.B.Warfield & wife Alice C.of Wash. Co.Ms.;Elisha W. Hunt,Mary Hunt,Catherine Hunt,Rebecca C.Hunt all of Fayette Co.Ky. The Warfield's give 160 ac.+ improvements for natural love and affection.Rebecca still a minor.

P.226:23 Apr.1851-Release:The last Will and Test. of Benj.Smith, left his plantation in Wash.Co.Ms.in trust to Mrs.Irene Smith & Miss Frances E.Smith,for his neice Sarah F.Johnson. The pltn. was known as"The Black Place",now "Glenora",@640 ac. Robt.W. Johnson,Sarah's husband, has bought adjoining land, and they have enjoyed the use of both tracts for 4 yrs.1847-1850. Robt. is solvent and releases all claim to Sarah"s property,and forms a trust for Sarah and her ch. Wit:Thos.H.Buckner,John L.(S?) Buckner.[NOTE:The Will of Benj.Smith is not recorded in Wash. Co.Ms.]

P.246:9 May 1851-Deed:Marcus F.Johnson & wife Mary of Chicot Co.Ark.,sell to Edward P.Johnson of Wash.Co.Ms.land in same.

P.248:9 May 1851-Deed:EDW.P.Johnson & wife Betsy W.of Wash.Co. Ms. to Marcus F.Johnson of Chicot Co.Ark. They are swapping land on Bayou Granicus (Wash.Co.Ms.)

[NOTE:Many Public Sales by Tax Collector & Sherf.Thos.Shelby]

P.265:21 Apr.1851-Perfection of Title:John Fulton & wife Anne of Wash.Co.Ms. to Daniel Brannum of Henry Co.Ky. & Abram O. Smith of Louisville,Ky.:On 7 jan.1836-Anne Crow,widow of Henry Crow decd.,now Anne Fulton,wife of John Fulton,petitioned for her dower rights and share of her husband's land in said Wash. Co.Ms. and received as her share Lot 6,Sec.2,Twp.16,R8W on 8 Apr.1836. Anne and her present husband John, then sold Lot 6 + dower rts.to Ben Taylor of Chicot Co.Ark. The deed has been lost,and property has since been sold to Brannum & Smith. They seek perfection of Title.

DEED BOOK "O": WASHINGTON CO.MS.
1 Oct.1850-28 Mar.1855

P.268:PALMETTO PLANTATION-Jan.18,1851:Survey completed this day on Palmetto Pltn.as 1550 ac.behind the levee-all of S9,10 some S29,8;T14;R9W-Choc.Dist.signed by M.L.Peters,Surveyor.

P.268:21 June 1851-Deed Wm.C.Barrett,of Wash.Co.Ms.sells to Mrs.Elizabeth S.Shelby,wife of Thomas Shelby,of same:Barrett sells land on Deer Creek to Eliz.S.Shelby with her father-Augustus W.McAllister acting as security.

P.270:1 July 1851-Deed:James Rucks of Wash.Co.Ms.buys from Orlando Brown of KY.-1 undivided 5th in a tract of land known as"The Brown Place"-1076+ ac.+ slaves, located in Wash.Co.Ms. Rucks mortg's.the place to Robert W.Scott & wife Elizabeth W. Scott on 24 July,1851(see page 279).On page 303-Robt. W.Scott and wife Eliz.W.of Ky.& James Rucks of Wash.Co.Ms.-both heirs & distributees of Dr.Preston W.Brown & wife Elizabeth Brown, both decd.They settle a dispute over the "Brown Place"and Rucks buys the Scotts out.

P.300:12 May 1851-Deed:Artimecy(X)Harrison of Wash.Co.Tex. states;"My brother Starling Gorman, departed this life AD 1839, leaving a last Will & Test."..leaving all property to his Bros. & Sisters. The Adm.of Starling was Leonard A.Weissinger of Marion Perry Co.Ala.(copied as written)and the Est. has never been settled. She sells her share of Starling's Est. to Felix Gorman(Note;her brother) for $400. Wit:J.M.Harrison,Wm.McDowell. For details of the Est.of STARLING GORMAN,see EMR-VOL.II.

P.307:17 Feb.1849-Perfection of Title:New Orleans-Andrew L. Baker(also sp.Barker)of New Orleans purchased from the Liquidating Commissioner of Bank of N.O.-land in Wash.Co.Ms..certain lands patented to Wm.R.Campbell,which he held for A.M.Scott ofMs.,which,by mistake, were not conveyed by Scott to T.O. Stark-the Bank was supposed to have taken possession of this tract. Whereas Eliza J.Scott,by inheritance is ½ owner of all purveyed by A.M.Scott,and whereas Eliza Barker of N.O.is the mother and "universal legatee of said Andrew",buys from Eliza J.Scott,together with her husband Preston W.Farrar the missing tract. Signed by P.W.Farrah,Eliza J.Farrar.[NOTE:ELIZA JUDITH SCOTT was the dau. of GOV.ABRAM MARSHALL SCOTT and SUSAN(GRAY) SCOTT.]

P.308:29 Jan.1851-Deed:Fielding Davis,Marshall of Southern Dist.of Ms.is commanded to sell 1201+ ac.on Deer Creek conveyed to James C.Wilkins by Charles Cocke of Albermarle Co. Va., on 31 Mar.1836 + much more land in Wash.Co.,Issa.Co.,Yazoo Co., as judgement in a suit styled Wm.W.Frazier & Joseph Frazier vs Jas.C.Wilkins,decd.whose descendants are Catherine C.Boyd (or Boyer),Saml.Boyd(or Boyer)in right of his wife Catherine; Anna B.Wilkins;Maria L.Wilkins;Frances C.Wilkins;Rebecca Wilkins; Louisa Wilkins;Jas.C.Wilkins;Stephen M.Wilkins;Wm.H.Wilkins-heirs of said decd.Property in question is sold to Robert Mott, at the Courthouse in Issa.Co.Ms.

¶[NOTE:There are 2 page 310's]
P.310(2)26 Sept.1851:Deed:Alexander Yerger & wife Elizabeth B. of Wash.Co.Ms.sells to James Rucks of same, all rights and claims to property Eliz.B.Yerger inherited from Louisa V.Rucks

DEED BOOK "O": WASHINGTON CO.MS.
1 Oct.1850-28 Mar.1855

(Cont)decd.(her mother).Land adjoining Saml.Worthington,Isaac Worthington & Wm.F.Hammett on KY.Bend(Wash.Co.Ms.)known as "The Brown Place",Louisa was entitled to 1/5th by virtue of a purchase made from her bro.John P.W.Brown + 1/5th of her own rt.by virtue of Superior Court decree.

P.311:9 Sept.1851-Deed"For love and affection I have for my dau.Mary Ford Offutt and her ch."..a gift of slaves Dr.Offutt, her husband, has been permitted to take to their Miss. pltn., 5 slaves. Signed by Ben.B.Ford. wit:Ann R.Smith,A.Smith.

P.315:4 July 1851-Deed Wm.B.Reese & wife Henrietta M.sell their inherited portion of "The Brown Place" to James Rucks-the undivided 1/5th-as heirs of Dr.Preston W.Brown.

P.319:31Mar.1851-Deed:Wm.Murdock,Adm.of Est.of Francis Murdock, decd.,of Jeff.Co.Ms.,seeks permission to sell Francis's land that he owned in Wash.Co.,stating that all legatees named in Francis's Will have been notified..The buyer was George Terry, of Jeff.Co.Ms.

P.329:6 Nov.1851-Deed:Willis L.Robards,Commissioner appointed by Prob.Court of Wash.Co.Ms. to sell certain lands belonging to Est.of Starling Gorman,decd. Pet.of heirs,Charles W.Allen, Felix Gorman,Eliz.G.Reed show the land lyin in Twp.17,R7W;and Twp.15,R7W-@108+ac. The purchaser is John W.Smith. The next document concerns the same Est.,Pet.by same heirs-purchased by Daniel P.Marr.

P.336:25 Feb.1848:"At the Instance of Ben Roach,Jr.,I have surveyed a tract of land in Wash.Co.Ms.known as the"Bachelors Bend Plantation"of the Est.of Ben Roach,Sr. @1312 + ac. Map attached".(Only blank space where map is supposed to be) signed by J.G.Beerry(copied as written)

P.350:24 Mar.1849-Deed:Claib.Co.Ms. Probate Court + Warr.Co.Ms. The Adms.of Est.of Jas.L.McCaleb,decd and the Est.of Thos. M. Briggs,decd.did on 17 Feb.1849 offer at Public sale certain property jointly owned by McCaleb & Briggs,both decd. Mrs.Eleanor Burwell(late McCaleb)and her 2 ch.James McCaleb & Ann C.-McCaleb by their agent Fletcher Coughton(also sp.CREIGHTON) purchased the property. Many slaves,farm tools,crops,stock, household furn.;medical books belonging to THOS.M.BRIGGS,etc. The Adm.of McCaleb was Johnathon McCaleb.Adm.of BRIGGS was John G.Guion.

P.357:28 Feb.1850-Deed:John Montgomery & wife Sarah of Madison Co.Ms.give to the Zion Seminary, under the care of Miss.Presbetery for promotion of Education and learning-a tract of land in Wash.Co.Ms.located in T17;R6W.

P.383:P.O.A.2 Mar.1852:Alfred G.Carter of Wash.Co.Ms.gives his Power of Atty.to Robert G.Carter of Carter Co.Ky. to handle Alfred's interest as one of the heirs of Wm.G.Carter,decd.of that Co.

P.393:1 Jan.1852-Deed:Sebelia A.Messinger of Berkshire Co.,Mass. sells to Alfred C.Downs of Warr.Co.Ms. land in Wash.Co.Ms.250 ac.located in T16,R7W. She signed in Vicksburg.

DEED BOOK "O": WASHINGTON CO.MS.
1 Oct.1850--28 Mar.1853

P.398:11 Dec.1851-Deed:John C.Richardson,M.D.and wife Mary A. sell to Saml.B.Richardson-all of Lexington,Ky.land on Yazoo River,Wash.Co.Ms. Written in margin"examined and sent to A.J. Downing in Jackson,Ms. Apr.20,1852."

County Officials in 1852 were:
Sheriff and Tax Collector-JAMES H.YERGER
Justice of the Peace-CHAS.S.ROBARDS
Clerk-J.J.CAUGHEY
Dep.Clerk-S.N.CAUGHEY

P.438:2 Mar.1852-D/T:Thos.Kershaw & wife Mary Jane convey for $5,to John Peavie Cunningham-land in Wash.Co.Ms.and Harrison Co.Ms. The Wash.Co.property, known as Plantation of Mrs.Mary Jane Kershaw and land in Pass Christian known as the residence of Mrs.Kershaw-220 feet fronting on Gulf of Mexico + slaves. Said property being by Ms. law(now)the sole property of Mrs. Kershaw.[NOTE:MARY JANE KERSHAW is the sister of J.P.CUNNINGHAM]

P.456:8 June 1852-Deed:Augustus W.McAllister,Treasurer of Wash. Co.Ms.buys land from the heirs of Thomas Bernard,decd.and Wm. Connor.

P.463:14 Feb.1851-Deed:Geo.W.Campbell & wife Martha of N.O. to Wm.R.Campbell of Wash.Co.Ms.

FROM P.472--498 many sales for taxes:

SHERF.	DATE	OWNER	BUYER
SHELBY	1849	ROBT.E.CRANE	BAYLISS E.P.SHELBY
"	"	CATHERINE M.CRANE	Willis S.Robards
"	"		" "
"	"	JAS.M.CRANE	" "
"	"	HENRY W.ALLEN	" "
CONNELLY	1846	W.R.&J.W.COCKRAN	T.J.LIKENS
"	"	STEPHEN R.FORD	"
"	"	T.B.J.HADLEY	"
"	"	JOHN WOODHOUSE	"
"	"	W.N.HARDWICK	"
"	"	T.D.DOWNS	"
"	"	W.& B.DUNN	"

P.498:3 Sept.1851-Deed:Jacob Barker & wife Elizabeth born Hazzard sell to Louisa M.Young wife of Wm.H.Young 320 +ac.in T17,R7W for Louisa's sole use.

P.508:29 Sept.1852-Deed:Isaac Roth of Wash.Co.Ms.sells to Jacob Roth of same for $1, a two story frame house in Greenville + accounts owed said store Roth & Roth.

P.512:29 June 1852-P.O.A.:Yuba Co.Calif.:Montague Endecott of said Co.gives his P.O.A.to his sister Ann M.Endicott of Lafayette Co.Mo.,to act for him in all matters in Mo.

P.609:15 Dec.1851-Deed:Maria J.Church,Guard.of Catharine,Wm.& Edw.Church,minor heirs of Edw.B.Church,late of Wash.Co.Ms.,decd. of 1st part:Willis L.Robards of same,bought property ordered sold-59 ac.in town of Greenville,part of the Est.of EDW.B. CHURCH,husband and father of 1st pt.Maria signed in KY.Next docu.-WILLIS ROBARDS quit claims the same prop.to MARIA CHURCH.

DEED BOOK "O": WASHINGTON CO.MS.
1 Oct.1850--28 Mar.1853

P.614;The lateWm.R.Campbell,decd.,had agreed to sell to Wm.P. Montgomery a certain parcel of land. Campbell left a Will and his Execx.& wife was Margaret Campbell, on order by the Superior Court of the Chanc.of Ms.does so on 17 Dec.1852

P.638:11 June 1851-Deed;On 15 Jan.1840,I,after having reserved a certain portion for myself, divide my property, land,negroes, situated and lying on Lake Washington,between my son Wm.R.Elley & son-in-law John W.Keene and took from them 4 promissory notes for payment of $25,000".(Land in Twp.14,R8W)1,000 ac. They have paid the notes and "Iam conveying said deed".signed by Henry Elley with Wm.R.Burch,Wm.Wayland. Wit:W.C.Harney,Wm.Upton,W.L. Upton. Henry Elley signed in Randolph Co.Mo.

P.639:10 Jan.1853-P.O.A.:Willis L.Robards gives his power of Atty.to Chas.L.Robards, both of Wash.Co.Ms.

P.641:14 July----:Zenas K.Fulton of Lawrence(Lavelle-?)Tx.sells to Marcus F.Johnson of Chicot Co.Ark. Zenas appeared in N.Y.,N.Y.

P.643:8 Jan.1853-Deed:Marcus F.Johnson of Chicot Co.Ark.,sells to Alfred D.Offutt & John W.Bradley of Scott Co.Ky. Marcus's wife is Mary.

P.712:18 Oct.1852-P.O.A.:Asa Smith of Boyd Co.Ky.,gives his P.O.A.to Sidney R.Smith of Louisville, Ky.,to collect for lands Asa sold to J.L.Roberts in Wash.Co.Ms.

P.713;12 Aug.1852-P.O.A:Sidney R.Smith of Louisville,Ky.appointed"as my agent"to receive payments from J.L.Roberts of Ms. -signed by W.Samuels of Scott Co.Ky., Wit:B.W.Samuels,Joel J. Offutt.

P.721;Alexander M.Paxton & wife Mary L. sell a plantation to John Bell,Jr.-land on West side of Deer Creek in T.17;R7W-500ac.

P.723:17 Aug.1850-Deed:Andrew J.Paxton & wife Hannah M.sell to Mary L.Paxton,wife of A.M.Paxton,land on West of Deer Creek in T17,R7W,for her sole use.

P.735:8--1853-Mortg:Grant A.Bowen,Jacob S.Yerger and wife Mary H.Yerger of Wash.Co.Ms.mortg.prop. to Thos.Shelby of same. The security for the loan is Wm.Yerger.

P.737:27 Dec.1850-Deed:Patsy Shall of New Orleans, for love and affection for"My son George Shall and to his wife Martha and their children"a gift of real estate located on Fish Lake (Wash.Co.Ms.)S.14,15;T18;R8W + slaves-under the following agreement;All profits including increase in slaves,to be used by Geo.and his family, but at his death, the ownership descends to his children with a life-time-or until Martha should remarry-enjoyment of the gift by Martha.

P.743:17 Feb.1853-Deed:James Rucks sells to Arthur Rucks & Jas. T.Rucks, land on Deer Creek in S11;Twp.18;R7W-87½ac.

==
END OF DEED BOOK "O"
ADDITIONAL HUSBANDS & WIVES IN DBK"O":Date of Doc.,Residence
BARNEY,MILTON and wife.SOPHIA Chicago,Cook Co.,Ill.1851
BILL,Chas.W.and wife ELIZA.D. Wash.Co.Ms.   "

HUS.& W.IN DBK"O"(CONT.)
```
BROOKS,J.M. and wife VIRGINIA L.-Wash.Co.Ms.        1853
CARSON,Saml. and wife PHEBE- Wash.Co.Ms.            1850
CRAIG,Joshua M. and wife ELIZABETH-Chicott Co. Ark. 1853
CRAWFORD,E.S.and wife ELVIRA ANN- Vicksburg         1851
DURFY,Robt.W. and wife ELIZA C.- Wash.Co.Ms.        1853
ERSKINE,Alex.and wife S.CATHERINE-Mad.Co.Ala.       1851
HANNA,John H.and wife MARY S.- South Frankfort,Ky.  1852
HILL,Caleb and wife SUSAN-Chicot Co.Ark.            1851
JAMES,T.J.SR.and wife FRANCES B.-Wash.Co.Ms.        1851
JOHNSON,EDW.P.and wife BETSY W.-Lexington,Ky.       1852
JOHNSON,Jas.(of Granicus)and w.Mary R.Wash.Co.Ms.   1852
MILLSAPS,Wm.W.and wife MARY-Copiah Co.Ms.             "
MORRELL,Michael P.and wife MILDRED A.-Wash.Co.Ms.   1851
NELSON,Newman J.and wife MARY-Wash.Co.Ms.           1852
OSWALD,Thos.H.and wife LUCY M.- Wilkinson Co.Ms.    1852
PATTON,Wm.Y.and wife MUNTORA C.-Claib.Co.Ms.          "
PINKARD,Geo.M.and wife SARAH ANN-New Orleans          "
RUNDELL,Ezra and wife MARTHA -Mad.P.La                "
THRASHER,John B. and wife ELIZA-Calib.Co.Ms.          "
WHITLOCK,Benj.M.and wife AMELIA M.-New York           "
```

SUPPLEMENTARY INFORMATION:

*¶Jacob Shall Yerger-born 1809,Md. according to Census-1850 Wash. Co.Ms.(Goodspeed's says 11 Jan.1816-Pa.) d.14 July 1867-marr. 1833 in Smith Co. Tn. to Mary H.R.Bowen a sister of Grant A. Bowen. She was b.1817/20(Census 1850-1870)Tn.,probably Smith Co. Her Will is probated Wash.Co.Ms.10 Oct.1892,.Wash.Co.Ms.W. Bk.1-p.496. Their Children were:
George S.Yerger who decd.while deer hunting
Wm.Gwin Yerger b.1840,Vicksburg,Ms. marr.1866 to Jennie Hunter
Harry,called Hal,Yerger b.1843, marr. Sallie Miller
Bowen Yerger who d.1864 in the Civil War, in Tenn.
Grant Yerger
*Taken from:Census Records-1850-1870 Wash.Co.Ms.;PWCHS;GOODSPEEDS:
MARRIAGES FROM EARLY TN.NEWSPAPERS,1794-1851
Court records-Wash.Co.Ms.

WARREN CO.MS.,WILL BOOK "A":
P.91;Will of Thomas Ferguson;Written 12 Aug.1838-Prob.Sept.Term 1838. Names;Nephew Andrew Ferguson Haynes;½ bro.Edw.S.Downs, "if he relinquishes all claim to his father's Est.",to Caroline M.Ferguson,my wife:bro-in-law Andrew Haynes to be co-exec.,with wife. Wit;R.H.Robinson,Lorenzo Port,Alexander Miller, C.D.Gibson, Dr.Wm.P.Dewer-his attending physcian.[NOTE:Thomas Ferguson marr. Caroline Downs,Warr.Co.Ms.,18 July 1830]

P.170;Will of Caroline M.Blake;written 25 Sept.1842-no prob.date; Proceeds from the following deed to go to her Husb.;Deed between Alfred C.Downs & wife Mary Jane-1st part;Beman Blake & wife Caroline M.-2nd;James R.Robinson-3rd part;Names sis.,Mrs.Charlotte Payne;Neph.Andrew Ferguson Haynes;Neph.Henry Payne the ½ bro.of Andrew Haynes;To Edw.Downs-prop.from ½ bro. Thos.Ferguson;Exec. Beman Blake,husb.[NOTE:Caroline M.Downs was 1st marr. to Thos. Ferguson-see above-and after his death,marr. Beman Blake.]

DEED BOOK "P": WASHINGTON CO.MS.
DATED: Mar.1853-May 1856
708 pages-badly water-marked;tightly rebound so that the documents are difficult to read,volumn in fragile condition. On microfilm, Indexed in Master Deed Index Book 1.

First 40 pages concerning many sales for taxes. The present Sheriff & Tax Collector is JAS.H.YERGER- 1853.

P.41;Sept.1852:Thos.B.Warfield,Trustee of Mrs.Catherine A.Warfield and ch. of.Lexington,Ky.and Henry C.Offutt,Wm.C.Offutt, Bartlett M.Hall of Shelby Co.Ky.and Ezra N.Offutt,Alex.Offutt, Ben B.Ford of Scott Co.Ky.,all of the 1st part;Zachariah C. Offutt of Wash.Co.Ms.2nd pt.:Zac,on Mar.1845,executed a Mortg., to Warfield,Trustee, on ½ of Plantation(+ slaves)"Utopia". The loan was paid off,all but the last note, when Zac took out a 2nd mortg.,to the Offutts,Hall,and Ford-named above. Zac.then paid off Warfield and remained in debt to "his brothers"and Hall. BenF.Ford releases his claims to his dau.MARY who is Zac's.wife. By 1852, all claims against "Utopia" have been paid and mortg."forgiven".

P.52:--1852-Deed:Jonathon McCaleb of ---Co.to R.J.Turnbull, C.F.Hampton, Wardens, and W.Hampton,W.Hampton,Jr.,John L.Chapman,Henry P.Duncan,John Butts,C.F.Howell,T.J.Likens,A.F.Smith all vestrymen of St.Johns Church(Wash.Co.Ms.).McCaleb sells to the church,for $1,a parcel of land bounded on the South by Lake Jackson(scratched out)Independence:On West by the public road leading along Lake Washington,420 ft.;thence East 420 ft. to Lake Independence--for the erection of a parsonage and for the celebration of Service.(St.John's was a Protestant Episcopal Church)Deed states the property to be used for "no other purpose whatever".

P.71;12 Apr.1853-Deed:Henry Rodewall of New Orleans sells to Sylvia Ann Penny,wife of Thos.Penney of Wash.Co.Ms.all that tract of land that she now resides on-in Twp.16,R4W-563 ac. + slaves on said Pltn.+ tools,etc.

P.81:15 June 1853-Deed:John James & wife Mary sell to T.J.James all of Wash.Co.Ms.

P.107:7 Dec.1848-Harris Co.Texas-P.O.A.:fromJoshua Hendy & wife Hettie O.Hendy,formerly HETTY O.FALL,widow of Jas.Fall, whose maiden name was Hetty O.Crutcher,only child and heir of Geo. B.Crutcher,late of Miss.,now decd. The Hendy's,who now reside in HOuston,Tx. give their P.O.A.to Wm.Yerger to handle their Ms.business.

P.113:18 Mar.1853-Deed:"For love and affection and $50 paid me by my son Waldo W.Putnam,now of Hinds Co.Ms." a certain tract of land in Wash.Co.Ms.-320 ac. Signed by A.W.Putnam in Davidson Co.Tn.(HIS signature)[NOTE:From Marr.'sEarly Tn.Newsp.- A.W.Putnam marr.19 July 1848 to Mrs.Mary W.Edwards of Columbia, Tenn.]

P.115:27 July 1853-Deed:Mary S.Roberts is Execx.of Est.of Jos. 1.Roberts,decd.-land to be sold for taxes and Mary bought it.

P.125:7 Aug.1853:Susan L.Hardaway,Execx.of Est.of Thos.P.Hardaway,Warr.Co.Ms.buys land for taxes owed.[NOTE:Will of THOS. P.HARDAWAY,Warr.Co.Will Dk."A"p.199-written 1 Apr.1853,Prob. June Term 1853:names,Wife-SUSAN S.:Neices MARY ANN FISHER, (cont.

DEED BOOK "P": WASHINGTON CO.MS.
Mar.1853-May 1856

(cont.)MARY J.R.HAWKS;Neph.ROBT.B.SCOTT:JULIANA S.RANDOLPH;
MINERVA B.SCOTT,dau.of my decd.neph.THOS.B.SCOTT. Wit:H.H.Hill,
Jos.N.Parks,Saml.G.Parks

P.129:12 Oct.1853-P.O.A.:Montague Endecott,late of Wash.Co.Ms.
now decd.,owned divers lots alone and with others in Wash.Co.&
whereas Ann Maria M.Endecott,Emma Endecott,Henry Smock & wife
Kate H.Smock formerly Kate H.Endecott are the only surviving
heirs at law of said Endecott,decd...heirs employ Chas.L.Robards
to perfect the titles to the lands. The heirs are all of Lafayette,Co.Mo.

¶[NOTE:Over the rest of Deed Bk."P", the heirs of Montague Endecott begin to sell out his Est.-to WM.HUNT, ANDREW CARSON,
CARTER B.HARRISON,FELIX G.GAMBLE,WM.BAILEY. Did not document
because the heirs and their residence remain unchanged.]

P.145:22 June 1853-Release:Thos.D.Carneal & Thos.B.Warfield
pay off the mortg. on "Highland Pltn."held by Elisha Warfield,
Sr.,of Fayette Co.Ky.,and Wm.P.Warfield of Shelby Co.Tn.

P.159:26 Sept.1853-Deed:Alfred D.Offutt & wife Sophronia &
John W.Bradley all of Scott Co.Ky.,of the 1st part;to Chas.S.
Morehead of Frankfort,Ky.

P.161:26 Feb.1853-P.O.A:Benj.F.White of Wash.Co.Ms. to Wm.W.
Willoughby of same. White wants Willoughby to sell his prop.

P.163-Deed:On 12 Dec.1853,Benj.F.White(inP.O.A.above) was "of
Rappahannock Co.Va.,and the prop.was sold by WILLOUGHBY in his
capacity as Atty.for White, to Wm.Hunt.

P.166:26 Dec.---Deed:T.D.Elliott & wife Mary Keene of Wash.Co.
Ms.sell to John Woodburn & John R.Woodburn of Louisville,Ky.
land,+ slaves,+ household furn.[Will of John Woodburn is in
Vol. I of this series,p.82, Wash.Co.Will Bk.I p.247]

P.169:4 Apr.1844-General Warantee:Jas.C.Wilkins & wife Cath.
L.Wilkins & Levin R.Marshall & wife Sarah E. all of Natchez,
sell 900/1000 ac.of land to Robt.G.Carter of Wash.Co.Ms.

P.188:24 Nov.1853-Mortg:Wm.Alson Hayne & wife Margaretta L.
of Charleston,S.C.to Matthew Watson,Pres. of Planters Bank
of Tenn.

P.189:24 Jan.1854-Deed:Jas.G.Gordon & wife Harriet of Tensas
P.La.(signed in N.O.)of the 1st part;Eliza G.Mosby wife of
Gervas S.Mosby of Wash.Co.Ms.,Ann M.Burks of Louisville,Ky.,
widow of the late Saml.Burks,decd.,of 2nd:Saml.and wife Ann
M. did on 25 June 1842 convey to said GORDON by deed, proper-
ty.(DBk."L"p.259-260).This property being that which ELIZA &
ANN M.would inherit.GORDON releases the mortg.-2/3rd to Eliza
1/3rd to widow Ann for natural life + personal Est.+ slaves.

P.214:2 June 1853-Deed:Jno.E.Smith of Wash.Co.Ms.sells to
Wm.F.Smith of same.

P.219:Following document recorded Philadelphia,Pa.,21 Apr.
1853 and recorded in Wash.Co.Ms.8Feb.1854:Bertha Burns,Gert-
rude P.Burns,Mary Burns, Archibald W.Burns,Isabella Norcross,
Chas.D.Burns,Wm.Burns-heirs at law of Wm.Burns,decd.of(cont.)

DEED BOOK "P": WASHINGTON CO.MS.
Mar.1853-May 1856

(cont.)Hinds Co.Ms. by their Atty.in fact, Jos.W.Allen,sell to Danl.P.Marr. Wit:John H.Frick,Wm.A.Mursey.

P.223:Feb.1853-Deed:Guignard Scott of Wash.Co.Ms.sells to Jas. S.Guignard,Jr. of Columbia,S.C.-land belonging to the Est.of John A.SCott,decd.and known as "Scotland Pltn."-1560 ac.Guignard Scott's share being 1 undivided 6th.

P.226:3 Mar.1854-Deed:Thomas Y.Heard of Wash.Co.Ms.sells to Sarah H.Heard-slaves + household stuff $700 cash.

P.229:21 Oct.1853-Deed:A.Waldo Putnam & wife Mary W.of David. Co.Tn.,sell to Waldo W.Putnam & Jas.P.Smith of Hds.Co.Ms. for $3100-397 ac.

P.238:27 Mar.1854-Deed:John J.Caughey & wife Mary H.sell to Alex.B.Montgomery & Alex.M.Kirk all of Wash.Co.Ms.

P.239:27 Mar.1854-Est.of Alfred Longeley,decd.,Adm.is Thos. Shelby of Wash.Co.Ms.

P.263:29 Mar.1854-Deed:Jas.B.Brabston & wife Roche H.of Warr. Co.Ms.sell to Stephen Barefield-$13,000-land on Deer Creek in Wash.Co.Ms.-East bank,T15,R6W @1050 ac.

P.264:1 June 1853-Deed:John M.Selser & wifeSybelia A. of Warr. Co.sell to Alfred C.Downs of same-land locatedinT16,R7W,809+ac.

P.272:10 Apr.1854-Deed:James Rucks of Wash.Co.Ms.-1st part: Wm.B.Reese of Knox Co.Tn.,Orlando Brown & Robt.W.Scott of Frank. Co.Ky.,2nd:Jas.Rucks owes Reese a large sum of money for which Reese holds 8 notes of said Rucks along with Arthur Rucks. Jas. Rucks also owes Brown and Scott for land on Ky.Bend,known as "The Brown Place"which he has mortg.-1068 ac..Jas.Rucks asks that the mortg.be released in favor of mortg.on another place he owns on Deer Creek,Wash.Co.in T18,R8W. The parties of the 2nd part agree to release the land, but not the slaves.

¶[NOTE:Dr.Preston W.Brown of Ky.,decd.,1826 and his wife Elizabeth,decd.May 1843,had the following children.
LOUISA V.BROWN,marr.1827,as his 2nd w.,JAMES RUCKS
HENRIETTA M.BROWN,marr.30 Jan.1834 in Frankfort,Ky.WM.B.REESE
MARY W.BROWN,marr.1830 ORLANDO BROWN in Frankfort,Ky.
JOHN P.W.BROWN,marr.16 Nov.1837,JANE NICHOL of Nashville,Tn.
ELIZABETH W.BROWN,marr.Oct.1831,Frankfort,Ky.to ROBT.W.SCOTT.

¶JAMES RUCKS had several children by a former marr.-ARTHUR,JAMES T.,HAL.T.,& MALVINA. In May 1827 James,an Atty.in Nashville, marr.LOUISA V.BROWN in Nashville,Tn. In 1843 LOUISA V.(BROWN) RUCKS filed suit for divorce in Adams Co.Ms.(Case#3022-Superior Chanc.Court of Ms.-Drw.92)stating she had 6 children. Louisa is decd.by 1852,when Jas.becomes legal Guard.to the minor ch.MARIA LOUISE, HENRIETTA,MARIAN,LEWIS TAYLOR. Also believe BETTIE B.to be dau.of Louisa. Many Rucks marr.many Yergers. ARTHUR RUCKS marr.MARY MARG.YERGER;BETTIE B.RUCKS marr.ALEX. YERGER;MARIA LOUISE marr.JAS.YERGER;MALVINA marr.Wm.YERGER; HENRIETTA marr.Wm.SWAN YERGER;JAS.T.marr.SALLY B.HUNTER;MARIAN marr.FRANK VALLIANT. There may have been additional ch. Many descendants remain in this area.]

DEED BOOK"P": WASHINGTON CO.MS.
Mar.1853-May 1856

P.300:14 Apr.1854-Deed:John L.Finlay,Treasurer of Wash.Co.Ms. of 1st part,sells for taxes,land in Wash.Co.to Nicholas L.Marr, Agatha S.Inge,Sarah V.Cameron,Mary E.J.Marr,Tennessee E.Venable, of 2nd part.

P.307:18 Mar.1854-Deed:John Willis & wife Annie M.of Warr.Co. Ms.,1st part;Henry W.Vick of same,Trustee of Sarah Vick. Both parties claim title to land in Wash.Co.Ms.located T14,R6W-833 + ac. They sign an agreement to swap & buy other land to settle dispute.

P.314:29 July 1853-Deed:Andrew J.Paxton and wife Hannah M. sell, for $12 per ac.land on East side of Deer Creek-T.7,R7W-bounded on West by creek @1300 ac.to Hugh Barefield.

P.326:29 June 1854-Deed:J.D.Goode sells a parcel of land to Thos.H.Hill,Guard.,of Nicholas Warren,minor,for Nicholas's sole use.

P.328:3 JUly 1954-Deed Alex.Yerger & wife Eliz.B.(Rucks)Yerger & Jas.H.Yerger of Wash.Co.Ms.,to Grant A.Bowen & Jacob S. Yerger of same[Note;GRANT ALLEN BOWEN is brother to JACOB SHALL YERGER"S wife MARY H.(BOWEN)YERGER]

P.334:29 July 1854-Marriage Contract:Morris Ash of Wash.Co.Ms. is contemplating marr. with Ernestine Ash,formerly of City and State of New York. Morris settles a trust fund of $5,000 with 8% int.to be taken out of the merchandise of firm of ASH & HORWITZ located in Greenville,Ms. Michaels Horwitz is to be Trustee.[NOTE:It is clear that ERNESTINE was an ASH before she marr. MORRIS ASH.]

P.338:21 Oct.1845-Deed:Jas.B.Chaplain;Chas.L.Chaplain and wife Frances E.;Anna Maria C.Chaplain;Geo.Henry Chaplain all of Dorchester Co.Md.,and Edw.K.Chaplain and wife Ameniade(sp.difficult to read)C.,of Adams Co.Ms.,heirs at law of Wm.R.T.Chaplain,late of Claib.Co.Ms.,decd.Quit claim to John Murdock of Claib.Co.Ms.,their undivided 1/3rd part of land in Wash.Co.Ms. located in T15,R6W.

P.353:4 Aug.1854-Deed:Surviving Heirs of Matthew Smylie,decd., late of Ms.,sell to Thos.L.Terry of Claib.P.La.. Signed in Hinds Co.Ms.by Mary C.Wilkinson-by authorization of D.M.Wilkinson;L.J.Smylie,Rabecca A.McFatter,Eliza J.McPherson.

P.386:25 Jan.1853-Deed:Evan Stevenson & wife Lydia of Scott Co.Ky.,and Edw.Stevenson of Macoupin Co.Ill.,sell to Alfred D.Offutt & John W.Bradley,Jr. the land that Thos.H.Bradford and wife Sarah sold to Evan and Edw.Stevenson in 1847.

P.407:15 July 1854-Deed:Victor M.Flournoy and wife Elizabeth J.*;Marcellus Flournoy and wife Polly; Henry Johnson and wife Eliza J.*;Robt.J.Ward and wife Emily;------Sanders-all parties of the 1st part;toMary J.Kershaw,wife of Thos.Kershaw. A title bond executed by M.(Matthew)Flournoy to Cornelius Haring;and from Haring to Kershaw. Heirs of Matthew Flournoy release full rights(*Denotes those who signed in Fayette Co.Ky.)

P.408:20 May 1854-Deed:Mary Jane Kershaw and husband Thos.Kershaw,both of Pass Christian,Ms.,sell for $30,000 to (Cont.)

DEED BOOK "P":WASHINGTON CO.MS.
Mar.1853-May 1856

(cont.)Mrs.Ann Matthew of S.C. @1600 ac.of land in Wash.Co.Ms.

P.410:6 Sept.1851-P.O.A.:At Georgetown,Ky.:Thos.P.Johnson of San Francisco, gives his P.O.A.to Wm.Warren Johnson of New Orleans to protect the rights of Thos.'s wife Laura Johnson,late Laura Miller dau.of John C.Miller,decd.,(a later document in DBk."P",p.497-dated 1855 gives W.W.Johnson,full powers to act in all matters pertaining to the inheritance of Laura from the Millers.)

P.413:30 Dec.1854-D/T:Henry Johnson,Sr.& wife Eliza J.of Fayette Co.Ky.,of 1st part;Thos.S.Redd of same-2nd pt;Margaret A.Erwin of same-3rd pt; The Johnsons sell "MT.HOLLY PLTN".-1699 ac.for $100,000.Henry Johnson bought this Pltn.from John C.Miller in 1833. Miller then sold part to Junius R.Ward + 110 slaves.

P.425:26 Jan.1855-Deed:F.A.Metcalfe and wife Martha Pricilla of Wash.Co.Ms.,sell to Wm.H.Hammet of same. "Lammermoor Pltn." for $32,000,Located in T14,R9W,+some in T15,R9W-640+ac.

P.437:5 Jan.1855-Deed:"Mistress Elizabeth Barker,formerly Hazard,Wife of Jacob Barker"of New Orleans, sells to John H.Sims, Chas.Sims,Wm.R.Sims,all of Wilkinson Co.Ms.

P.438-439:10 Feb.1855-Mortg:Ann D.Halsey of Vicksburg,negotiates with Sterling Neblett of Brickland,Va. for time to pay off Loan made to the late Stephen M.Jackson in 1837. Neblett agrees to swap some land he bought from Herbert W.Hill located at Bachelor's Bend(Wash.Co.)for some other of hers.[NOTE: Ann Dunn Hill,dau.of Richard Hill & Nancy Dunn,marr.1st-Stephen M.Jackson. He decd.,Jan.1847,and ANN D.(HILL)JACKSON marr. 2nd,Dr.Seymour Halsey in 1851. He decd.,soon after their marr. and ANN D.(HILL)JACKSON HALSEY returned to Wash.Co. The Will of NANCY DUNN HILL-Warr.Co.Ms. Will Bk."A",p.313;Written-5 Apr.1860-No Probate date.
Names;Daus;FRANCES E.ELLIOTT,MINERVA G.MILLS,ANN D.HALSEY
    Gr.dau;MARY FRANCES HILL
    Gr.sons;THOS.H.HILL,C.H.HILL,WM.E.HILL
    Son:HERBERT W. HILL
    Gr.Dau.;NANCY D.HILL
    Exec:son,HERBERT W.HILL
Wit:F.C.Jones,O.H.Mixson.
Warr.Co.Ms.Will Bk."A",p.314-Will of Wm.E.Hill-writ.18 Feb. 1862:He states he has ch.,but does not name them;names his wife Virginia execx;Wit;H.W.Hill,Robt.Wm.Harris,Matthew J.Harris Robt.T.Tucker.taken from Jackson Family papers:Census 1850 Wash.Co.,Warr.Co.,;Court Rec.Wash. & Warr.Co.'s]

P.440:16 Nov.1854-Deed:Claib.P.La.:Bird Williams,for "myself and heirs of John Williams,decd."and Fanny Williams,wife of said John late of Hds.Co.Ms.and Eliza Whittington,heir of said John ofthe 1st part;sell to Thos.L.Terryof Claib.P.La.-land in Wash. Co.Ms.Wit:J.R.Wilder,F.M.Hays.

P.445:26 Dec.1854-Deed:Endora Likens of Wash.Co.,Ms.Widow of Thos.J.Likens,decd.,of same,sells land to Edw.W.Jack of Warr. Co.Ms.[NOTE:for the Will of T.J.Likens-see Vol.I,this series]

DEED BOOK "P": WASHINGTON CO.MS.
Mar.1853-May 1856

P.450:1 Jan.1855-Deed:Wade Hampton,Jr.makes a series of Prom. notes to Wade Hampton for $170,000+-notes endorsed by WADE HAMPTON & C.F.HAMPTON-land + slaves. All parties are of Columbia,S.C.

P.456:17 Feb.1855-Deed:Wm.H.Paxton of New Orleans sells to Alex.M.Paxton of Vicksburg-1 undivided ½ int.in land located in Sunflower Co.Ms.,+ land in Wash.Co.Ms.

P.457:5 Jan.1855-Petition for Partition:Jas.H.Yerger,Commissioner and Jas.Rucks acknowledge a decree by Sup.Court in June 1854 in case of Jas.Rucks,Maria Louisa Rucks,Henrietta Rucks, Marion Rucks,Lewis Taylor Rucks(Case #5282)over "The Brown Place"located in T15,R9W-Wash.Co.Ms.-1076 + Ac.

P.461:8 Jan.1855-Quit Claim:Orville M.Blanton & wife M.R.; Wm.C.Blanton & wife Georgia-heirs at law of Wm.W.Blanton,decd. sell to Robt.M.Carter.

P.496:27 Apr.1855-Deed:Benj.Whitfield and wife Lucy E. of Hinds Co.Ms.sell to Fletcher Creighton,Exec.of Est.of Jonathon McCaleb,decd. of Calib.Co.Ms.

P.512:14 Apr.1855-Deed:John James & wife Mary of Wash.Co.Ms. sell lot to Thos.V.James of same.

P.517:17 Feb.1855-P.O.A.;State of Texas-Co.of Nacogdoches. Achsah Brasher,wife of Essex P.Brasher appoints him her Atty. to handle her inheritance from her brother's Est.-the late Sanders Ward(Jeremiah Sanders Ward),who died while residing in Ms.[NOTE:Est. of J.S.Ward;Wash.Co.Ms.Pkt.#148,Drw.4.Abst. in Vol.II,p.148 EMR.of this series.In this Est.Achsah is called AMY,and Essex is called ESSIE. But she signed the above document ACHSAH.]

P.522:19 Apr.1855-Deed:Wm.H.Lee of Wash.Co.sells to Nathl.W. Lee,Harry Percy Lee, John M.Lee of same, tracts of land located on Deer Creek-all in T18,R7W-740+ ac.

P.523:6 June 1855-Deed:John H.Sims,Chas.Sims & wife Philadelphia,Wm.R.Sims and wife Lizzie(she signs E.L.)all of Wilk.Co., Ms.,sell to L.L.Taylor of Wash.Co.

¶Many pages of land being sold for non-payment of taxes.County Officials at this time-1855 were:
Sheriff & Tax Collector-Jas.H.Yerger
Clerk-J.J.Caughey
Dep.Clerk-M.L.Worthington

P.560:30 June 1855-Deed:John L.Finlay,Adm.,with Will annexed of Wm.H.Lawson,decd.,of Wash.Co.Ms.,whose Will appoints Wm. Tompkins his exec.-but he renounced and the court accepted Finlay,who in turn, under the terms of the will sold slaves + property at Public Auction to Wm.Hunt.[NOTE:Will not recorded in this Deed Bk. but is rec.in Will Bk.1,p.207-and abst. in Vol.I of this series,p.77.]

P.561:7 Mar.1855-Deed:New Orleans,La.Alex.C.Bullett & wife Frances Elizabeth of New Orleans sell her share of the Pltn. "Longwood"for $200,000,+ slaves to Mistress Irene Smith of Louisville,Ky.widow of Benj.Smith,decd.,of KY. The (Cont.)

DEED BOOK "P":WASHINGTON CO.MS.
Mar.1853-May 1856

(Cont)portion of land and slaves were devised to Frances Eliz.
by her late father Benj.Smith,containing 1800 ac.+ a tract called the Basin Tract and adjoining "Longwood"-1600 ac.-having
been purchased from David Threkled & J.M.Brooks(DBk."N"p.544-
546)+another tract adj. the other 2-1200 ac.bought from W.Vogel,
agent. The 3 tracts bounded on North by Pltn.of Seth Cox & wife,
and lands of Robt.W.Johnson,Dr.Buckner,& Jeoffrey James;on
South by Pltn.,of Ward & Miller, land of Junius Ward and others;
on East by PLtn.of Jas.A.McHatton & A.Lashley & Jeoffrey James;
on West by Ms.River,+ a parcel lying between the Pltn.of Seth
Cox and Phil Cox known as Hill Field-140 ac.:+ 210 slaves now
upon said lands,+ stock,etc. + a lot lying in Louisville,Ky.
where the residence of Mistress Irene Smith now stands. Conveyance follows on p.563.[NOTE:a follow-up in Deed Bk.A-3,p52
dated 1889(Wash.Co.),in a deed to the R.R.,and in 1862 parts
are sold to levee right of way. Signed by Irene Williams,Fanny
Bullett & Merritt Williams. WILL OF ALEX.BULLETT-Vol.I p.94
of this series-and Wash.Co.Will Bk "1"-p.390. WILL OF IRENE
SMITH- Will Bk."1"p.95, abst.in Vol.I-p.95 of this series.]

P.568:Jos.G.James and wife Sarah P. of Wash.Co.Ms.sell to Edw.
C.James of same.11Aug.1855.

P.572:7 Oct.1855 Deed:Chicot Co.Ark.-Essex(Essie)Brasher,hus-
band & Atty.of Achsah(Amy)Brasher,transfers to Henry Smith of
same, for $750 of their undistributive share of the Est.of
Jeremiah Sanders Ward,late of Wash.Co.Ms.decd.,intestate. The
Brashers then appoint Smith their Atty.to handle their affairs.
(See Note on page 103)

P.579:3 Dec.1855-Deed:Irene Smith buys "The Black Place"at
public sale,Loc.in T16,R8W + some in T16,R9W,@800 ac.for $5
per acre.

P.581:19 Nov.1855-P.O.A.:A.T.B. Merritt of Richmond,Va.,appoints
Wm.H.E.Merritt & H.E.Merritt or either of them,to buy lands
in Ms.,or act on lands owned jointly with W.H.E.& John G.Parham
+ lands owned separately.

P.609:26 Nov.1855-Deed:John Bull of Shelby Co.Ky.,both for
himself and as exec.of Est.ofRobt.Bull,decd.,of 1st part:
Abram Auter of Vicksburg-2nd part;Auter, in 1842,executed a
Mortg.to John Bull and Jacob Cardwell as joint exec.of Will
of said Robt. Jacob Cardwell has now decd.and a mortg.exists.

P.610:26 Jan.1856-Deed:Andrew Foster Elliott & wife Mistress
Marie Antoinette Odile of New Orleans sell to Henry T.Lonsdale
of same-land in T18,R7W-502 ac.+ 32 ac.-a Pltn.now being work-
ed as a cotton farm + slaves that Elliott and Lonsdale purchased jointly from Wm.Yerger Jan.1855-Schedule of pay.follows.

P.635:3 Feb.1856-P.O.A.:"We,Nathan(X)Freeman & wife Winnaford
(X)Freeman,formerly Winnaford Harris,& Exum Dunning & wife
Martha(X),formerly Martha Harris, all of Shelby Co.Tn.,give
their Power of Att.to Wm.C.Dunlap to Collect their share of
Est.of Turner Joyner,decd.late of Wash.Co.Ms. Martha and Winna-
ford are Daus.of Sally Harris,decd.,who was the sister of said
Joyner. The said Harris sisters ask Dunlap to determine the
validity of the Will of Turner Joyner, and if it is not(cont.)

DEED BOOK"P":WASHINGTON CO.MS.
Mar.1853-May 1856

(cont).valid to immediately file suit.[Note;for Will of Turner Joyner,see Vol.I of this series p.78.Abst.from Will Bk.1.p.212 Wash.Co.Ms.]

P.637:P.O.A.-State of N.C.:Aaron Neale & wife Elizabeth,formerly Eliz.Fox of Franklin Co.N.C.,appoint Jacob Fox of Wash.Co. N.C.,to sell their share of Est.of Burrell Fox of Ms. as "his only heirs". Next document Jacob sells out to Jefferson Compton of Wash.Co.Ms. 1 undivided ½ interest-being all that Burrell owned of a certain parcel of land.

P.642:1 Jan.1856-Deed:Gervas S.Mosley and wife Eliza G.Mosely who was Eliza G.Burks,dau.of Saml.Burks,decd.,late of Wash.Co. Ms.and Ann M.Burks-widow of said Burks sell to Wm.P.Montgomery of same-land along Williams Bayou.[Correct spelling is MOSBY]

¶1856-County Officials;Sherf.-Geo.T.Blackburn;Clerk-J.J.Caughey; Dep.Clk. Arthur 'Hanes.

P.666:26 Mar.1856-Deed John H.Likens,Adm.with Will annexed of Est.of Thos.J.Likens,decd.of Wash.Co.Ms.,sell to Sidney R.Smith of same.

END OF DEED BOOK "P"

ADDITIONAL HUSBANDS & WIVES IN DBK."P",Residence,date of Doc.
ADAMS,DANIEL W.& wife ANNA M.-New Orleans-1856
ALEXANDER,AMOS & wife LAVINIA F.-Adams Co.Ms. -1856
AUTER,ABRAHAM & wife JULIA- Vicksburg,-1854
BOLAND,JOHN & wife ELLEN MARIANE-Warren Co.Ms.-1853
BROWNING,JOHN A. & wife MARY L.-of Va.-1854
BURNEY,ROBT.W. & wife MARY F.-of Madison P.,La.-1855
CARTER,ROBT.M & wife E.M.-Wash.Co.Ms.-1851
CLARK,JOHN C. & wife GEORGIANA-Wash.Co.Ms.-1852
COLEMAN,LOYD & wife HARRIET L.- Warren Co.Ms.-1853
COOPER,JAS.A. & wife ELLEN E. -Wash.Co.Ms.-1856
COX,ROBT. & wife LAURA LEMINDA-Jeff.Co.Ms. -1855
DAVIS,JOS.E. & wife ELIZA Warren Co.Ms.1854
DOWNING,RUBEN N.& wife ELIZABETH-Vicksburg-1853
GAMBLE,FELIX G. & wife MARY V.- Wash.Co.Ms.-1854
GOODE,J.D. & wife SOPHIA-Wash.Co.Ms. 1854
GREARES,THOS. & wife ISABELLA F.-Jackson,Ms. -1854
HARDEMAN,WM. & wife MARY M.-Hinds Co.Ms. -1853
HARVEY,JAS.R. & WIFE ELEANORA- Wash.Co.Ms.-1853
HAYES,JAS.B. & wife CHARLOTTE M.-Warr.Co.Ms.-1848
HUFFSTICKLER,ABEL & wife CAROLINE-Wash.Co.Ms. 1856
JAMES,THOS.V. & wife NANCY-Wash.Co.Ms.-1855
JETER,JOHN J. & wife ANN W.-New Orleans-1853
KILPATRICK,ELIHU & wife JARUSHA A.-Wash.Co.Ms.-1853
LASHLEY,ARNOLD & wife LUCRETIA C.-Louisville,Ky.-1854
LIKENS,JOHN H. & wife MARY J.-Berkeley Co. Va.-1855
MARSHALL,THOS.A. & wife LETITIA-of Vicksburg-1855
MILLER,JAS.W. & wife MARTHA A.----1853
PERKINS,WM.P. & wife JANE M.-Madison Co.Ms.-1844
PICKENS,JOHN O. & wife F.H.- Wash.Co.Ms.-1852

(Cont.)

(CONT.)HUSBANDS & WIVES FROM DBK."P".Res.& date of Doc.
RIGBY,DAVID & wife ELIZABETH- Warren Co.Ms.-1853
SHEPHARD,JOHN E. & wife MARTHA-Hinds Co.Ms.-1853
SMEDES,ABRAHAM & wife THOMASINA-Warren Co.Ms.-1854
SMITH,HENRY & wife CECILIA L.-Chicot Co.Ark.-1854
SMITH,JAS.P. & wife SARAH-Hinds Co.Ms. -1854
SMITH,S.T. & wife BETTIE B.-Louisville,Ky.-1854
TARPLEY,C.S. & wife ELIZA W. -Wash.Co.Ms.-1853
THRELKELD,D.H. & wife ORPHA E.-Wash.Co.Ms. -1850
WARD,GEO.W. & wife JOSEPHINE -Fayette Co.Ky.-1855
WEST,JOS.M. & wife MARY JANE-Holmes Co.Ms.-1856
===
SUPPLEMENTARY INFORMATION:WARREN CO.MS.,WILL BOOK"A":

P.60;WILL OF RANDAL GIBSON;Written 1 Nov.1835-Prob.26 Aug.1836
Sons;Ambrose & Wm.Winans Gibson to be Exec.
Wife;Harriet
Sons;Tobias, Claudius, Gideon Gibson
Gr.Ch.-Randall Gibson Higgins,son of Joel & Ann Higgins
 "   -Randall Gibson,son of Tobias & Louisana B.Gibson
 "   -Harriet Gibson Faulk,dau.of Wilson & Martha Faulk
 "   -Harriet Nelson Nailor,dau.of Jefferson & Eliza Nailor
 "   -Son of Wm. & Harriet Gibson
 "   -son and dau. of Ambrose & Marg.C.M.Gibson
Codicile; 7 Jan.1836:Added the name of Gideon & Adline Gibson's
dau.-Harriet Lionly(a gr.ch.)

P.105:WILL OF DAVID HORN:of Warren Co.;Written 4 Aug.1840-Prob.
Oct.1840;Sister-Elizabeth Green, wife of Wm.Green of Ga.
Kinsman;Thos.H.Christmas, Henry Christmas
To affectionate friends and relations Mary E.Christmas and her
son Wm.Hardeman Christmas. Exec. Thos.H.Christmas.

P.107:WILL OF WILLIAM TURNBULL:of Vicksburg;Prob.July 1840.
Native of Cumberland Co.,England. Wants all debts owed to him
to go to his bro-in-law James Brough of England, to be divided
between"my father & 3 sisters-Mary,Elizabeth,Jane. Exec.John
M.Chilton of Vicksburg.

P.242:WILL OF ALFRED C.DOWNS:Written 10 July 1844-Prob.Oct. Term
1857;Cousin Abijah Downs to be exec. with Elijah Pace-my par-
ticular friend who is to also be the Guard. of his 2 ch. Wife-
Mary Jane;2 ch. Henry Augustus Downs & James R.Downs.

P.306:WILL OF WM.A.LAKE:of Vicksburg.Written 13 Aug.1857-no
prob.date:Wife-Ann E.;Children Mary,Louisa,Alice,Willie Ann.
Friend-Geo.S.Yerger.

P.311:WILL OF JOHN HEBRON:Written LaGrange,Warr.Co.Ms.,1 Mar.1862
no prob.date:Wife-Adaline L.Hebron;Dau.Jinny Hebron;Sons-Dr.
John S.(L?),George B.,Daniel N.,Alexander C.:"my two boys Bell
Everett & Everett Bell Hebron;½ of the Est.goes to his ch. by
1st wife-Sarah J.Cameron, John L.Hebron, Geo.B.Hebron,Jinny
Hebron;½ of Est. to wife Adaline and her Children: Exec. son-
in-law Daniel A.Cameron,sons John L.and Geo.
===

DEED BOOK "Q":WASHINGTON CO.MS.
DATED:June 5,1856-May 22 1858--700 pages.

P.8:16 Apr.1856-Deed:Harvey Miller of Ky.,sells to Alex.C.Bullett & Irene Smith of State of Ky.-land in Wash.Co.Ms.

P.12:18 July 1841-Relinq:George Winchester was appointed a Trustee for Frances E.Sprague;at the time she was the wife of Sturgis Sprague,now decd.Sturgis Sprague placed in trust,for Frances E.,land in Natchez set aside in a deed from Thos.Metcalf & Robt. H.Adams. The trust for Frances E. was dated 26 Apr.1827. Also in addition,land in Wash.Co.Ms.,entered at Mt.Salus in 1833 + other tracts since purchased by George Winchester, the Trustee. George now transfers this property to Frances. Recorded 6 Feb.1856.[Note; At the time of the first part of the Trust for Frances E., Sturgis was protecting her rights by having a trusted friend care for her property. She was not allowed to hold title if she had remarried, but the law had been amended by 1848, in favor of Marr.women retaining their own possessions apart from their husbands.]

P.16:2 June 1856-Deed:John M.Milliken & wife Mary G.Milliken-Exec.of the Est.of Joseph Hough,decd.,for purpose of advancement to Minor Milliken,one of the legatees of said Hough, for $5,000-a parcel of land.[Will of Jos.Hough-Wash.Co.Ms.WB1.1, p.183-abstr.in Vol.I EMR-states that Mary G.Milliken is the only child of Jos.Hough, and Minor is one of her children.]

P.18:4 June 1856-Deed:Hannah H.Caldwell of Claib.Co.Ms.,sells to Jane E.Pattison(her sister),land in Yazoo Co.,Hinds Co., Wash.Co.all Ms.,property of late father-Isaac Caldwell. Hannah H. signs Anna H.Caldwell.

P.36:10 July 1856-Deed:Martha W.Bland,wife and now widow of James Bland,decd.;John C.Bland & wife Lucy A.;Robert D.Howe & wife Sarah Eliza;Juliet H.Bland-which said John C.Bland,Sarah E.Howe,Juliet H.Bland are Children of the said James decd., all of Warren Co. and Jas.Bland Littlejohn of New Orleans who is only child of Olivia E.Littlejohn who was also the child of Jas.Bland,decd.,all sell land in S.6;T14;R6W Choctaw Dist. -320 ac.in Issa.Co. to John Willis of Warr.Co.Ms.

P.41:9 Aug.1856-Deed:Sarah F.Buckner & Thos.Freeland Buckner,and all heirs of Robt.H.Buckner agree to let Sarah F. buy out Thos. Freeland's interest in Est.,of his decd.father-for $26,000. They sign in Hinds Co.[All heirs are listed in DBk."N",p.382, also this Vol. Sarah F.Buckner,widow of Robt.H.Buckner was the dau. of Thomas Freeland, whose will is recorded in Claib.Co.Ms. WBk."B"p.218-Rec.28 Jan.1856-nameing his daus. Sarah F.Buckner, Catherine Daniell wife of Smith C.Daniell, and a son Frisby A.Freeland.]

P.47:5 May 1855-Deed:Sybelia A.Selser of Warr.Co.,sells to Geo.Messinger of same-$3,000-land in Wash.Co.,located in T.15, R6W-370 ac.(her brother). Next document-a schedule of payments from Geo.Messinger and wife Sophia to Sybelia.

P.114:13 Feb.1856-Deed:For love and affection-Benj.Whitfield and wife Lucy E. of Hinds Co.Ms. give a gift of land to their dau. Sarah A.E.Griffith wife of Richard Graiffith of Hinds Co. --lands loc.in T18;R8W-Wash.Co.Ms.,1402 ac.

DEED BOOK "Q":WASHINGTON CO.MS.
DATED: 5 June 1856-22 May 1858

P.116:30 Apr.1856-Lease:John J.Caughey,Clerk of Prob.Court of Wash.Co.Ms.,of 1st part;Mary Ann Robb, lately Mary Ann Evans-widow of McLin Evans,decd.,of 2nd part;Caughey states that Evans became Lessee of school lands in 1837-and has paid all notes and the right to continue renting the said lands is extended to Evans' heirs for the rest of the term of 99 yrs.From 1837.

P.127:Christopher Gillespie & wife Nancy E. of Sunflower Co. Ms.,relinq.to Lucellus Gillespie of Wash.Co.Ms.,and to his heirs forever-land in Wash.Co.Ms. Wit:W.W.Hunt; A.Heathman.

P.136:11 Nov.1856-Deed:"I,Jackson C.Hooks of Wash.Co.Ms.,-one of the heirs of Charles Hooks,decd",sells to J.R.Hooks his share in 2 tracts of land in Stewart Co.,Tn.,on North side of Cumberland River, on Cubb Creek.

P.152:17 Mar.1855-Deed:Ralphe North,Commissioner of Prob.Court of Adams Co.Ms.,cites a decree issued 3 Jan.1855 in a certain cause between Thos.Sharp and other heirs and next of kin of Absolom Sharp,decd.,late of said county-were plaintiffs and Clarissa Sharp,Admx. & Alex.K.Farrah,Adm.of said Est.,of Absolom + others, were defendants. A public sale of some of the property of Absolom Sharp,decd.,was conducted, and the buyer was George W.Baynard & wife Mary Jane Baynard of Adams Co. [Note;the other heirs are not listed here]

P.170:29 Dec.1856-Deed:Thos.H.Buckner and wife Louisa of Wash. Co.Ms.,sell 391 ac. + slaves to Edward C.James & wife Martha Ann of same Co.

P.179:--1857-Memo:Title Perfection;On 26 Oct.1846-"I,Samuel Garland"and my wife Mary L. of Lynchburg,Va.,conveyed to Col. Wm.Woods of Albermarle Co.Va.,as Trustee of others who professed to be creditors of "my bro. Wm.Garland,decd.",gave all my rights and interest in a tract of land in Wash.Co.Ms.,formerly owned by Archibald Kinney & Robt.C.Menefee(Menifee,Menessee?) now decd.,the same land bought by Burr Garland at a public sale of land of Menefee's @387 ac. Wm.Wood,now decd.,never recorded the deed and the land was sold for taxes, and John Wood,Jr. of Alber.Co.Va.,agent and Saml.Garland relinq.their claims in favor of Alfred B.Carter & Wm.F.Randolph-both of Wash.Co.Ms. who bought the tract in good faith.

P.188:2 Dec.1855-Deed:Not recorded until 12 Jan.1857:"I,Hubbard Hind Kavanaugh,one of the Bishops of the Methodist Episcopal Church South, under the protection of the Almighty God and with a single eye to his glory--have set apart Wm.F.Camp for office of Deacon in said Church--a proper person to administer the ordinances of Baptism,Marriages,and Burial of the dead, and in absence of an Elder, to feed the flock of Christ."

P.194:9 Jan.1857-Deed:G.W.B.Messinger & wife Sybelia A.,now residents of Issa.Co.Ms.,sell a parcel of land to John Willis of Warren Co.Ms.

P.197:26 Apr.1854-Deed:"Shell Ridge,Wash.Co.Ms.": Heirs of Mrs.Sophia H.Bookout,decd.,of Wash.Co.Ms.and wife of B.R.Bookout,through said B.R.,their natural Guard., pay levee taxes-heirs-Benj.C.Bookout,Anna M.Bookout,George W.Bookout,Sophia H.Bookout.

DEED BOOK "Q":WASHINGTON CO.MS.
June 1856-May 1858

P.207:15 Mar.1856-Deed:David L.Clore and wife Susannah B. & Henry B.Clore & wife Emeline of the State of Ind.;sell to Jacob Roth the former place of residence of Jas.Prince in town of Princeton,Wash.Co.Ms.,where Roth now resides.

P.236:23 Nov.1851-Agreement of Separation:Andrew Carson & wife Elizabeth J.--Owning to great difficulties of disposition and circumstances growing out of same which has destroyed all hope of living together hapily -Agree to live separately and apart. on following conditions:Andrew must put in trust-to J.J.Ross - for Eliz.J.,several slaves + $1466 on 15 Jan.1852 + added payments in lieu of any dower rights to any prop. of Andrew's. Andrew will pay for the Ed.of his 2 ch.and oversee the ed.and upbringing of their son,Andrew B.Carson. Eliz.J.will ed. their dau. Mary L.(orS.),and she will live with her mother. All parties sign this doc. in Bolivar Co.Ms.[Note;"Ms.Court Rec.Superior Ct".by Hendrix p.184;1851-Wash.Co.Ms.,Drw.97,Case #4637- Eliz. Carson vs Andrew Carson,Divorce Petition. Married,1831 at Point Chicot,Ark.]

P.262:10 Sept.1856-Deed:Bythel Haynes & wife Delia of E.Feliciana P.La.,and Wm.Monroe Quin of Pike Co.Ms.:Bythel & wife Delia,formerly DELIA McCAY,were exec.and exectx.of Est.of Robert McCay,decd.,of Pike Co.Ms. The Will instructed the exec. to use the profits from certain lands for the use of Courtney Ann Boatner,dau. of said Robt.McCay,decd.,and wife of Jas.W. Boatner of Morehouse P.La. The Boatners release all claim to "the worthless lands" in Ms.

P.275:12 Feb.1857-Article of Division:John F.Warren & wife Agnes F.,formerly Agnes F.Miller;Thos.P.Johnson & wife Laura M.formerly Laura M.Miller & Jane H.Miller,widow and relict of John C.Miller,decd.,left a large Est. He was the father of Agnes and Laura. The widow Jane H.chooses to take 1/3rd instead of dower rights, and a division of slaves follows.

P.277:23 Jan.1857-Deed:New York City;Eliz.Barker,born Hazard, with consent of husband Jacob Barker,sells land to Montgomery & Kirk.

P.280:11 Feb.1857-Deed:John Tackett & wife Eliza.A.;George W. L.Byrd & wife Eliz.B.;James M.Roberts & wife Sarah A. all of Holmes Co.Ms.,sell 3760 ac. to Lewis G.Galloway.

P.292:-- Mar.1857:Deed:Henry Davison & wife Matilda of N.Y. City and Elias Davison & wife Charlotte of same, sell a lot in town of Greenville,Ms. to Morris Ash, & Michael Horwitz of Greenville.

P.301:31 Mar.1857-Deed:Richard Brenner of New Orleans sells to Lionel Walden:Zoe Walden,nowMrs.Morgan wife of Thos.G.Morgan who consents to this act;Ellen Walden now Mrs.Walden,wife of Phillip E.Walden who consents;Tredwell Walden:& Lowd T. Walden,-all being over 18 yrs.and being children & heirs of Daniel T.Walden,decd.,who during his lifetime was a citizen of N.O.and all heirs reside in N.O.,Land title muddied by the bankruptcy of Passmore Hoopes & Wilhemine Bogart in 1842 under the firm name of BOGART & HOOPES of N.O.when certain tracts of land were sold.

DEED BOOK "Q":WASHINGTON CO.MS.
June 1856-May 1858

P.311:19 Feb.1857-Deed:Carroll P.La.:John W.Keene,Esq.,"my decd.husband"sold to Wm.R.Elly 1 undivided ½ of certain lands-992 ac.in all. The widow of Keene,decd.,Frances E.Keene,signs a relinq. Wit:Keene Richards;R.A.Johnson.

P.315:8 Sept.1854-Mortg.:John E.Fitzpatrick of Hinds Co.Ms. of 1st part;Abram K.Smedes & Geo.A.McAlpin- both of Vicksburg of 2nd part;George Smedes of New Orleans and Chas.E.Smedes of Vicksburg-merchants doing business as SAYLE,GEORGE SMEDES & BRO. of 3rd part.

P.323:14 Mar.1857-Deed/Gift:Aug.W.McAllister,Sr. & wife Caroline S.give to their son, for love and affection, a tract of land @480 ac. The son's name is Augustus W.,Jr.,all of Wash.Co.

P.415:28 Feb.1856-P.O.A.:Gonzales Co.Tx.,Jas.T.Matthew and wife Eliza Ann appoint Wm.Harris of Warr.Co.Ms.,to conduct their business in Ms. and La.-and "anywhere else".

P.430:1 June 1857-Quit Claim:Catherine Segur(?),John Irish, Wm.Irish of Attala Co.Ms.,-heirs of Wm.T.Irish,decd.sell for $1240, land located in T14,R6W and in T14,R7W to Elijah H.Sanders of same. Land in Wash.Co.Ms.

P.431:30 May 1857-Deed:Oliver Barrett & Lucy Cordill,relict and widow of Richard Cordill,decd.,of Hinds Co.,sell 1500+ ac. to R.L.Dixon of Wash.Co.Ms. Land bought from Jas.C.James by Dixon and Rich.Cordill and now owned and occupied by Dixon as a plantation.

P.432:9 June 1857-Deed:G.N.Jordan employed Sharkey,Withers, & Daniel Mayes as counsel in a suit entered against Jordan about his right to 1/5th part of Est.of Benjamin Roach,decd., as derived through Jordan's late wife-May Jordan(who was the dau. of said Benj.Roach.).Jordan is claiming in right of his decd.children who survived their mother. Jordan agreed to pay counsel 15% of amount of said Est. Schedule of payments follow. Jordan signed in Warren Co. Ms.

P.450:2 Apr.1857-Right of Way:J.N.Nelson of Wash.Co.Ms. grants ROW to Messrs.Montgomery & Kirk for a road from "this pltn. on the line between S15 & 16;T14 to or near Fish Lake Bridge in T18,R8W-by Gate or lane as may be best suited for N.J.Nelson.

P.456:1 Apr.1857-Deed:Wm.McKinstry & wife Mary;Wm.D.McKinstry & wife Margaret of Frankfort,Ky.,sell to Miles S.Browne of Yazoo Co.Ms.,land in Wash.Co.Ms.

P.470:1 Dec.1856-P.O.A.:Henry A.Rodewall & Eliza M.Rodewald, widow of late Henry Rodewald,decd.,acting both in her separate right as Guard.of the minor children Frederick & Henrietta Rodewald--all of Baltimore,Md.,appoint John Rodewald of New Orleans their lawful atty.,to sell land in Wash.Co.Ms.

P.472:2 Apr.1857-Deed:Henry A.Rodewald,Eliza M.Rodewald,widow of late Henry Rodewald, Frederick Rodewald & Henrietta Rodewald all of Baltimore and Henry Rodewald & wife Eliza J. & John Rodewald of New Orleans sell to Harvey Latham of Hds.Co.Ms.

DEED BOOK "Q":WASHINGTON CO.MS.
June 1856-May 1858

P.475:30 June 1857-Mortg:T.J.James,Jr.of Wash.Co.Ms.1stpart;
Jos.G.James & wife Sarah J.of same,of 2nd.

P.476:16 Mar.1857-Mortg:Catherine Segar(sp.Sequr in another
doc.),Guard. of Wm.,David, & James Irish,minor heirs of Wm.T.
Irish, late of Attalla Co.Ms. and now decd.;sell to Elijah H.
Sanders of same Co.

P.516:21 May 1844-Deed:Durant H.Arnold & wife Mary M.;James
R.Shackleford and wife Elizabeth;Levi W.Arnold & wife Arreanne
(sp.varies,Arra Ann,etc.);Mary Arnold;Stephen B.Arnold;Allen
Arnold- all of Carroll Co.Ms.,and heirs of their decd.brother
Peter Arnold;sell to James R.Enloe of Bolivar Co.Ms.

P.520:30 Jan.1857-Deed:Susan L.Hardaway,et al to Horatio W.
Spencer. Susan L. Hardaway & Minerva Scott of Warr. Co.Ms.;
Jacob W. Payne & wife Charlotte B.Payne; Jilson P.Harrison &
wife Sidney Ann of New Orleans, sell to Horatio W.Spencer of
Claib.Co.Ms.

P.522:3 Feb.1855-Deed:Robt.B.Scott & wife Louisa J.;Jos.P.Hawks
& wife Mary Jane Rebecca;Jos.P.Hawks as Guard. for Juliana S.
Randolph;Mary A.Fisher- all of Warr.Co.Ms.;Jacob W. Payne &
Jil P.Harrison of New Orleans, known as Payne & Harrison; Division of property, as set out in the Will of Thomas P. Hardaway,¶
decd.in Warr.Co.,-Adm. is Susan L.Hardaway. The following division was made;ROBT.B.SCOTT-$6,000;MARY J.B.HAWKS-$3,000;JOS.
P.HAWKS-$3,000 as Guard.to JULIANA;MARY A.FISHER-$6,000. Written
opposite signatures,"this act does not convey any right title
or interest belonging to JULIANA S.RANDOLPH under the Will of
THOS.P.HARDAWAY,decd.as a reversionary legatee,in the event
that she survives MISS MINERVA B.SCOTT--this done before sign-
ing- J.P.HAWKS,Guard."
¶[NOTE;Warr.Co.Ms.Will Book "A"p.199:Will of Thos.P.Hardaway-
Written 1 Apr.1853- Probated June Term 1853;
Wife;SUSAN S.(or)L.HARDAWAY
Neice;MARY ANN FISHER
   "   MARY J.R.HAWKS
Neph;ROBT.B.SCOTT
To JULIANA S.Randolph
To MINERVA B.SCOTT,dau.of my decd.neph.THOS.B.SCOTT
Wit;Herbert H.Hill, Jos.N.Parks,Saml.G.Parks.]

P.532:30 June 1857-Deed:Georgetown Dist.,S.C.:Daniel Tucker
& wife Sarah- late Sarah Allan;Joseph R.Tucker & wife Claudia
T.;Mary J.Allan heirs of Robt.M.Allan,decd.,of S.C. sell to
Geo.M.Pinckard of New Orleans. WHEREAS: on 11 Apr.1844,Thos.
D.Conday,as exec.,of Robt.M.Allan,decd.,sold to John L.Chapman
of Wash.Co.Ms.,land in said county called the "Glen Allan Est".
and described as follows;Bounded on West by Lake Washington;
On South by lands of Jonathon McCaleb;on East by lands bought
by Chapman from Frederick G.Turnbull; on North by lands of
Wade Hampton-@500 ac.+ slaves.On 14 May 1857,Andrew Turnbull
and parties of 1st part noted above, obtained a decree in Chan.
Court of Wash.Co.Ms. against Chapman for $53,000 or more, and
Pinchard has become entitled to that land.[NOTE:Robt. M.Allan
and Andrew Turnbull were Bro.-in-law.]

DEED BOOK "Q":WASHINGTON CO.MS.
June 1856-May 1858

P.540:5 Sept.1857-Deed/Gift;"For love and affection I bear for my neice Sally Myra Edgar" a gift of a negro girl named Linda, about 6 yrs.of age. Should the neice decd.without heirs, the negro girl will become the property of "my sister" Julia A. Edgar for her natural life. Docu.signed by Wm.H.Browning of Wash.Co.Ms.

P.552:.0 Aug.1857-Deed/Gift;"For love and affection" Andrew Turnbull,Sr.gives to his 2 sons-Dr.Robt.James Turnbull of Wash. Co.Ms. and Andrew Turnbull,Jr.of Issa.Co.,a tract of land in Wash.Co.known as the "Mound Bayou" tract to be divided equally. An O.P. Division of this prop.on p.554.10 Aug.1857,Issa.Co.

P.555;22 Dec.1856-Mortg:John M.Bott & wife E.F.Bott of Wash. Co.Ms.,of 1st part;borrow from Pamelia B.Swan of Phillips Co. Ark.

P.559:11 Mar.1856-Deed:Jonathon T.Sims Commissioner, in response to a decree in case known as Zenas K.Fulton vs John H. Robb,et al #4810 in Superior Court of the Chanc.,13 Feb.1856, transfers land in Wash.Co.Ms. to Annie L.Robb and her infant children Ann Robb,Eugene Robb,Laura Robb,Jos.Robb,Martha Robb, F.Robb. John H.Robb being the husband of said Annie L. and father of minor children.

P.604:12 Dec.1857-Deed:Thos.E.Vick of La.& H.O.Vick & Jas.M. Brabston and wife Roche H.(Robinson)Brabston of Warr.Co.,sell to John Willis.[NOTE:From the John Wesley Vick Bible;John W. Vick marr.,1828,Anna Maria Brabston,dau. of Thos.Brabston-issue,4 children.1.Thos.Eugene,2.Hartwell Overton,3.Harriet, 4.Martha. JOHN WILLIS is a cousin of the Vicks.]

P.618:30 Aug.1857-Deed:Peyton H.Skipwith and wife Catharine A. of New Orleans,sell lands that had been patented to Jas.B. Griffing and wife Martha L.Griffing,to Philip St.George Cocke of Powhatan Co.Va.

P.630:May 1857-P.O.A.:Jas.Wallace & wife Frances A. of Holmes Co.Ms.,appoint Robt.Wallace of Yazoo Co.to handle all of their affairs.

P.650:11 Dec.1857-Partition Agreement:Benj.Roach,exec.of last Will and Test.,of Benj.Roach,decd.,makes settlement with G.N. Jordan,who is entitled to 1/5th part of said Est. Benj.seeks a settlement on Jordan's claims against crops on various pltns. One in Adams Co.Ms.,shall be appraised, and Benj.must deliver to Jordan a Pltn. on Silver Creek in Yazoo Co.-1400 ac.known as "Pedandiere" which joins Jordan,+ all slaves on Pltn. with a few named exceptions, all stock except David Roach's horse. Each chooses arbiters.(Jordan was marr. to May Roach,now decd.)

P.658:22 Nov.1857:Bishop John Earley of Meth. Epis.Church So. appoints Wm.G.Millsaps for Deacon.

P.663:22 Mar.1858-Deed:Henry H.Morris sells to Robt.H.Carter, A.Grayson Carter,Elizabeth L.Carter-all of Wash.Co.Ms.

P.690:6 Apr.1858-Deed:Henry W.Vick of Wash.Co.Ms.,Trustee of minor heirs of Sarah Vick,decd.and Henry G.Vick of Wash.Co.-one of the heirs. Other Heirs and children of Henry W.Vick(Cont)

DEED BOOK "Q":WASHINGTON CO.MS.
Jume 1856-May 1858

(Cont.)and Sarah now decd.,Mary B.Vick,Geo.R.E.Vick; Land conveyed in deed 1850; Also land from Gray J.Vick,decd. Henry W. & Henry G.Vick then appoint referees,E.M.Lane,W.T.Barnard,H.O. Vick to handle the partition. P.680:Henry G.Vick receives control of slaves left to him in the Will of Burwell Vick-dated 19 Mar.18--,left with Henry W.Vick,Trustee.

END OF DEED BOOK "Q"
HUSBANDS & WIVES FROM DEED BOOK"Q":RESIDENCE,DATE OF DOCUMENT
Ambrose,Jas.and w.Almira D.,Holmes 1856
Archer,Jas.and w. Mary Ann, Jeff.Co.Ms.,1857
Bagley,John G. and w.Cornelia, Madison Co.Ms.,1855
Biddell,John A.and w. Frances Ann, Wash.Co.Ms.,1856
Boice,Squire B. and w. Mary Ann, Wash.Co.Ms.,1856
Brecount,Soloman and w. Mary Ann, Warren Co.Ms.,1856
Briggs,Wm. and w. Susan A.,Wash.Co.Ms.,1857
Buck,John W. and w. Mary Bell, Wash.Co.Ms. 1857
Caughey,Saml.N. and w. Rebecca E., Chicot Co.Ark.,1857
Crawford,Erasmos S. and w. Elvira A., Wash.Co.Ms.,1857
Farrar,Alex.K. and w. Ann M., Adams Co.Ms.,1856
Ford,Jas.C. and w. Mary Jane, of Louisville,Ky., 1858
Ford,Wm.G. and w. Mary L.,Memphis,1856.[Note;The Fords owned
    thousands of ac. along the levee right-of-way]
Gains,Wm.F. and w. Ann D., Warren Co.Ms., 1857
Gray,Nicholas and w. Ellen N., Warr rn Co.Ms.1849
Harper,Thos.J. and w. Mary J., Warren Co.Ms. 1856
Harwood,John C. and w. Mary E. Warren Co.MS. 1857
Hines,Wm. and w. Ann F., Warren Co.Ms.1856
Holt,A.C. and w. Mary W., Wilkinson Co.Ms.1856
Hopkins,Arthur F. and w. Juliet A.,Mobile,Ala. 1856
Katz,Simon and w. Triezy, Wash.Co.Ms.,1857
Kelly,Alex.B. and w. Anna M., New Orleans, 1857
Kinney,Nicholas C. and w. Mary Ann, Aug.Co.Va.,1856
Langley,Wm.S. and w. Sophia D.,Hinds Co.Ms. 1856
Lofton,Walter C. and w. Mary Ann, Issa.Co.Ms. 1856
McDougall,John and w. Minerva, New Orleans, 1856
McLeod,Benj.P. and w. Mary, Green Co.Ms.,1858
Marshall,Thos.A. and w. Letitia, Vicksburg, 1856
Miller,Jas.W. and w. Martha A., Hinds Co.Ms.,1854
Mims,Levingston and w. Emma, Vicksburg, 1857
Moore,John M. and w. Mary Virginia, Hinds Co.Ms.,1857
Morehead,Chas.S. and w. Margaret, Frankfort,Ky.,1857
Newman,S.B.and w. Mary Bell, Wash.Co.Ms. 1857
Paxton,Alex.M. and w. Mary S.(or L), Warren Co.Ms.1856
Putnam,Waldo and w. Eliza J., Hinds Co.Ms.,1856
Richardson, Saml.B. and w. Eliza Juliet, Louisville,Ky.,1855
Rucks,Henry and w. Sarah J.,Washington Co.Ms. 1857
Sanders,Wm. and w. Marg.A.,Carroll Co. 1856
Scott,John F. and w. Frances-----1857
Simms,Jonathan T. and w. Anna V., Hinds Co.Ms.,1856
Sullivan,David and w. Martha, Wash.Co.Ms. 1858
Summers,Geo.W. and w. Maria Jane, Hinds Co.Ms. 1856
Taylor,Saml.P. and w. Jane L., Tipton Co.Tn., 1857
Thompson,Jacob W. and w. Catherine A.,Lafayette Co.Ms.,1857

(CONT)HUSBANDS & WIVES FROM DEED BK."Q":RES.,DATE OF DOCUMENT

Watson,Jonathan and w. Joanna L., Titusville,Crawford Co. Pa.
West,R.C. and w. Frances M., Wilkinson,Co.Ms. 1858
Wood,Wm. and w. Margaret, N.Y.City ,1857

SUPPLEMENTARY INFORMATION:THE VICK FAMILY
NEWITT VICK,son of WILLIAM VICK was born Va.Mar.17,1766-decd.
Ms. 5 Aug.1819
Marr. 16 Apr.1791,Va.-Elizabeth Clark who died on the same day
as her husband-5 Aug.1819

The Children of Newitt and Elizabeth(Clark)Vick:
1. Hartwell Vick b Va.,5 Mar.1792-decd.Ms.,Marr.Va.,Sylvia Cook
2. Sally C.Vick b Va.22 Jan.1794-marr.John Lane 1820 in Ms.
3. Nancy Vick b.Va.9 Dec.1794-d. Memphis 1832,Marr.Dr.R.A.Irion
4. Mary Tirza Vick b.Va.3 Oct.1797,Marr.John Henderson
5. Martha Vick b.N.C.20 Feb.1800-never married
**6. Eliza White Vick b.N.C.10 Dec.1801,marr.Col.Henry Morse,who
    was b.21 Dec.1794,Sharon,Vt..They were marr.10 Mar.1822,Vicks-
    burg,Ms. Both buried present Cypress Grove Cemetery,N.O.,La.
7. Lucy W.Vick b.N.C.--1803,marr.John Lawson Irwin
8. John Wesley Vick b.Ms.1806-marr.Maria Ann Brabston in Adams
   Co.,8 May 1828:John Wesley Vick marr.2nd Letitia Francis Booker
   on 22 Oct.1839:He marr.3rd Catherine Barbour in Danville, Ky.
   7 Oct.1845.
9. William Vick b.Ms.22 Dec.1807,d.1859.Never married.
10. Matilda Louise Vick b.Ms.16 Mar.1810,marr.Dr.Sam'l D.McCray
11. Emily Franklin Vick b.Ms.
12. Amanda Maria Vick b.Ms.12 June 1812,marr.Rev.C.K.Marshall
13. Newitt Holmes Vick b.Warren Co.Ms.11June 1819,d.Ms.1855,nev.marr.

**Issue of Eliza White Vick and Col.Henry Morse
1. Rev.Henderson Anthony Morse marr.2nd Mary J.Stenlinger
2. Emily Vick Morse b.9 May 1834,marr.8 May 1851 John George Glover
   She died 29 Jan.1892 New Orleans,La.
3. Alexander G.Morse b.27 Aug.1836 marr.Amanda F.Dortch.He decd.
   1867
##4. Eliza Hulda Morse b.1827 Vicksburg,marr.,Warren Co. as his
    2nd wife-John Greenway Parham. She decd.early 1889
5. Lucinda Morse marr.---Ponder of Camden,Ark.
6. The Henry A.Morse named in Deed Bk"E"p.415,app.died young.

##Issue of Eliza Hulda Morse and Dr.John Greenway Parham
1. James Greenway Parham b.1Dec.1847 Vicksburg,Ms.d.young
2. Henry Greenway Parham b.5 Apr.1849 New.Orleans,d.Anguilla Ms.
   marr.Mary Belle Andrews.
3. Rosa Morse Parham b.17 Jan.1851 N.O.,marr.Solomon Frank
4. Junius Greenway Parham b.28 Nov.1853 N.O. d 1937 Rolling Fork
   Ms.,marr.29 Apr.1877,Alice Gertrude Stevens.
5. Linus Parker Parham b.18 Sept.1855,St.Helens Parish,La.d.N.O.
   La.1857
6. Lucinda Morse Parham b.13 July 1859 St.Helens P.La.,marr.
   Williard Chamberlain
7. John Greenway Parham b.26 Feb.1863 St.Helens P.La.d. 1864

##Eliza Hulda Morse Parham marr.2nd Martin Haney

-115-

DEED BOOK "R":WASHINGTON CO.MS.
DATED:Apr.1858-25 May 1860
This DBk. has been divided into 2 Vols. Vol.1 contains pgs.1-384-Apr.1858-Mar.1859. Vol.II. pgs.385-718-Apr.1859-May 1860.
It is very faded,patched,writing very difficult to read. Its reduced size does make it easier to handle. On microfilm,but would be extremely difficult to read.

P.80:26 Apr.1858-Deed:Butler Co.Ohio-Minor Milliken & wife Mary Mollyneaux(carefully spelled)sell a tract of land to Edwin G.Cook & wife Olive M.-640 ac.[NOTE:Minor is a grandson of Jos.Hough]

P.82:21 July 1858-Deed:Jas.D.Blencoe,Comm.in Chanc.in the case of W.P.Barton and wife vs Chas.E.Smedes,et all #38 on Dkt.of Chanc.Court of Wash.Co.Ms.,Court orders Wm.Brodnax,Edw.Brodnax, Chas E.Smedes & wife Martha L.-formerly Brodnax,Abram K.Smedes & wife Thomasina L.-formerly Brodnax,Mary T.Brodnax,W.E.Brickell & wife Helen,formerly Brodnax,Adele Brodnax & Roberta Brodnax to turn over the land to Lucy H.Barton-wife of Wm.P.Barton of Warren Co.Ms.

P.87:17 July 1858-Deed:Harvey Miller of 1st part:Edw.P.Johnson-trustee-2nd:Mrs.Betty A.Miller-3rd. Betty owned a house and lot in City of Lexington,Ky.,in her own right and her husband Harvey Miller, was paid $10,000 of the purchase money. He,in turn transfers a tract of land in Wash.Co.Ms.,where the Pltn.and residence of said Betty and Harvey Miller was.

P.92:11 July 1858-Deed:Chas.A.Harris of Austin Co.Tx.,sells land on Sunflower River in Wash.Co.Ms.,to Minerva Harris of Vicksburg. P.93:11July 1858-D:Benj.F.Harris & wife Josephine of Tx.,sell all their rt.in land on Sunf.River to Minerva Harris.

P.95:16 July 1858-Deed:Randall Gibson & wife Louisiana of Warr. Co.Ms. give to David Gibson,Jr. a tract of land in Wash.Co.Ms.

P.96:15 July 1858-Deed:David Gibson,Jun. & wife Jane N.of Warr. Co. sell to E.B.Willis whose wife is Margaret E.

P197:17 July 1858-Deed:Thos.J.Gibson & wife Minerva N.-for $1 paid by David Gibson,Jr. of Warr.Co.Ms.

P.117:3 Apr.1858-Deed:Jos.Woods & wife Jane;John Bell & wife Jane:James Woods & wife Rebecca;Jas.Woods as Exec. of Robt.Woods decd.,(See Vol.I,EMR for Will of Robt.Woods)of Davidson Co.,Tn. sell to George Torry of Jeff.Co.Ms.

P.122:13 Apr.1858-Relinq.:2400 ac.Mrs.Elizabeth Caroline Swaine, wife of Jethro B.Bailey of New Orleans & A.C.Ferguson receiver.

¶Note;From P.139 to 183 very faint and hard to decipher.

P.192:30 Nov.1858-Marr.Contract:Between Robt.H.Hord of Brownsville,Tx.Cameron Co.,and Mary I.Jackson of Wash.Co.Ms. After their marr.she is to keep control of her property.

P.199:21 Dec.1857-Deed:Abram Y.Smith and wife Sally Myra of Wash.Co.Ms.,sell to Benj.Roach;David Roach;Wilkins Roach;Eugene Roach, heirs of Benj.Roach,decd.,of Adams Co.Ms.,for $22,000. Land located in S10,T18,R9W-@420 ac.

P.201:1 Jan.1852-D:Alex.Erskine & wife S.E.:Robt.Fearn & wife Eliza Maria;Thos.Fearn-all of Huntsville,Ala. Arthur F.Hopkins
(cont.)

DEED BOOK "R":WASHINGTON CO.MS.
Apr. 1858-May 1860

(cont.)of Mobile,Ala. All are equally and jointly owners of land in Wash.Co.Ms.,who sell to Hugh Craft of Holly Springs, Ms.,as trustee. Land descriptions in Wash.Co.,Issa.Co.,Rank. Co.,Scott Co.,all in Ms.

P.230:7 Aug.1858-Article of Agreement & Div. of Property:"For Love and affection I have for my mother Mrs.Annie Fulton,and for my ½ brother Andrew J.H.Crow,and feeling that the property has been judidiously managed since the death of my father,John Fulton"- Sallie Fulton,now Buford, asks that the Est.of her father be appraised, and her Mother to take first choice, which ever portion she wants.Sallie to get ½-her mother and Andrew to share the other½. At her mother's death, her½ of ½ to be disposed as mother sees fit. Should Andrew decd.without heirs, Sallie is to get his ½ of ½. Signed Sallie Fulton,G.H.Buford, Sallie Buford. Wit:John James,Andrew J.H.Crow on Aug.9. A further division of slaves follows, in addition to stating there are 2 tracts of land, Mrs.Fulton and Andrew living on 1, and Sallie and G.H.Buford on the other.P.233:Mrs.Fulton and Andrew buy out the Bufords.

P.237:21 Jan.1859-Deed:John A.Scott sells to Wm.Little:Benj. Little:Montgomery Little of Wash.Co.Ms.

P.238:25 Oct.1859-Deed:Frances E.Kempe,widow of Sturgis Sprague, decd.,of New Orleans,sells to Henry T.Lonsdale of N.O.[NOTE; The La.records frequently give the maiden name of the females]

P.246:11Jan.1836-Deed:A.Waldo Putnam and wife Cornelia V.(Sevier) of Overton Co.Tn.,to Passmore Hoopes & Jos.H.Moore. Clerk of Overton Co.Tn.,in 1836 was Geo.W.Sevier.

P.253:30 Dec.1858-Deed:German N.Jordan & wife Sallie V. of Yazoo Co.Ms.,sell to Benj.Roach,David Roach,Jas.Wilkins Roach, Eugene Roach of Adams Co.Ms. The Roach's buy out Jordans share of "Woodland", the last residence of Benj.Roach,Sr.- 475 ac.in Adams Co.+ the "Ball Ground Pltn."in Warr.Co.-3300 ac., the "Prairie" & "Duck Pond Pltns."in Yazoo Co.-5,500 ac. +"Wolf Lake Pltn."-3500+ in Yazoo Co.,Also the "Bachelor Bend Pltns"in Wash.Co.Ms. 1313 ac + slaves-around 900. The Jordans sign in Adams Co.Ms.

P.270:9 Feb.1859-Deed:Mary Ann Hood,widow of Wm.S.(J?)Hood,decd. and Eliz.W.Hood,dau. of said Hood,decd.,of Ky.,sell to Wm.N. Hood of Wash.Co.Ms.,land on Deer Creek known as the property of Smith & Hood-"Magenta PLTN.",which was ordered sold by a decree of Chanc.Court of Wash.Co.in a case"Mary Ann Hood and Wm.N.Hood vs Sidney R.Smith,et al".Signed,Mary A.Hood and Lizzie Hood.[NOTE:Sidney R.Smith was the bro.of Mary Ann Smith Hood, widow of Wm.S.Hood. Wm.S.Hood & Mary Ann Smith Hood had 3 children-Elizabeth Waller who Marr.Wm.R.Fleming-she decd.7 Apr.1863 in Lexington,Ky:Wm.N.Hood the oldest-b 1832,marr.1856 Clara Hickman of Paris,Ky.and they had a large family- settled at "Magenta Pltn.";and Dr.Thomas Harwood Hood who lived Cynthania,Ky.,and decd.Nov.1900]

P.291:21 Feb.1859-Title of Slaves:Wife and all the heirs of lateWm.S.Hood,with exception of minor heir,Thos.Harwood Hood sign-Mary A.Hood,W.N.Hood,Lizzie Hood.

DEED BOOK "R":WASHINGTON CO.MS.
Apr.1858-May 1860

P.296:28 Jan.1858-P.O.A;E.Livingston Hord of Lafayette Co.Mo., appoints his bro.,Lewis Hord of Cincinatti,Hamilton Co.Oh. to act "for me as one fo the heirs and children of Lewis Hord,decd." Property in Vicksburg or elsewhere in Ms.

P.297:18 Jan.1859-Deed:Lewis Hord & wife Mary B.of Cincinatti, Ohio sell to Thos.C.Clarke of Warren Co.Ms.

P.299:Feb.1859-Deed:Edward S.Hord of Covington,Ky.sells to Thos.C.Clarke.

P.302:20 Jan.1859-Deed:Margaret S.Ware,by her atty.Geo.M.Barnes of Hinds Co.,sells to Ellen L.Lynch of same for $1-640 ac.

P.303:20 Dec.1858-Deed:Geo.Torrey and wife Mary Ann of Jeff.Co. Ms.,sell to John Torrey of same.

P.305:8 June 1858-Deed:Sarah B.Woods,Davidson Co.Tn.,relict of Robt.Woods,decd.(see Will,EMR Vol.I)of said Co.,sells to Geo.Torrey-her dower rights to land in Wash.Co.Ms.

P.308:6 Apr.1858-P.O.A.:Chas.Y.Hutchinson & wife Virginia A. & Eugene M.Riddle-all of Gonzales Co.Tx.,appoint Edwin G.Cook of Vicksburg,Ms. their atty.to handle Virginia A.Hutchinson's,widow of Robt.Riddle,decd.,and Eugene M. Riddle's-child of said decd., share of the decd.Robt.Riddill's lands in Ms.

P.331:Superior Court of Wilkes Co.Ga.:Petition of Sarah Ann Reeves a "femme covert wife"of John L.Rives and her children Thos.L.(S?)Reeves(Sp.interchangeable)Jas.W.Reeves,Mary B.Reeves, Francis N.Reeves,Leonora Reeves-by their next friend John L. Reeves. A marr.settlement was executed 14 Sept.1852 as each was entitled to considerable separate property for which Wm.M. Reeves was appointed trustee. He was dismissed and Edward R. Anderson was appointed in Feb.1857,but has since decd.,and they wish Francis L.Wingfield to be appointed. He was, on 25 Mar.1857.

P.333:1 Jan.1858-Deed:Margaret Allen,single woman of New Orleans,sells to Chas.W.Allen of same.

P.336:22 Nov.1858-Deed:Henry B.Kidd,Adm.of Est.of Andrew Patterson,decd.,intestate,sells to Wm.Parker Scott under Court Order.

P.352:29 Jan.1859-Quit Claim:James M.Brabston of Warr.Co.sells to Ambrose J.Foster & wife Elizabeth E.;L.D.Harris & Daniel Harris-heirs of Ezekiel Harris,decd. Brabston buys a lot for $50. P.353:Alfred C.Holt & wife Mary W.-quit claim to Elizabeth Foster,Leanna Harris & Daniel Harris-sole heirs of Ezekiel Harris decd.-land in Wash.Co.Ms. 19 May 1858.

P.360:NoDate on Doc.Wit:26 Feb.1859:Edw.H.Bryant & wife Lucilla E.;Thos.F.Folkes;Frances C.Green;and Albert A.Folkes of Warr.Co. sell to Edwin G.Cook,for $3,000 their interest in 320 ac. The grantors Lucilla E.-his widow-,and Thos.F.,Frances, & Albert A. are children and heirs of James Folkes,decd.,who lived in Warr. Co.and died about the yr.1840.[NOTE:Doc.on p.395,Dbk."R",states they are the only children of Jas.,and Lucilla was his widow]

P.370:4 Feb.1859-Deed:Thos.Rigby and wife Mary A.B.;Miles C.Folkes & wife Rebecca H.Folkes;Sophia E.Moore all of Warr.Co.Ms.sell to Edwin G.Cook, for $2,000,land in Wash.Co.Ms.[NOTE:Goodspeeds-states that Thos.Rigby Marr.Mary Ann(Jewell)widow of Mr.Stovall]

DEED BOOK "R":WASHINGTON CO.MS.
Apr.1858-May 1860

P.380:25 Apr.1859-Deed:M.L.Peters & wife Harriette H.of Wash.Co.
sell to Dr.W.W.Worthington for $36,000 land in Wash.Co.located
in S3,T16,R8W @330 ac.+ 20 slaves.

¶Note:The Southern Railroad has begun to buy R.O.W.

P.425:24 Mar.1859-Deed:Rebecca C.McElroy wife of Rev.Dr.Joseph
McElroy,Execx.,& David B.Crane,Exec. of last Will and Test.
of Robt.Jaffrey,decd., & Edward S.Jaffrey & wife Anna Frances
and said David B.Crane in his own right-sell to W.Hopkins of
Memphis,Tn.,749 ac.in T.4,R7W. The first parties all signed
in New York City.

P.449:1 Jan.1856-Warr.Co.:Geo.Messinger of Warr.Co.Ms.sells
to Nelson T.Warren,minor heir of Admiral N.Warren,decd.,of
Wash.Co.Ms. Nelson's Guard.is Thos.H.Hill,who pays Messinger
$7200 for 723 ac.of land in T16,R7W in Wash.Co. An earlier
Guard.of Nelson's was John M.Selser, now decd.

P.457:22 June 1859-Deed:M.L.Peters of Wash.Co.Ms.,sells to
Thos.,Belinda, & Laura James-heirs of Gabriel James,decd.of
same.

P.471:7 Apr.1859-Deed:Robt.E.Crane & wife Octavia of Sunflower
Co.Ms.,sell to Saml.Crane of same, their right to prop.in Wash.
Co.,in T18,R4W.

P.477:18 Aug.1858-Deed:Samuel Rose & wife Eliza & David B.Smith
and wife Ann H.-all of Sunf.Co.,sell to John A.Kline,of Vicksburg

P.481:No date:P.O.A.:Martha A.Burgess of Mason Co.Ky.:Charles
S.Savage & wife Elizabeth late Elizabeth Burgess of Bracken
Co.Ky.:Chas.S.Savage as Guard.for Francis A.Burgess & John B.
Burgess-infant heirs of H.J.Burgess,decd.,of Mason Co.Ky.,do
hereby appoint W.H.Savage of Maysville,Mason Co.Ky.,to insti-
tute proceedings for land in Wash.Co.Ms.

P.484:1 Jan.1859-Deed:John W.Robinson & wife Mary Jane of Hinds
Co.Ms.,sell to Letitia S.Shearer,wife of Wm.B.Shearer of Madison Co.Ms.

P.502:11 Jan.1859-Deed:Margaret Duvall of Issa.Co.,execx.of
Will of Alex.D.Duvall,late of said Co.,sells to Edwin G.Cook.

P.518:20 July 1859-Deed:Oramel B.Burgess of Mason Co.Ky.,to
Marg.Campbell,execx.,of Wm.R.Campbell,decd.of Wash.Co.Ms.

P.537:12 Oct.1859-Deed:Amos Alexander of Adams Co.Ms.,for natural love and affection for "my son Virgil Flornoy Alexander"
a gift of land in Wash.Co.Ms.inT19,R8W-600 ac.+ * slaves.

P.539:8 Nov.1858-Deed:Geo.T.Blackburn,Special Commissioner in
caseof James W.Browder,et al & Jas.Yerger,Adm.,vs John Willis.
The Browders and the Yergers ordered to sell to John Willis
@138 ac.subject to the dower rt. of the widow of Jesse R.Fields,
decd. The Property belonged to Est.of Jesse R.Fields.[NOTE:For
the settlement of Jesse Fields'Est.-Vol.I of this series]

P.541:16 Feb.1848-D:Chas.I.Chamberlain & wife Pamelia of Jeff.
Co.Ms.,sell to John P.Watson lands lately sold by Matilda Sle-
mons as Admx.for Est.of Wm.B.Slemons & Guard of Williamnora
Slemons.(Just now recording the deed)

DEED BOOK "R":WASHINGTON CO.MS.
Apr.1858-May 1860

P.545:21 Dec.1858-Deed:Wm.Cannon & wife Jane E. of Adams Co.Ms. sell to Elizabeth J.Chotard;Mary A.;Corinne;Wm.S.;& Thos.Barnard heirs-at-law of Thos.Barnard,decd.,all of Adams Co. The Cannons sell to the Barnard heirs,for $1, an undivided moity of a certain tract.

P.547:2 Nov.1859-Deed:John P.Watson of Pt.Coupee Pa.La.,ordered by Dist.Court of Madison Pa.La.,(Suit #2530)delivers to Mrs.Mary K.James,widow of Joshua James of Mad.P.,1 undivided ½ of 799+ac.

P.548:1 Nov.1859-Mortg:Emily A.Ferriday wife of Jos.C.Ferriday,- and said Jos.C. who joins and assents- of New Orleans, of 1st part;Edw.P.Johnson & Saml.Worthington of Wash.Co.Ms.,2nd pt; Robt.J.Ward of Louisville,Ky.,3rd. 1st bought of 3rd a Pltn. + slaves-the"Granicus Place".2nd part are the securities.

P.565:30 Oct.1859-Deed:David Roach of Adams Co.Ms.,to his mother for love and affection,Mary Eliza Montgomery of Warr.Co."for supporting him in a genteel way and paying his debts",gives her his undivided share in his late Father's Est.,Benj.Roach. See p.253 of this DBk."R" for descriptions of lands.
Wit:John Hutchins, N.Roach.

P.561:15 Nov.1859-P.O.A.:Edward Hord appoints his bro.Lewis Hord of Hamilton Co.Ohio his Atty.

P.571;24 July 1859-Deed:James W.Browder & wife Elizabeth W.,of Wash.Co.Ms.,Geo.W.Faison & wife Ellen R. of Issa.Co.,sell to John Willis of Warr.Co.Ms.,land owned by Jesse Fields,decd., father of Elizabeth W. & Ellen R.

P.580:9 Dec.1859-Release:Maria J.Church became Guard. of her minor children and gave bond along withSusan P.McCutchen(now Taylor)as surety. She has disbursed money to her dau.,Kitty S.Church,now marr.to John H.Warterman(also sp.Waterman).Maria J.Church was the widow and exec.of Est.of Edw.Church,decd., asks relief of her Guardianship.

P.596--Mar.1859-Deed:Wm.N.Hood & wife Clara H. of Scott Co.Ky., sell to Eliz.W.Hood of same.

P.606:James Osgood Andrews,Bishop of Methodist Epis.Ch.South, sets apart Green C.Fore for Deacon. 8 Feb.1860.

P.610:10 Aug.1859-Deed:F.Anderson & wife Mary A. sell to Warren P.Anderson all of Hinds Co.Ms.

P.611:21 Mar.1859-Deed:Mobile,Ala.:"Mary Jones in my own right and as Guard.to Amanda & James B.Joyner"-minor heirs of John Joyner,decd.,the bro. of Turner Joyner,decd.,for consideration of payments, made to me of the distributive share of said Amanda, Jas.E.(C?) & John A.Joyner in sale of said Est. as sold to Junius R.Ward.

P.612:1 Aug.1858-Est.Settlement:Benj.D.(X)King;Anna Oliver & husband Wm.Oliver;S.A.Mills & H.M.Mills:M.T.Anderson & T.D.Anderson:Elizabeth Ray & W.G.Ray by atty.,in fact,Elijah Oliver; Louisa Bryant & Eliza King by Guard.Elijah Oliver;-children & heirs of Permelia King,decd.,who was the sister of Turner Joyner,decd.,of Itawamba Co.Ms., & Elijah Oliver,Guard.(Cont.)

DEED BOOK "R";WASHINGTON CO.MS.
Arp.1858-May 1860

(cont.)of the persons and Est.of Eliza Bryant & Louisa King-minor heirs of said Permelia King.--Sell to Junius R.Ward,Exec. of Will of TURNER JOYNER.

P.613:7 June 1858-Deed:Eli Joyner,brother of decd.Turner Joyner, and Eli Lewis or Whitehead & wife Mary(X)Lewis or Whitehead (Copied as written);John Henry(x)Harris-son and heir-at-law of Sallie Harris,decd.;the said Mary Lewis or Whitehead and Sally Harris,decd.,being sisters of Turner Joyner,decd.-all of Halifax Co.N.C.,sell to Junius R.Ward.

P.615:28Feb.1859-Deed:Wm.C.Dunlap of Wash.Co.Ms.,agent and Atty. for Winefred Freeman & Martha Ann Denning-sell their share of Turner Joyner's Est. to Junius R.Ward.

P.616:14 Aug.1858-Deed:Hardeman Co.Tn.;Isham Sills & wife Milly (X)formerly Harris;Isaac Brewer & wife Charlotte-formerly Harris; West Harris;James H.Harris & wife Isabel L.;Eli Harris & wife Susanna;John J.Lambert-Guard.of J.Abner Lambert minor heir of Ailees Harris,decd.-all heirs at law of Elizabeth Harris,decd., sister of Turner Joyner,decd.,-sell to Junius R.Ward

P.617:8 Sept.1858-Deed:Turner J.(X)Harris of HOt Springs,Ark. is paid for his share as heir of Elizabeth Harris,decd.,sister of Turner Joyner,decd. He sells to Junius R.Ward.
NOTE:The Will of Turner Joyner is recorded in Will Bk.1,p.212; Wash.Co.Ms. and abstracted in Vol.I in this EMR Series,p.78.

P.623:23 June 1859-P.O.A.:J.T.Foote & wife Charity(X)Foote of the State of Tenn.,appointHenry T.Branch of Issa.Co.Ms.,their Atty.,to handle a certain matter concerning Charity's dower rights in the settlement of the Est.of Jesse Fields,decd.,her former husband.[Goodspeed stated that Jesse was marr.4 times]

P.626:20 Oct.1859-Deed:Ann M.Sands-Widow:Austin L.Sands,Jr. & wife Julia M.;Saml.S.Sands & wife Mary E.;Wm.R.Sands;and Andrew H.Sands-all of N.Y.City.& John Rodgers of U.S.Navy & wife Ann E. Late Hodge;Theodosia M.Hodge of City of Washington; and J.Ledyard Hodge of Philadelphia,Pa.,sell tracts of land left in Ms.,by the demise of the late Andrew Hodge of P.of Jefferson,La. The buyer is John S.Hodge of Philadelphia,Pa. Andrew Hodge,decd.,left a Will in Jefferson Parish La.

P.631:18 Oct.1859-Deed:David Geo.Humphreys & wife Mary C. of Claiborne Co.Ms.,sell to Charles S.Buck of Warren Co.Ms. 319 ac. in Wash.Co.Ms.

P.632:1 Jan.1860-Deed:J.W.Vick & wife Catharine Ann of Warren Co.Ms. sell to H.O.Vick of same.

P.633:22 Nov.1859-Deed:W.W.Hill and wife Martha Jane of Louisville,Ky., & Jas.C.Ford and wife Mary Jane of same, sell to A.Downing of Jackson,Ms.

P.635:24 Feb.1860-P.O.A.:Emily D.Harper,widow of late James T.Harper;Geo.W.Allen & wife Olivia T.-formerly Olivia T.Harper: Thos.M.Harper & wife Mary G.R.Harper: only surviving heirs of James T.Harper,decd.,late of Claib.Co.Ms. Appoint Henry V.McCall of New Orleans their Atty.

DEED BOOK "R":WASHINGTON CO.MS.
Apr.1858-May 1860

P.641:12 Mar.1860-D/Gift:Stephen Castleman gives his dau.Virginia M.Burton,wife of John Burton a tract of land in Wash.Co.Ms., in T15,R3W-170 ac. They are all from Wash.Co.Ms.

P.644:13 Feb.1860-Deed:John Corlis & wife Mary Ann, Peter Corlis, unmarried, Munford Perks & wife Mary Perks all of New Orleans sell to Nathan W.Motherall of Williamson Co.Tn.

P.662:29 Dec.1859-Deed:State of S.C.,Wade Hampton,Christopher F.Hampton & John S.Preston all of S.C.,being firmly bound unto Flowden Charles Sennett Weston,deliver slaves-223.

P.671:24 Feb.1860-Deed:Abner Heathman & wife Jane M.,of Sunflower Co.Ms.:Burrage Heathman & wife Elvira M.,of Shelby Co. Tn.,sell to Duncan McAnn of Jeff.Co.Ms.,land in Wash.Co.Ms. 2,441+ac.in T19,R5W.

P.678:9 Mar.1860 Deed:David B.Cook & wife Mary B.,formerly Mary B.Hageman of Chicago sell to Lucius Livingston & James Livingston of Wash.Co.Ms.,-land in Wash. and Yazoo Cos.Ms.

P.708:3 Sept.1859-Deed:Geo.Torrey & wife Mary Ann sell to John Torrey all of Jeff.Co.Ms.

P.709:4 Apr.1860-Deed:Mrs.Sarah L.Barnes of Madison P.La.,sells to Robt.P.Briscoe of Fort Bend,Tex.,land that had been sold to Parmenas Briscoe in 1844-land formerly in Wash.Co.-now in Issa.Co.Ms.

END OF DEED BOOK "R"
HUSBAND & WIVES NAMED IN DBK."R",RESIDENCE & DATE OF DOCUMENT
Alcorn,Jas.L. & w. Amelia W.   Cohoma Co.Ms. 1858
Archer,Jas. & w. Mary Ann   Jeff.Co.Ms. 1858
Baker,John & w.Mary   Fauquier Co. Va.   1855
Black,John & w. Sarah   Hinds Co.Ms. 1837
Bland,Maxwell W. & w. Mary L.,   Claib.Co.Ms. 1855
Bostick,Ferdinand & w. Elilee C.   Yazoo Co.Ms. 1857
Burwell,Armistead & w. Pricilla W., Warren Co.Ms. 1859
Byrne,Edw. & w. Susan V., Wash.Co.Ms. 1860
Byrne, John Bligh & wife Azemia Remy, New Orleans   1840
Caffal,Carl & w. Mary, Madison Parish La.   ----
Cannon,Wm. & w. Jane E. Natchez,Ms. 1849
Cobb,John D. & w. Harriet Ms., of New Orleans   1859
Cook,M.L. & w. Jennett S., Hinds Co.Ms. 1859
Daniel,Wm.E. & w. Sarah S. Wash.Co.Ms. 1858
Gillespie,Christopher & w. Melissa D., Wash.Co.Ms. 1859
Griffing.Jasper C. & w. Martha L., Shelby Co. Tn.   1857
Hampton,Wade & w. Mary S., Richland Dist. S.C., 1858
Haynes,Jas.M. & w. Mary D., Holmes Co.Ms. 1858
Hill,Horace B. & w. Susan, Lexington,Ky. 1858
Holmes,Saml.A. & w. Mary W., New Hanover Co. N.C.,1857
King,Rufus & w. Margaret R., Cincinatti,Ohio, 1857
Lee,Thos.J. & w. Nancy J. ,Wash.Co.Ms.   1858
Littlefield,Jas. & w. Mary C.,   Newton,Mass. 1859
Manlove,Christopher & w. Ann E., Warren Co.Ms. 1859
Marsh,Shelby B. & w. Dorinda J., Giles Co. Tn.   1859
Mears,John L. & w.Betsy A., New Hanover Co. N.C.   1857
Mellen,Wm.P. & w. Sarah C.,Natchez,1859(They own Locust Grove Plt.)

DEED BOOK "R":WASHINGTON CO.MS.
Apr.1858-May 1860

(cont)Hus.& wives in deed book "R"
Nailor,Jefferson & w. Eliza C. Warren Co.Ms. 1859
Nelson,Newman J. & w. Mary, Wash.Co.Ms.1859
Nye,N.G. & w. Lucy A., Yazoo Co.Ms. 1858
Pierce,Granville S. & w. Elizabeth V., Rutherford Co.,Tn. 1842
Pugh,Wm.M. & w.Josephine P., of Assumption Parish La. 1858
Putnam,W.W. & w. Eliza J., Coffee Co.Tn., 1859
Smith,David B. & w. Ann H., Sunflower Co.Ms., 1859
Sumrall,Thos.L. & w. Margaret, Jackson Co. Ms.,1859
Willis,Edw.B. & w. Margaret E., Warren Co.Ms., 1859
Winn,Orasamus & w. Eliline S., Yazoo Co.Ms.,1858

SUPPLEMENTARY INFORMATION:WARREN CO.MS.,WILL BOOK "A":

P.330:WILL OF GEORGE MESSINGER;Written 10 Dec.1865
Wife-Emilie L.to receive"Baconham Pltn".on Big Black River in
Warren Co.and Hds.Co.,"where I now reside"-2200 acs. Also prop.
in Vicksburg. Neice-Sarah Lucinda Warren,wife of Nelson Y. Warren;
To Saml.Raney;2 sisters-1.Mary Sebrina Moore of Harrodsburg,Ky.-
and 2.Sybelia A.Foote of Macon,Ms.[NOTE;Wife of Judge Hezekiah
Wm.Foote];Cousin D.B.Messinger of Hillsdale,Columbia Co.N.Y.
"all I now possess in Egremont Co.or Berkshire,Mass."
Wit:David Raymond Fox,T.Blanche Fox,R.Sarphy.
[NOTE:Marr.Rec.of Warr.Co.,Ms.-Emilie L.Messinger marr.7 Oct.
1869 to George W.Howard]

CENSUS 1850-WARREN CO.MS.
George Messinger	32	b.S.C.
Sophia "	39	b.Mass.
Mary "	18	b.Mo.
Sarah L.Andrews	7	b.Va.
Lucinda Vaughan	78	b.Va.
George W.Sisson	38	b.N.C.

WARREN CO.,MS:WILL BOOK "B":

P.126:WILL OF MARY JANE DOWNS:Written 2 July 1879
Neices;Annie R.Noland,Jennie R.Batcheler
Gr.Sons;Alfred C.Downs & Jas.R.Downs
Nephs;John R.Brabston,W.H.Brabston
Sister;Roche H.Brabston
Friend:Henry P.Noland,Exec.
Wit:James E.Kennan,Sarah L.Robinson,Victoria C.Batchelor

P.355:WILL OF HENRY AUGUSTUS DOWNS:Names his mother-Mary Jane
Downs-dated 15 Oct.1862. Warren Co.Ms.Will Bk."A".

WILL BOOK "A":MADISON CO.,MS.
P.247:WILL OF WM.BALFOUR:Written 17 Apr.1857-prob.1857:"My pltn.,
in Mad.Co.Ms.on which I now reside and the Pltn.in Yazoo Co.&
Carroll P.La.to be kept together until my youngest son Horace
B.Balfour reaches 21":4 sons-James, Jos., Lewis, Horace B.:Sister
Eliza Alice James(?):Bro.Charles Balfour-land in Sunf.Co.Ms.:
Dau.,Mrs.Mary Blackman and her ch.-Wm.S.,John H.,Chas.R.,Jas.R.,
Jos.D.,Lewis C.,Horace B. Blackman.

DEED BOOK "S":WASHINGTON CO.MS.
DATED:25 May 1860-9 Jan.1867
Dog-eared,but repaired. Handwriting very difficult to read.

P.2:16 Jan.1860-Deed:Samuel Putnam & wife Margaret M;James H.
Moore;Susan B.Moore:Richard C.Moore; & Cordelia Moore-widow
and heirs-at-law of Wm.M.Moore,decd.,all of Vicksburg,-sell
to Henry Lawrence of Yazoo City at $2 per acre,the proceeds
to be divided as follows;
Putnams-1 undivided 1/8th
Jas.H.   "   "   "
Susan   "   "   "
Rich.C.   "   "   "
Cordelia-1/3rd of 1 undivided 1/8th
Land located in Wash.Co.all in T16,R3W-@480 ac.
Next document:P.3;Mrs. Margaret Moore relinq.dower rights as
the widow of William Moore,decd.,of Warren Co.-doc.signed in New
Orleans-to Henry Lawrence-16 Jan.1860
Next doc.;P.3;16 Jan.1860-Loyd R.Coleman & wife Harriet Louisa
of New Orleans sell"Our right and title"-being 1 undivided
1/8th to Henry Lawrence.

P.9:12 Dec.1859-Deed:Wm.F.Martin;Richard D.Chotard & wife Elizabeth;J.Chas.Chotard & wife Mary Ann:;Corinne Barnard;& Wm.I.Bar-
nard sell to Frances E.Gale(Yale?)Guard. of Margaret J.Gale
& Anna M.Gale..all of Adams Co.Ms.,lots lying on Miller's Bend
and being part of Barnardstown, and 1 undivided ½ which has
been lately purchased from Joshua James & wife Mary K. by said
Wm.T.Martin as trustee of said Eliz.Chotard, Mary A.Chotard,
Corinne Barnard,Wm.I.Barnard & Thos.Barnard.

P.23:8 May 1860-Deed:John H.Sims & Wm.A.Sims,Adms.of Est. of
Chas.Sims.late of Wilkinson Co.Ms.,- an undivided 1/3rd in cer-
tain wild lands sold at public auction at"Sligo Pltn.",in Wash.
Co.Ms. The Est.holds 1 undivided 1/3rd for $10,000-S19,30;W½
NE1/4 of S31;T17;R7W +E½ of S29;E½S30;NE1/4 S38;T17;R8W-bought
by John P.Dillingham.
Next Doc;30 Dec.1859:John H.Sims,Wm.R.(sometimes A.)Sims & wife
Elizabeth S.of Wilk.Co.Ms.,sell to John P.Dillingham land known
as the Black Bayou tract owned by John H. & Wm.R.(A)Sims-2,570ac
Next Doc:Wm.A.P.Dillingham-his wife is Martha R.-co-signs a
note to Edw.J.Elder with J.P.Dillingham.

P.37:7 July 1860-DeedJas.H.Yerger is decd.,and his Adm.is Jas.
T.Rucks & Maria Louisa Yerger of Wash.Co.Ms. They sell the Est.
to Maria Louise Yerger at public auction[NOTE:MARIA LOUISA(RUCKS)
is the widow of JAS.H.YERGER,decd.,and the sister of JAS.T.RUCKS]

P.61:Will of Andrew Hodge,Jr. of Jeff.P.,La.,late of New Orleans
Written:N.O.27 May 1852
Codicil:16 Dec.1853,1 June 1856-written,Plantation"Bavataria"
Proved:2 Aug.1856
Andrew states he"has no ascending or descending Heirs"and ap-
points E.A.Bradford & Wm.M.Randolph exec.and gives each $5,000.
To friend:Pierre C.D.Peyster
Neices:Ann & Theodora Hodge and to their bro.John L.Hodge,Jr.
    the children of W.S.Hodge.
Sister;Ann-wife of Austin L.Sands,New York & to her 4 sons-
    Dr.Christian L;Samuel L;Wm.;& Andrew Hodge Sands.
(Cont.next page)

DEED BOOK "S":WASHINGTON CO.MS.
May 1860-Jan.1867

(Cont.)To the Bible Society;Orphanage;Firemen's Assn.,etc.
Bros:John L.HOdge & WM.S.Hodge-Cancels their debts to him.

P.64:21 Feb.1860-Deed:John Ledyard;John Rogers & wife Ann;Theodora Hodge;Ann Hodge,wife of Austin L.Sands;Austin L.Sands,Jr.
Samuel S.Sands-all legatees of Andrew Hodge,Jr.decd.,sell to
WmR.Sands & Andrew H.Sands.
¶[NOTE:Difficult to tell whether these are LANDS OR SANDS. After double checking in Deed Index "2"- believe them to be SANDS]

P.73:Alfred B.Carter & wife Elizabeth H. of Fauquier Co.Va.,sell
to A.C.Brown and ----Tupper.

P.75:20 Dec.1859-Deed:John H.Newman & wife Permelia of Warren
Co.Ms.;Simon B.Newman & wife Mary Bell of Madison Co.Ms.;Arra
Ann Brabston of Warr.Co.;all sell to Sam.T.Taylor & Fred N.Macklin of Wash.Co.

P.95:24 Nov.1860-Deed:Emily D.Harper;George W.Allen & wife
Olivia T.,formerly Harper;Thos.M.Harper & wife Mary G.R.-only
heirs of Jas.T.Harper: Wm.B.Harper;Sarah McCarroll;Drucilla
J.Chambliss;Maria Darden;& Martha West-heirs at law of Jesse
Harper,decd. by their Atty.Henry V.McCall sell to Alexander
P.Montgomery & Alexander M.Kirk-"all our rts.and title" to
11/12th interest in lands in Wash.Co.Ms. in T18,R7W.[NOTE:
Another doc.states that OLIVIA T.ALLEN & THOS.M.HARPER are the
children and only surviving heirs of JAS.T.HARPER,and that EMILY
D. is his widow]

P.109:12 Nov.1860-Deed:Mrs.Catherine Egg,Mrs.S.C.Cox,P.A.Cox
& wife Annie,& Marcus F.Johnson of Wash.Co.Ms.,-for "the affection and goodwill"they bear A.J.H.Crow-they swap some lots of
land on Eggs Point in return for free shipping of Mrs.Egg"s
cotton for her lifetime.

P.171:25 June 1860-Deed:John C.French & wife Sarah F.French
of San Antone,Bexar Co.Tx.,to Samuel G.French of Wash.Co.Ms.
$65,000 for 1 undivided ½ interest on Deer Creek,located in
T19,R8W called Matilda Place, which was conveyed to Saml.G.French
and said John C.French by Jas.H.Yerger,Commissioner-1,030 ac.
+ 1 undivided ½ of slaves,stock,buildings,etc.

P.175:22 Jan.1859-Deed:James S.Walker of Wash.Co.Ms. & Freeman
Walker owe Daniel Grant of Ga.,as trustee of Francis C.Coleman,
and put up slaves as collateral.

P.176:13 June 1860-Deed:Gracia M.Turnbull releases her dower
rights to land Andrew,her husband, has already given to their
sons Dr.Robt.J.Turnbull,& Andrew Turnbull,Jr. Wit:Claudia B.
Turnbull,W.P.Walker-Charleston,S.C.[NOTE:CLAUDIA is a dau. of
GRACIA & ANDREW TURNBULL]

P.186:4 Feb.1861-Mortg:Wm.H.Rose of Wash.Co.Ms.,to Jas.S.Lamphier,Stephen O.Nelson,Thos.A.Nelson,Henry C.Walker-Merchants
of New Orleans.

P.189:20 Oct.1860-Deed:On21 Jan.1842,David Fitzpatrick buys
1 undivided ½ of certain lands from Peter Fitzpatrick. In 1860-
Lauderdale Co.Tn.,Peter buys it back.

DEED BOOK "S": WASHINGTON CO.Ms.
May 1860-Jan.1867

P.190:31 May 1859-Deed:Stephen A.Douglas in his capacity as
Exec.of Est.of Robert Martin,decd.and Guard. of his 2 sons-Robt.
M.Douglas & Stephen A.Douglas,Jr. who are the heirs-at-law of
said Est.of Robt.Martin of Chicago---to Jas.A.McHatton of Baton
Rouge,La. Douglas and McHatton entered an agreement in 1857
to co-work a cotton plantation in Wash.Co.Ms. The contract will
continue until Robert, the oldest of the 2 boys,becomes 21 on
28 Jan.1870, and continue,if Robt.so desires, for 2 more years
until Stephen is 21. Wit:A.Lashley,Bob Lashley.

P.201:21 Nov.1860-Deed;Susan E.Chambliss of Jeff.Co.Ms.,sells
her share,as an heir of the Est.of Peter C.Chambliss-for $5
to Lewis W. Thompson of Madison Co.Ms., Sue signed in Claib.Co.Ms.
P.202:25 Feb.1860-D:Cortez Chambliss & wife Lizzie(She signed
E.N.);Calvin F.Chambliss & wife Mary;Jackson Chambliss & wife
Kate V.;Wm.H.Corbin & wife Martha D.;& Susan E.Chambliss; &
Drucilla J.Chambliss-sell to Lewis W.Thompson,for $6,000,land
in T15,R7W-227 ac+1 undiv.½ of land in T15,R6W.[NOTE:GEN.PETER
CORBIN CHAMBLISS and his wife DRUCILLA HARPER had the following
children:CORTEZ who marr.1847,ELIZABETH N.BOLLS;CALVIN who marr.
MARY___;LACONIA who marr.JAMES M.BERRY;MARY who marr.1st--WIL-
KINSON,2nd DR.R.E.RICHARDSON;JACKSON who marr.KATE.--:MARTHA
who marr.her cousin WM.H.CORBIN and moved to Ga.(It was here,
while on a visit that Peter C.decd.);and SUSAN E. who apparently
never marr.]

P.220:10 Nov.1860-Deed:Wm.T.Barnard & wife Endora J. of Issa.Co.
Ms.,sell to Edwin G.Cook of Warr.Co.Ms. their interest -1/5th -
of ½ -the ½ belonging to the heirs of A.G.Creath,decd.,and the
1/5th of that ½ belonging to Mrs.Barnard,she being one of the
5 said heirs and whose interest is conveyed above.[NOTE:ENDORA
CREATH marr.1st T.J.LIKENS, then WM.T.BARNARD]

P.236:2 June 1860-Deed:Richard C.Moore of Warren Co.Ms.,Guard.
of persons and property of Sophia M.Moore & Mary S.Lewis minor
heirs of Wm.Moore,decd.,-sell part of the Moore Est. to Henry
Lawrence of Yazoo Co.Ms.

P.239:24 Jan.1861-Agreement:Between Bowman Stirling & his wife
Penelope J.Stirling, late Stewart. Penelope had received $20,000
from her father-Jas.Stewart,and her husband promised to pay
interest on her money. Doc.signed in Wash.Co.Ms.

P.241:6 May 1861-Deed:Andrew B.Carson,Sherf.of Wash.Co.Ms.:
a Decree from Chan.Court dealing with a case in which Wm.L.Nugent
was the complainant and David Harrison,Exec.of last Will and
Test.of Henry Shaifer,Clarissa Shaifer-his wife;Emily C.Briscoe;
Sidney B.Briscoe;Lizzie S.Briscoe;Emma Harrison;James Parmenas
Harrison;Robt.Briscoe and other unknown heirs-at-law of Parmenas
Briscoe,decd.,--for legal fees and other costs,land put up for
public sale and Nugent was the buyer.

P.274:29 May 1861-Deed:Wm.N.Hood to Rich.D.Dixon,trustee for
Clara H.Hood,wife of Wm.N.Hood, all of Wash.Co.Ms. According
to their Marriage contract, Clara was entitled to her own Est.,
a large sum of money inherited from her father,Wm.Hickman of
Bourbon Co.Ky.,and also from the Est.,of her brother David
Hickman,a part of which has been received by W.N.Hood from(Cont.

DEED BOOK "S":WASHINGTON CO.MS.
May 1860-Jan.1867

(Cont.)John H.Shackleford,her Guard.,and a part from Robt.Davis. Wm.N.converted the funds to his own use $7,000.Now Wm.N. conveys to Dixon property in Wash.Co.Ms.+ slaves and his interest in a Pltn.on Deer Creek known as Smith and Hood.

P.292:22 Oct.1860-P.O.A.:James H.Myers & wife Elizabeth A.give their Power of Atty.to Alexander B.Montgomery to sell the Dry Bayou Place-1880 ac. Myers signed in E.Feliciana P.La., On P.293:Montgomery sells the land to John J.Kirk,land located in T17,R8W-400 ac.

P.300:19 Mar.1857-Mortg:Wm.G.Lane of N.Y.City & wife Mary C. mortg. to James P.Boyce of Greenville,S.C.,Exec.of last Will and Test.,of Ker Boyce,decd.,-for 149,222 ac.

P.318:25 June 1861-Deed:Alfrd B.Carter & wife Eliz.H. to Robt. M.Carter.

P.327:13 Mar.1861-Release:Elizabeth Omahondro, wife of Richard Omahondro of Va.,releases dower rts.to land sold to Orville C.Reeves of Ms. Witnesses sign in Fluvana Co.Va.[NOTE.The correct spelling is Rives]

P.330:12 Dec.1860-Deed: Andrew J.Patton,Exec.of Est.of John G.Patton,decd.,sells to Orville C.Rives-all his rights to certain land according to terms given in a deed from the Omahondros.

P.340:13 May 1859-D/G:For love and affection to my son Wm.Morehead an undivided ½ of my new place in Wash.Co.Ms.,located in T16,R8W and a lot of negroes purchased from W.L.Vance of Ky. Signed by C.S.Morehead.

P.343:28 Sept.1861-P.O.A.:Evelina M.Hammet of Wash.Co.Ms.,appoints F.A.Metcalfe of same,her Atty.to collect her rights as widow of W.H.Hammet,decd.[NOTE:EVELINA MATILDA McCALEB marr. 1st,A.G.METCALFE,by whom she had a son-F.A.METCALFE;she marr. 2nd Wm.HENRY HAMMET.]

P.348:5 Oct.1861-Quit Claim:Samuel Carson of Jeff.Co.Ark.,quit claims land to his nephew Andrew B.Carson of Wash.Co.Ms.

P.349:18 Nov.1861-D/G:Andrew Carson of Wash.Co.Ms.-for love and affection to son Andrew B.Carson,lands in Bolivar Co.Ms.

P.359:20 Nov.1860-Deed:James T.Rucks of Hinds Co,Ms.of 1st part; Mary Margaret Rucks widow of Aurthur Rucks,decd.;Amanda Y.Rucks; James Rucks,Jr.;Grant B.Rucks;Sally Rucks-heirs of said Aurthur. Est.partition.[NOTE:JAS.T.RUCKS was a bro.of AURTHUR RUCKS. MARY MARGARET RUCKS was the former MARY MARGARET YERGER,dau.of JOHN K.Yerger.]

P.364:26 Dec.1861-Deed:Alfred Willis & wife Emeline L.Willis sell to James M.Sutton.(All of Wash.Co.Ms.)[NOTE:EMELINE was the dau.of JAMES M.SUTTON and his wife ELIZA VAN NORMAN.Emeline marr.2nd ----MELCHOIR.]

P.369:5 Jan.1859-D/G:Edward P.Johnson,Sr.to his son Jas.Wm.Johnson-1 equal undivided moity of"Granicus Pltn"on which Jas.Wm. is now living.

DEED BOOK "S":WASHINGTON CO.MS.
May 1860-Jan.1867

P.456;12 Oct.1865-Deed:State of Texas,Co.of Smith:Jos.G.James
sells his share of the Est.of Theodore E.Jackson,decd.to Nancy
James of Tx."my undivided interest as a legatee-1/5th portion-
land in Wash.Co.Ms.,located in T16;R8W and known as the homestead place of T.J.James,Sr.,decd.

¶NOTE:Harriet B.Theobald begins to sell off lots in the town,
created by her on her plantation of"Blantonia",later named Greenville,and referred to as "New"Greenville.Initial sales were
to Rich.A.O'Hea;to Wash.Co.;Jennie Raffington;Anne Finlay;Jona-
than Pierce;John Harbicht,Milroy,& Kuker;Mrs.L.Meisner;Louis
Caffal;Jas.H.Lynch of Chicago;R.W.Baker;C.J.Field;Wm.L.Nugent;
David Kirk.]

P.461:18 Nov.1865:Samuel G.French is bound to Wm.A.Haycraft,
Clerk of Chanc.Court of Wash.Co.Ms.,for $83,000-Est.of late
Jos.L.Roberts that was ordered sold in 1855 Term of Court.
Portions are to go to Roberts' 3 daus. The suit Titled E.Z.Van-
*Cockelberghe & others,complainants vs A.K.Farrar and others,
defendants-#5313 on Gen.Docket. The husbands of the 3 daus.
were to act as trustees. Saml.G.French is the husband of E.
Matilda R.French late E.MATILDA ROBERTS. On p.462;the widow
of Jos.L.Roberts,decd.,was Mary S.Roberts,also decd.,so that
her Est. is to be divided between"her"3 daus....one of whom
is E.Matilda R.French,late wife of S.G.French. ½ of Matilda's
portion is to go to her only dau.Matilda R.French,a minor.(same
date)P.464;Saml.G.French is appointed trustee for Miss Margaretta J.Roberts and posts bond..at her death he pays her share
to E.Z.VanCockelberghe as trustee for his wife Mary B.VanCockel-
berghe and her children. Saml.G.French also pays John C.French,
as trustee for his wife Sarah F.French and her Children.[NOTE:
Marr.rec.Adams Co.Ms.,SAM'L G.FRENCH to ELIZA MATILDA ROBERTS
*26 Apr.1853. JOHN C.FRENCH marr.SARAH F.ROBERTS,14 Feb.1854]

P.468:26 Dec.1865-Deed:Eben N.Davis sells for natural love and
affection land in T15;R7W and R6W in Wash.Co.Ms.,to Eben N.
Davis,Jr.;Jonathan P.Davis;Mary Elizabeth Davis;Ann Winnefried
Davis;Augusta Virginia Davis...all of Marshall Co.Ms.

P.471:P.O.A.;13 Jan.1866:"Know all men by these present,that
I, Andrew Turnbull of Co.of Issaq.and State of Ms.,do hereby
appoint,constitute and nominate O.N.Cutter of the Co.of New York
and State of N.Y.,my lawful agent for the purpose of prosecuting
to a final judgement my claims against the Treasurer of the
United States in the matter of two hundred and eighty one(281)
bales of cotton which were seized by the authority of Maj.Gen.
U.S.Grant of the U.S. Army." The clerk of Wash.Co.Ms. was Chas.
F.Turnbull.

P.477:1Nov.1865-Deed:Thos.Shelby,to wife Elizabeth Shelby,agrees
to turn over the annual rent from land-470 ac. on Deer Creek
conveyed by A.W.McAllister to said ELIZA.SHELBY,his dau.,and
used by her husband.@$4 per ac.+Int.Also the rent from 400 ac.
on Black Bayou conveyed by Dr.O.M.Blanton to said Elizabeth.

P.479:18 Jan.1866-Deed:G.S.Mosby of Wash.Co.Ms.,mortg. land
to Mrs.M.C.Cunningham of Fayette Co.Ohio,+ 12 mules branded
S.B.on shoulder. Mosby owes $1379.31,to be paid in gold.
*see end of Deed Book "S"

DEED BOOK "S":WASHINGTON CO.MS.
May 1860-Jan.1867

P.499:19 Feb.1866-Mortg:Thos.H.Hill Mortgages "Forest Home Pltn." 880 ac.in T16;R7W to Wright & Allen of N.O.

P.466:26 Dec.1865-D/T:A.C.Holt & wife Mary W. of New Orleans are indebted to Daniel Williams,and for security he puts in trust to Robt.G.Sims land in Wash.Co.Ms.,located in T17,R7W-having been purchased of J.H.Sims,W.R.Sims,Chas.Sims,A.M.Paxton.

P.402:24 Dec.1862-Deed:Wm.T.Ashford and wife Mary J. sell to Chas Caffal- all of Wash.Co.Ms.

*¶NOTE:Documents jump from 1862 or early 1863 to 1865 with 2 documents recorded. Obviously, the records were hidden and pre-served somewhere, when Grant ordered the burning of Greenville]

P.428:12 July 1865-D/T:Wm.R.Elley sets up a trust for his wife Louisa to be held by Wm.L.Nugent-"considering the troubled times" so that she would be secure financially. Land lying in T14,R8W @992 ac.

P.430:8 Nov.1865-D/T:Orville M.Blanton gives a D/T of"Belle Aire Pltn.",in T18,R8W to be held by Jos.M.Smith for Orville's wife Martha R.

P.433;P.O.A.-3 Oct.1865:H.Mary Irish,Mary B.Irish,Volney S.Irish all of New Port,R.I.,nominate and appoint Henry T.Irish of same their Atty.to take possession of Est. real or personal in Ms. of the late Henry Irish.Volney signed in Suffolk Co.Mas;Hannah Mary and Mary B.signed in Newport.

P.435:13 Sept.1865-Agreement:Archie Baugh & Mrs.M.S.Brashear for the heirs of H.Carpenter,decd.,of Wash.Co.Ms.,to Thos.H. Johns of Wash.Co.Ms.,all parties agree to a co-partnership for the purpose of cultivating"Peru Pltn"-located at the foot of Lake Washington. The Heirs of H.Carpenter furnish the plantation and Johns does the work.

P.436;1 Aug.1865-Agreement:Gabriel W.Robb & Thos.H.Johns-for the purpose of working "Lake Island Pltn".owned by ROBB.(NO land description).

¶NOTE<The instruments have changed their tone and purpose. After the slaves were freed, the problems of working thousands of fertile acres with the newly liberated negro, the almost complete lack of cash or any concrete financial backing, compounded by the death of thousands of the men responsible previously for the direction of these huge land operations, left many floundering. Much of the land was transferred into the name of the wife, to ward off complete loss if foreclosure became a reality. ED.

P.437:5 Sept.1865-Deed:W.R.Sims sells his undivided 1/3rd int. in"Sligo Pltn",now held and occupied by said W.R. to W.E.Sims of same. Both heirs of J.H.Sims,decd.,and the heirs of Chas.Sims, Decd. W.R. signs for himself in Wilk.Co.Ms.;W.E.for Himself in same.

P.438:15 Nov.1865-Deed:Gordon Robinson & wife Martha P.sell to Charles T.Robinson -all of Wash.Co.Ms.

*see end of DBk"S"

DEED BOOK "S":WASHINGTON CO.MS.
May 1860- Jan.1867

P.439:OFFICE FREEDMENS BUREAU,Greenville,Wash.Co.Ms. 6 Oct.1865
Know ye that Patsey(X)Cately,colored,aged 10 yrs. the dau of
Lee Cately & Sallie his wife, both decd."The said Patsey Cately
has lived with me from her infancy,has voluntarily expressed
a willingness to live with and be bound"to Harriet B.Theobald
of"Blantonia Pltn".'in Wash.Co.Ms. for a term of 6 yrs..when said
Patsey will be old enough to choose for herself. Mrs.Theobald,
in turn,binds herself unto Col.Saml.Harris,Ass.Commissioner
for Freedmen Bureau of State of Ms.

P.504:9 Feb.1866-Deed:T.A.Harris mortg.land to John W.Harrow-
Pltn."Hollywood"

P.506:15 Nov.1865-Mortg:Pricilla W.Gregory mortgages "Elmwood
Pltn." to Lacy & McGhee of Shelby Co.Tn.

P.507:20 Feb.1866-Deed:George R.Fall and wife Elizabeth A.Fall
sell to James M.Collier all of Wash.Co.Ms.,for $10-81 ac.S½
of SE 1/4,Sec.36;T17,R7W.

P.510:10 Feb.1866-Deed:George Torrey & wife Mary Ann of Jeff.
Co.Ms.,sell 640 ac. to B.A.Bullen- exec.of last Will and Test.
of Wm.Stewart,decd.;to Martha J.Stewart widow of Wm.Stewart;
Mary L.Stewart;Isaac D.Stewart;Francis E.Stewart;Wm.Claudine
Stewart;Martha Stewart-children and heirs-at-law of Wm.Stewart,
late of said Jeff.Co. All said Grantees of Co. of Jeff.Ms.

P.511;20 Jan.1866-Deed:Wm.R.Elley,Mortgages "Swan Isle Place"
to Given Watts & Co. of N.O.La.

P.521:31 Jan.1861-Deed:John M.Bott & E.F.Bott of Wash.Co.Ms.,
to Josephine M.Worthington of same.(Josephine is their dau.)

P.532:4 Mar.1866-Bill of Complaint:Filed June Term 1848-Super-
ior Court of the Chancery,State of Ms. by Susan P.Herring,and
others-complainant vs Shepherd Brown,Jas.Johnson and others.
Brown and Johnson are to Quit claim all interest on certain
lands. Susan P.Herring, now the wife of Saml.Brown;and also
Winford Herring;Saml.Herring,Jr.;Bailey Peyton Herring-child-
ren of said SUSAN P.BROWN by her first marr. with Saml.Herring
Sr.,decd.

P.535;19Mar.1866-Mortg:Lyman G.Aldrich and wife Bettie A. of
Wash.Co.Ms.,Mortg.Pltn."Oak Hill" in T16,R8W to Buckner Newman
& Co.,N.O.La.

P.540:P.O.A-14 Apr.1866:George T.Blackburn & wife Mary Belle
of Wash.Co.Ms.nominate Robt.A.Johnson their Atty. to handle
a deed delivering their share in the Est. of "ourdecd.father:-
Henry Johnson,late of said Co.,and to cover any liablity "of
our mother"Elizabeth J.Johnson,Exec.of last Will & Test.of said
Johnson. The Justice of the Peace was Ben Johnson.[NOTE:HENRY
JOHNSON marr. ELIZABETH JULIA FLOURNOY dau. of MAJ.MATTHEW
FLOURNOY and his wife EMILY W.SMITH. MARY BELLE BLACKBURN was
a dau.:ROBT.A.JOHNSON & BEN were sons;a dau.LOUISA marr. WM.R.
ELLEY;another dau.MARGARET A .marr.1st an ERWIN,2nd a DUDLEY.
<For the Will of Henry Johnson see EMR Vol.1-p.91-Will recorded
Wash.Co.Ms.WBk.1,p.346>]

DEED BOOK "S":WASHINGTON CO.MS.
May 1860-Jan.1867

P.541:17 Apr.1866-P.O.A.:Henry J.Johnson of Desha Co.Ark.,and Ben Johnson & Matthew Johnson of Wash.Co.Ms.,give their P.O.A. to (their bro.)Robert A.Johnson for handling their share of the Est. of their father,Henry Johnson and to protect their mother Elizabeth Johnson. P.542;Chas.F.Johnson of Louisville, Ky.,does the same thing.

P.547:2 Apr.1866-Mortg:Sidney R.Smith of 1st part:George W. Burch & James D.Smith of 2nd;1 undivided ½ of Pltn.on Deer Creek and Fish Lake in Wash.Co.Ms. @6 miles from Greenville-joining John C.Courtney,also the land of the late Chancelor Buckner now in possession of his widow-Mrs.Sarah F.Buckner,and also joining Dr.S.S.Taylor being now occupied by Wm.N.Hood & Wm.R. Fleming who are cultivating same under the name of SMITH & HOOD -@2150 ac.

P.638:Saml.Worthington and wife Amanda mortgage "Mosswood Pltn"- 1866.

P.650:30 Jan.1866-Agree.:Saml.G.French signs lease to rent all of the portion of"Matilda Place"belonging to Sallie C.French of New Jersey.Located on N.side of BlackBayou-@600 ac.

P.659:17 Apr.1866-P.O.A.:Sarah H.Gunnison of Bibb Co.Ga.,to Arvin N.Gunnison of Wash.Co.Ms. Sarah signed in Hillsborough Co.N.H. In the Clerk's proof,it is stated Arvin is Sarah's husband.

P.690:4 Aug.1866-Deed:Philadelphia Sims,Admx.of Est.of Chas.Sims decd.of Wilk.Co.Ms.,sold,under court order,certain lands belonging to said Chas.-2575 ac-1/3rd int..Land sold to G.G.Sims and his heirs.

P.694:15 Nov.1866-Agree.;"Whereas John T.Courtney,did during the late war and during my absence and in the yr.1864 on my account, loan to my mother and sister the sum of $500,which money has not been paid"-gave a lien on"Matilda Place".Signed by S.G.French.Onp.696;Also gave a lien to Clayton French,of Philadelphia,Pa.,on "Matilda Place".Saml.French owes Clayton French $1,000,loaned in 1866.

P.700:7--1866-Mortg:W.H.Lee of Wash.Co.Ms.,an agent for H.P.Lee, John M.Lee,a minor,Catherine Ferguson -on their PLtn."Ditchley" deliver to S.W.Ferguson,husband of Catherine,11 bales of cotton, + an a/c from Judge Hughes of Tx.to Catherine. Document also mentions property belonging to the Lees' in Texas.

END OF DEED BOOK "S"

ADDITIONAL HUSBANDS AND WIVES LISTED IN "S",+ RESIDENCE + DATE
Baird,Jas.M. & wife Eliza T., Lowndes Co.Ms. 1864
Bland,Maxwell W. & wife Mary L., Yazoo Co.Ms. 1861
Brown,Shepherd & wife Louisa N., New Orleans,La.1865
Calhoun,Gustavus & wife Eliza Jane, Adams Co.Ms. 1861
Catchings,Augustus,Sr. & wife Fanny M.W., Hinds Co.Ms. 1860
Clark,Chas. & wife Anne E., Bolivar Co. Ms.,1860
Clitherall,George B. & wife S.A., Mobile,Ala.,1866
Echols,John H. & wife Medora E., Jackson,Ms., 1863
Fleming,Wm.R. & wife Lizzie Hood Fleming, Fayette Co.Ky.,1860
Gholson,Thos.S. & wife Corry Ann, Petersburg,Va.,1863
Goza,Dupuy & wife Mary P., Bolivar Co.Ms.,1865
(cont.)

ADD.HUS.& W.LISTED IN "S".(cont.)
James,John & wife Mary, Wash.Co.Ms.1866
Klein,John A. & wife Elizabeth B.,Vicksburg,Ms. 1865
Lane,Lafayette N. & wife Mary Julia,NewOrleans,La.,1860
Latham,Harvey & wife Lucy Ann, Warren Co.Ms.,1865
Lee,Thos.J. & wife Mary J., Wash.Co.Ms.,1863
Nelson,John H. & wife Mattie J.,Wash.Co.Ms.,1862
Peebles,Henry W. & wife Anna W., St.Marys P. La.,1860
Powell,Edw.U. & wife Susannah P., Warren Co.Ms.,1861
Rives,Orville C. & wife Mary W., Wash.Co.Ms.,1863
Roberts,Percy & wife Mary S., Memphis,Tn.,1866
Rose,Wm.H. & wife Susan E., Hinds Co.Ms.,1863
Royall,Tecumseh F. & wife Ellen B., Yazoo Co.Ms. 1865
Scott,Wm.Parker & wife F.M., Yazoo Co.Ms.,1862
Sims,Robert G. & wife Felixina, Wash.Co.Ms.,1866
Smith, Sydney R. & wife Bettie B.,Lexington,Ky.,1860
Smylie,Thos.B. & wife Eliza J.,Chicot Co.Ark.,1866
Worthington,Wm.W. & wife Elizabeth P., Wash.Co.Ms.,1866

*p.127,this Vol.,Deed Book "S"p.461.The name VanCockelberghe
sp.VanCoeckelberghe,Van Coekelbergh_,in same document.

*¶NOTE:Documents are also out of sequence.

SUPPLEMENTARY INFORMATION: THE FRENCH FAMILY

Saml.G.French,b 22 Nov.1818,Gloucester Co.,N.J. graduated from
the U.S.Military Academy at West Point.He fought in the Mexican
War,and served in the U.S. Army until he became an officer in
the Conf.Army.On26 Apr.1853 he marr.Eliza Matilda Roberts,dau.of
Jos.L.Roberts & Mary(Symington)Roberts.A sister ,Sarah F.Roberts
marr.the bro.of Saml.-JohnC.French,in 1854.Saml.& Matilda's dau.-
Matilda Roberts French was b.16 Aug.1855.Saml.G.French was sta-
tioned at Ft.Smith,Ark.,when he and his bro.John C.French bought
a plantation in Wash.Co.Ms.in T19,R8W(DBk."S"P.171)
In the spring of 1857,Matilda French and her small dau.went to
San Antonio,Tex.to visit Sister Sarah & John French. Saml.joined
them there,and tragedy struck. Matilda(Roberts)French died,giving
birth to a son. Her body was returned to Laurel Hill Cemetery
in Philadelphia,Pa.,and buried in the family vault,with her mother,
father,and infant son. During the early part of the War,Gen.French's
mother & sister Sallie C.French lived with the little girl,Mat-
ilda, on the pltn.in Wash.Co.Ms.,called "Matilda Place".They
returned to N.J.late in the War.
After the end of the Civil War,Gen.Saml.G.French returned to his
Pltn.in the Ms.Delta,and described his homecoming thusly:"The
Captain of the steamer put me on shore at "Argyle Landing",near
my home..When I dismounted at my door,God only knows my agony
of heart..Fences were burned,bridges destroyed, the pltn.a forest
of tall weeds:horses,mules,cattle,sheep,poultry,provisions,wagons,
implements of every kind--all gone;Wealth,servants,comfort--all
means of support for my family gone..I sat down and surveyed
the desolation around me."
Saml.G.French marr.2nd Mary Abercrombie in 1865,and the family
regrouped on "Matilda Place"by 1866.Gen.French struggled to bring
order out of chaos.
Taken from"TWO WARS" by Gen.Samuel G.French.

-131a-

The following is an abstracted document, in which Harriet B. Theobald authorizes the donation and sale of lots on her plantation Blantonia, to form "New"Greenville.

DBk"S"Wash.Co.Ms.

P.411-412:18 May 1865:P.O.A.:"Whereas I,Harriet B.Theobald of the Co.of Wash.,State of Ms.,am about to leave my home on a visit,and as I may by accident or death,be prevented from returning and executing business and arrangements herein after to be mentioned,and whereas it has been suggested to me that it may become necessary to change the location and site of the court house and other public buildings of the county from the place at which they are now located to some other more safe and desirable location,and whereas, it has been also suggested to me that it may be desirable to locate the same on some portion of my"Blantonia Plantation"on the front part thereof lying immediately on and bordering on the Miss. River and that it has also been suggested that I consent to such location,and the designation thereof. Now,therefore I do,in the event that such location shall be made upon my land,consent thereto under the stipulation and conditions herein after to be named...nominate and appoint my sons Orvill M. & William C.Blanton my agents for me and in my name, whenever the site of the public buildings shall be so located upon my lands, by persons legally authorized so to fix and locate the same, to convey by deed as a donation from me to the Board of Police of Wash.Co.,a lot of ground for such purpose not exceeding 2 acres.

And Whereas...it has been suggested to that it would be advisable and promotive of the public convenience to lay off a portion of my land in streets and town lots to enable parties so desiring to erect dwelling houses,offices,stores,warehouse, workshops...I authorize and empower my said sons...lay off streets,squares and lots...and when numbered,sell same to such persons as may desire to make purchases...for cash,or upon credit...It is however to be expressly understood that no such division of my land into lots,etc.,shall be made until after the location of the public buildings have been permanently made ...I assign all proceeds of the sales to be applied to the payment of such debts as I owe to Samuel Theobald,Augustus W.Newman and the bills of my phisicians...I wish each of my sons children to have conveyed to them one lot so layed off at such point as may be selected by their fathers...persons may lease and pay rent on lots before public buildings erected...option to buy...cannot engage in shipping,cotton,goods,wares and merchandise and other commodities...I reserve the use of the landing on my front for shipping and recieving freight...I do further declare that the acts of my agents O.M. & W.C.Blanton shall not be binding upon me if made and done during my absence unless the same have the written approval of J.S.Yerger, or in the event that he cannot act therein,of such person as he may appoint...and if either agent dies...survivor shall be authorized to act...

Signed by H.B.Theobald, accepted by Clerk of Probate Court of Wash.Co.Ms.,William A.Haycraft.

Left Margin Notation:Examined and delivered to J.S.Yerger.

Know all men by these presents that I Harriet B Theobalds of the County of Washington State of Mississippi having caused to be laid off and surveyed a town out of the lands belonging to me situate in said County & State on the Mississippi River and Known as the Blantonia plantation a plat and survey of which town is hereto annexed for record. Now therefore be it known that I the said Harriet B Theobalds do hereby dedicate to the use of the purchasers of the Lots in said town and the public all the Streets as designated in the said plat running through the said town, and to the public road and river landing to be used as such public highway only but expressly and unconditionally reserve to myself all the land and all accretions hereafter made thereto lying between or adjoining the said town and the said River or Chute of the same. In testimony whereof I have hereunto subscribed my name & affixed my seal this 1st day of Septm 1865

Witness
Richd A. O'Hea
H B Theobald [seal]

State of Mississippi
Map of a Town laid off in The Blantonia Plantation showing the Streets Lots and Blocks with their numbers; situated in Section 4 Township 18 Range 8 West in Washington County Miss. the property of Mrs Harriet B Theobalds. And further described, to wit: Begining at the S.E. Corner of Section 4, a piece of Marble thence along the Section line N 55½ W 37.24 four pole chains, to a stake thence N 34½ E 5 chs to a Stake the S.E. Corner of the town; thence 15 chs to a Stake the N.E. Corner of the town thence N 55½ W 31 chains to a Stake the N.W. Corner of the town thence S 34½ W 15 chs to a Stake the S.W. corner of the town; thence S 55½ E 31 chs back to the S.E. corner of the Town

By Richd A. O'Hea
Civil Engineer

See Addition to City P. 544 this book.

GREENVILLE, MAY 1st, 1866

I hereby certify that the annexed is a correct sketch of the Town laid off by me on the Bachelor Bend Plantation. Situated in Section 6, Township 18, Range 8 West, Washington County Mississippi. The property of Benj. Roach Esq. described as follows. The N.E.Cor of the town "A", bears N55½ W17.24 chains, from the N.E.Cor of Section 6. Thence along North Boundary to N.W.Corner of Town "B" N.55½, W.56.95 chains; Thence along West Boundary S.34½ W.250 chains to "C": Thence on a line parallel to the West Boundary 7.50 chains to "E", the SW Corner of the town: Thence along South Boundary on a line parallel to the North Boundary 51.95 chains to "F", South East Corner of the town; Thence along East boundary on a line parallel to the West Boundary 10.00 chains to "A" the point of beginning.

   S.J. Butler
  of Hodges & Butler

Civil Engineers & Surveyors
   New Orleans

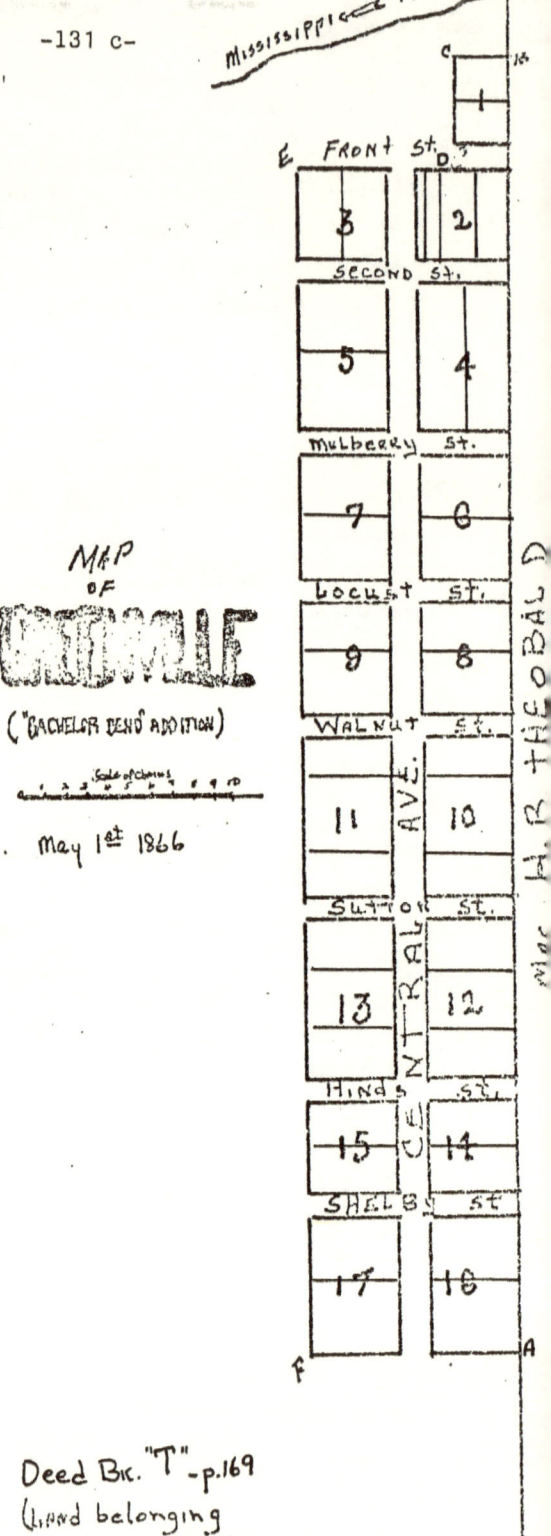

Deed Bk. "T" - p.169
(Land belonging to Ben Roach)

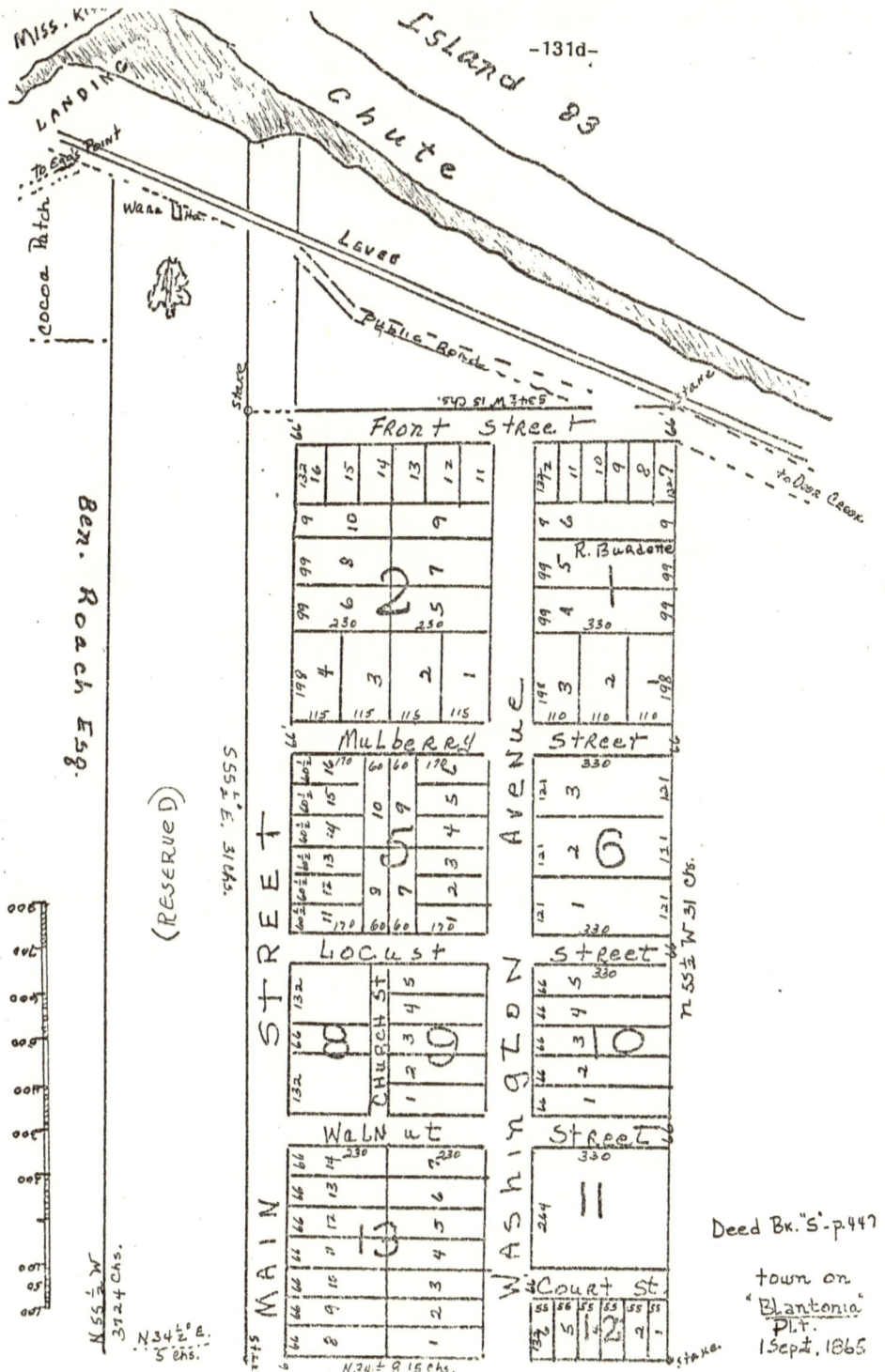

DEED BOOK "T":WASHINGTON CO.MS.
DATED:9 Jan.1867-8 Feb.1869
Indexed in front,also in Master Index Bk.1;Water marked,mended,
640 pages. This book is dominated by the selling of lots in the
town marked off from "Blantonia Pltn."and from the new addition
marked off from"Bachelor Bend Pltn."to be known as GREENVILLE.

Ben Roach sells lots in Bachelor's Bend to B.Hanway;T.Greary.
On 4 Jan.1867 Roach sells to Wm.B.Wheatley & McKinzie Davis for
Wheatley & Davis-L3;Bl.2;65ft. Fronting on 2nd st.,running back
264 ft. On Condition that they must never sell their frontage
for a public road or a wharfboat landing. Others buying were
N.J.Johnson & J.Manifold;Susan V.Byrne;Mrs.Rebecca Roberts;A
lot donated to the Catholic Ch.for $10;Moses Selig & J.O.Welles.

P.9;1867-Mortg:Mansfield Wilmot mortg.all crops on"Ashland Plt"
to Williamson Hill & Co. of Memphis.Ashland Pltn.,belonged to
the Est.of E.P.Johnson,decd. Wilmot leased it for 1867.

P.10:15 Jan.1867-Deed:Saml.Theobald & wife Harriet B.of Wash.Co.
Ms.,to Saml.Theobald,Wm.L.Nugent,Robt.M.Carter,Andrew J.Paxton,
Jas.McClennan all of Wash.Co.Ms.:For great love and respect,the
Theobalds give to the Methodist Episcopal Church South 2 lots
laid out in Blantonia Pltn.-L#1,Block#9-center lot in reserved
Block 8-to be used for the dwelling house of the preacher and
a house of worship.

P.19:23 Jan.1867-Mortg:Shepherd(X)Blackburn(freedman)of Wash.Co.
Ms. to Elijah B.Thornton,agent for J.H.Lynch & wife M.A.Lynch.

P.23:16 Jan.1867-Quit Claim:Emily Angelina Ferriday,of full
age, wife of Joseph C.Ferriday of New Orleans sells to John
James of Wash.Co.Ms.-200 ac.

P.25:29 Jan.1867-Mortg:Harry Yerger-Guard.of person and Est.of
Maggie, Malvina & Harvey Miller & Sallie Yerger his wife,seek
funding from E.B.Kimball & Co.of N.O.[NOTE:Maggie,Harvey,Sallie,
Malvina are the ch.of Harvey Miller,decd.]

P.59:7 Feb.1867-P.O.A.:Eleanor N.Percy of Nashville appoints
Wm.Nichol of David.Co.Tn.,to conduct business for her in Wash.Co.
Ms.as an heir of the Est.of "my late father,Chas.B.Percy",make
settlements with the late J.Walker Percy's successor as Adm.for
my late father's Est.,and Wm.A.Percy,my Guard.-all of Wash.Co.
and of my Grandfather,the late Thos.G.Percy.(For the Will of
Chas.Percy,J.Walker Percy,Thos.G.Percy see Vol.1,Vol.11 of this
series,EMR.)

P.60:18 Jan.1866-Release:Theodore G.Walcott rents,for 7 yrs.,the
plantation on Deer Creek belonging to Nelson T.Warren,and cancels
lease.Nelson's wife is Lucinda Warren:Walcott's wife is Bettie C.

P.62:16 Feb.1867-Deed:Nelson T.Warren & Sarah Lucinda acknowledge
receipt of $7,000 from Bettie C.Walcott-her husband is T.G.
Walcott-as 1st payment for land in Sec.19;& Sec.30;T16;R6W +
some in R7W-@723 ac.

P.68:27 Feb.1867-Agreement:J.W.Harrow declines to pick up document in which T.A.Harrow turned over the unexpired lease for
"Hollywood Pltn."made on 9 Feb.1866.

P.87:26 Mar.1867-Deed:Albert W.Dunbar & wife Matilda B.sell
to Wm.A.Phietus(Phetus)all of Adams Co.Ms.,-1996 + Ac.in Sec.21
and Sec.20;of T14;R8W that Dunbar bought from D.H.Humphreys,

DEED BOOK "T":WASHINGTON CO.MS.
1867-1869

(cont.)Benj.G.Humphreys,Sarah S.Barnes in 1848.+ land entered
by Dunbar as O.P.known as "Marathon Pltn.".

The following bought lots in "New"Greenville;Josephine Johnson;
Benj.H.Sutton-L1 & 4 on Bl.4 on Mulberry St.& Davis;Jas.R.Cox
bought L10,B5;Harry G.& John Dixon bought L11 on Main:Lawrence
D.McMeekin bought L2,B2 fronting on Mulberry St;Wm.L.Nugent
bought L1 & 2,B1-also L1 &2 in 2nd Addition on Walnut St.;Barlow
W.Wheatley in Front Addition.

P.103:6 Mar.1867-P.O.A.:Peter D.Gregory of Southampton,Burlington Co.,N.C.,gives his P.O.A.to Wm.L.Nugent to take hold of "Elmwood Pltn"and to act as his agent.

P.106:22 Mar.1867-P.O.A.:John R.Blanchard gives his P.O.A.to
Chas.G.Morehead & Wyndham R.Brigg-or either of them-to take
possession of "my property" as late partner in firm of J.R.Blanchard. All in Wash.Co.Ms.

P.107:1 Feb.1867-D/T:J.M.Montgomery,W.E.Montgomery,D.C.Montgomery
all of the 1st part:Wm.L.Nugent of the 2nd part;Saml.H.Kennedy,
Paul E.Mortimer,Julius Jarvin of the 3rd part,acting under the
firm name of J.H.Kenedy & Co.(Sp.on Kennedy,different)

P.121:22 Apr.1867-Mortg:C.G.Morehead is indebted to Maj.Wm.Hunt
for notes dated 1860,1861,1866. Wm.Hunt and his Exec.,advanced
more. Morehead paid Geo.B.Hunt & Wm.E.Hunt-Exec.of Wm.Hunt,decd.
by mortg.to them all his rights to "Catalpha Pltn."which he
is now residing on and cultivating + "Greenleaf Pltn."now occupied by Saml.Murrell & Harmon-all land in Wash.Co.Ms.

[NOTE:Many Mortgages followed-a large number to"Cotton factors"]

P.128;6 Feb.1867-Mortg:James Archer,Sr. & wife Mary Ann of Jeff.
Co.Ms.,mortg."Haiford Pltn."in T17,R8W of Pearl River-1600ac
to Ann B.Hunt.

P.130:15 Apr.1867-P.O.A.:"Woodlawn",Jeff.Co.Ms.,a release (of
mortgage above)of James Archer and wife,in favor of David Hunt
and signed by Ann B.Hunt,Exectx.& Dunbar Hunt who give their
P.O.A.to J.B.Gray.James Archer was the Exec.of the Est.of David
Hunt,decd.

P.131;6 Feb.1867-Deed:James Archer,Sr. & wife Mary Ann of Jeff.
Co.Ms.-for natural love and affection for their son Rev.Stevenson Archer for managing "Haiford Pltn."-give him a part of
said pltn.adjoining Alex Montgomery + 320 ac.,sold by David
Hunt and wife to said James Archer and wife-dated 18 Aug.1857,
and recorded Bk.#2,p.563,564. Land in Wash.Co.Ms.

P.151;7 Feb.1857-Mortg:Saml.G.French-for $1 to Chas.Scott
Chandlor,French's undivided ½ of land on Deer Creek,known as
"The Matilda Place"described as L-8 of Sec.26;E½ S34,L-1-3-4-
5-6-7-S35 + 74 ac.of W side of Sec.36,L-5 of Sec.25-all in
T19,R8W-1030 ac. and conveyed to Saml.G.French and John C.French
+ 85 slaves.S.G.French is under a bond for $83,000 as trust
for his wife and child and according to a verdict in case of
E.Z.VanCockelbergher & Others. On p.152:next document dated
12 Feb.1867, S.G.French of Wash.Co.Ms.,leases Matilda Place
to Mrs.M.L.Berry of Ala. French states he is now residing(CONT)

DEED BOOK "T":WASHINGTON CO.MS.
1867-1869

(cont.)on this place. The rent is $5,000 unless there is an overflow...in which case a refund of no more than $500 will be made.

P.154:10 Dec.1866-Deed:Wm.P.Montgomery sells for $20,000,"Locust PLtn.:to Wm.E.Montgomery,D.C.Montgomery,J.M.Montgomery. Land in T17,R8W;some in T18,R8W;T17,R9W;T18,R9W-@1571 ac.

P.156:28 May 1867-Gift:Absolom Petit,Sr.for love and affection to his son Absolom Petit,Jr.-land in T17,R8W @240 ac.known as "Forrest Home Place".

P.162:2 Feb.1867-Mortg:A.C.Hutchins and wife Anna of Claib.Co. Ms.,of 1st part owes John Hutchins of Sumner Co.Tn.,$2700. Saml.Hutchins of Claib.Co.Ms.,is security.All signed Claib.Co.

P.200:10 July 1867-Quit Claim:for $100 W.A.Haycraft quit claims to Amelius C.West,Hector R.West,E.Winston West,Lizzie M.West, Sallie R.(?)West,land in T15,R6W and R7W.

P.225:12 June 1867-Deed:James Cooper,late of Nueces Co.Tx.,and now temporarily residing on a part of "Woodstock Pltn"in Wash. Co.Ms.,sells to John Cooper,Hamilton Co.Ohio,all growing crops, etc.on said pltn.,leased from Robt.H.Carter,Adm.of ----Caithers Est.,lying on portion of Woodstock. @80 ac.on which "I(Jas.) am.. now living and have leased for 1867".

P.325:13 Feb.1867-Mortg:Gervis S.Moseley,Exec.of last Will and Testament of Eliza G.Mosley,decd.,mortg."Loughborough Pltn." to Newman J.Wilson. [NOTE:Gervis Storrs Mosby marr.Eliza Glover Burks-1851.The correct sp.is Mosby.From the "Montgomery Paper."]

P.268:1 Oct.1867-Release:Christopher F.Hampton was Guard.of Ann H.Hampton(note;his dau.)during her infancy, under the approval of the Court of Equity of S.C. On 19 Oct.1849, Christopher took charge of the estate she was entitled to under Wills of Mrs.M.E.Richardson and Mrs.Ann Lovell,and rendered a true a/c in 1861. Land known as "Linden Pltn."in T14,R8W-1280 ac.+ notes given to Wade Hampton and W.Hampton,Jr.(for Will of Ann H.Hampton see Vol.II this series or Will Bk.1,p.440 Wash.Co.Ms.)

P.273:10 Jan.1868-D/T:Robt.G.Sims & Geo.G.Sims of Wash.Co.Ms., sell to A.J.Paxton 2 undivided 1/3rd interests in "Sligo Pltn" in Wash.Co.Ms.

P.274:7 Jan.1868-D/T:F.G.Wingfield,nameing son- W.J.Wingfield-sells his plantation to A.J.Paxton,lying between Bogue Phalia and Sunflower River in T17,R6W.

P.281:14 Feb.1849-Marr.Agreement:Between Margaret Eliza Montgomery & Benj.Roach of Adams Co. They are to be marr. on the 15(of Feb.)..Margaret is to retain control of her property, but Benjamin is to manage it, under her approval.[NOTE:From "The Montgomery Papers":Benj.Roach marr. the dau.of Alexander Montgomery & Jane Gilbert Montgomery. After the death of Jane, Alex.marr.Benj.Roach's mother Mary Eliza Wilkins Roach. In Census 1850-Adams Co.,Alex.Montgomery & Mary Eliza are living in Natchez with David,Wilkins,Eugene,Mary Roach in the household.]

DEED BOOK "T":WASHINGTON CO.MS.
1867-1869

P.287:P.O.A.7 Feb.1868:Elizabeth Hynes of Warren Co.,Exectx.:
Madeson P.Hynes,Exec.of Est.of John Hynes,decd.appoints W.H.
Henderson their atty.,to see to their undivided interest in
land in Wash.Co.Ms.

P.291:7 Feb.1867-Deed:Thomas Hinds of Wash.Co.Ms.,sells a portion of "Plum Ridge Pltn."on Rattlesnake Bayou to Wm.L.Nugent,
trustee;Rich.J.Nugent,agent for S.H.Kennedy & Co. The wife of
Wm.L.Nugent is Mary Catherine.

P.299:15 Feb.1868-Deed:Tobias Gibson of Terrebonne P.La.,sells
to Hart Gibson of Woodford Co.Ky.,land loc.in T16,R3W,an O.P.
entered in 1835-1675 ac.

P.343:1Mar.1868-Deed:Christopher F.Hampton of Wash.Co.Ms.,sells
to Kate Hampton,Ann M.Hampton,C.L.Hampton of Richl.Co.S.C.,
household furnishings at "Linden Pltn."-1100 books,beds,china,
wine cellaret,billiard table,stone ware,glass,pictures,etc.+
all silver and plate.(Christopher owes his sisters $6,000.)

P.351:2 Mar.1868-Deed:John Butts,Adm.de bonis non with Will
annexed of Ambrose Knox,decd.of Wash.Co.Ms.,is ordered to sell
property in order to pay debts-1036 ac. being the plantation
called "Solitaire" loc.inT14,R9W bought by Edward S.Butts with
C.F.Hampton as security.(Will of Ambrose Knox, Vol.I of this
series or in Will Bk.1,p.280-Wash.Co.Ms.)

P.353:2 Dec.1867-Deed:Gustin W.Thomas to Illinois C.Thomas
(female) of Madison Co.Ms.

P.436:1 Oct.1867-Deed:A.Wickliffe sells to A.W.Wickliffe,for
$1370, 12 mules with brand "W" + 40 head of cattle,brand "W"
& "J.P."

P.439:6 May 1868-Deed:John A.Scott has owed Sarah E.Scott 2
notes for $21,300 for "sometime". John sells his interest in
a Pltn.,known as "Scotland Pltn.:situated in Wash.Co.Ms.,belonging to the heirs of John A.Scott,decd. and lying between
the plantations of Dr.&Mrs..Orville Blanton,and that belonging
to Est.of Wm.R.Campbell,decd.+all other land he owns in Wash.Co.
+ his interest in certain lands in the counties of Archer,
Wichester in Texas, which lands were conveyed to the father
of both parties of this instrument-John A.Scott,decd...by O.P.
in 1855-@9600 ac.+ John's interest in 1/6th of John A.Scotts',
decd.,Est. + 1/4th of 2/6ths as heir-at-law of his 2 bros.
Guignard & Calhoun Scott,both decd.(Guignard and Calhoun were
killed in the Civil War. Sarah E. was the sister who Marr. Harry
Percy Lee on 23 Nov.1868-Wash.Co. & there were 2 other ch.,
Caroline and Fannie- all being the issue of John A.Scott and
wife Sarah Slann Guignard of Columbia,S.C.)

More Sales for Bachelor Bend Addition to the town of Greenville;
Annie E.Lampkin-L-1,B-11 fronting on Central,going through to
Walnut:H.C.Lipowsky-L-1,B-8 fronting on Central & Locust.

More sales for lots in New Greenville on Blantonia Plt.+ 1st
and 2nd additions:Evie H.Comstock L-15 in 2nd add.on Walnut
and back to Locust;Wm.A.Haycraft L-3-4-6,B-21;Hannah Fischer
L-18 in 2nd Add.on Walnut,back to Locust;Nannie J.Trigg owned
E½ of B1-1stAdd.fronting on Poplar,Davis & Court-now buys(Cont)

DEED BOOK "T":WASHINGTON CO.MS.
1867-1869

(cont)E½ of B-11 fronting on Wash.,to Court +certain land lying between B-11-12;A.W.Newman L-1,2 B-2 of 1st Add.;Rich.A. O'Hea-lot in Reserved sec.L-5 fronting on Main St.;Betty Howard Nelson-L-25,2nd Add.on Locust St.;James R.Cox of Wash.Co.Ms. sells L-10,B-5 for $2200 to Ellen M.Cox of N.O.

P.453:30 June 1868-D/T:Chas.Bosley and wife Eliza A. of Nashville sell "Swiftwater Pltn." in T17,R8W @2552 ac.to Victor Montgomery and his brother and sister-Wm.F.Montgomery & Davidella Montgomery as tenants with full power of partition or sale or mortgage.

P.455:6 Jan.1868 Deed:Wm.A.Broadwell of 1st part;Jacob P. Broadwell of 2nd;Whereas-on 6 Jan.1859 Jefferson Nailor & wife Eliza Nailor gave a D/T to the late Wm.A.Lake,& Wm.A.Broadwell was a trustee to secure payments from Andrew F.Haynes,decd.,on notes overdue. The Nailor's mortg.,land in Yazoo and Wash.Co.Ms. After non payment of notes,land went up for public sale and Jacob was the buyer.

P.462:15 June 1868-Mortg;R.H.Hord & wife Mary J.Hord mortg. mules,crops on"Cold Spring Pltn."on which they live, in Wash. Co., to Jos.Hoy.(No land description)

P.478:20 May 1868-Crop Loan:"Pltn.Ditchely" to be cultivated by W.H.Lee & wife Emma. Harry P.Lee is part owner.

P.484:13 Jan 1868-Agreement:Between Jas.P.Hammett of Wash.Co. Ms.,and Lawson A.Melchoir of same-co-partnership agreement for purpose of cultivating "Lammermoor Pltn."

P.485:2 July 1868-Deed:On 15 Nov.1867 a final decree rendered in Circuit Court of U.S.for Southern Dist.,of Ms.,in case #18,R.Marsh Denman & Mary R.Denman,Exec of J.Marsh Denman,decd., vs John T.Courtney;Ordered to sell "Oakland Pltn."loc.E.side of Deer Creek + some on E.Bank of Black Bayou- all of E½ of Sec.9,& N½ of Sec.12; all of Sec.7,All of Sec.8 except for a roadway;N½ of Sec.13, & all of N½ Sec.14 on N.side of Dr.Creek and Fish Lake road,all lands in T18,R8W. Lands were sold and "struck off" to said Mary R.Denman,widow of said J.Marsh Denman, decd.,and to Isaac R.Denman,Abraham C.Denman,Frederick A.Denman of N.J.-only heirs-at-law of J.Marsh Denman,decd.

P.490:25 Dec.1867-Deed:F.A.Metcalfe sells,for $5,000,his inherited portion of "Lammermoor Pltn"to Mrs.Pricilla Metcalfe. F.A.'s portion came from division of Est.of Dr.Wm.H.Hammett.

P.493:20 Apr.1868-Chattel Deed:Gustavus Calhoun of Adams Co. Ms.,sells for $1, to Robt.Harwood Calhoun of Wash.Co.Ms.,all farming utensils now attached to "Glen Allan Pltn".on Lake Wash. + mules brought from our "Park Pltn." + other stock and crops.(No land description)

P.495:18 Apr.1867-Deed:Thos.H.Buckner & wife Louisa sell a lot on Eggs Point Road-situated on Lake Lee-to Frances Griffin wife of John Griffin-all of Wash.Co.Ms.

P.505:23 Dec.1867-P.O.A.:Fannie Theobald of Baltimore,Md.gives P.O.A.to W.R.Trigg of Wash.Co.Ms.,to act as her agent in her undivided right as Admx.,with Will annexed,of Samuel Theobald, decd.[NOTE:No record of this will in Wash.Co.Ms.]

DEED BOOK "T":WASHINGTON CO.MS.
1867-1869

P.518:Dist.Court of U.S.For Southern Dist.of Ms.:"In the matter of Saml.G.French," Bankruptcy- S.W.Ferguson was appointed assignee of Est.of Saml.G.French-"all the Est.,Real and Personal,all property of whatever kind he owned,interest in,etc." on 29 Feb.1868.

P.522:6 Jan.1868-Deed:Leroy P.Percy of 1st part:Fannie E. & Maria W.Percy of 2nd-all of Wash.Co.Ms. Fannie relinq.all dower rights of marr.with J.Walker Percy,decd.,and all of said rights of Maria from her father,J.Walker Percy,decd.,to land on Deer Creek call "Percy Pltn."described in a deed from Leroy P.Percy to Nannie J.Percy-in exchange for 120 ac.of cleared land to be laid off wherever Fannie and Maria want it + ½ undivided interest in dwelling house on said pltn.,with Nannie J.,the wife of W.A.Percy,owning other ½.(W.A.& Leroy P.Percy are bros.) "Percy Pltn."is loc. S½ Sec.22,N½ Sec.22...all in T18,R7W-@1590 ac. Reserving the right of Leroy P.Percy to convey some of the land to heirs of Chas.P.Percy,decd.[Note;for further information on this Percy Family see Vol.II of this series.E.M.R.]

P.532:24 July 1868-Deed:Wm.A.Haycraft,Treas.of Board of Levee Comm.for Bolivar,Wash. & Issaq.Co.'s of 1st part;Rosanna Jane Pace,Ida Briscoe Pace,Alfred Claiborne Downs Pace, Minor Ch. of said Rosanna Jane Pace, buys land from Haycraft loc.,in T16,R7W.

Further declarations of Bankruptcy by Dist.Ct.of U.S.Southern Dist.:

Thomas S.Redd,p.533
Matthew F.Johnson,p.534
Morris Weiss,p.535
Ben Johnson,p.536
Thos.G.Polk,p.537
Geo.P.Worthington,p.538
Thos.V.James,p.539
Chas.G.Morehead,p.540
Geo.T.Blackburn,p.541
W.P.Montgomery,p.542
Wm.F.Smith,p.543
Wm.R.Campbell,p.544
Thos.Hinds,p.545
Chas.W.Dudley,p.546
Wm.N.Hood,p.547
Robt.M.Carter,p.548
Edw.P.Byrne,p.549
A.B.Montgomery,p.552
Robt.Howe & Hamilton Wright,p.564
Chas.G.McHatton,p.617

P.550;8 Nov.1867-Gift:Jas.M.Sutton & wife Laura - for love and affection for Benj.H.Sutton,land in T19,R7W-40 ac.

P.553:4 Nov.1867-Deed:Andrew B.Carson,Sherf.of Wash.Co.Ms.,on order from Probate Court in Hinds Co.Ms.,Case #894 and issued 16 May 1867 concerning a tax levied against Sarah F.Buckner, sold at public auction some property. The buyers were Emily E.Evans,Sarah Roberta Parker,Kate Buckner,Nellie F.Buckner-heirs and distributees of R.H.Buckner,decd.,of Wash.Co.Ms.[NOTE:Robt. H.Buckner d.11Sept.1845 & his wife Sarah F.Buckner d.9 Feb.1892. Emily E.,S.R.,Kate,and Nellie F. were their daughters.]

P.555:30 JUne 1868-Deed:John M.Powell & wife Cordelia A. of Circleville,Pickaway Co. Ohio,sells land loc.in Issaq.Co.Ms., in T12,R6W, to Philip F.Giesse(Giefse?)of Willsville,Columbiana Co.,Ohio.

P.561:Greenville,15 Sept.1868:"For and in consideration of invaluable assistance and support in my business of Keeping Hotel in town of Greenville-by my wife Hester A.Cawell...and her suffering & discomfort to which she has been subjected"...(cont)

DEED BOOK "T":WASHINGTON CO.MS.
1867-1869

(cont.)+ the fact that she loaned him $625-conveys to said Hester his lease of building known as the Stonewall Saloon in Greenville,all fixtures,stock,etc. Signed by Jacob Cawell.

P.562:8 July 1868-Deed:S.J.Henderson of 1st part:Helen M.Finlay,Annie P.Archer,John P.Finlay,Bettie D.Finlay,Eliza B.Finlay, Mary N.Finlay,Saml.D.Finlay,Pricilla W.Finlay,Thos.P.Finlay of 2nd; Henderson sells land on Williams Bayou to the Finlays. Land loc.in T19,R8W.

P.568:13 Jan.1868-Mortg:Ulyses Merchant sells to Henry R.Merchant for $5-land in Wash.Co.Ms.

P.573:--Aug.1868-D/T:Illinois C.Thomas,widow;Oscar D.Thomas; David P.Thomas;Caroline A.Vaughn & Geo.W.Vaughn her husband; heirs-at-law of J.P.Thomas,decd.;Whereas-J.P.Thomas left a plt. on Deer Creek in Wash.Co.Ms.,loc.in T15,R6W + a lot of wild land in vicinity of said plt. & whereas G.W.Thomas,one of the heirs of said J.P.Thomas,sold out to Illinois,assignee of Said G.W.and other heirs-seek partition of property. Geo.W.Vaughn and Caroline get the portion on which they now live, with Oscar joining them on the back,and release other lands to Illinois and rest of the heirs. Diagram of division on p.576.

P.582:24 Dec.1867-Deed:Rankin Co.Ms.-Chas.T.Robinson sells @217 ac. to Martha P.Robinson,wife of Gordon Robinson.

P.591:Mrs.H.H.McGregory received a patent"for a new and useful improvement in making Butter-not known before".Mrs.McGregory is from Grayner,Mich.,and records the patent before allowing rights to local sales.

P.596:18 Oct.1868-Deed:John Griffin & Isabella G.Johnson-formerly Isabella G.Griffin-heirs-at-law of Francis Griffin,decd.,and Ed.P.Johnson,husband of said Isabella of Wash.Co.Ms.,sell land that was ordered sold by the courts-"Hollywood Pltn." +"Refuge Pltn."and lands adjoining to John T.Foote of New Jersey.

P.602:8 Nov.1867-Gift:James M.Sutton and wife Laura for love and affection give land in Wash.Co.Ms.to Mrs.Kate R.Douglas.

P.631:11 Nov.1867-DeedHarry Percy Lee & John M.Lee of Wash.Co. Ms.of 1st part;W.A.Percy of same 2nd; The Lees own "Ditchely Pltn."on Deer Creek described as L-1,2,3,4,5,6,7,Sec.34;L-3, Sec.35, all in T18,R7W,@740 ac. except 1/9th undivided interest of Kate Ferguson. The Lees want to make provision for their father Wm.H.Lee and permanent provision for the edu.and maintenance of minor bro.& sis.Clarence P.Lee & Mary L.Lee-for love and affection,puts 1 undivided 3rd part of "Ditchely" in trust to W.A.Percy- also to any other ch. that may be born to Wm.H. Lee & Emma Knight Lee.

P.633:-------Deed:Jas.M.Collier,for $10,paid by Levetta L.Collier & Levand James Collier,minor children of Learew(?)H.Collier-land inT17,R7W in Wash.Co.Ms.,bought"by me"from Geo.R.Fall and wife.

END OF DEED BOOK "T"

SUPPLEMENTARY HUSBANDS & WIVES FROM DEED BOOK"T":RES.& DATE

BLACKBURN,(X)Shephard & wife Phillis(X)Wash.Co.Ms.1868
BOYCE,F.H. & wife V．Ltherine a.,Wash.Co.Ms.1868
BURDETT,Richard & w. Emily S.,New Orleans, 1867
CRUTCHER,Wm.& w. Elizabeth H. Warren Co.Ms. 1867
DILLINGHAM,John P. & w. Martha R.----1864
FERGUSON,S.W. & w Catherine W. Wash.Co.Ms.1867
FERRIDAY,Jos.C. & w. Emily S. New Orleans 1867
GRIFFIN,John and w. Sarah, Wash.Co.Ms.,1867
JUDSON,Wm.H.& w. Jacintha, Vicksburg 1864
LYNCH,Jas.H. & w. Margaret A. Vicksburg, 1867
MARSHALL,Thos.A. & w. Letitia Vicksburg 1866
PAXTON,A.M.& w.Mary S. Wash.Co. 1856
PETTY.A.J. & w. Laura Wash.Co. 1867
PUCKETT,Walter R. & w. Ann Matilda Vicksburg 1837
TURNER,Robt.J. & w. Laura Wash.Co. 1867
WHEELER,W.S. & w. Margaret L. vicksburg 1867
WOODBURN,John R. & w. Nannie W. Louisville, Ky. 1867
YERGER,Alex & w. Elizabeth B. Wash.Co. 1867

CENSUS 1850-WILKINSON CO.MS.:House hold numbers are messed up, impossible to tell heads of house and occupants if neighbors have same name..i.e. Sims.

SIMS,							
John C.	48	Carpenter	bMs.	JOOR,Emily	67	b S.C.	
E.A	40		"	Amanda	14	Ms.	
Jas.C.	19		"	Louisa	12	"	
John C.	10		"	John C.	35	"	
Mary E.	8		La.	Sophia	26	"	
Jessae F.	(M)5		"	John P.	6	La.	
Wm.T.	3		"	Alice	3	"	
Sallie A.	6/12		"	Emily	1	Ms.	
Wm.R.	31	M.D.	Ms.				
Eliz.L.	24		"	JOOR,Peter H.	42	b.S.C.	
Chas.	37		"	Charlotte	35	"	
Philidelphia	29		"	Ella E.	15?	Ms	
Jordan	8		"	Maria P.	10	"	
Leanora	5		"	John	8	"	
Frank	2		"	Peter	5	"	
Nannie	1		"				

HOLT,A.C.	30	M.D.	b.Germany	SIMS,Elizha S.	41	b.Ms.
Mary W.	23		Ms	Martha	3-	"
SIMS,John	77	Planter	b.Va.	Edward	12	"
Ann	59		N.C.	Baby	7	"
				Baby	2	"

DILLINGHAM,John	23	Lawyer	b.Me.	m/w
Martha	22		Ms.	yr.
Lilian	6/12		"	

SIMS,John H.	43		b.S.C.
John	16		Ms.
Eliz.A.	14		"
Robt.G.	11		"
Wm.E.	7		"

PROBATE COURT MINUTES-"1"
WASHINGTON CO.MS.
Small book, heavy binding-unindexed

JUNE TERM 1827
P.1:Orphans Court-June 18,1827:L/A to Rutha Mathews & John Mc-
Fadden with Wm.B.Prince, Elijah Bunch as Sec. for EST.OF ISRAEL
MATHEWS.Inv.p.5 by P.A.Gilbert,Wm.Penrice,Wm.Britton
P.2:ALEXANDER BAIN,decd.,intestate with Joseph Wallace appoint-
ed Adm. Inv.P.4.
AUGUST TERM 1828
P.7:EST.JOHN REED(also sp.READ),to be appraised by John McFadden,
Abell Rolls,Wm.Thomas.Collector-Jesse Jones presented Inventory
NOV.TERM
P.10:EST.WM.BABBITT,decd.,intestate-Lomas Brasher appointed Adm.
with Joseph Wallace sec. Appraisal by Thos.Marney,John Blue,John
Morrison.Inv.p.13,sale ordered at New Mexico 1Feb. next.
P.11:EST.OF ROBT.PRINCE,decd.-Alexander G.Prince Adm.with Wm.
B.Prince as sec. Aprs.by Saml.Worthington,Henry Johnson,John
Miller.
P.12:Jos.Wallace seeks Guard.of infant ch.of ISRAEL MATTHEWS
decd.,Lavinia Berry Matthews & Elijah Matthews of Wash.Co.Ms.
P.14:Ordered that a negro boy named Peter,the prop.of John Reed,
decd.,be hired out for 12 mo.,he must be furnished with a full
suit of clothes,etc.
JAN.TERM 1828:
P.14:JOSEPH EGG gives $500 bond for an agreement between he and
EDWARD SELLERS,binding Sellers 3 children to Egg until they
reach majority.The ch.were-James,about 15,Thomas,@14,Margaret-
noage given.Sec.for bond-Jesse Jones,John Morrison.
P.16:JOSEPH EGG gives bond$500,for agreement with R.H.PRINCE,
binding said Prince's 2 ch.-Louisa Savannah-age6,& Darthula
Rosean age 3,until they are 16.Sec.John Morrison,Jesse Jones.
FEB.TERM 1828
P.17:JOHN FLANAKIN,late of Wash.Co.,decd.,intestate;Mary(X)Flan-
akin & Wm.Williams apply for Adm.with Royal Bill & Elijah Bunch
as sec.(Name later sp. Flanagan)
APR.TERM 1828;
P.19:Sale of Robert Prince's Est.
      "   " John Flanakin's Est.
P.19:EST OF WM.B.PRINCE,decd. of Wash.Co.,intestate.L/A by Sarah
S.Prince with Catharine S.Prince,P.A.Gilbert,Francis Penrice sec.
P.20:Appraisal for EST.WM.B.PRINCE-by Turner Joyner,Francis
Penrice,F.G.Turnbull.
P.20:EST.SAML.SHAYWOOD(Sherwood),decd.,intestate.L/A by Augustine
(X)Geaw(?)with Elijah(X)Bunch,sec. Apprai.by James Lane,Wm.
Peterson,Wm.Rife. (29 Apr.1828)
JULY TERM 1828
P.22:JAMES PERRY,decd. Appraisal by JohnClark,Wm.McKee,Barnet
Dempsey.
P.22JAS.HUTCHESON,decd.,intestate,same appraisers as above.
P.23:Inv.of ROBT.PRINCE(large Est.)
NOV.TERM 1828
P.26:JAMES P.WOOD,Wash.Co.,decd.,intestate.Appraisal by Jos.O.
Campbell Adm.,with E.Bunch & P.A.Gilbert as sec. Apprai.by Saml.
Sojourner,Edw.Doughty,Burges French.
DEC.TERM 1828
P.29:EST.JAMES BABBIT,decd.:Court allows claim of Ichabod Allen
& also that of Mary Monhollands against Est.

PROBATE COURT MINUTES-"1".
WASHINGTON CO.MS.

P.29:EST.OF JOHN READ:Court allows a/c against Est.by Thos.Tunstalls for transporting Jane Reed to and back from Vicksburg.
FEB.TERM 1829
P.31:EST.OF ALEXANDER BAIN:Thos.Bailey seeks appointment of Guard.to infant heirs of Bain,decd.,with Jos.Wallace & John W. Delaney,sec.
P.32:Inv.of ISREAL MATHEWS,decd.
P.32:Court ordered John W.Delaney to be appointed Guard. for James Reed, of Wash.Co.Infant son of John Reed,decd.
P33:Inv. of prop.of James Hutcheson,decd.(Aug.1828)
JUNE 1829
P.36:EST.OF ELIJAH BUNCH,decd.intestate;L/A by Nancy(X)Bunch with P.A.Gilbert,F.G.Turnbull as sec. Appri.by Wm.A.Dromgoole, Jos.O.Campbell,Saml.Sojourner. Inv.P.39
    (Note:a list of notes due the Est.followed, with comments
    by the Widow Nancy written below each entry)
    1819-1note of John Fulton's(Iknow nothing of this)
    1823-Amos Paxton-1 note(was given in this country,but
        since that time he has removed to some of the North-
        ern states)
    1822-1 note-P.S.Prichett(sent to N.O.,but he had gone to
        the Isle of Cuba)
    1828-1 note E.R.McFadden(considered good)
    1830-1 note S.B.Hawley(good when due)
Apprai.of Est.Wm.A.Dromgoole,John Monholland,Saml.Sojourner, 23 May 1829
P.40:EST.OF THOS.COLLINS,decd.,intestate.L/A by Wm.Collins & John Collins.Bd.$4000 with Francis Penrice as sec. along with Alex.G.Prince.Appra.P.42 by John McFadden,Wm.Thomas,Emanuel Millsaps.
JULY TERM 1829
P.42:Court ordered final a/c in Est. of Isreal Mathews, John Flanagan, John Reed.
P.43:Court approved a deed made out to Charles Reed from John Reed,decd.
AUG.TERM 1829
P.43:EST.OF JOSEPH LAIRD,decd.,intestate,L/A by Mary T.Laird with Wm.Penrice,Wm.W.Worthington as sec. Apprai.by Lomax Brasher, Seborn Brasher,Allen Wynens.
SEPT.TERM 1829
P.45:HENRY M.BOWLING,late of Wash.Co.,decd.,intestate,L/A by James H.Bowling with Lomax Brasher, P.A.Gilbert as sec. Apprai. P.46,by Henry Fake,Walter Trimble,& Gilbert.
P.46:EST.OF WM.THOMAS,late of this Co.,decd.,intestate,with Jos.Egg appointed Adm. Sec.Gilbert,& Jas.H.Bowling. Apprai.Henry Crow,Cephus Smith,Zekiel Black,Sr.
OCT.TERM 1829
P.51:Mary Flanagan,one of the heirs of John Flanagan,decd.,seeks Guard. of Pricilla & Sarah Flanagan,minor heirs. Daniel Rowland, one of the heirs of John Flanagan,decd.,wants to be notified of Est.sale.
NOV.TERM 1829
P.52:WILL OF ALEXANDER G.PRINCE:Presented by Joseph McQuillen Names; My wife Sally H.Prince-negro slaves
To the Children of Jos.& Cynthia McQuillen-slaves to be(cont.)

PROBATE COURT MINUTES-"1"
WASHINGTON CO.MS.
P.52;(cont.)divided equally between them when youngest is 21.
To my sis.Myra Jane Prince-rest of slaves,should Myra Jane decd.
     without issue,her portion to be divided between Mary Jane
     & Eliza Ann Pennington,children of sis.Sarah Pennington.
My friend and bro-in-law Jos.McQuillen,exec.with sis.Myra Jane.
Written:11 Nov.1828
Wit:Francis Penrice,Alfred Cocks,Wm.Thomas,Wm.Jenkins
P.54:EST.OF WINSDOR TAYLOR,decd.intestate.L/A by Wm.Taylor with
Enoch Rose,Manuel Ferreno as sec. Apprais.by WmW.Blanton,Augustus McAllister,Wm.P.Montgomery.
P.55;INV.OF WM.THOMAS
DEC.TERM 1829
P.56:EST.EPHRAIM C.DAVISON,decd.intest.L/A by Polly Davison
with John C.Miller as sec.
P.57:EST.ALEX.G.PRINCE:L/A by Jos.McQuillen,Andrew Knox on behalf
of his wife Myra Jane. Philip A.Gilbert,Wm.A.Dromgoole sec.
Adm/Bd $30,000.
JAN.TERM 1830
P.59:EST.OF ROBERT PRINCE:Andrew Knox applies for L/A with Sally
S.Prince. Catharine Prince as sec.$30,000.
P.61;inv. of A.G.PRINCE
FEB.TERM 1830
P.63:Inv.of WINSDOR TAYLOR
P.64:Inv.of EST.OF THOS.COLLINS
MAY TERM,SPECIAL 1830
P.6 :Andrew Knox applies for L/Guard.for Ann Pennington, infant
dau.of EDWARD PENNINGTON,decd. 17 May,1830
JULY TERM 1830
P.67:Est. of DR. ROYALL N.POWERS,decd. Apprais.Dr.B.H.Moyler,
Seborn Brasher,Thos Stephens. Wm.Penrice is authorized to sell
said Est.
P.68:Est.of JOHN LOVE,late of said Co.,decd.,intest. L/A to
F.G.Turnbull with John G.Cocks,P.A.Gilbert,Fielder Offutt as
sec. Apprais.by Turner Joyner,Saml.Tanner,Jos.Briggs,Saml.Briggs,
     Lee-23 Aug.1830.-Adm/Bd.Turnbull states that Love left a
Will.
JAN.TERM1831
P.69:EST.HENRY FAKE,decd.L/A to Saml.Scott with F.G.Turnbull,
Edmund Bass as sec.
*P.71:EST.DR.BENJ.H.MOYLER,decd.,L/A to F.G.Turnbull with Alfred
Cox & R.P.Shelby as sec.
P.72:Court order to Alfred Cox to be Guard.of Seth & Sarah M.
Cox,minor heirs of SETH COX,decd.
FEB.TERM 1831
P.73:EST.JOHN MCFADDEN,decd.intest.,L/A to John G.Cocks and
  blank McFadden. Adm./Bd.by Elizabeth(x)McFadden,John G.Cocks,
Edm.P.Bass,Wm.Penrice for $5,000.Apprais.Wm.Penrice,Owen Jones,
Harvey Shelby.
P.74:EST.P.A.GILBERT,DECD.,INTEST.L/A by Wm.A.Dromgoole
P.75:EST.HARVEY WILKINSON,decd.intest.L/A by J.J.CHewning with
John G.Cocks,Thos.Stephens,Harvey Shelby as Appr.Sale of Est.
APR.TERM 1831
P.78:EST.OF ELIZABETH HARLAND,decd.,intest.Inv.& a/c,with order
to sell. Same order for EST.OF PETER H.BENNETT.
P.79:Inv.of P.A.Gilbert. JULY TERM 1831
*Copy of Moyler Est.inv.on pg.147a-147d,this vol.

PROBATE COURT MINUTES-"1"
WASHINGTON CO.,MS.

OCT.TERM 1831
P.82:Court ordered that Saml.Wallace,an orphan boy,age about 12,be bound to Joseph Egg until he is 21.
P.82:EST.OF J.MCFADDEN-Wm.W.Collins ,appraiser.
DEC.TERM 1831
P.84:EST.SION BASS,decd.,intestate.L/A to Edmund P.Bass with Champ Terry,Council R.Bass as sec(12 Dec.1831)
¶[NOTE:. This is the first mention of court being held at Princeton,Ms.]
JAN.TERM 1832
P.87:John Cocke applies for L/Guard.for Martha Cocke & Benj. Cocke,minor heirs of Wilson Gibson,decd.
P.87:Dower rts.for Eliz.McFadden,widow of John McFadden,decd.
P.88:Est.DR.ELIJAH CARROLL,decd.,L/A granted to Jas.D.Hallam with Council R.Bass as sec.
SEPT.TERM 1832:Court order that June 18,1832,Richard a freeman of colour,formerly the property of Benjamin Moore and his wife Polly Moore,be permitted to remain in the state as "he is of good character,and honest...He is about 40 yrs.old,dark complected,about 6 ft.high". He was liberated by the Moores in consideration of the services he had rendered,by deed of manumission, regularly recorded in Court of Gallatin Co.,Ill.
OCT.TERM 1832
P.97:WILL OF JOHN FOSTER,decd.,produced and admitted for recording.(See Deed Bk.B,p.163-and this Vol.p.14)
P.104:EST.OF MALACHI LANE(Also sp.LAYNE),decd.,intestate,L/A by Chas.B.Lane with Turner Joyner,T.W.Morris,John Swan as Apprai.
JAN.TERM 1833
P.105:EST.OF RICHARD MURPHY,decd.,L/A by Jesse Murphy with Moses Green,James Boyce,Wyatt Boyce, Apprs.
P.107:EST.OF THOS.B.RILEY,decd.L/A Wm.F.Jeffries with Apprs.by Allen Wynens,Geo.Ward,John Hunter.
P.107:Sale of Est.of JOHN WOLFE,decd.,by Henry Crow,E.Black,Jr. E.Black,Sr.
P.110:WILL OF JOHN LOVE,of Wash.Co.Written New Orleans 20 Mar. 1830-Filed Wash.Co. Jan.1833;
My mother Peggy Love of Wilkes Co.,N.C. to have everything. Allen Wynens,exec.:Wit.-J.B.French,Wm.H.Covert
In.follows(L/A filed 23 Aug.1830 by F.G.Turnbull)
P.114:Est of WM.COCKE,decd.,L/A by Conway Oldham.Adm'/Bd.with Stephen Arrington,Wm.Boyce,Wyatt Boyce.
P.115:Est.of EDMUNG P.BASS,decd. L/A by Council R.Bass & Jesse Bass with F.G.Turnbull,Jordan Bass as sec.
MARCH TERM 1833
P.117:Est.A.G.METCALF,decd. Appraisal ordered.
P.117:HENRY WEATHERS applies for license for operation of a ferry boat on Ms.River opposite Helena in Wash.Co.:$1 for one man and horse;25¢ for single horse;25¢ a head for stock.
APRIL TERM 1833
P.118:Est.of Wm.FRAZIER,decd. Appraisal ordered by Claudius Gibson,W.W.Blanton,Pinckney Montgomery.
P.118:Ordered WILL OF JOHN COWDEN be recorded as presented by Elizabeth Cowden--22 Apr.1833
Will: Wife Elizabeth to have full control"as they went hand in hand and dearly earned it"She will be fair with the children (unnamed)(cont.)

P.118;cont.Cowden;He left the Will with Eliz.on the eve of departing for N.O. 21 June 1832.
OCT.TERM 1833
P.123:Noncupative Will of JOS.WALLACE;(previously covered in this EMR series Vol.I,Vol.II)
P.127:WILL OF JAMES BARR-ordered to be received and recorded and L/Test.be granted to John C.Snow with David Thraickill and Saml.Worthington as sec.
WILL OF JAMES BARR:
½ Est.to only child-Margaret Ann Gilmore,dau.of Nancy Gilmore an unmarried woman.
½to sis.Margaret Barr, my only sister
If dau.Marg.Ann decd.,then my mother,Katherine and my only bro. (living)John Barr to get her share.(no date when written)
P129:EST.EPHRAIM G.LUNY(Looney)L/A Alexander B.Montgomery.
P.130:EST.EZEKIEL BLACK,SR.,decd/ L/A to Ezekiel Black,Jr.
P.133:EST.OF JOHN WHIPPLE,decd. L/A to J.T.P.Yeargain with Wm. W.Collins as sec. Apprai.by Thos.Stephens,Thos.Chambers,Allen Wynens.
P135:EST.OF GEO.SHANKS,decd. L/A by W.W.Collins
P.136:EST.OF ELISHA SELSER,decd.with L/A by John Selser
P.140:Est.of Jenkins W.Shelby,decd. L/A to Thomas J.Chambliss
P.141:EST.OF Wm.James,decd. L/A Zachariah Janes
DEC.TERM 1833
P.143:Est.of HARTWELL COCKE,DECD.,Adm.Elizabeth Cocke seeks to be removed as Adm.and asks that Rowland M.Whitman & Thos.J.Cocke be appointed in her place.
P.146:EST.OF SEBORN BRASHER,decd.L/A to Alfred Cox & Louisiana Brasher.
P.147:EST.OF DANIEL SLAGEL,decd.L/A to Saml.Carson
P.149:Court order that Rowland M.Whitman,Thos.J.Cocke be appointed Guard.,of Mary Jane, Louisiana & Elizabeth Cocke-minor heirs of HARTWELL COCKE,decd.
"This day John H.Cocke came before the Court"and requested that Whitman and T.J.Cocke be his Guard.
James Cocke also asks for the same Guards.
Also appeared Lucinda Cocke seeking same. 16 Dec.1833.
JAN.TERM 1834
P.153:EST.WM.PENRICE,decd.,L/A Alfred Cox.
P.155:Inv.of Est.of SEBORN BRASHER.(In listing the debts owed to the est.-the ones by Lomax Brasher were listed as"desperate")
P.157:Court Order that Louisiana Brasher be appointed Guard.to infant heirs of Seborn Brasher,decd.,to wit:Chas.H.Brasher age 10, Lomax age 7, Asa D. Age 8 mo.-27 Jan.1834.
P.159:EST.BARNET DEMPSEY,decd.,Bennet M.Hines,Francis Patterson to be appraisers,since John Guetry left the country.
MARCH 1834
P.163;Est.of SAULTER ACRES,decd.,intestate,L/A to Wm.Johnson & Wm.Rife for $150 bd.(15 Oct.1833)
P.164:Andrew Knox to be appointed Guard.,of Myra Jane Penrice, minor heir of WM.& ELIZABETH PENRICE,decd.,with Robt.P.Shelby,sec.
P165:Est.of ELIZABETH PENRICE,decd.,L/A by Robt.P.Penrice with Andrew Knox and Francis Penrice,sec.
P.167:Robt.P.Penrice seeks Guard.of Joseph Berry Penrice and Thos.S.Penrice,minor heirs of WM.& ELIZ.PENRICE,decd.
APRIL 1834
P.169:Est.of blank-DOAK,decd.L/A John M.Doak

PROBATE COURT MINUTES-"1"
WASHINGTON CO.,MS.

P.175:Est.JOHN DeHART,decd.,with L/A to Mildred DeHart .
Thos.James sec.
P.176:EST.OF JOHN DOKE,decd.with L/A Wm.Doke and a request that
"the whole business be removed to Tallahatchie Co."
NOV.TERM 1834
P.183:EST.Adkin Cornell,decd.L/A Jas.D.Hallam
P.184:Application of John A.Miller that he be allowed to take
the oath of Adm.for EST.OF WM.B.PRINCE,decd.,in lieu of his wife
Sarah S.Prince,Adm.of said Est.as her lawful husband.
JAN.TERM 1835
P.191:Belinda B.Hudson & Thos.Tunstall give Adm./Bd.in EST.OF
FERGUSON HUDSON,decd.
P.195:EST.A.G.METCALF,decd.L/A to Jonathon McCaleb & David Mc-
Caleb of Wash.Co.
P.199:EST.OF BARNET DEMPSEY,decd.L/A to Rachel(X)Dempsey and
Alfred Cox.
P.200;John M.Doak seeks L/A on Est.of his father WM.DOAK,decd.,
late of Wash.Co.(19 Nov.1833)
P215:Inv.of Est.of DR.BENJAMIN H.MOYLER,decd.
P.233:INV.WM.DOAK:names among others-Betsy Doaks,J.S.(or.L.)
Doak,B.M.Doak.
Pages from 240 to 249 blank
JAN.TERM 1836
P.250Jos.O.Campbell seeks Guard.of Narcissa H.,Eliza and John
Henry Shanks of Wash.Co.
P.250:EST.OF THOS.Y.CHANEY,decd.,Adm.Emily Chaney with sec.,
Mordecai Powell,Walter C.Lofton.
P.252:Est.of DEXTER ARMS,decd.,intestate,Wm.F.Jeffries,Adm.
P.254:Est.JOHN C.JONES,decd.,intest.,Adm.David F.Blackburn(25 Jan)
P.256:Est.WM.F.JENKINS,decd.intest.,L/A Wm.Jos.Jenkins with F.G.
Turnbull & Thos.W.Longley as sec.
P.260;Inv.of ALLEN WYNENS
P.261:Est.WM.McFADDEN,decd.,intest.,Adm.Hector Lastly,22 Feb.1836
P.263:Est.JAMES M.HODGES,decd.intest.,Adm.Wm.P.Hodges,22 Feb.1836
P268:Inv.T.Y.CHANEY
P.270:"   WM.McFADDEN
P.271:"   JACOB W.PHILLIS
¶[NOTE;they've stopped putting---Term---and place date by docu.]
P.274;EST.WM.F.GEORGE,decd.,Adm.Walter C.Loftin-24 Oct.1836
P.275:Emily M.Powell seeks Guard. of Wm.Isaac,Sarah Eliz.,& Thos.
Young Chaney,infant heirs of THOS.Y.CHANEY,decd. of said Co.
Signed by Emily M.Powell,Mordecai Powell, Wm.Rushing.24 Oct.1836
P.276:EST.OF FURNEY F.F.G.HERALD,decd. Adm.is James G.Herald
23 Jan.1837.
P.279:EST.WILLIS SMALL,decd.,intestate,Adm.Wm.E.Hall 25 Jan.1837
P.281:Pet/Guard.by Wm.W.Blanton for Guard.of Louisa & Joseph
Berthe of Wash.Co. 27 Feb.1837
P.282:EST.OFJOHN TURNBULL,decd.,intestate. Adm.John Turnbull,Jr.
27 Feb.1837
P.287:EST.OF SIDNEY S.FISHER,decd.,Adm.Bd.by John Fisher.,Emily
Fisher, John L.Fisher,Alfred Cox of Wash.Co. 27 Feb.1837
P.293: Inv.WILLIS SMALL
P.296: " S.S.FISHER
P.299:L/Guard.by Emily Fisher for John E.,Saml.F.,infant heirs
of SIDNEY S.FISHER,decd.,late of Wash.Co. 24 Apr.1837.Inv.follows

PROBATE COURT MINUTES-"L"
WASHINGTON CO.MS.

P.304:L/Guard.,WALTER C.LOFTIN for Guard.,of Martha Jane Eliza Loftin infant_ of said Loftin-(later in doc. it speaks of children but there is no punctuation between the names.)23 Mar.1837
P.315:EST.DAVID K.MCALLISTER Adm.Zenas K.Fulton May 1837
P.317:L/Guard.by STEPHEN CASTLEMAN for James Wren of Wash.Co. with Adam Shirley sec. 25 Sept.1837
P.319:EST.CYRUS GRIFFIN,late.of Wash. Co., Adm.Isaac M.Glidewell Oct.1837
P.320:23 Oct. 1837:Guard/Bd.to Elizabeth Cocke,Geo.W.Reynolds, Alfred Cox of Wash.Co. for infant heir Louisiana Cocke, heir of Hartwell Cocke,decd. Signed E.Walker,G.W.Reynolds.
P.321:EST.HENRY CROW,decd.,intestate,Adm./Bd.by John H. & James Cocke
P.326:EST.HUGH MONTGOMERY,decd.,Adm.Alexander B.Montgomery 25 Dec.1837
P.327:EST. HIRAM R.THOMAS,decd.,Adm.Wm.T.Price-Dec.1837
P.329:Inv.D.K.MCALLISTER
P.330:Guard/Bd.by Wm.E.Hall to minors Haywood & Catherine Small, heirs of WILLIS SMALL,decd. 22 Jan.1838
P.331:EST.ISAAC SHELBY,decd. Adm.Jeremiah Dashiell,22Jan.1838
P.334:INV.OF HENRY CROW
P.339:EST.WM.W.BLANTON,decd.,Adm/Bd H.B.Blanton,S.R.Dunn,John Turnbull 23 Apr.1838
P.341:EST.WM.F.JEFFRIES,decd.,Adm. Thos.Endecott 23 Pr.1838
P.342:Inv.of WM.W.BLANTON
P.350:Pet/Guard by Frederick G.Plant for Guard.of minor Benjamin F.Cocke,infant orphan of JOHN COCKE,decd. 28 May 1838
P.351:Guard/Bd.by Wm.White & Henrietta E.White & Mordecai Powell. "An act passed by the La.Legislature" when Wm& Henrietta were the Guard.of Emily M., Melissa Jane Chaney, minor heirs and children of WOOD L(S)CHANEY,decd. of Parish of W.Felic.,La. They seek permission to move their Ward's property to another state.May 1838
P.353:Inv.of WM.F.JEFFRIES
P.356:Est.of ELIZ.WALKER,decd. Adm.Jeremiah Dashiel 23 July 1838
P.358:Pet/Guard.by Jeremiah Yellott Dashiell for Guard.over Mary Jane & Louisiana Cocke, infant orphans of HARTWELL COCKE, decd. .23 July 1838
P.359:Est.SALMON PHELP(S)decd. Adm./Bd.John Fulton,W.W.Collins 23 July 1838
P.362:Est.ANDREW MCCORMICK,decd. Adm.Council R.Bass.26 Dec.1838
P.364:WILL OF THOS.JAMES,late of Wash.Co.
To sister Frances Steer-$300 per yr.during her widowhood
Neice-Susan Steer
Dau.-Melinda Jackson --all the rest.
Written:31 Aug.1838
Wit:Jos.Burgoyn,Thos.Grimes,Jonathon Young
Recorded 26 Dec.1838
L/A for Est.Thos.James by Jas.B.Jackson filed same day as record.
P.366:Est.THOS.J.COCKE,decd.,Adm.John H.Cocke 26 Dec.1838
P.368:Adm./bd by John H.Cocke,Jas.Cocke,Stephen Arrington,Adam Shirley-$20,000 for Est.of ELIZABETH WALKER 26 Dec.1838
P.369:Guard/Bd. by John H.Cocke for Guard.of minors Mary Jane & Louisiana Cocke.
P.372:EST.WM.B.WREN,decd.,Adm/bd.Council R.Bass,Thos.Grimes, Jas.B.Jackson. 26 Dec.1838

PROBATE COURT MINUTES-"1"
WASHINGTON CO.MS.'

P.376:Est.JAMES MILLER,decd.,Adm.Wm.S.Wells 25 Feb.1839
P.382:Guard/Bd by Harriet B.Blanton for infants Orville M.,W.C.,
and Reed H.Blanton,Inf. orphans of Wm.W.Blanton,decd.29 Mar.1839
P.383:Est.of THOS.J.CHAMBLISS,decd.of Wash.Co. Adm.Jas.D.Hallam
20 Apr.1839
P.385:Adm/Bd:Est.of JOHN TURNBULL,decd. by John Turnbull,Jr.,
F.G.Turnbull, Andrew Turnbull. 27 May 1839
P.388:EST.SINCLAIR GERVAIS,decd. Adm.John Turnbull 29 May 1839
P.389EST.JOHN Y.SINGLETON,decd.,Ann J.Singleton,Sardine G.Stone,
George Lake, Wm.Bridges,Levin Disharoon of Claib.Co.Ms. with
Will annexed.29 May 1838(Note: no Will rec.here)
P,392:Warren Co. 23 June 1839
WILL OF AUGUSTINE B.FAUST
To my mother Sarah C.W.Faust-my only heir & exectx.
Wit:A.G.Creath,L.P.Cunningham,D.Hardeman
Prob.29 Oct.1839

¶NOTE:Next Probate Court Min.Bk."2"skips to 1849

SUPPLEMENTARY MATERIAL:
WILL BK."A":Madison Co.,Ms.1829-1892
P.81:Will of Enoch Rose:Written 1 July 1843-Prob.Nov.Term 1843:
Wife-Mary to be exectx.along with friend Robt.Tucker & H.C.Bennett;
Son-Wm.Walls Rose:Dau.-Mary Stokes Patten:Son-Paschal Rose;Dau.-
Rebecca Bennett:Dau.Elizabeth Graves:Dau.Mary Jane Irwin(Irion):
Dau.-Margaret Rose:Son-John Rose who is not capable of attending
to his inheritance,so it is put in trust for him to H.C.Bennett.
Wit:D.W.Haley,Harrison Jordan,Geo.W.Stewart.

MARRIAGES FROM EARLY TENN.NEWSPAPERS 1794-1851:by Lucas.
P.532:Mr.Isaac Worthington of Ms. marr. at Lexington,Ky.,to MIss
Margaret Higgins,youngest dau. of Rich.Higgins,Esq.(Nat.Banner
& Nash.Whig.-Mon.Nov.11830)

"THE AMANDA WORTHINGTON DIARY"-Carter Room,Greenville,Ms.Library.
Mary Worthington(Aunt'Polly')-sister of Sam,Sr.& Dr.W.W.,and
Isaac,Sr.Worthington, Marr. Aaron Wickliffe-they had no children
& adopted Nephew Aaron Wickliffe Worthington, son of Thos.Worthing-
ton. The nephew changed his name to AARON WORTHINGTON WICKLIFFE.

¶EST.OF HENRY BRAWNER & WIFE MARIA CAMPBELL BRAWNER:See pg.57.
Charles County,LaPlata,Md.
The Will of Henry Brawner is recorded Charles Co.Md.Bk#16,Folio
131.The Pltn."Ellerslee",was still in existence Nov.1983. The
clerk added a Will for another Henry Brawner,written 17 Dec.1842,
Rec.3 Jan.1843,and a copy of a Renunciation of the children
of Henry & Maria as follows:
Est.of Henry & Maria C.Brawner----Renunciation.
The undersigned Eliza C.Barnes & Mary F.Brawner renounce in
favor of Henry H.Dent their respective rights to Adm.the estate
of their late father & Mother,Henry & Maria Brawner.12 Aug.1847.

WASHINGTON Co.-PROBATE COURT DOCKET
P.77;Wm.Hecford-Alien-becomes a citizen-28 Oct.1844

P.118:Wm.T.Seacock-Alien-becomes a citizen-26 Oct.1844

-141a-

Inventory of Appraisement of a trunk of clothing &c
belonging to the estate of Benjn H Moyler dec'd

2 linen shirts at 4 50		9 00
2. do not made		6 00
1 dressing glass		1 00
1 black hat		1 50
1 frock coat badly shot to pieces		2 00
1 pair casinet pantaloons do		50
1 black velvet vest do		1 50
2. linen shirts	2 50	5 00
1 pr black cloth pantaloons		5 00
2 flannel shirts		2 00
1 black cloth vest		1 00
1 silk do		75
2 pair drawers		1 00
3 pair wool socks	25 ea	75
1 lot articles razor & &c		1 00
4 handkerchiefs		2 00
1 seal skin trunk		2 50
		$42 50

We the undersigned appraisers having been duly sworn do value and appraise the trunk of clothing of Doct B H Moyler dec'd as above stated this 28th day of May 1834
   Wm W Collins
   Malachi Layne } Appraisers
   Allen W [Ivins]

Inventory of money belonging to the estate of Doctor Benjamin H Moyler deceased which hath come into my hands and of the debts due to the deceased which have come to my knowledge.

Statement 1 shews the amount of money rec'd		Baker	2 00
		Bass E P	149 27
		Blue Jesse	50
Received from Jas. U. Smith taken from the pockets of the deceased at Rodney	1 50	Blue John	57 88
		Brady C	5 00
		Brasher Leabons	22 01
		Brasher Louisa	3 50
		Briscoe John	6 50
2 This statement shews the accounts for medical services on his books viz		Bowling Harvey	43 00
		Broadnax filler	11 50
Abbot Stephen	15 50	carried forward	

Name	Amount	Name	Amount
Brought forward		Brought forward	
Briggs Joseph (estate of)	213.89	Jones Pjes'a O'Drangodes'	15.50
Boatman & C Jones	50.34	Joiner Turner	2.00
		Jourdens James	13.50
Campbell Charles	2.00		
Campbell John	5.00	King William H.	2.00
Carius Joseph	3.50	Knox Andrew Army	54.53
Clark James	53.39	Keulischan	.50
Cox Alfred	173.52		
Cocks J G	135.49	Leslie Hector	3.13
Cocks J (est'e of P & G)	11.76	Lane Malichi	17.10
Cocks Robert	54.00	Lee Henry	1.00
Collins William (L P)	3.13	Ladbetter Sneed	15.13
Collins William R	19.65	Leflore Walter	6.13
Cook Wm B	12.13		
Cook Susan A	5.00	McFadden James	9.00
Creath A G	71.88	McFadden John (estate of)	269.63
Cross Richard	42.14	McFadden John (for ___)	23.33
		McIntosh	5.00
Dehart Abraham	39.00	Martin Christopher	10.71
Delany John A	3.50	Marney Thomas	10.3
Dinnigale John	13.00	Maryho D R	13.33
Dinnigale Wm A	25.62	Metcalf A G	2.
		Merriweather Frances	16.00
Fake Henry (estate of)	86.88	Merriweather John	336.2
Flournoy Matthew	9.26	Millsap Emanuel	13.26
French A B	54.62	Montgomery Alex	59.6
		Montgomery Jas S	11.00
Gilbert P A (estate of)	67.57	Montgomery Kim.	18.50
Godfry	38.50	Moore	10.00
Guire Paul	4.00	Morris E	13.13
Guy James	7.25	Morrison John	31.70
		Morse Jos O	19.50
Hogan James	27.00		
Hogan Wm B	29.63	Odell Samuel	5.70
Howard Philip	80.39	Offutt Fisher	286.51
Jenkins Mrs	1.13	Peebles John W	33.00
Jenkins William	2.00	Pennel Frances	2.13
Jones Elias	.50	Pennel William	95.13
Jones Owin	19.30	Phillis Joel R	4.00
Carried forward		Carried forward	

			-147c-		217
	Brought forward			Brought forward	
5.50	Phillips		12.50	Hutchinson Harvey (estate of)	90.65
2.00	Pinial Bath S		65.63	Wilkinson Jefferson	1.50
3.50	Pinia Sarah S		196.91	Woodward Edward	1.50
				Workman of Thos Tunstale	7.60
2.00	Rex Enoch		3.00	Worthington Sam'l	1.00
1.32	Roberts		8.00		4401.37
.50	Shank George		16.75	Statement 3 shews list	
	Selby Thos (estate of)		106.34	of accounts & found in	
3.13	Selby R P		215.19	the pocket book of the de-	
1.10	Shadrack Wench		34.00	ceased not charged on his	
1.00	Sheriff of Nashn Co		1.50	books and made under	
5.13	Short		1.76	or to his settling in this County	
5.13	Simms Thomas		10.00	John Espers 1824	17.30
	Snow John		26.13	Alfd Llewellyn 1824	21.83
1.00	Stallon		3.00	Wm G Hardy Exto 1825	10.50
1.13	Stillings William		4.00	Miss Wallace 1825	2.00
3.50	Smith James M		4.50	William Myrick 1826	.50
1.00	Stephens Thomas		1.13	Alfd Hampton 1826	3.00
.76	Stone Asher		55.26	Chambers 1826	6.00
.39	Stewart Lewis		41.39	William Dodd 1826	9.50
1.50	Stranger at Halemans		3.00	J Jardous 1826	3.50
1.13				William Taylor 1826	6.00
.01	Thornsbury John		9.26	J White 1826	2.00
1.65	Trathoone William		2.00	Wathr Nevsom 1826	9.50
21	Trimble Walter		16.02	W Nicholson 1827	8.00
1.13	Tunstale George		.50	L Throckmorton 1829	1.25
.01	Tunstale Lynch		1.50	Eleazar Tharp 1830	3.00
.51	Tunstale John Senr		57.00		172.13
.11	Tunstale John O		47.38	Statement 4 shews the account	
1.5	Tunstale Richard		1.00	on the medical books of the	
74	Tunstale Thomas		64.63	deceased which appear to have	
51	Tunstale William		10.76	been settled by himself viz	
	Turnbull Andw		124.25	Boatman a O Jones	50.39
11	Turnbull F G		26.25	Crop Richard	42.14
.1				Dehart Abram	39.00
	Vanclave John		1.50	Delany John No	3.50
1	Vanclave Thomas		7.50	Goulding Mrs	1.13
15	Vickers		15.00	Jones Elias	.50
15	Wade		21.3	Leslie Hector	3.13
6	Well		.63	Merriwather Francis	16.00
	Carried forward			Carried forward	

218 —147d—

Brought forward			Brought forward		
Smith James M	4	50	Leadbetter Snead	15	13
Trelhonie Williams	2	00	McFadden James	9	40
Trimble Walter	16	82	Martin Christopher	10	76
Things at Houlsmins	3	00	Meagho D F	13	50
Wade	2	13	Moore	10	00
Montgomery Alexr	59	63	Peebles S. M.	33	00
	$243	07	Phillips	12	50
Statement 5 shews Desperate			Roberts	8	00
and doubtful debts viz			Short	1	16
Baker	2	00	Simmes Thos	10	00
Broadnax John	11	50	Talyon	3	00
Cairns Joseph	3	50	Stone Asher	55	26
Clarke James note	56	39	Webb		63
Cox J G agent of R A Gilbert	11	76	Wilkinson Henry estate will		
Fercold A B	54	02	pay part of $90.65		..
Gilberts estate $67.51 will pay a			Woodward Edward	1	50
Small dividend probably 1/4	20	00	Workmen of Thos Truslalo	7	00
Godsey	35	50	The amt rendered in		
Guy James	1	25	statement three	172	13
Aquivires Philip	80	39		$667	10
Joyoden James	13	50			
Kentuckian		50			
carried forward					

June 2nd 1831. I F G Turnbull administrator of Docter Benjamin H. Moyler deceased do certify the with Inventory contains an accurate account of all the monies which have come into my hands and all the debts which have come to my knowledge due the deceased
F G Turnbull Admr
of B H Moyler decd
Sworn to before me and
subscribed this 22nd day
of June 1831 F S Smith
C J E C

An Inventory of the estate of Henry Fakes decd State of Mississippi Washington County

1 Negro man Daniel valued at	550	00
2 Charles	300	00
3 Bill Murray	300	00
carried onward		

WASHINGTON COUNTY PACKET GLEANINGS
DRAWER#164B -#175
C.C. means Chancery Court Record.
EST. means Estate Probate

#164B:Est.of Alfred G.Carter,decd.:Robt.H.Carter,Adm. Packet contains no Adm.Bond or Est.papers, only vouchers. From these it would seem that the heirs of A.G.Carter are:Widow Elizabeth L.:Robt.H.:Mary E.called Mittie;Eleanor S.;Will G.;Ann B.called Nannie;Grayson. A.G.Carter decd.by 27 Nov.1855. Vouchers show the family enjoyed a holiday at Olympian Springs,Ky. 2 Sept.1857 with R.H.Carter, Mrs.E.L.Carter, Mary E.,Eleanor S.,W.G.and a servant girl staying 14 days. Bill-$234.50. Clothing bills from Wash.D.C.,Lexington,Ky.;N.O.;One of the girls went to school at Patapsco Institute(?) Robt.J.Archer Principal;Nannie went to school at Walnut Hills,Ky.,in 1858. Another bill from "Kirkwood House"Wash.D.C.;Bills for Woodstock,Ms.,for transportation for Mr.A.M.Moseley on the steamer "Belfast". Many bills from "Penrice & McMeekin",Greenville,Ms.

#165:C.C.-M.G.Crockett vs E.P.Brown,et all
Bill of Complaint,Chancery Court term Jan.1896-Court sitting at Clarksdale. M.G.Crockett a citizen and resident of Litchfield, Ill. vs E.P.Brown,& wife Delia Brown,Napoleon Scott-all of Wash.Co.Ms.,and Wm.Hightower of Bolivar. Co.Ms.,-defendants. Land dispute.

#168(inside marked #158);C.C.-Andrew B.Carson vs Junius L.Johnson,et al. Exhibit"A"filed 28 Sept.1866;An indent made on 18 May 1844 between,Edw.P.Johnson of Lexington,Ky.,his wife Betsy of same & Geo.Downing of Wash.Co.Ms. Edw.P. gave a D/T to Downing for benefit of Betsy-deed dated 8 Jan.1841(DBk."M"p.240,241). A sale of the property was made 1 Jan.1845 to John Hanna & John G.Chiles. Downing then loaned the money to Edw.P. in return for which, Edw.P. gave a mortg. to Downing in Trust for wife Betsy on other Prop. in Wash.Co.Ms. @1000 ac. on Ms.River in T16,R8W. Another document filed 11 Nov.1868-Commissioner reports sale of said prop. to F.Lonsdale,E.Richardson with E.P.Johnson and F.H.Boyce as securities. Answer of Complainants:Junius L. Johnson,Edw.P.Johnson,Jr.,Nannie Lonsdale(late Johnson)and her husbandFitzwilliam Lonsdale,plus Betsy Erwin,who is a minor (Another Doc.states that BetsyE.is the dau.of Edw.P.Johnson and Betsy's decd.dau. Margaret E. who marr.Henry C.Erwin,also decd.. Betty Erwin,being an orphan and only child is to inherit a childs share of her gr.parents Est.)Shortly after the original D/T,Downing decd. By 1866-Edw.P.Johnson and his wife Betsy are both decd. Case sent to the Supreme Court by Pet.of Betty Erwin who became 21 in July 1875.

#172;C.C. "Thornhill & Richardson"vs Jas.M.Johnson,et al.John Thornhill is from La.,Edm.Richardson is from Hinds Co.Ms., vs Junius L.Johnson, Edw.P.Johnson,Fitz.& Nannie Lonsdale,& Bettie Erwin a minor. Suit over mules, and other stock. Case states that Edw.P.Johnson decd. May 1866 in Wash.Co.Ms. It further states that after the death of Edw.P.Johnson the family found a Will among some old papers. In said Will he appointed his sons Edw.P.,Jr. and James Wm.Johnson, now decd., his exec. without bond. He wanted 1/4 of "Ashland PLtn."where Junius and Lonsdale were farming with Edw.P.Sr.,to go to Bettie Erwin(CONT.)

Wash.Co.Packet Gleanings
Drw.#164B-#175

(cont.)his gr.dau..He further states that Betsy W.Johnson decd.
1863.Pkt. also contains Will of Jas.W.Johnson-written N.O.13
Dec.1864(See Vol.I.this series. Will Bk."1"p.361,Wash.Co.Ms.)

#174;C.C. Agnes Warren vs Wm.Warren,Adm. Agnes Warren of Ark.
was the dau. of John C.Miller,decd.1841 Wash.Co.Ms..leaving
a Will,(Recorded WBk.1,p.9,10,11--Abst. in Vol.I of this series)
Agnes's father left her a large amount. She then married John
T.Warren who took control of her property until he died 7(?)
Apr.1863. Agnes states that John T.Warren, her husband, bought
a place called"The Percy Tract" in 1856 from James Rucks. She
further claims it was financed with her money. The Will of John
T.Warren is recorded in Sangamon Co.Ill. A copy is included
in this pkt.
WILL OF JOHN T.WARREN;Written 26 Mar.1861-Recorded and filed
18 Nov.1863-Scott Co.Ky.,Adm.s-Phil Warren & Wm.Warren in New
Berlin,Sangamon Co. Ill. States that he wants Mother,Father and
"All my family" to be interred in lot in Georgetown Cemetary
and a monument errected;a bequeath to the Christian Church;demands that his slaves not be allowed to go to either Laura or
Jane H.Miller. He leaves everything to his wife Agnes;Neice
Agnes Warren Johnson;his sister Margaret L.Johnson and her 3
youngest children-Annie,Jinnie,& Warren Johnson;bro. Wm.B.Warren
and his 3 girls-Louisa,Marg.& Agnes Warren;to Wm.Warren,Phil
Warren,Wm.Johnson,John T.Johnson,Thos.P.Johnson,& Wm.Warren
Johnson,& Maria Turney- $5,000 each. States that Thos.P.& Wm.
Warren Johnson are bros.
Agnes then states that 15 Nov.1860,John T.Warren sold the land
bought from Rucks to Oliver T.Morgan,and that John T.& Agnes
sold the land she inherited from her father, to W.W.Worthington.
Agnes has a sister-Laura(Miller)Johnson[note;Laura marr.Thomas
P.Johnson]and their mother Jane H.Miller who shared land from
John C.Miller. The guardian of Agnes,when she was a minor was
her Uncle Harvey Miller. Under the terms of JOhn C.Miller's
Will, if either Dau. died without issue, the prop. was to revert to their Uncle Harvey Miller. Laura and her mother sold
out to John A. Miller. Agnes further states that John T.Warren
decd. leaving no issue and that Phil and Wm.Warren are his
nephews. Stating firmly that the funding for John T.Warren's
Est.came from her inheritance from her father, she wants the
legacies named in the Will of John T. set aside.
May 1869 Depositions followed;Dr.W.W.Worthington,age 68 stated
both Agnes & John T.Warren were raised in Georgetown,Ky.,and
were marr.there.
Zack Offutt states they were marr.1843
Robt.A.Johnson,age 52 of Louisville,Ky.,knew them both
Geo.T.Blackburn,39 yrs. of Wash.Co.Ms.
Junius R.Ward,66 yrs. a farmer
M.L.Peters,48 a planter
Geo.W.Ward
John A.Miller,upwards of 60 yrs.,a planter
All stated that they never knew John T.Warren to have any money
until he marr.Agnes,and then he spent his time managing her
Est.All are originally from Ky. No dispensation given in Pkt.

WASH.CO.PACKET GLEANINGS
Drw. #164B-#175

The following pkt.#181 is misfiled,& includes pkt.#176
#181;EST.OF JAMES ABELL,decd.who was Guard. of T.Edw.Jackson,
decd.,late his ward. Final a/c of Jackson's Est. was 1862. No
new information. This Pkt. also contains PKT.#176;S.W.FERGUSON
ADM.vs.ORVILLE M.Blanton-1868.A C.C.

DRAWER:#176-195A

#176;Est.;Wm.T.Wilson,decd.-G.T.Blackburn,Adm.;Pkt.contains
Inventory,all tattered,dated 22 Mar.1859; + a P.O.A. from
Edlott Wilson & Mary A.Wilson ofLoudoun Co. Va., and Sarah A.Cole
of Wash. D.C.,& John Wilson of Ill.,gives P.O.A. to Jas.H.Wilson
to attend to the Est.of "our"brother Wm.T.Wilson,decd.of Wash.
Co.Ms. States that Jas.H. is also a Bro. Filed in Ill.12 Jan.
1859; An appraisal of Est.included.

#179;Est. of JOHN J.CAUGHEY;Let.of Adm.filed by Mary H.Caughey,
widow and Admx.of Est. with security by John M.Bott,O.M.Blanton
25 May 1857; Pet.for sale states that Mary H.is widow and Annie
W.Caughey the only surviving child-23 Apr.1857. The Guard.,ad
litem, of Annie is James D.Blincoe. Land in the town of Old
Greenville.

#187;EST.JAMES H.YERGER,decd.-James T.Rucks,Adm.,Pet.for Let.Adm.
states that James H.Yerger departed life on or @12 May 1858
leaving a widow-Maria Louise Yerger,and a small Est.in Wash.
Co.Ms. Rucks asks to be Adm. along with Arthur Rucks,Henry Rucks
as Security. Filed 28 June 1858;Writ of Dower-Mar.1859-M.L.Yerger
states her husband decd. intestate and she is entitled to ½;
Citation to Edwin M.Yerger, Orville Yerger in Wash. Co.Ms.;
to Geo.S.Yerger & Wm.Yerger in HindsCo.Ms.;to Alex.Yerger in
Bolivar Co.Ms.;to J.S.Yerger in Wash.Co.Ms.[NOTE:Maria Louise
was the dau. of James Rucks & Louisa V.Brown. Her Bros.were
James T.,Arthur,Henry. You'd have to be a Yerger to unscramble
them!]

#188;Intestate JAMES B.MONTGOMERY,decd.May 1855-A.P.Montgomery
is Adm.;Pkt.contains Inv.;A/C;Vouchers/Receipt from Est.of
Jas.B. signed by Edwin S.Fly & wife Mary A.Fly, A.J.Montgomery,
D.J.Montgomery,Atty.sole distrib.of the Est. 22 Nov.1859; Proof
of Part.Apr.1860;The Flys and A.J.Montgomery are from Gibson
Co.Tn.,give P.O.A. to D.J.Montgomery of Johnson Co.Ark.,on 24
June 1859;Inv.-$2,000 to be Divided between the Flys,D.J.& A.J.
Montgomery

#190;EST.OF JAMES A.FLOWERS,decd.on 4 Oct.1858,leaving a small
est.@$500. His brothers have requested Wm.L.Nugent to be Adm.
and pay off the debts, as relatives live away from Wash.Co.Ms.
17 May 1859. On 25 Feb.1861,Wm.L.Nugent declares Susan Jones
and her husb.Sidney Jones,Deadama(sp?)Jones and her husb.Hy
Jones are distributees of the Est.,and believes them to be residents of this state. Citation to Bolivar Co. to summon John
B.Flowers,Wm.Flowers on 28 Feb.L861.

#190;C.C.;EDW. McCABE et al vs. JUNIUS L.JOHNSON,et al;Edw.Mc-
Cabe & wife Mary R.(late Mary R.Johnson),Albert S.Johnson &
May Alice Johnson-last 2 minor children of James Johnson,decd.,
who sue by next best friend Wm.A.Haycraft-all four parties(cont.)

WASH.CO.PACKET GLEANINGS
DRAWER:#176-195A cont.

#190;cont.-heirs at law of James Johnson, whose Adm.is McCabe, vs Edw.P.Johnson,Junius L.Johnson,Fitzwilliam Lonsdale & wife Nannie(late Johnson),& Bettie Erwin,children and heirs of Edw.P. Johnson,decd.,and against Edw.P.Johnson Exec.of last Will & Test. of Edw.P.Johnson,decd., and ___Londale,Exec.of last Will & Test. of Jas.W.Johnson,decd.,all defendants. Case states that Jas.Johnson decd.11 Jan.1853,leaving his wife Mary R., now McCabe. Further stating that said James Johnson sold land that he left the widow to Edw.P.Johnson. That Jas. left a widow,Mary R.,and 4 children-Albert S.,May Alice, Anna & Jane Johnson... that Jane died 30 Dec.1856, Anna died 25 June 1858. Edw.McCabe and the widow Mary R.Johnson were marr.23 Oct.1854 and that Edw.McCabe was declared Adm.of the Est.of said Jas. Johnson, decd. in Marion Co.Mo.,Feb.1867. Case further states that Edw. P.Johnson, then sold the land he bought of Jas.Johnson to his (Edw.'s)son Jas.W.Johnson(½)while still owing the said Jas.- That Jas.Wm.Johnson decd.1863 leaving his last W.&.T.with Lonsdale as Exec. E.P.Johnson decd.1865 leaving Junius L.,Edw.P., Nannie & her husb.Fitz.Lonsdale, and Betty Erwin-who was a minor in 1867 when the sale of the property was ordered. Very large PKt.contains the original contract between Jas. and Mary R.Johnson with Edw.P.Johnson; File on Complaint asking for 10%int. on $10,000 note due; Pet. of Defendants; The defendants lost, appealed and the High Court of Appeals reversed it Jan.1869. In meantime McCabe resigns as Adm. of Jas.Johnson,Marion Co.Mo. 1870 and Wm.B.Phillips was appt. They were still filing motions in 1874.

#191;Guard.of M(ARY)A.THOMPSON & C(YNTHIA)C.THOMPSON by M(arion) M.Wallis. Est. of Alfred T.Thompson of Ark. of whom Mary and Cynthia are minor heirs. 1859.

#195A.:EST.OF JOS.M.BROOKS,decd.intestate 9 Aug.1858-Pet.of Va.L.Boyce,stating she intermarried__ day of 18__ with Jos.M.Brooks and he departed this life intestate 9 Aug.1858 leaving your pet. his lawful widow and David Emerson,Bettie,& Lucy B.Brooks all minors under 21. He left them land in Twp.17,R8W,and some in Twp.17,R9W in all 1207 ac. called"Deer Field Pltn."and that said decd. owed money on other land in said Co.of Wash.Ms. He also left a large personal est. which is now destroyed. Virginia has intermarried with Felix H.Boyce who is still living. Virginia seeks her dower rights. Filed Oct.24,1865. F.H.Boyce is the Adm. of Brooks Est.,and resigns in order that his wife can co-. llect the dower;she received 1/3rd. The Adm. in Apr.1859 was John T.Buckner, stating he was related to the widow and children. Pkt.contains Guard.of Bettie B. & Lucy Brooks to E.J.Comstock 28 Sept.1868,stating V.L.Boyce decd. before June Term 1868

DRAWER #195B-219

#199;EST.OF AMBROSE KNOX,decd.(Will rec.WBk.1,p.280,also Vol.1 of this series)Additional Info.;Adm.Was D.F.Blackburn,now decd. and Adm.Pet is filed by Thos.Shelby in Mar.1861. Pkt.contains;Copy of Will. Invoice for Mrs.Elizabeth Knox at "Bloomingdale Asylum". for Martha L.Knox; Co-Exec.with Blackburn was Ambrose's bro.Thos.D.Knox.(cont.)

WASH.CO.PACKET GLEANINGS
DRAWER #195B-219 cont.

#199(cont.)
Petition of Martha Lowry Knox-gr.dau.of Ambrose Knox by next
best friend John Butts & Mary Berry Butts his wife, late Mary
Berry Knox,Mother of said Martha L.;Pet.states that Ambrose
decd. 10 Dec.1859, leaving a Will;That Dr.Blackburn decd. and
then her gr.f's brother Thos.Knox became sole Exec.and made them
leave the house. She wants Thos.,of small means and from Tenn.,
to be removed as Adm. Filed 24 Dec.1861.
Pltn.named"Solitaire". Thos.B.Knox answer filed 28 Jan.1862;
states that as long as Mary Berry Knox remained unmarr. she
was entitled to live in the house on "Solitaire",but when she
marr.Butts,she forfieted that right. Soon after John Butts be-
comes Adm.of Est.

#200;EST.OF HENRY G.VICK,decd.-AdmH.C.Pendell(Will of Henry
G.Vick-WBk.1,p288-Also See Vol.1,this series)Add.info.Will
probated4 Feb.1860.By Mar.15,1866 Mrs.A.J.Phelps formerly Mary
B.Vick is the only surviving heir of H.G.Vick(she was his sister).Before her marr.the Guard.of Mary B.Vick was Jona.Pearce
(Peace-Peice)[Note;Henry W.Vick & wife Sarah were large land
holders in the Indian Lands. Henry W. was a bro.to Grey P.Vick,&
Martha Vick who marr.1816,Wm.Willis . Henry W. & Sarah Vick
had 3 known Ch. Henry Grey,who was killed in a duel on the eve
of his marr. to Helen Johnston;Mary B.who marr. Alonzo Phelps.
& Geo.R.E.]

#204;EST.OF ELISE SCHWARTZ,decd.-Adm.G.T.Blackurn;Inventory
    1 trunk of clothes $75
    1 Guitar   15
    2 Violins   50
    1 Violin   25
    1 lot of music   5
                         $170
Filed 23 Oct.1860

#212;C.C.:JOSHUA GREEN,et al vs LOUISA N.BROWN,Issaq.Co. Ms.
Filed Apr.Term 1880(what is this doing here?)Joshua Green,Geo.
Green,Liddie Stevens and her husband John P. Stevens,
Emma Stevens & Mary Shelton with their husbands W.T.Stevens
& Jas.Shelton (Writing difficult,spelling terrible)
vs Louisa V.Brown and her husband Shephard Brown.
Clarification of Title:in 1871 Joshua Green & Thos.Green the
father of the other Complainants and since decd.bought land.
Cross Bill, also filed.

#214:Est.DR.SAML.R.DUNN:(Will in WBk."1",p.298-See Vol.I,this
series) In Will he states that he has 3 children;Wm.,Saml. &
Mary "nearly grown" and other smaller ones. Add.Info:Saml.R.
Dunn decd.May 1860.
Let./Adm.filed May 1860 by Wm.B.Dunn,Exec.
Proof of Will-Citation;Andrew Lawson & wife Mary R.Lawson:
Chas.W.Johnston & wife Annie F.;Saml.R.Dunn;Bettie M.Dunn;
Pricilla W.Gregory Guard.of Thos.K.Dunn;Harriet B.Dunn-children
and heirs of Dr.S.R.Dunn. Dated 20 June 1867.
Wm.R.Trigg states that he went to the Army and when he returned
he couldn't collect any of the debts owed the Doctor, and that
the Dr. had a medical library that was carried off by Chas.W.
Johnson of Memphis. Final a/c 27 Mar.1867   (Cont.)

WASH.CO.PACKET GLEANINGS
DRAWER #195B-219 cont.

#214(cont.)
A citation to Andrew Lawson & wife Mary R.;Chas.W.Johnson & wife Annie F.;Saml.R.Dunn;Pricilla W.Gregory-Guard.of Thos.K., Bettie M.;Harriet B.;Orville B. & Sallie R.-children and heirs-at-law to show cause why Est.should not be closed.(See Pkt. #220,221, this Vol.)

#216: JOHN B.PELHAM,decd.Intestate;Let/Adm.filed 29 May 1860 by John L.Finlay;states that John decd.on the"the 23rd"intestate,leaving a wife and 1 infant dau .under the age of 14 as only survivors. Does not name them.

#217:EST.JERE W.COLLINS,decd.-Adm.Wm.S.Collins;
Inv.-1 gold watch-$100, 1 bay horse-$100, 1 clock-$8,+ $2,500 in notes due him. Pet.for Adm.states that Wm.S. & Jere were bros. and that Wm.S. is the only living relative in this state- 27 Aug.1860.

DRAWER:#220-#235

#220;Also contains #221;SALLIE R. & O.B.DUNN,minors,Dr.S.R.Dunn; Guard.Pet.of Pricilla W.Gregory,Aunt of Thomas K.,Harriet T., Sara R.,& Orville Dunn-minor heirs of Saml.R.& E.A.Dunn,decd. Thos.K. & Harriet T. are above 14 years.-filed 25 Sept.1865.
Aug.19,1871-Saml.R.Dunn became Guard.of Orville B.& Sallie R.Dunn.
27 May,1871-Sallie R.Dunn pet.from Union City,Tenn.to Wash.Co. Chan.Court of Ms.,for Dr.Saml.R.Dunn to be her Guard.
10 July 1871-Orville B.Dunn pet.from Greenville, Ms. for Dr. Saml.R.Dunn to be his Guard.
Aug.1871 P.W.Gregory resigns as Guard.of above minors.
A loose paper-Peter Gregory in a/c with P.W.Gregory,Guard.(in pencil-1856)filed 25 Oct.1858,Rec.28 Feb.1860. A/c for yr.1856 signed Saml.R.Dunn,Agent,P.W.Gregory Adm.
#220;Est.of Elizabeth A.Dunn-Thomas Shelby,Adm.surrendered Let/ Adm.,25 May 1863. Citations to Saml.R.Dunn,Thomas K.Dunn,Mary R.Dunn,Mrs.(?)Bettie McDunn,W.A.Haycraft.Guard.Ad litem of Ann F.Dunn.

#222Est.of H.G.Vick,Decd.;H.C.Pindell,Exec.
15 Mar.1866 Mrs.A.J.Phelps-formerly Mary B.Vickis only surviving child of H.W.Vick. Jona Peace(Pierce)is Guard.of Miss Mary B. Vick before her marriage.
June 1861,Exec.Pindell states that H.W.Vick has decd.

#223;NIMROD T. LINDSAY,DECD.Let./Adm.to Andrew B.Carson,23 Apr. 1867.

#224;ROBERT MARSH;Decd.Intestate;Let./Adm.by John L.Finlay were filed 28 May 1861,who states after the war that he never tried to sell anything because of the war,that when Marsh decd.he was farming on someone elses land,but did own slaves,which he hired out.
Adm.sale of stock,furniture,equipment-Jan.1862 + slaves. Finlay stated that before the sale John Marsh took a horse.
Pet./Adm.states the personal prop.worth @$40,000,but the Est. was tied up in numerous lawsuits(unexplained),that Robt.Marsh had no near kin in the state- that John Marsh,only bro.and next of kin in this state asked John L.Finlay to be Adm.23 Apr.1861 Suits settled-1869

WASH.CO.PACKET GLEANINGS
DRAWER:#220-235 cont.

#225;C.C.JONATHON PEARCE vs MARY B.VICK;Hes her Guard.Pkt.
contains nothing but vouchers.

#226;EST.OF MICHAEL FARRELL,decd.20 June 1861.
Let./Adm.filed 28 Oct.1861 by Chas.B.Halbutt

#229;EST.OF JAMES ABELL,decd.;Pet/Adm.of the widow,Nannette
Abell,who states that her late husband decd.leaving a sizeable
Est.of slaves,and other prop. She waives her right to act as
Adm.and asks that W.A.Haycraft act in her stead. Filed 20 Aug.
1861. Final sale-Jan.1866. Tax Return filed 1 Apr.1862-
Signed by Miss Laura James.

#231;Est.of T.EDWARD JACKSON,decd.14 Oct.1861;Adm.is Thos.V.James.
Citations-John James,T.V.James,Nannette Abell,Franklin James,
Nancy J.Powell,Andrew Jackson,Lizzie Jackson on--Nov.1862.Also
to Lizzie,minor, to her Guard. Mrs. M.J.Hord,who is also the
Guard.of Andrew Jackson.
Pet/Adm. by Thos.V.James,states that he is one of the next of
kin, and that the decd. left no direct heirs but next of kin
John,Thos.V.,Gabriel,Edw.C.James & Nannette Abell,Uncles and
Aunt,living in 1863. The cousins are Franklin James,minor son
of Theodorick J.James,Jr.who died before T.Edw.Jackson;and
Andrew & Lizzie Anna Jackson, minor children of Jas.B.Jackson,
decd.before T.Edw.Jackson.
Est.divided between the living Uncles and Aunt.

#233;EST.OF THOS.W.WILSON,decd.21 Apr.1861,Intestate;
Widow is Bettie Ann Wilson,who intermarries with Lyman Aldrich.
Pet./dower rts.Oct.1868,stating there are also minor heirs.
Guard.Pet. of T.W.Wilson for minor David Emerson Brooks,heir
of Jos.M.Brooks,decd.-under 14-filed 28 May 1860 and included
in this pkt.
Adm.Bond for Est. of Thos.W.Wilson filed 25 Nov.1861
Citations filed June 1868-to Mary Wells Wilson,Bettie Buckner
Wilson,Ann Eliza Wilson,and to the girl's Guard. E.J.Comstock.
Bettie A.& Lyman Aldrich want to close out the Est.
Let./Guard.T.W.Wilson left the following minor children;Mary
age 8,Bettie age 5,Ann Wilson age 4 + considerable est.-filed
26 Feb.1866 by Bettie Ann Wilson-their mother.
Adm.Bond by Lyman Aldrich states he & Bettie Ann Wilson marr.
8 Feb.1866.Bond signed by Lyman G.Aldrich of Wash.Co.Ms.,
Lyman D.Aldrich & Thos.C.Reddy of Adams Co.Ms.

DRAWER:#236-254A

#236;Est.REBECCA FOLKS vs WM.HUNT,et al
Pkt.contains;Pet.for Dower-Jan.Term 1862-widow & relict of
Miles C.Folkes,decd.,states they were marr.--day of--yr.Miles
became possessed of certain prop. by this marriage.Miles decd.
July 1860 leaving his widow and one child. She never relinq.
her dower rts. The land in question is now the prop. of Andrew
Carson,Wm.Hunt,Thos.Shelby.
An instrument dated Nov.1861 list the following as possessors-
Jona.Pearce-trustee,John Willis,Geo.Messinger,R.M.Caither.
Rebecca and Miles's child is not named here.

WASH.CO. PACKET GLEANINGS
DRAWER:#236-254A cont.

#238;Est.of PETER M.WALKER,decd.-Widow & relict Margaret H.Walker,
Execx.--Pkt.contains;Adm.Bd.Aug.1862.
Report of sale 25 Nov.1865 by Margaret H.
Pet.23 Oct.1865-states that the U.S.Government confiscated all
their property since the appraisal was made in 1862. She has
children, and they own a pltn. of @750 ac.

#239;Est.of JAMES R.DOWNS,decd.-Letty Vick Downs,Adm.& widow
Pkt.contains;Adm.Pet.26 Feb.1866-she states that their residence,
corn crib,etc.,were burned by U.S.Military forces under the
command of Gen.Steele. All cotton confiscated by Confederate
States, negroes all freed--only $200 worth of personal prop.left.
Appraisal;
Adm.Bd.-citation on 21 Oct.1865-she Pet.Judge Frank Valliant
of Wash.Co.Ms.,stating that Geo.R.Fall and the others had not
yet made the appraisal,due to the War.

#240:Est.of ELIZA G.MOSBY,decd.-Geo.T.Blackburn Adm.
G.S.Mosby,husband,is Exec. In an a/c 1866 Gervas S. Mosby states
that Eliza decd.during the late war,and when he took over the
Est.all currency was in Confederate Bonds, the cotton had been
destroyed,and on 22 Jan.1866 there was a balance of $3,246 in
Confed.Treas.Notes. They lived on "Loughborough Pltn." @1,000
ac. of cleared land. Pkt.contains;Rental Contract for N.J.Nelson
to rent the land 1868.
Copy of Will(husb.to rec.1/6 of "Loughbourgh")
In 1871-Haycraft,Adm.says a suit is pending, mentions Eliza's
family, but does not name them.

#242;EST.ofEMEDICUS MURPHY,decd.:Pet.Let/Adm.by Eugenia Bass
of Wash.Co.Ms. on or @ 15 Sept.1865,states that Emedicus Murphy
passed leaving no wife so far as she, the petitioner knows.
He owned ½ int.in a pltn.on Lake Jackson in partnership with
Eugenia. The enemy took off everything,but one negro girl and
a small amount of personal property worth @$2,000,and since
5 months have passed since he decd.,she requests to be appointed the Adm.of his Est.
¶[NOTE:Eugenia Bate marr.Council R.Bass 1st and they lived in
Wash.Co.Ms. After his death,she marr.2nd Joseph Bertinatti,
and Italian Count with the Diplomatic Corps.]
Mar.26,1867 A.B.Carson,Adm. petitions for sale of property.
Franklin A.Burke,Exec.of Est.of Wm.B.Murphy,decd.,files petition 22 July 1867,stating that Wm.B.Murphy decd.,a citizen of
Tenn.,and a bro.of Emedicus Murphey,decd.,of Wash.Co.Ms. Further
states that Wm.B. died after Emedicus and was an heir of Emedicus. He believed that Mrs.E.P.Bertinatti(Eugenia Bass) owes
the Murphy Est. $10,000 or more. The other heirs reside in N.C.
Petition of S.W.Ferguson,Adm.states that Mrs. Bertinatti is
now a resident of Constantinople and out of jurisdiction and
her property is involved in much litigation, and that the heirs
of Emedicus may never see any portion of the debt.-filed 15
Jan.1868.
In 1867-Haycraft is Adm.:Annual a/c filed 1871.

#243;Est.ofJACK,KATE,& ELLA COX,minors-W.L.Nugent Guard.
Pkt.contains;Annual a/c's Nugent states the 3 children are above
14(1865),that they live on "Willow Glen Pltn.and Landing"(cont.)

WASH.CO.PACKET GLEANINGS
DRAWER:#236-254 cont.

#243;cont. in 1871-Nugent asks to be dismissed. Jack is aka John J.Cox. Katie and Jack file an objection to the manner of business dealings between Nugent & Betty McHatton, who rents the Pltn.
Other Doc.-a receipt from Ky.Military Institute for John J. 26 Feb.1866,Farmdale,Ky.
Depositions from Stevenson Archer & W.R.Trigg in relationship to the objection of Jack & Katie over the Amount of rent for their land,filed 23 July 1872.
Usual bills,some to State Female College for Ella.Final a/c with Ella 1873.She is now Mrs.T.R.Wallis
Final a/c with Kate 1871.
¶NOTE:John J.Cox marr.Alice Nelson 31 Mar.1870 Wash.Co.Marr. Bk."A"p.131;Miss Kate Cox marr.W.P.Kretschmar 20 Dec.1876-Marr. Rec.from the "Greenville Times".John J,Katie Belle,Ella(aka Sallie Egg,)were the children of Seth Cox & wife Sallie Egg.]

#244 Est.of CHARLES CAFFAL,decd.-Louis Caffal,Adm.,states that Chas.decd.,5 Dec.1865,intestate,Louis is his bro. That Chas. decd. leaving 2 children as heirs-Thomas & Wm.Caffal.

#245;Est.of STEPHEN CASTLEMAN-Admx.is Maria Louisa Castleman.
L/Adm.filed Aug.1866
Will of Stephen Castleman,not included
Pet.for sale by widow Maria Louisa Castleman.
Answ.for minor heirs of Stephen Castleman and George Dawson by their Guard.,E.K.Stafford...stating the heirs are Stephen & Lucy Castleman & George Dawson,minors. Filed 27 July 1872.
Final a/c 1874.
¶[NOTE:Hinds Co.Ms.Marr.Rec.;Stephen Castleman marr.M.L.Dawson 5 Apr.1860]

#247;Est.of EDWARD S. FRASER,decd.-Adm.is Alex G.Fraser:
Pet./Adm.,states that Edw.S.Fraser was killed in Confederate Army-and that his wife lives in Mass. Alex promised Edw.S. to collect all debts owed to him and send the proceeds to his wife-filed 27 Nov.1865.
Notice to heirs printed in "Greenville Times"-To Hannah S.Fraser Abby Jane Fraser,Sarah Fraser-all of Fall River,Mass...the sole heirs of E.S.Fraser,decd. 1872.Final a/c 30 July 1872.

#248:Est.of JOHN L.FINLAY,decd.-Admx.is Annie B.Finlay
Pet./Adm.filed 23 Apr.1867 in which Annie B. states that G.S. Mosby & wife Eliza were in debt to John L.Finlay for @$12,000. Eliza decd.leaving her Est. in heavy debt, with her husband G.S.Mosby as Exec.,but with little property of his own. Annie B. asks the courts' permission to compromise with the debtors.
Inv.23 Apr.1867
Pet.for Let.Test.-Annie B.states that John L.Finlay decd. July 1862,intestate,and that she is his widow and they have 8 children,minors.

#251:Est.ofEVELINA M.HAMMETT,decd.with F.A.Metcalfe,Adm.
Pkt.contains:Appraisal filed 25 Sept.1865
Adm.Bond 28 Aug.1865
Adm.Letters state that Evelina M.Hammett died Jan.1865,and F.A. Metcalfe declares he is her only heir,and that he has already received and inheritance from W.H.Hammett-17 May 1871.   cont.

WASH.CO.PACKET GLEANINGS
DRAWER:#236-254

#251;cont.
¶[NOTE:F.A.Metcalfe is the son of Evelina Matilda McCaleb who
marr. Albert Gallatin Metcalfe 1st, and W.H.Hammett, 2nd.]

#252;Est. of A.F.HUDSON,decd.-Admx.is Tabitha E.Hudson.
Pkt.contains;Pkt.253 also,which is the Guard.of Nannie & Frank
Hudson to T.E.Hudson Feb.1867-and Feb.1868.
Pet.of Guard.Nov.Term 1865-Tabitha states that her husband
A.F.Hudson decd.20 Oct.1863,intestate, leaving his widow,Tabitha
and 2 children-Nannie age 10-Frank age 4 as his heirs.
Filed 27 Nov.1865.

DRAWER:#254-259

#254B,C,D,E,F;Est.ofWM.HUNTdecd.-Execs.George B. & Wm.E.Hunt.
Will rec.Wash.Co.Ms.Will Bk."1"p.358, names his 2 sons Geo.&
Wm.E. as Exec.,but did not name his wife and other children.
Will prob.Apr.1866.Pkt.contains:Vouchers,vouchers,vouchers.
Names Pltns."LaGrange"and "Mont Rose".Bills pd.for Mrs.P.B.Hunt
& Mrs.E.F.Blackburn in N.Y.
C.L.Morehead,former Gov.of Ky.and Wm.Hunt,decd. were business
partners, and Morehead had gotten deep in debt. In 1866 Morehead
mentions his son Wm.in a letter to Wm.Hunt.
In 1868 the family went on a shopping spree at Rodman Bros.in
Frankfort,Ky...ForLizzie Hunt,Miss Katy Hunt,Mrs.P.B.Hunt,who
was the Guard.of Geo.Alex. To D.F.Hunt,Maj.Geo.Hunt,Pru & Alice.
5 fat Pkts.with Pkt."A" missing.
¶[NOTE:Wm.Hunt marr. Prudence Blackburn and they had the follow-
ing children;Geo.Blackburn Hunt who marr.Mary Nichol of Nashville Tenn.;Wm.E.Hunt-called Billy-who marr.Maria Crittenden
of Ky.;David Flournoy Hunt who marr.Lizzie Green of New Orleans;
Lizzie Hunt who marr. Frank Chinn of Frankfort,KY.;Kate Hunt
who marr. David L.Stone;Prudence Blackburn Hunt who marr. Russell
Rodman of Frankfort,Ky.;Alice Carneal Hunt who marr.Claudius
M.Johnson. Taken from PWCHS;Census 1850,Wash.Co.Ms.;Court Rec.
Wash.Co.Ms.]

#256;Est.of JOHN JOOR HAILE,decd.-Adm.Calhoun Haile
Pkt.contains;Will of John J.Haile,of Wash.Co.Ms.,written 5 Dec.
1861;States that he has a wife and a child or children. Asks
that his brother Calhoun Haile and friend J.B.Stirling be co-
exec. Wit:E.F.Brooks who witnessed Will in Wash.Co.,Thomas J.
Sutton of Bolivar Co.,Thos.Bracken of Wash.Co.-June 1866.
¶[NOTE:From the "Diary of Lavinia Bateman",Carter Room,Greenville
Ms.Library;John J.Haile was killed in the Civil War. Calhoun and
John also had a sister Emily Haile.]

#257;Est.of THOS.J.JAMES,decd.-John S.Nelson,Adm.
Pet./Adm.23 Oct.1865-Nelson states that James decd.1864,intes-
tate,and that Nelson is connected to James by marriage and that
his wife, the former Belinda James & Laura James,a minor, are
the only heirs of the Est.

#258;Est of HENRY JOHNSON,decd.-E.J.Johnson,exec.
Pkt.includes;Citation to-Benjamin Johnson, Matt Johnson, Henry
J.Johnson, Elizabeth Johnson,Louisa E.Dudley, C.W.Dudley, Mary
B.Blackburn, Geo.T.Blackburn, Victor F.Erwin, Emma Morgan,(cont)

WASH.CO. PACKET GLEANINGS
DRAWER:#254-259 cont.

#258;cont.--Johnson Erwin, Wm.Erwin, Chas--, Minerva M.Morgan
to answer Petition ofE.J.Johnson for dower rts.,filed 2 Dec.1868
C.W.Dudley is natural Guard.to Johnson Erwin and Oliver C.Morgan
is Guard to Emmma M.Morgan
Proof of Publication summons-Robert A.Johnson, Chas.F.Johnson,
Emily M.Bartley & her husb.W.T.Bartley, Vertner Johnson, Henry
Johnson, Claudius M.Johnson, Rosa V.Johnson,children and minor
heirs of Claudius M.Johnson,decd. and residents of Louisville,
Ky.,to hear cause of E.J.Johnson, Adm.of Henry Johnson.Filed
25 Jan.1869.
¶[NOTE:Henry Johnson and his wife Elizabeth Julia Flournoy had
11 children;Henry J.JOhnson-living Desha Co.,Ark.1866;Mary Belle
Johnson who marr.1st Geo.T.Blackburn, 2nd A.B.Carson;Robt.A.
Johnson;Claudius M.Johnson;Matthew F.Johnson;Eliz.J.Johnson:
Emily M.Johnson who marr.1st--Tilford,2nd W.T.Bartley;Benjamin
Johnson; Louisa Johnson who marr.1st W.R.Elly, 2nd C.W.Dudley-
her bro-in-law;Margaret A. is used in Henry's Will, but family
papers say she was Margaret Julia Johnson who marr.1st James
Erwin and 2nd C.W.Dudley; Chas.F.Johnson. From Wash.Co.Census
1850;Wash.Co.Ms. Will Bk."1";PWCHS.]

#259;C.C.;JOEL JOHNSON,Minor-Mrs.Ann Worthington,Guard.
Pkt.contains;Pet.for Guard.-Ann Worthington states that Isaac
Worthington,decd.(by 1860)leaving several children,two of whom
are Isaac M. & Thos.minors-age 18 and 10. Ann is their mother
and natural Guard. She further shows that Masie W.Johnson,form-
erly Masie Worthington, one of the ch. of Isaac Worthington
has also decd., and that Joel Johnson is an infant @6yr.old-
is the only child and heir of Masie. That Joel lives out of
the state(Ark.)with his father, but his inherited property is
in this county.(Wash.Co.Ms.) Ann asks to be appointed Guard.
of Joel,too,to be able to handle his inheritance.
Filed 28 Nov.1865.
Doc.dated 28 Dec.1869-states that Joel's father was Cyrus R.
Johnson. By May 1881 Joel was 21.
Other heirs of Isaac Worthington,decd.,were Leroy B.Valliant,
Tenie W.Valliant, James Ann Pratt(?) Ben Worthington, Isaac
Worthington, Wm.H.Worthington.

DRAWER #260-295

#261:C.C.:LARZ ANDERSON,TRUSTEE VS THOS.B.WARFIELD
Anderson is trustee for Alice D.Warfield and children. Thos.
Warfield gave notes to Thos.D.Carneal for mortg. In Bill of Complaint,Anderson states that Thos.D.Carneal wanted to make a dis-
tribution of his property to his children and the mortg. made
by Warfield is to be held in trust for Carneal's dau.Alice D.
Warfield and her children (She is the wife of Thos.Warfield)
Carneal then died,leaving a Will.Suit further states that no
part of the notes have ever been pd.and Mrs.Warfield being a
"married woman and until recently the children all minors"and
some still are...Anderson demands payment of mortg.-filed in
Chancery Court May Term 1868(Warfield owed $75,000)
Sale of property on Bachelor Bend ordered May 1868.

#261:EST.OF B.FRANKLIN JAMES,minor with Thos.W.Powell as Guard.
filed 23 Jan.1872.Guard.seeks to rent out"Opossum Ridge"(cont.)

WASH.CO. PACKET GLEANINGS
DRAWER #260-295(cont)

#261:(Cont)and "Oak Grove Pltns.",belonging to said minor for yr.1876
Minors petition by B.Franklin James stating he is an orphan @15 yrs.and legal heir of T.J.James his father and his mother was Nancy Jane Powell-both decd..B.Franklin James further states that his last Guard. was J.T.Switzer,who has decd.and the petitioner's Aunt,Nannett Switzer is seeking someone else to manage his large estate. He chooses Thos.W.Powell,the bro.of his late step-father-filed 19 Dec.1871.
Pet.For Guard.by John James,an Uncle,filed Dec.1866,says that Nancy Jane Powell decd.,leaving Frank James,minor heir at-law of T.J.James,Jr.decd.
Pet.for Guard.by Nannette Switzer and her husb.J.T.Switzer state that John James has decd.-this doc.not dated.The Switzer's are still Guard.in Oct.1869.[NOTE:Theodorick J.James,Jr.marr.Nancy Jane Miller.After he decd. she marr.George P.Powell on 4 May 1859,Wash.Co.Ms.]

#262:EST.THOS.B.WARFIELD,decd.Carneal Warfield Adm.:S.W.Ferguson, appointed Adm.of Est.in Wash.Co.Ms. states that Carneal,an heir of Thos.B.Warfield won't give him the information he needs to settle Thos.B.'s Est. States that the widow is Alice Warfield,and other heirs-filed Mar.1870
In Pet.for Adm.of Est.of Thos.B.Warfield filed Dec.1868,his surviving partners;A.L.Stewart,M.O.H.Norton,& Rich.Atkinson. Carneal Warfield's answer to Ferguson was to state that he is Thos.B.Warfield's eldest son,and that Warfield owned land also in Ky.,and that his father was a resident of Ky.,and not of Ms., and that he,Carneal,was the proper Adm.of his father's Est.and wants Ferguson dismissed.

#266:EST.OF F.G.KIRK,who decd.July 1866,Intestate:His bro.A.M. Kirk files Let/Adm.27 Dec.1867.

#267:EST.ISAAC RICHARD MOSELEY,decd.:Pet./Adm.by Alfred W.Moseley states that Isaac R. was killed in the 1st battle of Franklin,Tn.,sometime in 1863.(Will in WBk.1,p.345 Wash.Co.-EMR Vol. 1)That John H.Moseley(one of the legatees)has decd.,and the other legatee-John E.Denson resides in La. Filed 23 Oct.1865.
Security on Adm.Bd.:John Butts,Ira I.Powell
Pet. of John Denson,of Wash.Co.Ms.,complains that only 1 a/c has been made since the Will was probated in 1865,by Adm.A.W. Mosely, and said Moseley has had possession of everything"embracing among other things,large sums of money".Seeks partition of Estate. Moseley ordered to file a/c 1867,1868.

#267:EST.OF MAGGIE MILLER,et al,minors vs Harry E.Yerger & E.B. Simmons(should be Emmons).Pkt.contains:Let./Adm.filed 27 Dec.1866 by Harry(called Hal)Yerger,stating that Harvey Miller,decd. leaving 4 ch.,all of whom were minors-Sallie Yerger nee Sallie Miller, Maggie J.Miller, Malvina Miller,& Harvey Miller. Hal (husband of Sallie)seeks Guard.
Vouchers-1868 show the girls Maggie & Malvina went to school at Mt.Auburn in Cinncinati,.bill sent to "Stella Pltn."
1870-Yerger seeks release from the Guard.of Harvey
24 Nov.1870-Guard.to Harvey is E.P.Johnson & wife Eliza(cont.)

WASH.CO.PACKET GLEANINGS
DRAWER #260-295(cont.)

#267:cont.:with W.E.Hunt as security.
Voucher shows that Harvey is in school in Glendale,Ky.-Lynnland Institute, 1870.
24 Nov.1870-Pet.for Guard.of Harvey by Elizabeth B.Emmons,stating she has been an intimate(torn off)& advisor to the family, having resided with the family for 20 yrs.
23 Oct.1871,annual a/c by Hal Yerger,Guard.of MAGGIE,MALVINA, HARVEY-in which he states the the pltn."Stella" contains a tract of land called the "Tom Johnson Place".
20 July 1876-Pet.of Mrs.Eliza B.Emmons to be released as Guard. to Harvey Miller
5 Feb.1877-Harvey to choose his own Guard.

#271:EST.OF ROBT.G.PEAK,decd.-Jeff P.Peak,Adm.
24 Sept.1866-Let./Adm.filed-Jeff states that Robt.decd.,22 July 1866,Intestate,-no wife or children.Jeff is one of the brothers of said Robt. who decd.,leaving a small Est.in Wash.Co.-@$200.

#272:EST.OF NANCY J.POWELL,decd.John James,Adm.
Pet.for Adm.,John James states that Nancy decd.,Mar.or Apr.1866, Intestate,leaving a small Est.and John being the next of kin to one of the heirs-at-law,seeks to be Adm.,since Nancy's bro.-in-law Thos.W.Powell waived his right. 24 Dec.1866
Citation left with John James' wife in Feb.1868.

#273;GUARD.OF MARTHA & ROBERT M.POWELL,minors by Thos.W.Powell: G/Pet.by Thos.W.Powell states that Geo.P.Powell died leaving 2 children Martha & Robert,minors under 14, That said minors are heirs-at-law of Geo.& Nancy Jane Powell,both decd.,both died Intestate. Thos W.seeks to become their Guard.,-Permission granted, stating that Thos.W.Powell is the natural Uncle of Martha and Robt.Powell-filed 24 Dec.1866
Pet.for discharge of Guard.filed 24 Feb.1868.Thos.W.states that there is no Est.,that Nancy Jane's Est. will be used to pay the debts. He further states that on 26 Dec.1867,Robt.M. Powell decd. and that he,Thos.W.,had maintained the two minors at his own expense and would continue to do so for Martha..Granted.

#274:EST.OF THOS.F.PORTER:Pkt.contains Will-written 7 Sept.1866; "to beloved brothers Alexander L.Porter,James L.Porter,& Wm.M.Porter-$10 each:to brother John N.Porter the balance of my Est." Exec.Wm.H.Bunn;Wit.Thos.W.Sellers,Dr.A.O.Fox, J.A.Biddle. Will probated Oct.Term 1866(Not in WBk.1)
Sale of prop.approved by J.N.Porter,so ordered,22 Oct.1866.

#275:EST.OF GEO.P.POWELL,decd.Ira M.Powell,Adm.
23 Oct.1866;Let/Adm.filed.Ira M.states that Geo.decd.Oct.1866, intestate. That the place Geo.farmed had hands working on it that threaten to walk off unless they were paid,and the Est. needs an immediate supervisor,so asks,as a brother of Geo.,to be Adm.
Pet.for sale and Adm.Bond.
Pet.for Adm.filed 24 Dec.1866 by John James after Thos W.Powell sole surviving relative of decd.,waived his right to act as Adm.

#276:EST.OF IRA M.POWELL,Decd.(Pkt.in very delicate condition)
24 Dec.1866-Let/Adm.filed by Susan Powell,widow,who waives right as Adm.in favor of Wm.A.Haycraft(County Adm.)
May 1867;Citations to Franklin James,(torn)James,his Guard.:(cont.)

WASH.CO.PACKET GLEANINGS
DRAWER:#260-295 (cont.)

Martha Powell & Robt.Powell & Thos.W.Powell their Guard.:to
show cause why the annual a/c of Robert Millers' Est.,of which
Ira M.Powell was Adm.,should not be allowed.
Inv.& Apprais.and Adm.Bond.

#277:EST.OF ROBT.B.SMITH,decd.of Wash.Co.Ms.,Adm.Lucinda Smith
of Sunflower Co.Ms.-Sept.1865-Lucinda states that she is Robt.'s
widow, that he died 19 Oct.1864 leaving an est.-part in Ms. &
part in Alabama. Adm.Bond is $2,000.
(Half of this pkt. has disintegrated.)
#---:also included in this Pkt. is EST.OF E.J.PACE,decd.;Wm.A.
Haycraft,Adm. 29 May 1867- Adm.Bond only Doc.

#282:EST.OF WM.SATTERWHITE,decd.-Adm.S.W.Ferguson,(County Adm.)
Filed 29 May 1867.Pkt.contains a handwritten note signed by
M.A.Satterwhite,asking Mr.A.B.Carson to act as Adm.to keep her
from having to come to town, saying he"has nothing to fear from
the children",as she has raised them and they will do as she
says--filed 23 Apr.1866
No other Documents.

#284:EST.OF ISAAC M. & THOS.WORTHINGTON,minors-Ben Worthington
Adm.(Pkt.disintergrating) Pet./Guard. + Bond by Ann Worthington
for the 2 minors-28 Nov.1865
Voucher 1866-schooling for Isaac to St.Louis
Annual a/c 1867.Incl.vouchers for Joel Johnson,minor whose Guard.
is Ann Worthington(His gr.mother)
June 1869-Final a/c for Isaac
21 Feb.1876-Thos.is now over 21 and after examining all matters
pertaining to the Guard.by his Mother,is satisfied with her a/c/,
and asks that she be released.

#286:EST.OF SAML.I.WORTHINGTON,decd.-Mrs.Amanda Worthington,Adm.
[Note;for Will see WBk.1,p.364 or EMR Vol.I]
Let./Adm.filed 29 Dec.1866,Wm.M.Worthington states that his fa-
ther died 21 Nov.1866 in Washington,D.C.leaving a Will. The 3
witnesses to Will-Zenas Preston, who resides in Tensas P.La.,
W.J.Minor,who resides in City of Natchez, & L.M.Talbit,who resides
in Wash.D.C.,-
Pet.by Wm.W. to get his father's Will probated..wit.all live
or are at this time out of state. Asks that his mother Amanda
Worthington,widow, be app.Adm.-Oct.1867
Amanda takes dower share Apr.1868,stating that Saml.Worthington,
Decd.leaving a large Est.& 4 children-Wm.W. Worthington,Mary
W.Stone,Amanda Buckner,Saml.,Jr.,with Saml.Jr.as the only minor.
(written in and then scratched out-James Stone,Davis M.Buckner)

#290:EST.OF JONATHON BALLARD,decd.,vs.G.B.Hunt Adm.
Pet./Adm.by Geo.B.Hunt of Bolivar Co.Ms.,states that Ballard
decd.17 Jan.1866,intestate,leaving an Est.consisting of notes-
no next of kin in this state.
28 Mar.1866 Adm.Bond;W.P.Montgomery,N.J.Nelson
23 Apr.1866-Inv.& Appr.:main debtors to Est. are Wm.Hunt & G.S.
Mosby. Est.worth $26,500.(Ballard held the mortg.on "Belmont
Pltn"in Bolivar Co.,owners were the Hunts.)
15 Jan.1869-Ballard heirs are listed as Jonathon A.Ballard,
Jennie Ballard,Joshua Ballard,Helen M.Ballard,Sarah C.Burr(?)
& Eunice Ballard as Guard.to Orville Ballard a minor. Wm.Hunt
(cont.)

WASH.CO.PACKET GLEANINGS
DRAWER #260-295 (cont.)

#290;(Cont.):has decd. and Exec.of his Est.are Geo.B. & Wm.E.
Hunt.who take up their father's notes.
#---:Included in this Pkt.:Will of J.P.DUNNINGTON;Document from
Springfield,Robertson Co.Tn.,authorizing wit.to authenticate
the Will;The Will is a small scrap of paper,half of which has
crumbled,names picked out- John Dunnington,"to my sister"(gone)
-ohnson,wife of   Johnson: my sister   the wife of John
W.B.   :to Victoria & Roy who are now with my bro.Ep   :Wm.&
Geo.   ,refers to co-partnership with his bro. and they have
slaves in Wash.Co.Ms.;Wit:Christopher Babb,Saml.Glidewell,and
a statement by E.M.Dunnington's Atty.,about the Will-dated 27
Dec.1857. Thos.Groves states that J.P.Dunnington had "a conver-
sation with his bro.E.M.Dunnington",signed before Miles Draughn
Comm. of Robertson Co.Tn. Will declared Valid.

#292:EST.OF COLON FLOYD-James W.Murphy,decd;Let/Adm.states that
Floyd-in Spring of 1863, was captured by a portion of U.S.Forces
in this county and taken off by them as a prisoner. It was after-
wards reported & believed that said Floyd jumped off a steamboat
into the Ms. River with a view of making his escape & was drown-
ed & nothing has been heard from him since...he left no wife
or children or relatives living in this state- he owned some
slaves, and a few notes.

#293:EST.OF ROB.G.FRASER,decd.,Alexander G.Fraser,Adm.Let/Adm.
by Alex.G.Fraser,states that Robt.G.,late of sd.Co.,was killed
in Confed.Army,leaving a small Est.,consisting of notes and a/c
due @$1700-that Alex is the bro.of Robt.G.and no other relatives
in this Co.-27 Nov.1865
Citation-Chancery July Term1872-pub.in "Greenville Times"noti-
fying Walter M.Fraser of Ripon Wis.:Geo.Y.(T?)Fraser-Fall River,
Mass.;Mrs.Margaret A.Stone of Binghampton,N.Y.;Mrs.Ellen Ester-
brooks of Newport,R.I.;Mrs.Jane Holt of Providence,R.I.;Miss
Catherine Fraser of Providence.R.I.;Abby Jane Fraser of Fall
River,Mass;Sarah Fraser of Fall River,Mass;David R.Fraser res.
unknown-all the heirs-at-law of Robt.G.Fraser.

#295;EST.OF VICTOR M.FLOURNOY,decd.Eliz.Flournoy,Adm.
March Court 1866-Fayette Co.Ky. Will of decd.presented for Prob.
(22 Mar.1866) by M.C.Johnson & John R.Viley;Copy of Will;
"I,Victor M.Flournoy of Fayette Co.Ky."..gives his wife Elizabeth
J. full control of his Est.,asking her to liquidate his Ky.,hold-
ing to pay his debts,as no part of his southern prop. could be
sold because of the war...Wife keeps ½,rest to his bros.& sis.
Names sister-Betsy J.Johnson,$10,000 + int.due from Capt.Henry
Johnson;Sister Emily M.Ward-amount of R.J.Ward's note. Written
10 Jan.1865; Inv.& Appra.
Notes collected from B.F.Miller for rent of Pltn.in Ms.,also
from C.W.Dudley,Henry Johnson,R.J.Ward.W.T.Bartly,Benj.F.Bradley,
Mrs.E.M.Ward,Mrs.E.P.Bass,Thos.Kershaw,Thos.B.Redd,Ben Johnson,
R.A.Johnson,Chas.F.Johnson.
Will filed in Chicot Co.Ark.29 Nov.1866.(Not filed in Wash.Co.Ms.)

DRAWER:#296-332;

#297:Outside label-Est.of A.F.Alexander-T.B.Blackburn,Adm.
Pkt.contains;EST.OF AUSTIN F. ALEXANDER,decd.Intestate,Adm.(cont.)

WASH.CO.PACKET GLEANINGS
DRAWER #296-332

#297;(Cont.)is Geo.T.Blackburn.
Let./Adm.by Blackburn state that A.F.Alexander decd.22 Aug.1866,
owning land on Williams Bayou in Bolivar Co.Ms.,+ stock,etc.-
worth @$1,000. Inv.& Appr.Report of Adm.Mar.1868.
#;also contains;WILL OF ROBERT WOODS,decd.,recorded 11 Feb.1843
(WBk.1,p.257,Wash.Co.Ms.-EMR Vol.I)
Proof of Will in Wash.Co.Ms.,& Davidson Co.Tn.
#;Also contains:EST.OF WM.R.MUSGROVE,decd.of Ms.Co.,Ark. Adm.
Pet.filed by Mrs.Mary E.Musgrove of same county,who states that
he decd.about 14 June 1864,intestate,owning a small Est. Pet.
verified by county Clerk M.W.Nancey 29 Aug.1865-filed 2 Nov.1866.
A schedule for collection of notes due the Est.

#298:EST.OF PICKENS COMPTON,decd.-John Compton,Adm.(Will in WBk.
1,p.379-EMR Vol.I,P.94)Names mother,Mary. 2 bros.Jeff.& John.Let.
Adm.states he decd.Jan.1867,leaving an Est.worth @$10,000-Filed
25 Feb.1867 by John Compton.
Will.
His mother files suit,stating that the Will is invalid(Heleft
her $5)-that his father has decd.several years ago, that Pickens
left no wife,children or descendants-that most of his Est.lies
in Ark.,and she has taken out Let/Adm.there in Chicot Co. Ark.,
and that Pickens decd. in Wash.Co.Ms.,when said Will was signed
and published. Mother claims he decd.intestate,and at the time
of signing said Will was of unsound mind-25 July 1867
[NOTE:the Will left Mother $5,Jeff $200,and all the rest to bro.
John]
26 Mar.1867;Mary withdraws her suit. Will is accepted as valid,
and John Compton is appointed Adm.
Filed same day is agreement between Mary & John in which she
withdraws suit against John & Jeff.,over validity of Will.She
releases all claim to Est.,withdraws complaint that Pickens was
of unsound mind-in return John must pay all court costs,and release Mary from all counter-charges.

#305:EST.OF W.E.DANIEL(S).,decd, in 1866. Suit styled Franklin
Daniel,et al vs S.W.Ferguson,Adm.- Petitioner states that W.E.
Daniel is "my Ancestor" who departed this life 1866, leaving
lands in T19,R9W.He also left his wife Sarah S.Daniel,& 3 minor
heirs-at-law-Franklin, Wade & Thos.Lee Daniel.Asks that 160 ac.
and the dwelling house be released from the Est.- Decree so or-
dered-24 Aug. 1870. Proof of Pub.22 Feb.1869
20 Feb.1871-to Franklin Daniel,Wade Daniel,Thos.Lee Daniel,minor
heirs of W.E.Daniel,decd.and Wm.A.Wallis their Guard. who resides
in Pine Bluff,Ark.,to answer Adm.Ferguson's statement that the
Est.is insolvent.
Sarah Pet.for dower-30 Dec.1868
Pet.for homestead states that Sarah decd.1870.
Survey map of land holdings,creditors clamoring for most of it.
Sale of prop. ordered Feb.1871-Heirs accept $1500 in place of
homestead-25 May 1871.
THIS PACKET ALSO INCLUDES #385;which contains;LAST WILL AND
TESTAMENT OF SARAH S.DANIELS:Filed 22 Aug.1870-Noncupative Will
of Sarah,who decd.,Pine Bluff,Ark.,11Aug.1870.Spoken by her on
9 July in presence of John A.Wallis & Cornelia C.Thompson. Sarah
having been advised of her certain death,but of sound mind,left
all her prop. to Wm.A.Wallis for the education & maintenance
(cont.)

WASH.CO.PACKET GLEANINGS
DRAWER:#296-332

#305;(cont.)of her ch.Franklin,Wade & Thos.Lee Daniels. She requested that the ch. live on the old homestead in Wash.Co.Ms. known as "Tyrone Pltn." on the Ms. River. Rec.Jeff.Co. Ark.

#300;out of sequence;Est.of WM.R.DEAN,decd.-Ambrose G.Shrickl,Adm Let/Adm.were granted in Feb.,but Adm.states that among some old papers of Dean's was found a Will witnessed by E.Mount, A.Bunn, John Blattenburg.Mount is residing in Ark.,the other 2 in Wash.Co Ms. The said Will designated B.F.Taylor as executor, but he has moved to South America during the War,and never been heard from since, leaving his wife,who said Wm.R.Dean left no children, or wife, and the sole legatee under the Will is Wm.Jesse Irby,the neph.,and next of kin-a minor @12 yrs. who resides with petitioner. Seeks proof of Will...signed by A.S.Shrie£25 Mar.1867(also sp.Shriek)Pkt.contains the Will of Wm.R.Dean-giving everything to neph.Wm.Jesse Irby(whose relatives have abandoned him)Written 8 Aug.1863-Filed 25 Mar.1867

#306:Est.OF W.R.ELLEY,decd.-Adm.Louisa E.Dudley;In petition for dower rts.,Louisa Dudley,states that her late husband,W.R. Elly,decd.1866, intestate, in Wash.Co.Ms.,leaving her,his widow, and Lilly Elley,Mary Worthington-formerly Elley,& Henry Elley as his sole heirs. He owned several hundred acres of land known as the "Homeplace"-578 ac.T14,R8W,& 474 ac.,same Twp.& R,240 ac + 160 ac + 320 ac.T14,R8W called "Swan Isle Pltn."She seeks dower rts.,to land and the homestead.
Answer of Mary Worthington,wife of B.T.Worthington,formerly Mary Elley, Lilly Elley & Henry Elley-ch.and minor heirs of W.R.Elley -by their Guard.E.J.Comstock-dower granted to their mother-now marr.to Chas.W.Dudley.

#308:EST.OF GUIGNARD SCOTT,decd.-S.W.Ferguson,County Adm.,de bonis non:Pet.for sale of prop.by Adm.Ferguson states that he found no personal Est. of any kind,debts will wipe out all assets and the Est. is involved in a lawsuit in Circuit Ct.in Wash. Co.Ms.,and the judgement was rendered 14 Nov.1867 in a suit styled Saml.F.Phelps vs Guignard Scott.
In the original suit-Phelps vs Wallis & Byrne & Guignard Scott-filed 26 Mar.1861 dealt with a mortg.dispute...This was appealed, and reached the Supreme Court of Ms.,24 Mar.1873.
Ferguson further states that Guignard owned an undivided interest in land in T18,R8W and also in T19,R8W-1/5th of 1/6th of the whole. Guignard's share of this was that belonging to his bro. Calhoun Scott,who decd.intestate-leaving no wife or ch. Ferguson says a sale of all this prop. is necessary to pay debts. He further states that Guignard decd. leaving 1 bro. & 3 sisters: John A.Scott, Caroline S. Gibbs wife of Robert Gibbs, Sarah Eliza Lee,wife of Harry Percy Lee,& Frances Elizabeth Scott-all over 21. Since the death of Guignard, the bro.& sisters have sold Calhoun's int. in the undivided prop. and divided the proceeds among themselves-and Geo.M.Helm,D.B.O'Banion and Newman J.Nelson are never in possession, as claimed in the said suit... Filed 4 Nov.1871
Answer of heirs-state that Guignard decd.during the late war. The pet. states the defendants were unaware of part of Calhoun's Est.,being involved in Guignard's..The tract of land in Question was originally owned by their father,John A.Scott,Sr.now decd., (cont.)

WASH.CO.PACKET GLEANINGS
DRAWER#296-332

#308:(cont.)and after his death came to the 6 children. That at the time of the sale, the land belonged to the 3 girls and others who had bought out the brothers. Filed by Percy & Yerger-27 July 1874
In 1872 Sheriff states that Caroline Gibbs,Robt.Gibbs,& Frances Scott are non-res.of Ms.,and now live in Columbia,S.C.-Sarah & Harry Percy Lee live in Wash.Co.Ms.,and John A.Scott lives in Bolivar Co.Ms.
Last Doc.dated May 1874-order of continuance with leave to answ.

#309:EST.OF WM.SMITH,decd.-Adm.W.A.Haycraft:Pkt.contains Inv.& Appris.-29 May 1867-1 ferry boat license,$25, 1 shot gun + house hold goods-$84.50
Order for sale-stating that Smith decd. in 1867.
Bill of Discovery-Adm.found out that Wm.Smith made regular deposits of money with Norman McLeod of Sunflower Co.Ms.,25 Nov.1867 and asks that Est. be opened. Also that Smith deposited certain sums of money with Abner Heathman of Sunf.Co.Ms. Adm.demands an a/c of sums held. 1st Annual a/c-1871

#310:EST.OF WM.N.PAGE,decd.-Haycraft Adm.Sale of prop yearling calf-which Jas.W.Murphey bought- 23 Oct.1867.

#313:EST.OF ELI GIBBONS -Haycraft,Adm.:Pkt.contains-Inv.& Appr. June 1867,oxen and wagon-$250,+ note made by Wm.Gibbons for $200 who bought the stock.
23 Mar.1868 Wm.Gibbons is the oldest of 7 children left orphan by death of Eli Gibbons. There is one sister who is a cripple + 2 sisters and 3 bros., the youngest is 11yrs.old,and all depend on Wm.

#315:EST.of Ira Wilkins should read IVY WILKINS,decd.-Ferguson, Adm.(note;Pkt.badly deteriorated).Let/Adm,Elisha Wilkins, ___ Wilkins, Mary Arnett,& ___ Humphrey,res. of __ Ky. In Oct.1866, Ivy Wilkins,late of Wash.Co.Ms.,decd.,leaving a large personal Est. The said Est.has been in the hands of Thos.H.Buckner,res.of said Co. Petitioners say they are the only surviving bros.& sisters and heirs of said decd.,and ask Haycraft to be Adm.Filed 22July 1867. Copy of letter to Buckner-26 Aug.1867 notifying him.

#316:EST.OF SAML.WORTHINGTON,minor-Guard.Pet.by Amanda Worthington: Pkt.contains Pet./Guard...Saml.Worthington,Sr.decd.,leaving several children,one of whom-Saml.,Jr.is a minor 19 yrs.old, and a large Est. The Pet.is Saml.'s Mother and natural Guard. Filed 24 June 1867
Guard.bond 18 Sept.1867-with Wm.Mason Worthington as security.

#317:EST.OF G.B.WILMOT-Pet.for Let/Guard.(Note:the right side of all documents rotted off)Pet. of Geo.Bowman Wilmot,minor of 17 yrs. who,on behalf of his mother,now decd.,is entitled to inherit from his uncle John Gist(also sp.Gess),decd.,who was living in Ky. Pet. asks that his father John L.Wilmot be appointed his Guard.to collect his interest @$3,000. 26 Aug.1867
Guard.Bond with Wm.C.Blanton as security.

#318:EST. OF J.S.YERGER-Adm.Wm.G.Yerger: Let./Adm.-Wm.G.states that his father Jacob S(hall)Yerger decd.,about a month since in Warren Co.Ms.,intestate,leaving a small personal Est.,about $3,000:That Wm.G. is the oldest living son-Filed 26 Aug.1867
Sale of prop.-a receipt given by Mary H.Yerger-Apr.1868(cont.)

WASH.CO.PACKET GLEANINGS
DRAWER #296-332

#318:(cont.)Inv. & Apprai. Jan.1868.-Annual a/c.
The widow is Mary B.Yerger.

#318B:C.C.[Note;Many of the doc.included in this Pkt. have additional numbers-316,318,364,346] Suit styled PAYNE HUNTINGTON & CO.vs J.P.DILLINGHAM,ET AL:Bill of Complaint- Jacob M.Payne, Geo.W.Huntington, Wm.H.Dameron, Henry M.Payne,citizens of La., in business in N.O. under firm name Payne Huntington & Co.,bought some land for taxes in 1869, that J.P.Dillingham had defaulted on, in 1865. The land was previously owned by J.P.Dillingham, mortg.to Wm.A.P.Dillingham,and put in trust to Edward J.Elder..
15 Sept.1869.
Clerk of Wash.Co.Ms.,states-same day-that J.P. livesin N.O.,Wm.A.P in Chicago,Ill.,and Elder- unknown.
Answer 31 Oct.1870 of J.P.Dillingham,states he sold ½ int. while Wm.A.P.Dillingham was behind the U.S.Military lines, and Wm.A.P. knew nothing of it, but the war has diminished J.P.'s holdings, so that he can no longer repay the money (He filed bankp.)
By 20 Dec.1871-Geo.W.Huntingham has decd.
Sale of prop.ordered-@500 ac.in T17,R7W
Answer of Wm.A.P.Dillingham-referring to D/T of John P. & wife Martha R. Dillingham on 29 June 1860 in favor of Wm.A.P.,with E.J.Elder as trustee...Wm.A.P.Dillingham is living in Keenebee Co.Maine(his wife is Caroline P.Dillingham) 11 Dec.1865
Answer of Wm.A.P. to Hamilton(who bought the ½ int.) says the original D/T from J.P. was to repay a debt of $31,703. The war came about that time before payment was due. W.A.P.,a citizen of Maine, J.P.,of La.,Elder of Ms.,:W.A.P.fought on U.S.side-other 2 were in the Confed.Military, and all communication cut off between them. He and J.P. are kinsmen and friendly;Signed Augusta,Maine 29 Aug.1870.
Doc.filed 18 Dec.1871 states that Wm.A.P.Dillingham has decd., and his Adm.is Jos.W.Patterson.Report filed 27 July 1871.

#319:EST.OF HENRY L.MAYER,decd.:Adm.Mary B.Mayer:Let/Adm.,Mrs. Mary B.Mayer,Leopold H.Mayer, T.G.Birchett state that Henry L. decd. 23 Mar.1918-age 79, late of Issa.Co.Ms.,left a Will witnessed by Miss Nora Burchett & J.W.Garrett. He was buried at Magna Vista, Ms. No copy of the Will.

#320:EST. OF JOHN M.BOTT,decd.-Elizabeth T.Bott,Adm.,Pet./Adm. Sept.1867 by Eliz.T.Bott, stating her husband John M.decd.,intestate, leaving an Est. of @$10,000.
Pet. to declare Est.insolvent: Pet. prays that Josephine Worthington & husb. Geo.P.Worthington & Belle Bott a minor under 21 are the sole distributors. @ Sept.1868.
Creditors file suits against Geo.T.Worthington over sale of prop. Dec.1868, Final a/c 30 July 1872.

#321:C.C.:H.S.BUCKNER vs L.G. & B.A.ALDRICH:Pkt..contains Mortg. on "Oak Hill Pltn".inT15,R8W + T16,R8W to Buckner Newman & Co. of N.O. 19 Mar.1866. Lyman G. & Bettie A.Aldrich of Wash.Co.Ms. default on crop loan of $12,000.Sale ordered(prop.seems to have been hers).

WASH.CO.PACKET GLEANINGS
DRAWER #296-332

#321:EST.OF BETTIE COLLIER,et al,minors- Guard.by Jas.M.Collier.
Pet.for Let./Guard.by Jas.M.Collier a citizen of Wash.Co.Ms.
(Note;most of the Documents in this pkt.are rotted off one end)
Jas.M.Collier is the father of Elizabeth Ann Lewis Collier,Geo.
Collier & Mary Alice Collier,all minors-who have due them an
inheritance from the Est. of (blank) on behalf of their mother,
now decd.,the sum of $1,000 and he seeks Guard. 23 Sept.1867
Pet.for sale of Ward's prop. July 1869-bought by David Friley-
an undivided share of the Est. of Stephen Barefield.
Citation issued to L.H.Collier, Jas.M.Collier, J.N.Collier,
Catharine Friley, David Friley her husb.,and Jas.M.Collier as
Guard. of Bettie, Geo.& Mary Alice Collier. Citation Feb.1871
states that Jas.M.Collier has moved to Warr.Co.Ms.
Another Pet/Guard.,states that the Collier children need a Guard.
to protect their interest in Est.of their uncle Stephen Barefield
-scratched out and Hatcher written above--land in T16,R6W.(1/4th
of the Barefield's Est.:1/12th of Stephen Hatcher's-their uncle)
He further states that Leven H.Collier,J.N.Collier,& Catharine
J.Friley are the uncles and aunt of said minors, and nearest
of kin after your petitioner. Signed Jas.M.Collier, Apr.1869

#322:EST.OF SALLIE ISABEL HOGAN,Minor-Geo.R.Fall,Guard.
Pet/Guard.,states that Sallie is under 14, has no relative,guard-
ian, and for several yrs. has been under his care and protection,
a large portion of which time she has been an orphan. She has
due her from her father (blank)Hogan about $300, which Fall wants
to collect.Filed 23 Sept.1867,:Sec.signed by Jas.M.Collier.

#322A:C.C.:E.D.MORGAN & CO.vs P.W.& PETER D.GREGORY.
Edwin D.Morgan, John T.Terry, Solon Humphreys-partners under the
name of E.D.Morgan & Co.,of state of N.Y.,state that on 15 Nov.
1865, Pricilla W.Gregory, a resident of Wash.Co.Ms., borrowed
$2,000 from Lacy and McGee for crop loan on "Elmwood Pltn",700
ac in T17,R9W. The mortg. was transferred from Lacy and McGee
to E.D.Morgan & Co. They complain that Peter Gregory has removed
some of the stock. Filed 28 Oct.1869.(Note:fat pkt.contains sum-
mons to the Gregorys.Seizure order.)
P.Gregory's answer:1871 Peter D.Gregory states that Pricilla
is his mother, and accepts that she signed the mortg.,but at
the time he was a minor, and knew nothing of it. He owns 2/3rds,
while she owns 1/3rd of "Elmwood"as inherited from his father
Geo.G.Gregory. Peter states that his uncle Saml.R.Dunn,now decd.,
was the Adm. of Geo.Gregory's Est.,and sold off part of it to
pay the debts, to Wm.T.Taylor. His mother was his Guard.
21Dec.1871-Depositions follow:A.L.Lacy,Shelby Co.Tn.,age 50,
residence, Memphis, merchant, witnessed signature of Mrs.Gregory
to mortg.
Jan.19 1872-Carneal Warfield states he bought "Elmwood" from
Peter D.Gregory on 25 Oct.1870 and took possession 1 Jan.1871.
He purchased the place with his bro T.B.Warfield. He had lived
as a neighbor to the Gregory's since 1866, but did not know of
the mortg.or of the tax title held by Nelson & Co.
In July 1872,Peter D.states he is now 24 yrs.old and lives in
Greenville,Ms.
Court ruled E.D.Morgan & Co. was entitled to 1/3rd of land-
Feb.1873 in lieu of mortg.payment of $12,034.73 due.(cont.)

WASH.CO.MS.PACKET GLEANINGS
DRAWER #296-332

#322A:(Cont.) Appealed Mar.1873 by the Warfields.
Supreme Court dismissed the case after learning the parties involved had compromised.(Case #953) 20 Oct.1873.

#323½;EST. OF IKE W.ROBINSON,decd. Wm.W.Robinson,Adm.:Pkt.contains Pet/Adm.filed 28 Oct.1867, shows that Ike decd. 28 Sept. 1867,intestate leaving a small Est.-land in Bolivar Co.(Sunflower written above this)- stocks, +notes due him,@$3,00. He left his wife Caroline C.Robinson,D.Bill Robinson,C.M.Robinson-children of said decd.,minors. Wife Caroline renounces the right to Adm. Est.,in favor of Wm.W.Robinson-bro.of Ike Robinson the decd.. Inv.& Apprai. made at the late residence in Greenville,24 Dec.1867 and an allowance'of $2500 for the 1st yr.given widow and ch.

#325:EST.OF JOHN M.SMITHERST,decd.-S.W.Ferguson,Adm.-Included is the Will of Smitherst-in which he states he holds 2 notes at 10% int.of $480 each-1 to Mrs.Ann Worthington,1 to Dr.Polk. Also a legacy coming to him from the Olmstead Est.,because he's in his Will. The notes he leaves to Mr.Andrew W.Smith. Wit:Mrs. Catharine C.Smith-Apr.29,1863.
Proof of Will same day as filed.

#326:EST.OF FOSTER BROOKS,decd. S.W.Ferguson,Adm.-Pkt.contains; Pet/Adm.of R.J.Turner,a phy.,shows that Foster Brooks decd.1867, intestate, leaving a small Est.,but is in debt to him. Believes Foster left his mother Mrs.Ann Brooks on S.Summer St.,Nashville, Tn.,and a bro.of the same place, a sister Mrs.D.Fleming residing at Thompson's Station,Tn. No relative or next of kin in Ms. Filed 25 Nov.1867. John H.Estill states that Foster Brooks was his overseer.

#327:EST.PATRICK CUNNINGHAM,decd.S.W.Ferguson,Adm.:(more than ½ of rt.side of papers gone)Pet/Adm.shows that Patrick decd. 2 Nov.1867,intestate,and Pet.believes he left 1 bro. in Ga. or Ala. and (torn)residing in state of Nor(torn). No next of kin in this state. Signed by Dr.J.W.Phillips,a creditor Adm.appointes S.W.Ferguson. Bill of Discovery-Cit.to Mrs.S.F. Buckner,J.M.Davis-Jan.1868 for building a levee on Pltn.on Deer Creek in 1867.

#328:EST.OF CHAS.B.TALBOTT,decd.-Haycraft Adm.:Let/Adm.shows Chas.B. decd. Aug.1867,small personal Est. @$1,000, leaving a widow who waives Adm.rts. 25 Nov.1867.
Inv.of Est.declares that the "Est.consists of doubtful and desperate debts amounting to $2,454. $1807 being doubtful,$647 being desperate." The widow will try to collect said debts in lieu of a yrly.allowance. 27 Jan.1868.

#330:EST.OF JOHN KIRKLAND,decd.-Lucilla Kirkland,Adm.:Let/Adm. the widow,Lucilla,states he decd.,8 Dec.1867 intestate,leaving a large personal Est.-3 horses,notes and a/c-$10,000.Filed 23 Dec.1867.Inv.& Apprai.Adm.Bd.Zack Tampley,John Heath.

#331:Est.of J.Downs,Mary J.Downs,Adm.-Should read EST.OF A.C. DOWNS,DECD.,MARY JANE DOWNS,SURVIVING ADMS.
Pet/Adm.Mary J.Downs of Warr.Co.Ms. relict of A.C.Downs,decd., states that her husband make his Will in 1844, and appointed the exec.,and then in 1857, he decd.The named exec.refused(cont.)

WASH.CO.PACKET GLEANINGS
DRAWER #296-332

#331:(Cont.) to qualify, and others were named,but have now decd.
Your Petitioner alone now acting. **The** Will divided everything
between Mary J. & their 2 sons-James R. & Henry S.Downs. both
of whom are now decd. At that time A.C.Downs'Est. was worth
between $200,000/$300,000, but due to the war the Est. is now
insolvent. She is infirm,and not being provided for. She seeks
dower rts. to the Est. stating that one of their sons, James
Robinson Downs(who marr.Letticia Vick) left 2 ch.-Alfred C.Downs,
& Jas.R.Downs, now living in Danville,Ky. with their mother
Letticia V.Downs..the ch.are minors. **Filed** 5 Dec.1867
Danville,Ky.,a court order for a legal Guard.to be appointed
the 2 ch. 5 Dec.1867
Descriptions of land in Wash.Co.Ms.-mostly in T16,R7W-over 4,000
ac. **Answer** of minors,sons of Jas.R.Downs,decd.,by their legal
Guard.T.B.Gray,ad litem 1868 in Mar.--Illegible.

#332:EST.OF ALEXANDER MCCAUGHN,decd.-S.W.Ferguson,Adm.:Pkt.contains **Let**/Adm.by Jos.Key,Geo.P.Walu,John Estill,creditors-24
Dec.1867,states that Alex decd.24 Nov.1867,intestate,leaving
a real and personal Est. No relatives or kin in this state.
Pet.for Sale-Order for sale-Public notice-Alex lived on Sunflower River in Wash.Co.Ms.- **Inv.**& debts Mar.1868.
Pet. Filed 23 June 1868,stating that E.G.Booth had a partnership,
entered into 1 Dec.1860 for cotton Pltn.,Booth supplying the negroes. Booth a resident of Philadelphia,Pa. and surviving partner & Eliza-Ann-Harbersen-of-South-Hansen,Ind.(Name and res.
marked through in all 3 places mentioned) & Jane Humphrey of
Floyd,Carroll P.La.,the last two named being the only heirs of
A.McCaughan,decd. Pet.declares Ferguson mismanaged the Est.,
sold prop.belonging to partnership,etc. and asks his dismissal.
Ferguson's answer to pet. of Jane Humphrey denies any misdoing.
Ferguson files annual a/c 1868, 1871.

DRAWER #333-369

#333:EST.G.W.POTTS,decd.-S.W.Ferguson,Adm.:**Let.**/Adm.by Jas.S.
Wilson stating the decd. was killed sometime last winter in
this county, leaving no relatives or family in county at that
time and since no one else would go to the trouble of burying
him,"Idid it at my own expense".($28.25)Filed 29 Sept.1868
Original file date 28 Dec.1867. **Pet.** of creditor Mrs.A.B.Finlay
states that G.H.Potts decd., 8 Dec.1867,intestate.

#334:EST. OF D.A.STOATS,decd. D.A.Love Adm.: **Let**/Adm. 24 Dec.
1867.(Note:right side of these doc.are torn off)by D.A.Love,
states that Stoats decd. 21 Oct.last, intestate,leaving no relative in state. **Pet.**for release of Adm.filed 23 May 1871,states
that Stoats owned no prop.in Ms.,and was at the time of his death
a citizen of N.Y.

#335:EST.OF HENRY RUCKS,decd.-S.J.Rucks,Adm.:Let/Adm.filed 26
Dec.1867 by Sarah J.Rucks,widow of Henry,declared he decd.,2
Oct.1867,leaving a small Est.-land on Deer Creek@235 ac. + wagon
etc. He left as heirs,beside his widow, 3 sons-Arthur,Benj.N.,
Saml.T.Rucks-all minors under 14.

#336:EST.W.W.DEEVERS(Deavers)decd.-S.W.Ferguson,Adm.Let/Adm.
filed by B.F.Penny & John H.Evans creditors,stating that W.W.
(cont.)

WASH.CO.PACKET GLEANINGS
DRAWER #333-369

#336;(Cont.)decd. 26 Dec.1867,intestate,leaving a large personal Est.,and request that Ferguson be appointed Adm. as the nature of W.W.'s business demands prompt attention ("leases in action") Filed 26 Dec.1867-no relatives in this state.

#337;WM.ERWIN,ET AL,Minors-Victor Erwin Guard.;Pkt.contains 3 documents-Pet/Guard.by Victor F.Erwin shows that his mother Margaret A.Dudley,late of said county,decd.,intestate and left 6 children.2 of whom are minors over 14,namely Johnson & J.W. Erwin. The petitioner believes that after the debts are paid there will be but a small Est. Pet.is bro.of said minors. Filed 27(Torn)1868. Guard.Bond filed 25 Mar.1868 with D.F.Hunt as sec. Pet.of minors for Victor F.to be their Guard ¶[NOTE:Margaret A.Johnson marr.1st James Erwin,as his 2nd wife, and they had the following ch:Eliz.Julia, Emily, Victor Flournoy, Wm.,James, & Johnson Erwin;Marg.A.(Johnson)Erwin marr.2nd DR.Chas.W.Dudley in 1856 and they had one ch. Chas.W.,Jr. After Marg.A.'s death, Dr.Dudley marr. her sister Louisa (Johnson)Elly the widow of W.R.Elly.
From"Ky.Pioneers and Court Records" by McAdams,p.298:"Mrs. Margaret Dudley, wife of Chas.Wilkins Dudley;(decd.)at the residence of Dr.B.W.Dudley, Aug.28,1863. Taken from Extracts from Funeral Invitation, Lexington,Ky., now in the Lexington,Ky. Public Library.]

#338:EST.ANDREW CARSON,decd.-E.J.Carson,Adm.Let./Adm. shows that Andrew Carson decd. 22 Feb.1868,intestate, owning a tract of land on Black Bayou @1600 ac.in Wash.Co.Ms.,+ stock,etc.+ 160 ac.in Bolivar Co.Ms.,worth @$2,000. E.J. is his Widow, and said he left 4 other heirs. Andrew B.Carson,Geo.F.Ross,Andrew B.Ross & Mary E.Ross-last 3 are minors. Filed 25 Mar.1868.

#339:EST.OF WM.& JOHNSON ERWIN,minors-Victor Erwin,Guard. Answer of Victor to Citation to appear in court and give report of minor's Est.;He has never had any property belonging to said minors, but only represented them in case of E.J.Flournoy,Exec. vs. the Erwin Heirs, pending in Supreme Court of Ms. This answ. was filed 23 Oct.1871.

#340:BETTIE B.BROOKS,et al minors.-F.H.Boyce,Guard.:Pet/Guard. filed 26 Oct.1868(some of these doc. are numbered #346)shows that Jos.M.Brooks,late of Wash.Co.Ms.,decd. leaving 2 ch.Bettie B.Brooks & Lucy(torn),minors under 14. Boyce has had their legal custody for several yrs. and out of love and affection seeks permission to collect said orphans inheritance.Vouchers show the girls in a boarding school"Nazareth"in Bardstorm,Ky.

#343:EST.OF JOHN LOLLIN,decd.-R.S.Buck,Adm.:(Right side of Pkt. gone)Pkt.contains#341EST.OF NAT HOLMES,decd.vs Wm.Montgomery & D.J.Beecher-16 Aug.1865(All pertinent information gone!)Pet/ Adm. by J.S.Walker for Est. of Nat Holmes, states he decd.,intestate, Sept. 1867,worked in a sawmill and has wages due him from the owners,named above. No heirs named.
EST.OF JOHN LOLLIN,......... Let/Adm.by R.S.Buck says he decd. Sept.1868,intestate,leaving a small Est.,no wife or ch. Filed 13 Oct.1868.

WASH.CO.PACKET GLEANINGS
DRAWER #333-369

#344 Est.ALFRED WILLIS vs EMELINE WILLIS,Adm.Let/Adm.Alfred Willis decd.,18 Oct.1868,intestate,leaving a small Est. Emeline is widow and he left 5 other heirs-Arthur C.,James A.,Robert L.,Mary B., & Fanny E., all Willis'... and children of said decd.,and your petitioner. ¶[NOTE:Emeline T.Sutton,dau.of James M.Sutton & Eliza VanNorman, marr.2nd H.H.Melchoir, and had issue: She marr.1st Alfred Willis]

#347:Est.John, Littleberry, & Caroline Mosby-Paulina Mosby,Guard; Pet/Guard. by Paulina asking permission to rent out "Loughborough Pltn."which descended to them from their mother Eliza Burks Mosby decd.Cit.to Susan P.Taylor & Caroline L.McAllister-4 Oct. 1872 to answer proposition of Guard.Paulina to sell a certain piece of land of her ward's,John B.,Littleberry H.,Caroline M.,all Mosbys, minor heirs of Eliza Mosby,decd. @80 ac. In 1872 in petition by Paulina the ages of the minors were John B.-19,Littleberry H.-16, Caroline M.-14. John B.is in school at Va.Military Institute, Caroline is at Pala---Institute in Md.,and Littleberry will need to go off to school in next year. Susan P.Taylor & Caroline L.McAllister are aunts of said wards, as is your petitioner. 2 Jan.1871 minors to receive $700-$800 from a suit styled Barrow vs Mosby #22828 in Chan.Ct.,Louisville,Ky.

#349:Est.JOHN F.WARREN,decd.Wm.Warren,Adm.(see Pkt.#174. No add. info.)Included in Pkt. Est.Arnold Lashley,decd.1863,intestate, leaving a sole legatee-Robert M.Lashley.

#355:Est.of GEO.BLACKBURN ALEXANDER-Geo.B.Hunt,Guard.:Pet/Guard. by Hunt shows that Geo.T.Blackburn,late Guard. of Geo B.Alexander minor, has decd. Petitioner is 1st cousin of said minor and seeks Guard. Est.,consists of annual sums of $700 to minor-Filed 2 Dec.1871.Guard/Bd. entered Feb.1869 by G.T.Blackburn for Geo. Alexander,minor heir of Austin F.Alexander,decd. Filed 9 Feb.1870 Let/Guard. filed 9 Feb.1870 by G.T.Blackburn with W.E.Hunt as Sec.¶[NOTE:George Blackburn and his wife Julia Flournoy of Ky., had 3 dau.:Cassandra marr.Austin Fleetwood Alexander;Prudence marr. Wm.Hunt,and another dau.marr.C.G.B.Blackburn]

#357:Est.of JOSEPH GIBSON,decd.-Archie Baugh,Adm.:May Term-1869- Pet.for L/A by widow Clarissa(X)Gibson stating he decd. 30 Apr. 1869 leaving a small personal Est. She relinquishes rights to Adm. and asks Archie Baugh to act in her stead-to sell growing crops,etc.Filed 24 May 1869.Pet.of heirs to release Baugh as Adm.-filed 20 Feb.1871 and signed by Clarissa(X)Gibson,Jos. Strothers for self and wife, Maria Gibson,-Clarissa(X)Gibson for Winney, Mary, & Wilson Gibson.

#358:Est.H.W.ANDERSON,decd.-W.W.Stone,Adm.:Let/Adm by Stone state the decd.left a small personal Est.,no relatives in this state, intestate.Filed 30 June 1869. W.W.Stone petitions to declare Est. insolvent, and the following heirs answer:Ann Maughes and her husband G.M.B.Maughes,St.Louis Mo.:Geo.Anderson-residence unknown:Wm.Anderson of Fulton,Calloway Co.Mo.;Thos.L.Anderson of Hot Springs,Ark.;and the children and living heirs-at-law of Asa Overall res. of St.Charles,Mo.;all non-res.of Ms. Pet. of Ann & G.M.B.Maughes states she was the sister and heir of Henry W.Anderson.Sale of prop. 28 July 1874.

WASH.CO.PACKET GLEANINGS
DRAWER #333-369

#359:Est.of JOHN JAMES,decd.-A.J.H.Crow,Adm.:Let/Adm.states
James decd.1869,intestate,leaving considerable prop. and Mary
James,his widow relinquishes rights to Adm.and requests that
her bro. A.J.H.Crow act in her stead. 11 Oct.1869. Pet/Dower by
widow Mary James,names their 8 children.L.Annie C.Baker marr.
H.L.Baker;2.John H.James;3,Jos.G.James;4.Benj.F.James;4.Willie
James;6.T.J.James;7.Albert E.James;8.Percy James.Cit.to all but
Albert 23 Nov.1870 for sale of prop.located on Bayou Granicus
@1272 ac.T16,R8W.Notification to widow Mary James and other
defendants who are non-res.of Ms.,residing at Louisville,Ky.
13 Feb.1872.

#361:Est.of T.Jefferson Compton-John Compton,Adm.;Let/Adm. by
John Compton,bro.of decd.and co-partner in farming,states that
before his death, Jefferson had a contract with Bernard Doge
for construction of a house and it has been started, and John
thinks it should be finished since it would add to the value
of the Est.of the decd. Filed 22 Oct.1869. John states that the
only heir lives in the state of Calif. Agreement to disc.Adm.
signed by Emma C.Eastin & C.C.Eastin-Finala/c May 1872.

#363:Est.of EDWIN M.BLACKBURN,decd.-S.W.Ferguson,Adm.;Let/Adm.
by Anthony Britton & Geo.W.Koontz,bank partners in Natchez,state
that Edward M.Blackburn,a citizen of Wash.Co.Ms.,decd.,intestate,
owned equipment in use on"Glen Allan Pltn.",the prop. of Gus-
tavous Calhoun & his son Howard Calhoun. The petitioners ask that
an Adm. be appointed. 25 May 1869-Ferguson was App.Document
states that he left a widow-Charlotte B.Blackburn and several
children in Natchez. 25 Mar.1870.

#364;Est.EMELINE FRENCH,ward-Dr.Stiles,Guard.;Pet.for Let./Guard.
20 Oct.1869,states that James French and his wife Diana French
are both decd.,leaving 4 children-Lewis, Nelson, Esther Ann,
& Emeline,all minors. Dr.Stiles is their Uncle. Lewis and Nelson
are over 14. Guard./Bd. 22 Nov.1869.Stiles seeks Guard.of Emeline.

#365:Est.ESTHER ANN FRENCH,et al,minors,-Wilson Clark,Guard.:
Clark is the Guard.for Lewis,Nelson,Esther Ann French,children
of James French decd.(see#364 above).Pkt.also contains a C.C.
#365;THOS.C.BEDFORDS vs SAML.RANEY of La.over land sold for taxes

#366:Est.GEO.VAUGHN,decd.-Carrie & A.C.West Adm.;Pet.of Carrie
West and Amelius C.West shows that Vaughn decd.1868,intestate,
small Est.,leaving his widow Carrie Vaughn,now West. Carrie has
intermarr. with Amelius C.West. Vaughn left 2 minor children,
1 of whom is the child also of Carrie West. 22 Nov. 1869.
Sale of prop.Receipt of J.B.Vaughan,son of decd.,acknowledged
by F.M.Vaughan-Columbus,Ms.,11 Nov.1870. Also a check made out
to Marian Vaughn-for $200 by A.C.West. 27 Dec.1870

#367;Est.NASH OLMSTEAD,decd.-John Daniels,Adm:L/A by Daniels
states that Olmstead decd.,leaving a widow-Filed 22 Nov.1869
with Daniels appearing in Issa.Co.

#368:Est.BETTIE D.FINLAY,et al minors-John P.Finlay,Guard.:
Pet. for sale of minor's prop.,names Pricilla W.& Thos.P.Finlay,
minors by Guard.John P.Finlay-126 ac. on Williams Bayou 28 May
1877.Cit.to other heirs names Helen, Bettie, Saml., Eliza Finlay
& Annie P.Archer all of Wash.Co.Ms.;Mary N.Sims of (Cont.)

WASH.CO.PACKET GLEANINGS
DRAWER #333-369

#368;(Cont.)Ranking Co.Ms.,-Co-heirs and A.B.Finlay & Saml.D.
Finlay of Wash.Co.,2 of the nearest relatives of the said minors.
Answer of Ann B.Finlay,Helen M.Finlay, Bettie D.Finlay,Saml.D.
Finlay, Annie P.Archer,Eliza B.Moore,Mary N.Sims all bro.& sis.
of said minors-Filed Dec.1876. They approve the sale.Ann B.Finlay
is the mother of said minors, Saml.D. a bro.-over 21.

#369;Est.BENJ.F.COMEGY,decd.-Nathan A.Heard,Adm.;L/A of N.A.
Heard shows that Comegys decd.,Nov.1869,intestate,leaving his
wife Julia Comegys & an infant child-John B.Comegys,and that
Julia Comegys has since decd.bearing the infant and the infant
survived. N.A.Heard states that he was the father-in-law of
said decd.Benj.Comegy and the grand father of, and next of kin,
of the infant. That on 6 Dec.1869, Heard was awarded let. ad
collegendum, and has kept everything together. The appraisal
was made before the widow's death-value $310. Filed 24 Aug.1870
Inv.shows that Comegys was a merchant.

DRAWER #370-403

#370:Est. of ANDREW G.HAYNES,decd.-Benj.S.Wing,Adm.(Pkt.all in
shreds)Wing qualified in Ark.-Crittenden Co. 27 July 1869.

#373;ELIZA APPLETON,decd.-Lewis(x)Henderson,Adm.L/A say Eliza
decd.2nd day of,July 1869,small est.Pet.is next of kin,Filed
27 Dec.1869.

#374:Est.of WM.F.SHANNON,decd.-Rebecca Shannon,Adm.:She states
that Wm.F. decd. 20 Nov.1869,leaving no heirs but herself, the
widow. Filed 18 Dec.1871.

#375:Est.of A.J.SILL,decd.-Mary A.Robb,Adm.:L/A states that
Sill decd.20 Jan.1869,intestate,leaving 6 horses. She is a creditor and seeks Adm.,27 Dec.1869.Inv.postmarked"Lake Island"-
G.W.Sill was one of the buyers.Final a/c states that M.O.Wake-
field & his wife Malissa(Molly) living in this county, are the
only heirs in this state.

#376:Est.of JAMES H.DUNCAN,decd.-J.J.Person,Adm.:L/A states
Duncan decd.,1869,intestate,small Est. Person is a creditor
28 Dec.1869.Est.consists of a promissary note of Sampson Williams
for $4,000 in Circuit Court,Issa.Co.,Person believes that Samp-
son has given considerable prop. to members of his family to keep
from making payment. Williams proposes a compromise.

#377:JOHN H.JAMES,et al minors-Mary James,Guard. is the label
on the outside of the Pkt. Pkt.actually is #377;EST.ROBERT SCOTT
decd.-Julia(X)Scott,Adm.L/A Filed 16 Feb.1870 by the widow Julia,
stating he decd. on Wm.H.Offuts Pltn."Utopia" in Wash.Co.Ms.,
on--Mar.1869,leaving 2 ch. Eli age 5,(torn) age 2. A note signed
by Wm.H.Offut,states Robt.Scott,"collored"died on Utopia Pltn.
on 27 Mar.1869. Note signed 14 July,1870.Another note from the
Freedmens Insurance Co. stated that if Julia could prove he was
her husband & could give the death date she could collect.

#379:Inside of #377:JOHN H.JAMES,et al minors-Mary James,Guard.
Pet/Guard.states that John James,decd.leaving 7 minor ch. John
H.,Jos.G.,Benj.F.,Willie, T.J.,Albert,Percy-under 14.(see Pkt.
#359)

WASH.CO.PACKET GLEANINGS
DRAWER #370-403

#380:Est.A.C.BULLETT,decd.-Irene Smith,Exec.(Pkt.in poor cond.) No Adm.Pet.**Copy** of Will(EMR-Vol.I p.94);To Mrs.Irene Smith,mother of my decd.wife Fanny L.Smith-"Longwood Pltn".&"Basin Pltn.";to my wife Irene Williams all other prop.;Exec. Irene Smith

#381:FANNIE S.BULLITT,minor-Irene S.Bullitt,Guard.;**Pet**/Guard. by Irene S.Bullit,Widow of A.C.Bullitt,decd.,leaving an only child, a dau.age 3 years.9 mo. who was born after A.C.made his will and she is entitled to an undivided ½ of"Longwood"and"Basin Pltn".containg @3500 ac. Which said pltn's are also subject to the dower rights of said widow.Irene S.Bullitt,mother of Fanny Smith Bullitt,minor,seeks Guard.Filed 1Mar.1870.**Guard**.Bond $10,000 with Irene Smith as sec. **Pet**.by Fannie S.Bullitt seeks release of her mother as her Guar.,as she has reached 21.All a/c settled-19 Mar.1888. on 19 Mar.1888 the mother also seeks release and signs Irene S.Williams. **A voucher** July 15,1876 from the Grand Hotel at Cincinnati, made out to C.P.Williams for self, wife, & servant,& Dau.-Miss Bullett and Servant.

#383:RACHEL & ESTHER ALEXANDER,minors-Jacob Alexander,Guard. **Pet**.Guard. Jacob states that Clara Alexander,decd.intestate, leaving 2 ch. Rachel 33 mo.,Esther 17 mo., and a small Est.- amounting to @$4,000 for each child. Jacob is the father-23 Aug. 1870. **The Est**. consisted of some lots in Greenville, and Jacob petitions to sell them. This results in Citation being sent to other relatives of said minors-Lewis Eckstone & Mark Eckstone July 1875. **Pet**.to sell another lot sends a cit.to Louis Schles- singer & Hulda Schlessinger-May 1875:Jacob seeks a summons to Jos.Radjesky,Rachel Radjesky,& Louis Schlessinger in Aug.1870.

#384:Est.O.R.SPRAGUE,decd.-Esther Sprague,Adm.**Let/Adm** by Esther states that O.R.decd.5 Apr.1870,intestate, at his residence in Wash.Co.Ms. She is his widow, and there are 5 minor children all of whom are living with petitioner. Filed_____(Torn)

#386:Est.ALEXANDER BROOKS,minor-Soloman Alexander,Guard.:**Pet**. of Alex. Brooks for Soloman Alexander to be his Guard.,stating hes is his natural father & his mother is Mary Dorson. His mother always told him Soloman was his father. Mary has since intermarr. with one James Dorson,who mistreats him-...his step-father even went after him with an axe, and his mother does nothing. Alex.has been living with Soloman for some time and is well treated and seeks him as his Guard. as he is over 14. He further states that ___Brooks, the husband of his mother at the time of his birth has since decd.-said Brooks and Mary were at the time slaves. Filed 23 Aug.1870.So allowed.

#387;Est.HENRY CHASE,decd.-S.G.Worthington,Adm.;**Let/Adm**.state that Chase decd. Sept.1870,intestate,living on "Avon Pltn."on Lake Lee. Worthington is a creditor of Ann Chase,widow. Filed 1871.

#388:Est.SOLOMAN COLLIER,decd.-Richmond(X)Collier Adm.;**Let/Adm**. state that Soloman decd. June 1870,intestate,leaving Maud Col- lier his widow and one son Soloman,minor under 2 yrs. Richmond is Soloman Collier,decd.'s bro. Filed 26 Oct.1870

WASH.CO.PACKET GLEANINGS
DRAWER #370-403

#389:Est.BARTHOLOMEW HANWAY,decd.-Mary Hanway,Adm.:Let/Adm.state that he decd.23 Sept.(Torn) leaving 2 heirs Ellen & Eliz. Filed 24 Nov.1870. Pet./Dower-He owned a store, and Mary the widow, states he decd.Sept.1870,intestate,leaving 3 minor ch. Lizzie, Nellie, & Bertha Hanway. The decd.,was a partner of T.Greany, owning ½ of some lots in Greenville, She accepts 1/3rd of Est. Filed 20 Dec.1871.

#390:Est.of HILLIARD H.LEE,decd.-Jesse J.Duncan,Adm.:Let/Adm. state Lee decd.21 Sept.1870,intestate,leaving 2 ch. Mina D.Lee age 5, and Harris Anna Lee age 4.Also a small Est.-some stock, plus a lot in West Point,Ms. The petitioner Duncan states that his wife is ½ sister to 2 minor children and he is supporting the children anyway. 23 Nov.1870.In 1874,Duncan seeks to declare Est. insolvent and Harris Anna and Minnie Lee answer by Guard. ad litem E.K.Stafford.

#391:Est.ofJAMES S.Wilson-Caleb Stone,Exec.:(Pkt.nearly all gone)The Will of Wilson, Written 17 Aug.1870-Probated Boone Co. Mo.,26 Sept.1870;"left in possession of my cousin Dr.James Walker of Greenville,Ms.,a promissary note executed to me by him for @$300.(The decd. was in business styled "Eveman & Wilson);names his Uncle Caleb Stone to get his Est. to keep in trust for Uncle Caleb's 5 children. Proof of Will.

#392:Est.J.C.WILLIAMS,decd.-Henry J.Williams,Adm.:Let/Adm.of Thos.J.Williams states that J.C.decd.,7 July 1870,intestate,- leaving Nancy Williams,his widow and your petitioner Thos.J. Williams,Henry J.Williams,J.B.Williams & J.C.Williams his children under 21-all his heirs-at-law. Widow waives Adm.rights and asks that their oldest son,Thos.J. be Adm. Filed 10 Nov.1870. Henry J.and mother Nancy Williams file petition to remove Thos. from Adm. and to appoint his bro. Henry, "asThos.has left the state with no intent to return!". Filed 24 Feb.1871.

#393:Est.J.H.BAREFIELD,decd.-John W.Winpegler,Adm.;(Pkt.falling to pieces)Pet.of P.J.,widow of J.H.Barefield,who decd.5 Feb.1870 intestate,no children,and she renounces her right to serve as Adm. Filed Nov.Term 1870-rest of doc.gone.Pet.of John W.Winpeg- ler, for L/A of est. of JOhn H.Barefield,decd.,and for Let/Guard for person of Jesse H.Barefield. States that John H.-marked out and Jesse written over it-decd,intest.,no ch.or other heirs but torn ,widow, then Jane Barefield   Stinson,MaryJ.Winpegler & Jessie L.Carter   of said JesseN.Barefiled &   & are heirs of his bro.decd. The petitioner is husband of Eldest Dau. of said John Barefield,Mary J.Winpegler-and senior heir at law and he has custody of Jessie L.Carter,Minor heir-at-law of Jesse H.,19 Apr.1871--agreed,then revoked.(Note;very confusing doc. with much of the pertinent information torn off, and often the name John overwritten with Jesse.)

#395:H.R.DAWSON,decd.-Lewis Hornthall,Adm.:Let/Adm.dated Oct.1870,states he decd.,intestate,leaving a widow and several children-the number petitioner does not know. The widow,Mrs.S.A.Dawson waives Adm.rights in favor of Mr. Hornthall-5 Dec.1870 (Pkt.in pieces)

WASH.CO.PACKET GLEANINGS
DRAWER #370-403

#396:Est.SARAH E.KIRK,decd.-A.M.Kirk,Adm.:Let/Adm.state she decd. 9 Dec.1870,intestate,leaving 5 children:Elizabeth W. 14yr.:Wm.M.-age 8:Sarah Y.-age 6:Roberta J. age 4:Alexander M. 6 mo.;All are Kirks.Pet.by the husband of decd.Filed 3 Jan.1871-small Est. worth @ $1500.

#397;Est.A.S.BALLINGER,decd.-S.H.Brown Adm.:Let/Adm.state he decd. Aug.1870,intestate,leaving a widow and his only son W.F. Ballinger-his only heirs. Filed 17 Sept.1870

#399:Est.of WADE,FRANKLIN,& THOS.LEE DANIELS-Wm.A.Willis,Guard. (Pkt.unreadable)

#402:Est.CLARENCE GEOGHEGAN,decd.-John Fawn,Adm. Filed 12 Aug. 1872-Let/Adm.petition by Fanny T.Geoghegan,widow of C.T.,waives Adm.Rts. as she is a resident of a distant state-Louisville,Ky. John Fawn is appointed.IN Fawn's pet. he states the decd.,left a widow, Fanny and 1 minor child age 2 years.-1871.

#403:Est.CAPITOLA & GEO.JOHNSON,minors,Mary(x)Clark,Guard. Pet.for Let/Guard. states that Wesley Johnson decd.,leaving 2 children,minors under 14. Mary Clark was the widow of said Johnson and their mother. Filed 18 Apr.1871.

CHANCERY COURT PACKET #497:RICHARD BURDETTE vs GEO.P.BIERNE,et al Contains the WILL OF ANDREW BIERNE-written Monroe Co.,Va. 9 Jan. 1845-Filed Monroe Co.July 1845(Monroe Co.,Va.became Mon.Co.W.Va.)
Brother:Oliver Bierne
Nephew:Geo.P.Flanagan
The heirs of Saml.Black,formerly of Mon.Co.
The rest of the Est. to be divided between"my(7)children"-Andrew Bierne,Jr.(has ch.):Mary D.Steenberger(has ch.)and her share to be put in trust to "my"sons Geo.P.Bierne & Oliver Bierne,the executors of this Est...other 3 daus.,Susan Patton,Nancy MacFarland,Ellen Bierne.
When this suit #497 was filed 1874(over tax sale of some prop. in the Est. of Andrew Bierne)the heirs and places of Res.were;
Geo.P.Bierne,Garnett Andrews & wife Rosalie C.Andrews-Huntsville
Nancy McFarland & dau.Nancy,age 17-Greenbrier Co.,W.Va.
Eliz.Barksdale & Husb.Randolph Barksdale   "   "   "   "
Susan McFarland-Greenbrier Co.,W.Va.
Wm.McFarland,Mrs.Turner McF.Bierne wife of Wilcox---Brown,
Bierne T.Sanders wife of John Sanders-all of Baltimore,Md.
Oliver Bierne of Sweet Springs,Monroe Co.,W.Va.
Mary B.Middleton,wife of Thos.A.- Georgetown,S.C.
Ellen Blair wife of Adolphus Blair-Richmon,Va.
Eliz.Mercer wife of ---Mercer, late of Savannah,Ga.but now living in Europe and P.O. unknown.
Alice Blackford- Baltimore,Md.
Nannie Blackford- Georgetown,D.C.
Kate Holman-address unknown
Jas.Reid-Bedford Co.,Va.
Oliver Patton- Huntsville,Ala.
Martha L.Stevens of Brandon,Ms.
Mary Echols of Huntsville,Ala.

RANDOM CENSUS 1880-WASHINGTON CO. MS.

GREENVILLE				b.	Fa.b.	Mo.b.
122-131:W.R.TRIGG	46	Atty.		Va.	Va.	Va.
N.S. "	43	wife		"	"	"
E.G. "	13	dau.		"	"	"
S.P. "	12	"		"	"	"
C.P. "	8	son		"	"	"
M.H. "	6	dau.		"	"	"
T.K. "	6	son		"	"	"
139-149:H.B.THEOBALD	83			Ga.	--	--
W.R.HARVEY	32	boarder-Civil Eng.b.at sea			F.b.Scot-M.B.Ire.	
140-150:BS.SHELBY	49(f)			Ms.	MS.	Ms.
Alex(?)	24	son		"	"	"
Bettie	21	dau.		"	"	"
Katie	16	"		"	"	"
Bayless	15	son,clerk in sewing machine store			"	"
Hattie	9	dau.		"	"	"
142-152:HY WETHERBEE	38	Marshall		Ind.	Ind.	Ind.
Dora	25	wife		Ill.	Va.	Tenn.
Harry	5	son		"	Ind.	Ill.
Edna	3	dau.		Ms.	Ind.	Ill.
Ed	9	neph.		Ill.	Ind.	Ill.
159-170:A.B.FINLAY	55(f)			Va.	Va.	Va.
John "	32	son,druggest		Ms.	Conn.	Va.(single)
Bettie "	30	dau.		"	"	"
Alice A."	32	dau.-in-law(Mar)"		Md.	"	Ms.
Percy "	22	" (single)		Ms.	Conn.	Va.
John Lewis	3	Gr.son		"	Ms.	Ms.
Sallie Pelham,34 ½sis.(single)				Ark.	Va.	Va.
G.F.Archer	25	boarder(sin.)keeps book store-Ms.			Md.	Ms.
John G.Archer	22	" grocer		MS.	Md.	MS.
254-284:L.CAFFALL	52	shoemaker		Baden	Baden	Baden
Agnes "	48	wife		"	"	"
Agnes "	18			La.	"	"
Louisa "	16or14			Ms.	"	"
Chas. "	16			"	"	"
Lena "	5			"	"	"
293-330:STEVENSON ARCHER-41		Clergy		Ms.	Md.	Ms.
Annie	33			"	Ohio	Va.
Alice	13			Ms.	Ms.	Ms.
Ellen	12			"	"	"
Wm.H.	9			"	"	"
Anna May	7			"	"	"
Pelham	3			"	"	"
Dunbar	2			"	"	"
Kate Fields19 (b)				"	"	"
302-402:MARGARET MANIFOLD	40			Ms.	France	Ms.
Mary CHILDS	20	neice		KY.	Eng.	Eng.
Lelia MANIFOLD	19	neice		Ms.	"	Ms.
Maggie "	15	"		"	"	"
Willie Thomas --(b)				--	--	--
385-512:KRETCHSMAR,Kate	30			MS.	Ms.	Ms.
" W.P.	1	son		"	Mo.	"
COX,Malcom	5	Neph.		Tx.	Ms.	Tenn.
SMITH,Myra	57	Aunt		Ms.	--	--(widow)

RANDOM CENSUS 1880-WASH.CO.MS.

```
GREENVILLE                                        b.      Fa.b.   Mo.b.
397-517:S.R.DUNN       37    Phy.                 Ms.     Pa.     Pa.
        Amanda         27                         "       Tenn.   Tenn.
        Marian         5                          "       Ms.     Ms.
394-521:C.W.LEWIS      39                         Ky.     --      --
        Margaret       28                         Ms.     Ky.     Pa.
        C.W.,Jr.       3                          "       "       Ms.(?)
        Margaret CAMPBELL 64 Moth.in-law-Pa.      Prussia N.J.
        Rebecca TEIDEMAN 87  Gr.Mother   N.J.     ?       ?
        Lclin(?)PERKINS 13   neice       Ms
        Clara BON      15    adopted ch. La.
BEAT#3-WASH.CO.
no #    A.D.HALSEY 70(widow) Farmer               Va.     Va.     Va.
        D.D.JACKSON 50 son   Phy.                 "       "       "
        Henry W."      17 Gr.son                  Ms.     "       "
        Henry COOPER 35(B)servant
        Lucy       "   30 "     "
        Wm.        "   9  "
WASH.CO.:LEOTA LANDING
193-260:A.W.WICKLIFFE  41                         Ky.     Ky.     Ga.
        Mary    "      22                         Ark.    "       Ky.
        Thos.T. "      5/12 Son                   Ms.     Ky.     Ark.
353-494:TOM WORTHINGTON 27 single                 KY.     Ky.     Ky.
        Ann            60 Mother                  Ky.     "       "
371-523:W.W.WORTHINGTON 40                        "       "       "
        L.F.B.         30                         Ark.    "       "
        Henry          3                          Ky.     "       Ark.
        W.W.,Jr.       1                          Ms.     "       "
597-848:THOS.KERSHAW   76                         S.C.    S.C.    S.C.
        Geo.  "        28 son                     Ms.     "       "
        Adrille "      32 dau.in-law              S.C.    "       "
        Geo.,Jr.       2  gr.son                  Ms.     Ms.     "
        James          2/12 gr.son                "       "       "
LAKE WASH.PRECINCT
465-465:C.W.DUDLEY,SR. 58                         Ky.     Va.     illegible
        Mrs. C.W."     52                         "       Ky.     "
        Sallie ELLY    17 step-dau.               Ms.     "       "
ROBT.STONE'S DIST.
----    John H.JAMES   27
        Bettie E."     21
        Mary C.        5
        Grace V.       2
        Mary           48 mother
        Benj.F.        22 brother
ARCOLA PRECINCT
525-534:W.E.WEST       35                         Ms.
        Jennie D.      33                         "
        Lizzie L.      6                          "
330-348:A.J.PAXTON     64                         Va.     Va.     Va.
        Hannah         51                         Ms.     "       "
        Jack           22                         "       "       Ms.
        A.G.           21                         "       "       "
        Frank          19                         "       "       "
        Hannah         13                         "       "       "
        Carnelia       10                         "       "       "
        Elisha         8  son                     "       "       "
        Sam            6                          "       "       "
```

(cont.next page)

RANDOM CENSUS 1880-WASH.CO.MS.

			b.	Fa.b.	Mo.b.
(cont)A.J.PAXTON					
	Lulu BEASLEY	35 sis.in-law	Ms.	Va.	Va.
	John BUCKLEY	50 Serv.gardner-Ire.		Ire.	Ire.
---	Rich.BURDETT	40	Va.	Va.	Va.
	Minerva	36	Ar.	Ga.	Ga.
	Fanny	18	Ms.	Va.	Ark.
	Emma	13	"	"	"
	Wm.	11	"	"	"
	Nannie	8	"	"	"
-------	R.E.PAXTON	35	Ms.	Ms.	Ms.
	Anna	35	Ms.	Scot.	Ms.
	Charley	4	Ms.	Ms.	Ms.
	Robt.	2	"	"	"
	McNutt	3/12	"	"	"
-----	A.P.WINGFIELD	30	Ga.	Ga.	Ga.
	Mattie	25	VA.	Va.	Va.
	Lizzie	1	Ms.	Ga.	Va.
------	John S.WILMOT	62	Ky.	Ky.	Ky.
	G.Bowman WILMOT	31 son	"	"	"
	Lena "	17 dau.	Ms.	"	---
------	Mary W.RIVES	76			
	Christine(?)	47 step-son			
	Martha MURFF	35 dau			
	Dudley "	10 gr.son			
	Mary "	6 gr.dau			
	Harvey "	4 gr.son			
	Mollie "	1 gr.dau.			
	Camille RIVES	-- step-dau.			
	Arthur "	-- step-son			
	James "	35 son-in-law			
	Orville "	4 gr.son			
	Mary "	2 gr.dau.			

ROBB AND STONE DIST:

274-296:	Charles P.WILLIAMS	40	KY.	Ky.	Ky.
	Anne E. "	26 wife	La.	Va.	Ms.
	Irene S. "	5 dau.	Ms.	Ky.	La.
	Katie C. "	3 "	"	"	"
	Merrit "	1 son	"	"	"
	Minor V. "	1/12	"	"	"
306-332:	Nannette SWITZER	45 widow	Ms.	N.C.	La.
	Mary E.WELLS	29 widow dau.	"	KY.	Ms.
	Sarah F.ABEL	26 " "	"	"	"
	Nellie P."	20 Marr.dau.	"	"	"
	Willie B.WELLS	5 gr.son	Ark.	Ms.	"
	Minnie SWITZER	13 dau.	Ms.	Ark.	Ms.
	R.Norman ROWE	25 boarder	Ark.	Va.	Va.
313-341:	Jos.H.ROBB	37	Ms.	Ky.	Ky.
	Mattie B. "	26	"	Va.	Ms.
	Jesse B. "	8	"	Ms	"
	Jos.H "	6	"	"	"
	Louisa A. "	1	"	"	"
	Geo.DAUGHERTY	55(B)	Mo.	--	--
	Susan JOHNSON	50(B)	Ms.	--	--
	Robert GREGG	55 boarder	Eng.	Eng.	Eng.

RANDOM CENSUS 1880-WASH.CO.MS.
ROBB & STONE DIST.CONT.

```
315-349:Edward C.JAMES     53                      Ark.  S.C.   La.
        Sassie      "      34                      Ms.   Ky.    Tenn.
        Molly L.    "      19                      Ark.  Ark.   Ms.
        Effie C.    "       9                       "     "      "
        Paul P.     "       7                       "     "      "
        Guy R.              1                       "     "      "
        Cora E.STEVENS     11 neice                Ms.   Ms.    Ms.
        Robt.E.     "       6 neph.                Ark.  Ms.    Ms.
        Pauline F.  "       3 neice                Ark.   "      "
363-399:Thos.V.JAMES       63                      La.   S.C.   La.
        Nancy       "      54                      Ms.   Pa.    Ky.
        Saml.Y.     "      25                      Ms.   La.    Ms.
        Thos.V.            23                      Ms.   La.    Ms.
374-410;Morris ROSENSTOCK-23 bookkeeper N.Y.       --           Austria

418-455:Wm.J.RUSSELL       36 Planter             Ms.   Ala.   Ga.

604-702:Thos.POWELL        49                      Va.   --     --
        Harriet MARSH      63 moth.in-law Tn.      Ga.          Ga.widow
        Mattie POWELL      15 neice               Ms.   Va.    Mo.
        Robertie ROW       18 neice               Ark.  Va.    Va.
        Susie       "      14  "                   "     "      "
677-790:Davis BUCKNER      39 lawyer              Ms.   Va.    Ms.
        Amanda      "      32 wife                Ms.   Ky.    Ky.
        Wm.                11 son                  "    Ms.    Ms.
        Louisa              8 dau.                 "     "      "
        Mary                6 dau.                 "     "      "
        Philip      "      27 bro.                Ms.   Va.    Ms.
682-795:Rich.F.DUNBAR      25 Bk.Keeper           Ms.   Vt.    Ms.

688-802:James STONE        42
        Mary W.            35
688-803:Wm.W.WORTHINGTON   45 Planter             Ky.   Va.    Mo.
        Bettie             35 wife                KY.   Ky.    Ky.
        Carlisle            5 son                 La.    "      "
        Mary                1 dau.                Ms.    "      "
        Amanda             76 mother              Va.   --     --
        Saml.              30 bro.                KY.   Va.    Va.
        Mary MORRIS        19 nurse               Ky.   Ire.   Ire.
697-812:James M.SMITH      43 Phy.                Ms.   Va.    Va.
        Anna               35                     Ky.   Ky.    Ky.
        Gregory             9                     Ms.   Ms.    Ky.
        Alexander           7                      "     "      "
        Albert              1                      "     "      "

REFUGE PRECINCT:
1-1     Jessie E.BELL      49                     Ms.   Ms.    Ms.
        Mary A.            49(dysentery)           "     "      "
        Jas.R.             22 son                  "     "      "
2-2     Dr.J.W.H.KZARS     53 boarder-Phy.        Vt.   Mass.  Vt.(dysen'y)
        Wiley BURT         23  "                  Ms.   Ala.   Ms.
132-103:A.J.GREEN          22                     Ala.  Ala.   Ark
        Geo.G.CHAMBERLAIN  19 Boarder             Ms.   Ms.    Ms.

208-160:Dudley W.GRAY      23 dry goods clk.KY.         KY.    Ky.
```

RANDOM CENSUS 1880-WASH.CO.MS.
REFUGE PRECINCT(cont.)

209=161:	Geo.B.SHELBY	35	Farm manager	Ms.	Ky.	S.C.
	Janie P.	29		Ms.	N.C.	N.C.
	Fred P.	3		"	MS.	Ms.
	Janora	1		"	"	"

¶NOTE:Many Irish and now Chinese have appeared,intermingled with the negroes.

GREENVILLE,BEAT#3(JEWISH COMMUNITY)

11-11	John CHURCH	30		Ohio	Italy	Italy
	Fannie "	19		Ill.	Ill.	Ill.
	Annie PUTNAM	58	moth.in-law,	Ill.	Scot.	Germ.
	Allie CHURCH	11	sis.			
	Frank POPE	10	neph.			
	Fannie "	5	neice			
	Minnie "	3	neice			

RANDOM CHANCERY COURT PACKETS-WASH.CO.,MS.

#267:THOS.H.HILL vs NELSON T,WARREN,et al:Suit states-on 2 Nov.1865,Thos.H.Hill & Nelson T.Warren,both of Wash.Co.,Ms. but Warren now of Macon,Ms.,did trade 35 ac.of land in Wash.Co. but never recored the swap.Later Warren sold all his Deer Creek holdings to Mrs.Bettie C.Walcott,wife of Thos.G.Walcott,and it was understood that Mrs.Walcott would give a deed of conveyance,but she decd.before this could be done,leaving as heirs-her husb.Thos.G.Walcott and minors-Chas.A.,Robt.H.,Theo.G.Walcott. Court ruled the prop.be deeded to Hill(his res.was on it).Other papers filed 8 May 1875:Thos.H.Hill,decd.1872,intest.,leaving a small Est.,a widow-Mrs.Mollie Hill who lives in Petersburg,Va. and 2 children-Thos.H.,Jr.& Theodore W.Hill.

#402:CALHOUN HAILE vs AMANDA HAILE:Filed 13 Jan.1871-Calhoun, the bro.of John J.Haile,decd.acting on behalf of his neices-Nannie age 11 & Aliena age 9,minor heirs of said John J.Haile, decd.,and the widow-Amanda Haile, now of Albany,N.Y. Calhoun seeks permission to sell the Est.of the decd.for the benefit of the heirs.

#483:W.H.LETCHFORD & CO.vs R.G.SIMS,et al Mar.20,1872:The defendants in this case are Robt.G.Sims individually, and as Adm. of the Est. of his Father-in-law F.G.Wingfield,decd.:G.Gordon Sims:Felixiana G.Sims-wife of R.G.Sims:W.J.Wingfiled:A.P.Wingfield:Bowdin Wingfield age 10:Frank Wingfield age 7:Ann Wingfield age 17:Walter Wingfield age 3-last 4 being minors & the last 7 being ch. of said F.G.Wingfield, who decd.6 Mar.1871 in Wash.Co.Ms.Another suit styled Jacob Barker,Adm.Est.of Eliz. Barker,decd.vs.R.B.Sims:R.G.Sims & G.G.Sims owned"Sligo Pltn." as inherited from their father.Land was sold at Pub.Auc.and the other heirs are named:Chas.Sims,W.R.Sims,John H.Sims,Robt. B.Sims-heirs at law of Wm.R.Sims,decd.& Eliz.Sims-widow,Moses Phares as Adm.of Est.of Wm.R.Sims,decd.:John P.Dillingham;A.C. Holt;Saml.T.Taylor:A.J.Paxton:R.G.Sims,Wm.E.Sims & Eliz A.Sims-Wm.E. being Adm.of John H.Sims,decd.;G.G.Sims,Leonory Sims, Nancy Sims,Philadelphia Sims-widow & Adm.of Chas.Sims,decd. The Barker suit dated 28 July 1869.

BIBLIOGRAPHY

"A HISTORY OF MISSISSIPPI"-Vol.I:Edited by R.A.McLemore
"BIOGRAPHICAL AND HISTORICAL MEMOIRS OF MISSISSIPPI":Published
   by GOODSPEED
"CEMETERY AND BIBLE RECORDS":Published by Ms.Genealogical Society
"DIARY OF LAVINIA BATEMAN":Private unpublished manuscript
   in Carter Room,Greenville,Ms.Library.
"HISTORY OF SHARKEY COUNTY,MS.":Compiled by the W.P.A.and
   available in the Rolling Fork,Ms.Library.
"HOMETOWN MISSISSIPPI":-by James F.Breiger
"KENTUCKY PIONEER AND COURT RECORDS":-by McAdams
"MARRIAGES,DEATH AND LEGAL NOTICES FROM EARLY ALA.NEWSPAPERS,
   1819-1893": by P.J.Gandrud
"MARRIAGES FROM EARLY TENN.NEWSPAPERS 1794-1851": by S.R.
   Lucas,Jr.
"MISSISSIPPI COURT RECORDS-SUPERIOR COURT": by Hendrix
   Available in Ms.D.A.R.Traveling Library.
"MISSISSIPPI COURT RECORDS": by King
"NATCHEZ COURT RECORDS,1767-1805": by McBee
"NEWSPAPER NOTICES OF MISSISSIPPI,1820-1860": Ms.Gen.Society
"PAPERS OF THE WASHINGTON COUNTY HISTORICAL SOCIETY":Currently
   out of print(1984).Copies in State Archives,Jackson,Ms.
   and the Greenville,Ms.Library
"THE AMANDA WORTHINGTON PAPERS":Unpublished manuscript, Carter
   Room. Greenville,Ms.Library
"THE FOOTE FAMILY":Researched by Rupert Watson,unpub.manuscript
"THE JOURNAL OF LETTY VICK DOWNS":unpub.manuscript,available
   in State Archives,Jackson,Ms.
"THE MONTGOMERY PAPERS": compiled by Dr.Cameron Montgomery,
   privately published.
"TWO WARS": Autobiography by Gen.Saml.G.French
"WILL BOOKS OF JEFFERSON CO. AND CLAIBORNE CO.,MS.":abstracted
   by Gordon Wells
"MARRIAGES & DEATH NOTICES FROM COLUMBIA S.C.NEWSPAPERS-1792-
   1839" by Holcomb

INDEX

A

ABELL:150,154,179
ABERCROMBIE:25,35,131
ABNEY:27,54
ACRES:144
ADAMS:26,49,54,78,80,81
85,105,107
ADDISON:69
AIKEN:81,86
ALBAY:54
ALCORN:121
ALDRICH:129,154,166
ALEXANDER:9,44,48,53,56,
105,118,162,163,171,174
ALLAN:40,44,51,71,75,111
ALLEN:55,67,74,84,94,95,
100,117,120,124,128,140
ALLISON:48,53,56,82
ALLSTON:51
ALSOP:22
ALSTONECRAFT:88
AMBROSE;113
ANDERSON:5,9,13,53,69,
73,79,117,119,158,171
ANDREWS:70,75,114,119
122,176
APPLETON:173
ARCHER:113,121,133,138,
148,156,172,173,177
ARMS:145
ARMSTRONG:15,28,33,
ARNETT:165
ARNOLD;6,47,52,111
ARRINGTON:14,49,54,61,
143,146
ARTHUR:26,31,32,36,53,
73
ASH:100,109
ASHFORD:128
ATCHIS(N)SON:6,14,16,18,
27,28,38,43,59,67,83,
ATKINSON:83,159
AULLSON:4
AUSTIN:21,29,31,39,44,
52,53,54,62,78
AUTER:104,105
AUTEX:68

B

BABB:162
BABBITT:vii,viii,140
BACON:5,12,24,37,46,49,
56,82
BAGLEY:54,113
BAILEY:26,31,99,115,141,33
BAINBROOK:34
BAIN(S):33,34,85,140,141

BAIRD:130
BAKER:64,80,82,90,91,
93,121,127,147a,147d,
172
BALWIN:27,59
BALFOUR:30,61,122
BALL:31,71,81
BALLARD:4,15,161
BALLINGER:176
BANKS:71
BANKSTON:2,27
BARBOUR:114
BARCKLEY(BARKLEY)62,66,
BAREFIELD;88,100,101,
167,175
BARKER:93,95,102,109,
181
BARKSDALE:vii,176
BARLOW:32
BA(E)RNARD:16,20,31,32,
35,41,44,62,91,92,95,
112,113,119,123,125
BARNES:10,11,13,17,18,
36,54,57,65,117,121,133
147
BARNETT:78,90
BARNEY:96
BARR:19,45,62,144
BARRETT:2,47,82,93,110
BARROW:31,171
BARTHEL:50
BARTLEY:158,162
BARTON:69,115
BASS:3,4,5,6,10,11,19,
21,22,28,30,41,43,48,
78,82,87,89,91,142,143,
146,147a,155,162,9
BATCHELOR:122
BATE:89,91,155
BATEMAN;157
BAUGH:128,171
BAYLOR:67
BAYNARD:108
BEAL(L):6,7,12,15,81
BEATY:49
BEASLEY:179
BECK:1
BECHETT:39
BEDFORD(S):18,172
BEECHER:170
BEERY:94
BELL:vii,39,85,96,115,
180
BENBROOK(E):22,23,27,28
35
BENNETT:5,29,43,61,67,
142,147

BERRIEN:85
BERRY:77,86,125,133
BERTHE:145
BERTHOFF:80,82,91
BERTINATTI:155
BIBB:73
BIDDLE;113,160
BIER:40
BIERNE:176
BIGELOW:61
BILL:96,140
BILLINGSLY:18
BINGAMON:18,27,38
BIRCHETT(BURCHETT):166
BLACK:31,32,36,68,76,121
141,143,144,176
BLACKBURN:31,62,77,78,88,
89,105,118,129,132,137,139
145,149,150,151,152,155,157,
158,162,163,171,172
BLACKFORD:176
BLACKMAN:122
BLAINE:17,75
BLAIR:1,81,176
BLAKE:51,97
BLANCHARD:133
BLAND:107,121,130
BLANKS:2
BLANTON:2,3,4,5,6,7,9,12
30,34,44,58,76,78,81,86,88,91
103,127,128,131a,135,142,
143,145,146,147,150,165
BLATTENBURG:164
BLI(E)NOE:115,150
BLOCK:8
BLUE(BLEW,BLEU)1,22,54,55,
140,147a
BLUNT:56
BOATMAN:147b,147c,
BOATNER:109
BODLEY:7,14,26,43,46,62,68
69,82,84,89,
BOGART:109,
BOHANON:42,52
BOICE(BOYCE):1,2,18,21,27,
52,113,126,139,143,148,151
170
BOLAND:105,
BOLLING:32
BOLLS:58,125
BON:178
BOOKER:34,114
BOOKOUT:9,31,52,108
BOOTH(E):54,169
BOSLEY:136
BOSTICK:55,71,121

BOSWORTH:36,
BOTT:112,129,150,166
BOWEN:53,96,97,101
BOWLING:vi,vii,viii,3,31,
141,147a
BOWMAN:8
BOYD:93
BOYER:93
BOYKEN:69
BRABSTON:73,81,88,100
112,114,117,122,124,
BRACKEN:vi,157
BRADFORD:vii,90,101,123
BRADLEY:73,96,99,101,162
BRADY:147a
BRANCH:120
BRANDON:1,3,8
BRANHAM:77
BRANNUM:92
BRASHEAR(S):30,128,
BRASHER:1,8,9,12,23,103,
104,140,141,142,144,147a
BRAWNER:39,42,57,58,147
BRAZER:1
BRECKENRIDGE:23
BRECOUNT:113
BREIGER:18,28
BRENNER:109
BREL(BEIL):49
BREWER:120
BRIDGES:147
BRICKELL:115
BRIGG(S):35,51,94,113,133
142,147b
BRISCOE:3,54,71,75,90,121
125,147a
BRITTON(BRITTIAN):1,2,3,
140,172
BROADNAX(BRODNAX):32,34,
115,147a,147d
BROADWELL:136
BROOKS:14,30,70,76,97,104
151,154,157,168,170,174
BROUGH:106
BROWDER:118,119
BROWN(E):2,3,16,20,29,30
32,39,40,56,72,73,76,79,
81,82,93,94,100,110,124,
129,130,148,150,152,175
176
BROWNING:91,105,112
BRUDLORCK:50
BRYAN:35,61
BRYANT:117,119,120
BUCK:54,113,120,170
BUCKLEY:179
BUCKNER:5,26,29,31,32,46,
52,58,67,71,74,77,81,82,
84,86,92,104,107,108,130

136,137,151,154,161,
165,166,168,180
BUFORD:116
BUKENBOROUGH(BROKEN-
BOROUGH):15
BULL:40,41,50,68,104
BULLEN:31,129
BULLE(I)TT:103,104,107
174
BUNCH:140,141
BUNN:160,164
BURBRIDGE:4,10,11
BURCH:96,130
BURDETT(E):139,179
BURGESS:118
BURGOYN:146
BURK(S)(BYRKE):52,58,82,
99,105,134,155
BURNET:1
BURNEY:105
BURNS:65,99
BURR:161
BURT:180
BURTHE:50
BURTON:121,
BURWAR:18
BURWELL:94,121
BUSH:61,67
BUTLER:30,31,131c
BUTTS:88,98,135,152,159
BYME:2,5
BYRD:31,109
BYRNE:51,83,121,132,137,
164

C
CABANISS:6,
CABLE:91
CADWID:31
CAFFAL;121,127,128,156
177
CAIRNES:147b,147d,
CAITHER(S):134,154
CALDWELL:2,16,17,18,21,
22,25,26,27,34,35,44,46,
48,54,58,59,63,84,87,88,
89,107
CALHOUN:83,130,136,172
CALLENDER:26
CALVIT:30
CAMERON:12,25,69,72,101
106
CAMMING:6
CAMP:108
CAMPBELL:2,4,5,6,9,16,23
26,31,32,33,35,37,41,44,
51,55,59,61,76,93,95,96,
118,135,137,140,141,145
147b,178

CANNON:119,121
CANIEL(CAMEL):27
CARDWELL:104
CARNEAL:70,84,99,158
CARNES:4
CARPENTER:17,21,24,53,57,
128
CARRADINE:55,
CARROLL:48,53,56,57,64,79
143
CARSON:9,23,38,43,76,80,97
99,109,125,126,137,144,148
153,154,155,158,161,170
CARTER:31,34,42,49,51,54,55
71,84,85,94,99,103,105,108
112,124,126,132,134,137,
CASON:82
CASTLEMAN:vii,viii,4,17,27
73,121,145,156,
CATCHINGS:130
CATELEY:129
CAUGHEY:95,100,103,105,108
113,150
CAWELL:137,138
CHAMBERLAIN:80,114,118,180
CHAMBERS:144,147c
CHAMBLISS:13,21,24,36,41,50
54,58,64,86,124,125,144,147
CHANDLER:133,
CHANEY:8,28,36,39,47,48,88
145,146,
CHAPIAIN:80,87,101
CHAPMAN:31,43,44,52,71,75,
98,111
CHASE:174
CHENNAULT:43,47
CHEWNING:14,15,24,28,31,41
58,59,142,
CHILDRESS:75
CHILDS:177
CHILES:148
CHILTON:73,106,
CHINN:157
CHISHOLM:91,92
CHOTARD:119,123
CHRISTIAN:30
CHRISTMAS:30,59,61,62,66,
67,69,106,
CHURCH:80,85,86,95,119,181
CLAIBORNE:31,32,38,
CLAPP:24,
CLARK(E):1,17,18,24,29,36
76,79,105,114,117,130,140,
147b,147d,172,176
CLARY:10,
CLAYTON:1
CLIFTON:67

CLITHERALL:130
CLORE:109,
CLOY:18,
COBB:2,8,28,84,121
COCK(COCKE(S):1,3,4,8,
9,14,15,17,23,27,37,39
47,62,63,67,76,79,84,86,
89,93,112,142,143,144,
146,147b
COCKRAN:95
COFFEE:21,26
COFFETT:9
COFFIN:24,52
COLE:11,150
COLEMAN:66,105,123,124
COLLIER:129,138,167,174
COLLINS:vii,2,3,8,9,11,
12,13,20,23,26,29,36,37
39,46,55,62,63,64,65,68
70,76,141,142,143,144,
146,147a,147b,153
COMEGY'S:173
COMFORT:44,83,87,88,
COMPTON:105,163,172
COMSTOCK:135,151,154,164
CONDAY:111
CONDRAY:16
CONDY:71,75
CONNELLY(CONALEY):vii,24
26,27,31,32,42,46,52,58
77,79,85,86,95,
CONNOR:95
COOK:1,3,4,5,6,8,9,14,15,
27,33,71,114,115,117,118
121,125,147b
COONS:79
COOPER:52,54,105,134,178
CORBIN:125
CORDILL:110,
CORDWELL:68,
CORLIS:121,
CORNELL:145
COULTER:8,24,
COURTNEY:34,87,130,136
COVERT:143
COWDEN:16,143,144
COWPER:53
COX:2,3,10,13,20,21,23,
31,37,52,72,86,89,104,
105,124,133,136,142,144
145,146,147b,147d,155,
156,177
CRABTREE:74,76,82
CRAFT:116
CRAIG:97
CRAIN(E)(CRANE):1,6,26
27,30,52,95,117,118

CRAVEN:48,
CRAWFORD:97,113
CREATH:3,41,51,54,58
125,147,147b
CREIGHTEN:54,94,103
CRESWELL:89,
CRITTENDEN:157
CROCKETT:31,148
CROSS:3,25,84,147b
147c
CROW:24,39,43,92,116
124,141,143,146,172
CRUMP:44,54,60
CRUTCHEN(R):53,74,86,
98,139
CUARD:54
CUDDY:37
CUNNINGHAM:31,32,38,47
54,72,76,95,127,147,168
CUTTER:127

D
DABNEY:3,
DAMERON:17,30,33,36,166
DANCY:83
DANGERFIELD(DAINGERFIELD)
16,53
DANIEL(S):107,121,163,164
172,176,
DANNER:1,
DARDEN:87,124
DARK:8
DART:24,25
DASHIEL:146
DAUGHERTY:179
DAVENPORT:23,55,
DAVIDSON:37,42,44,142
DAVIS:vi,17,31,36,46,47,
49,53,60,61,62,93,105,
126,127,132,168
DAVISON:78,109
DAVY(DAVEY):48,53,56
DAWSON:15,24,31,37,39,41,
44,55,156,175
DAY:74,83
DEAN:164
DEARING:74
DEAVERS(DEEVERS):169
DEBRILL:75
DECOIN:42
DEFORE:52
DeHART:1,15,34,43,49,145
147b,147c
DELANEY:30,141,147b,147c
DEMISTONE:62
DEMOSS:71
DEMPSEY:1,2,66,140,144,145

DENHAM:31
DENMAN:136
DENNING:120
DENNISTOWN:84
DENSMORE:56
DENSON:159
DENT:42,57,71,147,
DENTON:81,83,
DEPEW:54
DERRAH:34,35,
DEWER:97
DICK:83
DICKENS:26
DICKEY:49
DICKSON(DICKINSON)
6,8,9,24,28,31,65,70
71,91
DILLINGHAM:15,16,123,139
166,181
DINWIDDIE:77
DISHAROON:147
DIVINE:6,
DIXON:31,36,70,86,89,110
125,133
DOAK(DOKE):144,145
DODD:9,147c
DOGE:172
DONELSON:76
DORSEY:11,54,76
DORSON:174
DORTCH:114
DOUGHTY:140
DOUGLAS(S):17,18,125,138
DOWELLS:19,
DOWNING:vi,vii,viii,31,
57,64,65,67,78,95,105,120
148
DOWNS:11,17,21,22,25,34,
36,44,55,56,57,58,59,63,
84,87,88,94,95,97,100,106
122,155,168,169,182,
DOX:65
DOZEWELL:17
DRAUGHN:162
DROMGOOLE:4,8,9,10,18,21
22,42,72,76,78,79,80,81,
86,141,142,147b
DUDLEY:129,137,157,158,
162,164,170,178
DUNBAR:vi,vii,14,18,19,
20,22,28,56,59,74,87,132
180
DUNCAN:6,13,14,16,18,20,
25,27,28,38,43,75,81,98,
173,175
DUNLAP:38,44,73,75,83,104
120

DUNN:6,58,78,91,95,102,
146,152,153,167,178
DUNNING:104,
DUNNINGTON:162
DURFY:97
DUVALL:118
DYASS:52

E
EARLEY:112
EARNEST:65
EASLEY:vi,vii
EASTIN:172
EASTMAN:12
ECHOLS:61,130,176
ECKSTONE:174
EDERINGTON:37
EDGAR:112
EDWARDS:98
EFFINGER:83
EGG:5,8,9,24,39,89,124
140,141,143,156
EGGLESTON:33,57
ELDER:123,166
ELLEXSON:35
ELLEY(ELLY):96,110,128,
129,158,164,170,178
ELLIOTT:8,19,44,47,76,
99,102,104,
ELLIS:11,18,20,25,30,
35,47,62,76,85,90
ELLISON:90
ELMORE:65
EMBRY:88
EMMONS:159,160
ENDECOTT:44,72,76,78,79,
80,95,99,146
ENLOE:111
EPHRAIM:68
EPPES:147c
ERSKINE:97,115
ERWIN:73,85,101,102,
129,148,151,157,158
170
ESTERBROOKS:162
ESTES:4,19
ESTILL:168,169
EUSTIS:87
EVANS:18,28,31,44,75,76,
108,137,169
EVEMAN:175
EVERETTE:31,36
EWING:75,90

F
FAISON:119
FAKE:13,141,142,147b

FALL:25,86,98,129,138
155,167
FARR:64
FARRAR:20,21,40,59,90,
93,108,113,127
FARRELL;154
FAULK:106,
FAULKNER:42,45,55,
FAUST:70,147
FAWN:176
FEARN:115
FELLOWS:49
FELTUS:44,47,67
FERGU(E)SON:1,8,15,21,
30,31,36,52,55,56,57,
97,115,130,137,138,139
150,155,159,161,163,164
165,168,169,170,172
FERRENO:16,142
FERRIDAY:2,5,11,43,62,
69,76,87,119,132,139
FIELDS:118,119,120,127
177
FINLAY:101,103,127,138
153,156,169,172,173,177
FINNEY:67
FISCHER(FISHER):17,31,
42,43,44,98,111,135,145
FISK:3,4,8,9,21,31,33,
35,36,73,84,85,90,
FITZ:vi,vii,viii,8,25,
31,59,60,63,64,66,68,
76,80,81,
FITZPATRICK:19,43,71,
110,124
FLAHERTY:47
FLANAGAN(FLANAKIN):140
141,176
FLEMING:67,116,130,168
FLEETWOOD:2,3,5,28,33
FLEWELLYN:147c
FLOOD:67
FLOURNOY:19,22,28,31,
38,41,57,70,74,80,101,
129,147b,158,162,170,
171
FLOWERS:49,150
FLOYD:162
FLY:150
FOLK(E)S:28,31,39,47,
76,84,117,154
FOOTE:27,31,33,42,53,
90,120,122,138
FORD:4,8,23,28,31,77,
85,94,95,98,113,120,
FORE:9,119
FORTNER:13

FORSTELL:50
FORSYTH:52
FOSTER:3,6,13,14,15,19,20,
22,23,26,74,117,143
FOX:105,122,160
FRANK:114
FRANKLIN:22
FRAZER(FRAZIER);4,9,15,22
23,27,28,34,35,62,88,93,
143,156,162
FREELAND:107
FREEMAN:104,120
FRENCH:124,127,130,131,
133,137,140,143,147b,147d
172
FRICK:100
FRILEY:167
FROST:57
FULSOM:31
FULTON:26,32,36,53,54,73,
76,83,92,96,112,116,141,
146

G
GADBERRY:48
GAINES:64,65,113
GALE(YALE?)123
GALLOWAY:13,109
GAMBLE:74,76,99,105
GANDRUD:30,
GARDINER:79
GARLAND:15,31,47,54,56,71
79,108
GARMON:92
GARNER:1,
GARRETT:76,166
GARTLEY:61
GATES:14
GAY:75,90
GAYLE:71
GEAW:140
GEMMILL:58
GENTRY:66
GEOGHEGAN:176
GEORGE:145
GERVAIS:147
GESS(GIST)165
GHOLSON:130
GIBBONS:165
GIBBS:38,75,164,165
GIBSON:3,4,5,7,10,11,16,
35,37,38,42,55,56,74,97,
106,115,135,143,171
GICE:23
GIESSE(GIEFSE):137
GILBERT:1,2,10,11,22,26,
72,81,86,140,141,142,147b
147d

GILLESPIE:108,121
GILLIAM:73,74
GILMORE:19,144
GINES:15
GINET:5
GISH:80
GLASS:41,49,84
GLIDEWELL:43,146,162
GLOVER:114
GODFREY:147b,147d
GODIN:31,32
GOOCH:28
GOODE:101,105
GOODLOE:76
GOODWIN:91,147c
GORDON:1,99
GORMAN:92,93,94
GOULDING:66
GOZA:130
GRAFTON:61
GRAHAM:50
GRANT:28,124,127,128
GRAVES:11,26,147
GRAY:41,113,133,169,180
GRAYSON:30
GREANY:175
GREARES:105
GREARY:132
GREEN:17,39,47,60,106,117
143,152,157,180
GREGG:179
GREGORY:16,64,129,133,152
153,167
GRIFFI(E)N:vii,viii,9,21,
43,136,138,139,146
GRIFFING:112,121
GRIFFITH:25,107
GRIMA:42
GRIMES:28,31,80,82,91,146
GROVES:162
GRUBBS:61
GRUMBALL:64
GUETRY:144
GUIEN:51
GUIGNAIRD:84,100,135
GUION:11,47,76,94,
GUISE:147b
GUNNISON:130
GUY:147b,147d
GWATHMEY:81
GWIN:21,28,30,46,56,59

H
HADLEY:64,90,95,
HAGA(E)N:2,47,48,
HAGERMAN,121
HAKE:27

HAILE:157,181
HALBUT:154
HALEY:11,52,147
HALL:15,19,45,54,67,77,
98,145,146,27
HALLAM:143,145,147
HALLEDAY:90
HALSEY:102,178
HAMBLIN:vi,vii,viii,65
66
HAMER:36
HAMILTON:166
HAMMEDIEN:55
HAMMET(T):94,102,126,136
156,157
HAMPTON:78,98,103,111,
121,134,135,147c
HANES:105
HANEY:114
HANNA:97,148
HANSON:45
HANWAY:132,175
HARALSON:35,
HARBERSON:169
HARBICHT:127
HARBIN:8
HARDAWAY:69,98,111
HARDEMAN:52,54,61,63,89
90,105,147
HARDING:15
HARDWICK:95
HARDY:59,147c
HARING:17,22,23,25,27,
28,35,38,42,91,101
HARLAND:18,142
HARMAN:14,30,48
HARMON:18,25,27,28,43,
47,49,88,133
HARMONSON:11
HARNEY:96
HARPER:38,44,58,67,86,
113,120,124,125
HARRELSON:58
HARRIS:18,22,23,26,34,
36,45,52,68,73,78,81,
102,104,110,115,117,120
129
HARRISON,18,21,22,26,27
34,37,47,48,53,74,83,93
99,111,125
HARROW:129,132
HART:31
HARVEY:17,105,177
HARWOOD:113
HASHBARGER:14,15,55
HATCH:61,71,
HATCHER:167
HAWKINS:14

HAWKS:99,111
HAWLEY:1,2,141
HAY:58
HAYCRAFT:127,131a,134,135
137,150,153,154,155,160,
161,165,168
HAY(E)S:102,105
HAYNES:55,56,58,97,99,109
121,136,173
HAYWOOD:76
HAXALL:42
HAZZARD:95,102,109
HEARD:100,173
HEATH:69,168
HEATHMAN:108,121,165
HEBRON:39,62,106
HECFORD:147
HEITE:43
HELBURN:31
HELMS(HELLMS):38,52,164
HENDERSON:11,24,37,50,51,
84,114,135,138,173
HENDY:86,98
HENL(E)Y:16,31,33,
HENRY:67
HERALD:13,145
HERMAN:51
HERRING:9,31,35,52,73,79,
129
HERRON:66
HERRYMAN:10
HESTER:4,8,19
HICKMAN:116,125
HIGGINS:10,11,23,106,147
HIGHTOWER:148
HILBURN:31,52
HILL:8,13,28,41,47,59,63,
66,68,69,71,76,82,83,90,
97,98,99,101,102,111,118,
120,121,128,132,181
HILLIARD:61,63
HINDS:4,7,14,15,20,31,135
137
HINES:4,27,28,113,144
HODGE(S):50,120,123,124,
131c,145
HOGAN:147b,167
HOGG:10
HOLLAND:8,9,18,31,66
HOLMAN:176
HOLMES:2,82,121,170
HOLT:113,117,128,139,162
181
HOOD:2,5,8,13,18,31,33,36
50,64,75,116,119,125,126,
130,137,
HOOKER:37,42
HOOKS:108

HOOPES:17,23,28,34,35,
38,109,116
HOPKINS:50,73,113,115,118
HORD:115,117,119,136,154
HORN:69,106
HORNTHALL:175
HORWITZ:101,109
HOUGH:1,5,6,12,35,39,107
115
HOWARD:21,22,31,37,45,122
147b,147d
HOWE:107,137
HOWELL:31,98
HOY:136
HUDNALL:30
HUDSON:84,145,157
HUFF:65
HUFFMAN:25
HUFFSTICKLER:105
HUGH(E)S:6,17,25,31,35,36
43,49,50,130
HUIG:51
HUMPHREYS:13,18,21,85,90,
120,132,133,165,167,169
HUNT:3,4,7,9,12,15,16,20,
22,23,28,30,37,44,52,86,
90,92,99,103,108,133,154
157,160,161,162,170,171
HUNTER:55,97,100,143
HUNTINGTON:6,166
HUSTON:16,63
HUTCHESON:140,141
HUTCHINS:119,134
HUTCHINSON:117
HYATT:38
HYDE:3,7,8,11,12,13,56,83
HYNES:135

I
INGERSOLL:16,27,29,30,31,
33,39,48,53
INGE:101
INGRAHAM(INGRAM):25,60,64
90
IRBY:164
IRION:114,147
IRISH(IREYS):21,22,24,28,
38,41,79,87,110,111,128
IRWIN(IRVIN):1,57,114,147

J
JACK:102
JACKSON:5,7,46,51,54,59,
60,67,69,76,77,81,82,83,
84,102,115,127,146,150,
154,178

JAFFREY:118,
JAMES:6,8,9,18,21,27,
41,43,44,46,52,55,67,
77,80,81,97,98,103,104
105,108,110,111,116,118
119,122,123,127,131,132
137,144,145,146,154,157
158,159,160,172,173,178
180
JANDON:71
JANES:12,18,144
JARVIN:133,
JASPER:31,32
JEFFERSON:71,
JEFFRIES(JEFFERIES):22,
30,44,54,70,143,145,146
JELKES:37
JENKINS:9,84,142,145,
147b,147c
JETER:105
JEWELL:117
JOHNS:128
JOHNSON:7,9,12,19,31,32
34,35,47,51,55,57,58,64
73,74,76,78,79,80,81,83
85,89,90,92,96,97,101,
102,104,109,110,115,119
124,126,128,129,130,132
133,137,138,140,144,148
149,150,151,152,153,157
158,159,161,162,170,176
179
JOHNSTON:17,76,152,
JOINER(JOYNER):17,76,104
105,119,120,140,142,143
147b
JOOR(IOOR):33,40,66,67,
68,139,
JONES:1,3,5,7,10,18,20,
37,44,58,64,65,76,77,82
119,140,142,145,147b,
147c,150
JORDAN(JOURDAN):110,112
116,147,147b,147c,147d
JOSEPH:77
JUDSON:139

K
KARSNER(KARSONER);42,51
58
KATZ:113,
KAVANAUGH:55,108
KEARNEY:16,25,63,87,88
KEENE(KEINE):1,2,96,99,
110
KELLY:113
KELSO:83

KEMPE:116
KENNAN(KINNAN):5,7,12,18,
122
KEN(N)EDY:54,133,135
KER:16,30,47,
KERSHAW:38,58,72,95,101
162,178
KEY:169
KIDD:117,
KILLEM:67
KILPATRICK:5,24,31,37,52,
53,105,
KIMBALL:132
KINCHELOE(W):59,71
KING:70,119,120,121,147b
KI(E)NNEY:51,62,69,78,108
113
KIRBY:24
KIRK:100,109,110,124,126,
127,159,176
KIRKLAND:168
KLIEN(KLINE):118,131
KNOX:2,5,8,15,17,21,33,36,
60,62,76,88,89,135,142,144
147b,151,152
KOONTZ:172
KRETSCHMAR;156,177
KRINGER:2
KUKER:127
KZARS:180

L
LAC(e)Y:3,7,14,129,167
LACOSTE:35,51
LAIRD:2,4,31,52,141
LAKE:42,57,58,73,106,136
147
LAMB(E):26,31
LAMBERT:47,120
LAMBETH:31
LAMPHREY:124,
LAMPKIN:135,
LAND:6,16,124,
LANE:13,23,29,31,32,73,
113,114,126,131,140,143,
147a,147b,
LANEY:66,
LANGLEY:6,7,9,113
LaROCHE:20
LASHLEY(LASTLY):31,32,85,
104,105,125,145,147b,147c
171
LATHAM:110,131
LAVERGNE:50
LAVILLE:27,
LAWRENCE:75,123,125
LAWRENS:51

LAWSON:86,103,152,153
LAYER:87
LEA:30
LEADBETTER: 147b,147d
LEARD:13,
LEDYARD:124
LEE:2,147b,164,165,175,
LEFLORE:45
LEGRAND:45
LEOD:2
LESTER:83
LETCHFORD:181
LEWIS:23,25,29,31,66,83,
91,120,125,177,178
LEY:34,39,42,47,57,63,68
LIKENS:74,78,80,81,82,84,
91,95,98,102,105,125
LILES:4,55
LINDLE:25
LINDSAY:153,
LIONLY:106
LIPOWSKY:135
LITTLE:116
LITTLEFIELD:121
LITTLEJOHN:74,107
LITTTLER:73
LIVINGSTON:42,78,121
LOBDELL:21,31
LOFLIN:37
LOFTI(O)N:10,24,25,52,113
145,146,147b
LOLLIN:170
LONG:46,73,74,78,79,
LONGER:51
LONGLEY:12,100,145
LONSDALE:104,116,148,151
LOONEY:83
LOVE:1,22,67,142,143,169
LOVELL:134,
LOWRY:30
LUCAS:147
LUDLOW:59,82
LUNCY(LUNEY):7,144
LUSTER:54
LYNCH:117,127,132,139
LYNE:38,40,47

M
MABREY:33
MACKLIN:124
MacMURDO:69
MAGEE:73
MAGOFFIN:50
MAGRUDER:20,28
MANDERVILLE:47
MANEY:90
MANIFOLD:132,177

MANLOVE:121
MANN:41,
MARABLE:80
MARBLE:80
MARKHAM:36,76
MARLOW:38
MARNEY:140,147b
MARR:94,100,101
MARSH:121,153,180
MARSHALL:5,7,12,15,25,
36,47,50,99,105,113,
114,139
MARTIN:9,13,31,33,45,
59,69,73,79,86,89,123
125,147b,147d
MASON:21,31,33,57,59,
73,84
MATTHEW(S):2,15,19,91
102,110,140,141
MAUGHES:171
MAULDING:64
MAURY:1,87
MAXWELL:26,63
MAYES(MAY(S)):3,16,23,
26,43,47,57,70,110,
MAYER:166
MAYFIELD:6,67,84
MAYHO:147b,147d
MAYLEE:3
McAFEE:43
McALLISTER:2,3,5,7,12,
15,27,28,30,37,39,44,
58,67,81,83,88,91,93,
95,110,127,142,146,171
McANN:121
McBEE:20
McCABE:150,151
McCALEB:25,51,52,94,98
102,111,126,145,157
McCALL:120,124,
McCAMMAN:6
McCANAWAN:9
McCARROLL:55,80.86,124
McCARTY:vii,viii
McCAUGHAN:35,36,47,61,
83,169
McCAY:28,31,83,109
McCLEARY:vi,vii,viii
McCLENNAN:132
McCLOUD:55
McCONNELL:51
McCORMICK:146,
McCOY:75,
McCRACKEN:47,
McCRAY:114
McCUDDY:31,37

McCULLOUGH:6,13,16,18,19,20
27,28,36,38,43,71,75,
McCUTCHEON:37,38,45,52,62,
78,88,119
McDANGERFIELD:63
McDANIEL(S);5,8,19,
McDONALD:vi,37,
McDOUGALL:113,
McDOWELL:93
McDUFFIN:71
McELROY:118
McFADDEN:15,19,140,141,142
143,145,147b,147d
McFARLAND:176
McFATTER:101
McG(H)EE:129,167
McGREGORY:138,
McGUIRE:4,6
McGLOTHLIN(STOTHLIN):1
McHATTON:104,125,137,156
McINTOSH:147b,
McINTYRE:52,
McJENKEN(S)(GUNKIN):3,4,9,
33,
McKEE:vii,4,11,20,24,76,140
McKIERMAN:73
McKINSTRY:110
McLAURIN(LAREN):17,47
McLEMORE:3,38,45,46,
McLEOD:113,165
McMEEKIN:133,148
McMURRAN:50,91
McMURTRY:10,16,38,43,45,
52,54,60,73
McNAIRY:75
McNEILL:26,27,30,31
McNUTT:9,11,14,15,25,28,29
37,45,62,88,
McPHAIL:vi
McPHERSON:101,
McQUILLAN:141,142
MEAD:25,60
MEANEY:65
MEARS:121
MEEK:67
MEGOWAN:14
MEIGS:39,75
MEISNER:127
MELCHOIR:126,136,171
MELLEN:121
MENEFEE:54,108
MERCER:176
MERCHANT:138
MERRIWEATHER:8,147b,147c
MERRICK:18,45,53,63,
MERRITT:34,56,104
MESSINGER:49,56,82,94,107,
108,118,122,154

METCALF(E):53,102,107,126
136,143,145,147b,156,157
MIDDLETON:25,176
MILAN:27,
MILES:87
MILLER:5,7,9,10,12,15,16,
19,23,34,37,43,50,51,55,
61,65,67,70,75,78,80,85
88,97,102,104,105,107,109
113,115,132,140,142,145,
147,149,159,160,161,162
MILLIGAN:50
MILLIKEN:20,107,115,
MILLS:23,43,59,69,102,119
MILLSAPS:97,112,141,147b
MILROY:127
MIMS:113
MINOR:20,161
MINTON:4,20
MINTOWN:50
MITCHELL:17,18,20,30,68,
80,85,
MITCHUM:41,54
MIXSON:102
MOFFET(T):25,60,
MOLLYNEAUX;115
MONGE:31
MONHOLLAND:140,141
MONTGOMERY:1,3,4,5,6,7,11
12,15,29,31,32,38,41,47,
48,51,52,53,54,56,57,60,
74,83,85,86,88,94,96,100
105,109,110,119,124,126,
133,134,136,137,142,143,
144,146,147b,147d,150,161
170,
MONTROY:31
MOONEY:15,34,49
MOORE:2,3,5,26,31,33,34,
36,43,44,52,78,113,116,
117,122,123,125,143,147b
147d,173
MOREHEAD:23,99,113,126,
133,137,157
MOREHOUSE:65,66,
MORELAND:46
MORGAN:28,29,39,41,49,59
63,64,68,90,109,149,157
158,167
MORELEY:89
MORRELL:97
MORRIS(S):31,32,65,71,75,
112,143,147b,180,
MORRISON:1,29,140,147b
MORSE:1,2,34,114,147b
MORTIMER:133
MOSBY:38,99,105,127,134

MOSBY(cont.)155,156,161
171
MOSELY(MOSLEY):83,105,
134,148,159
MOSS:10,16,38,43,45,54
60,64,67
MOTHERALL:121
MOTT:93
MOUNT:164
MOYLER:142,145,147a,147d
MUIR:31,
MULHOLLEN(AN);58,76
MUND(A)Y:69,72
MUNN:67
MURDOCK:87,94,101
MURFF:179
MURPHREE:61
MURPHY:4,49,143,155,162
165
MURRAY:88,89
MURRELL:133
MURSEY:100
MUSGROVE:163
MYERS:65,126
MYLINE:84
MYRICK:147c

N
NAILOR:42,106,122,136
NANCEY:163
NEALE:105;
NEBLET(T):44,69,76,102
NEIBERT:16,19,20,29,38
43,58,74
NELSON:97,110,122,124,
131,136,156,157,161,164
167
NEWBERRY:37,67,78,
NEWCOMB(E):22,23,27,28
34,35,75,
NEWMAN:8,10,11,12,15,
19,26,30,36,54,113,124
129,131a,136,166
NEWSO(U)M:48,53,56,57,
147c
NEWTON:79
NICHOL(S):100,132,157
NICHOLSON:viii,25,147c
NOE:23,37,48
NOLAN:122
NORCROSS:99
NORFLEET:61
NORTH:108
NORTON:21,159
NUGENT:2,25,125,127,128
132,133,135,150,155,156

NUTT:49,71,76
NYE:90,122

O
OATES:37,59,71,73,88,
O'BANNON(BANION):53,164
ODILE:104
ODLE(ODEL):2,5,147b
OFFUTT:23,31,32,69,77,85,
86,94,96,98,99,101,142,147b
149,173
O'HEA:127,131b,136
OGDEN:62
OLDHAM:143
OLIVER:119
OLMSTEAD:168,172
OMAHONDRO:126
OSBORNE:70
OSWALD:97
OUSLEY:8,19
OVERALL:171
OVERMAN:41
OVERTON:31,37,42,75
OWEN:10,49,67,75

P
PACE:106,137,161
PAGE:165
PARHAM:31,32,34,41,56,76,
104,114,
PARKER:13,35,51,137
PARKS:58,63,76,98,99,111,
PAR(R)ISH:66,71,
PARSONS:83
PARTEE:83
PATRICK:49,64
PATTEN:11,33,147
PATTERSON:18,66,117,144,
166
PATTISON:88,107
PATTON:31,37,54,90,97,126
176
PAXTON:15,25,31,39,42,56,
60,62,85,88,96,101,103,113
128,132,134,139,141,178,179
181
PAYNE:64,66,67,71,78,90,97
111,166
PEACE(PEARCE-PIERCE):69,71
122,127,152,153,154
PEAK:160
PEARER:68
PECK:51,54,61,80
PEEBLES:20,26,67,71,131,
147b,147d
PEGRAM:2

PELHAM:153,177
PENDELL(PINDELL):152,153
PENNINGTON:142
PENNY:70,98,169
PENRICE:1,2,3,5,6,9,12,
18,20,41,46,48,52,60,62,
70,72,73,74,76,79,80,83,
86,90,140,141,142,144,
147b,148
PENTECOST:73
PEPPER:75
PERCY:3,16,20,29,39,40,
48,70,81,82,87,89,132,
137,138,165
PERKINS:18,26,27,49,59,
90,105,178
PERKS:121
PERRIE(PERRY):85,140
PERVIS(PURVIS):7,10,
PERSON:173
PESCOD:46,88,89
PETERS:50,93,118,149
PETERSON:140
PETIT(PETTY):134,139
PEYSTER:123
PEYTON26,31,71
PFULLY:5
PHARES:181
PHIETUS(PHETUS):132
PHELP(S):146,152,153,164
PHILBRICK:33,38
PHILBROOK:30
PHILLIPS:4,36,50,61,147c
147d,151,168
PHILLIS:145,147b
PICKENS:83,105
PICKETT:58
PIERSON:49
PINCKARD(PINCARD-PINKARD)
6,42,45,46,54,58,59,62,
89,97,111,
PINTARD:71
PLANT:31,44,146

PLANTATIONS:
Andalusia,43,59,60,64;
Ashland,132,148;Avaly,90;
Avon,174;Bachelor Bend,94
116,131c,d,132;Baconham,
49,122;Bailey Tract 58;
Ballard 161;Ball Ground
116;Basin 174;Bavataria
123;Belle Aire 128;Bel-
mont 161;Belzoni 73,84,
90;Ben Lomand 58,63;The
Black Place 92,104;Blan-
tonia 81,127,129,131a,d,
132,135;The Brown Place
93,94,100,103;Catalpa

133;Cold Springs 136;
Deerfield 151;Ditcheley
81,130,136,138;Dry
Bayou 126;Duck Pond 116;
Dunbarton 59;Edge Hill
67;Ellerslee 57,147;
Elmwood 129,133,167;
Forest Home 128,134;
Glen Allan 51,71,75,111
136,172;Glenora 92;
Granicus Place 119,126;
Greenleaf 133;Haiford
133;Highland 99;Holly
Ridge 38,43;Hollywood
62,87,129,132,138;Home
Place 164;LaGrange 157
Lake Island 128;Lammer-
moor 102,136;Liberia 69
Linden 134,135;Locust
134;Locust Grove 121;
Lofton Tract 58;Long-
wood 103,104,174;Long
Island 72,78,81,86;
Loughborough 134,155,
171;Magenta 116;Mara-
thon 133;Matilda Place
124,130,131,133;Mena-
fee Tract 79;of Mitchem,
Creath & Pinckard 54;
MontRose 157;Mosswood
130;MountBayou Tract
112;Mt.Holly 102;of Mrs.
Mary Jane Kershaw 95;
No Mistake 83;Oak Grove
159;Oak Hill 129,166;
Oakland 136;Opossum
Ridge 158;Palmetto 93;
Park 136;Pedandiere 112;
Penford 44;Percy 137,
149;Peru 76,128;Pleas-
ant Hill 59;PlumRidge
135;Prairie 116;Refuge
138;Riverside 40;Roll-
ingFork Place 68;St.
Peters 56;Scotland 100
135;Sligo 123,128,134,
181;Smith&Hood 126,130;
Solitaire 135,152;Stella
159,160;Swan Isle 129,
164;Swiftwater 136;Tom
Johnson Place 160;
Tyrone 164;Utopia 48,77
98,173;WalnutGrove 40;
WalnutHills 74,88;Wash-
ington 1;Buckner Wilson
&Co.77;Willow Glen 155;
Woodland 116;Wolf Lake
116;Woodlawn 133;Wood-

stock 134;Wyche Tract 40.

PLEASANTS:73
PLUMMER:22,26,46,56,59
POINDEXTER:11,41,46,49,81
POINTS:78
POLK:46,137,168
POLLARD:69,71
PONDER:114
POOL:8,19
POPE:37,85,181
PORT:97
PORTER:37,61,66,67,160
POSTLEWAITE:90
POTTS:24,47,49,62,169
POWELL:12,28,31,35,39,45,
47,61,67,131,137,145,146,
154,158,159,160,161,180
POWERS:142
PRATHER:41
PRATT:17,158
PRENTISS:43,71,
PRESTON:18,25,27,28,47,48
50,59,121,161
PREWITT:16,20,38,43
PRICE:25,146
PRICHETT:141
PRINCE:1,2,5,17,18,23,30,
33,85,88,89,109,140,141,
142,145,147c
PROUT:28
PRYOR:76
PUCKETT:45,47,81,139
PUGH:122
PURCELL:5,71
PUTNAM:34,98,100,113,116,
122,123,181
PYLES:48

Q
QUIN(N):30,109
QUITMAN:2,30

R
RADJESKY:174
RAFFINGTON:127
RAGAN:44,55,62
RAGLAND:33,37
RANDALL:5,7,12
RANDOLPH:41,96,99,108,111
123
RANEY:122,172
RAPALJE(RAPPLYE)20,47
RAVEN:26
RAWLINGS:16,30,71,76
RAY:119
RAYBURN:5

READ(REED-REID):23,75,94
140,141,176
READING:28,61
REDD:75,102,137,162
REDDY:154
REESE:29,94,100
REILLY:vii,37
REMY:121
REYNOLDS:2,5,6,17,18,23
31,41,146
RHODES:16
RICE:4,9,14,
RICHARDS:viii,64,68,110
RICHARDSON:45,53,65,66,
73,95,113,125,134,148
RIDDLE:44,117
RIDLEY:75
RIFE:4,5,6,7,13,14,26,
36,140,144
RIGBY:11,23,41,106,117
RIGHTON:42
RIGLEY:20
RILEY:47,143
RITCHIE(RITCHEY)44,67
RIVES(REEVES);59,68,71,75
88,117,126,131,179
ROACH:vii,12,13,84,85,94,
110,112,115,116,119,131c,
131d,132,134,86
ROBARDS:61,76,87,92,94,95
96,99
ROBB:34,108,112,128,173,
179
ROBERDS:73
ROBERTS:13,41,96,98,109,
127,131,132,147c,147d
ROBERTSON:6,15,25,35,
ROBINS:62,84
ROBINSON:17,19,21,22,25,
27,34,35,44,57,58,59,63,
87,88,97,112,118,122,128
138,168
RODES:83
RODEWELL:98,110
RODMAN:157
RODNEY:20
RODGERS(ROGERS):47,120,
124
ROLAND:91
ROLLS:140
ROOD:38,42
ROSE:4,7,10,84,118,124,
131,142,147,147c
ROSENSTOCK:180
ROSS:7,14,15,16,25,50,109
170
ROSSER:51
ROTH:95,109

ROUSE:85
ROUSEAU:84
ROUTH:20,47,62
ROWAN:18,19,68,70
ROW(E):179,180
ROWLAND(ROLAND-ROLIN)
91,92,141
ROYALL:131
ROYSE:5,
RUCKS(ROUCKS):29,36,
39,72,75,87,93,94,96,
100,101,103,113,123,
126,149,150,169
RUNDBERG:87
RUNDELL:54,80,97
RUNES:52
RUNNELS:8,21,35,45,46
RUSHING:33,66,67,145
RUSK:2,8,11,15,25,40,51,
70
RUSSELL:2,5,27,69,180
RUSSUM:17,36
RUTHERFORD:75,81
RUTLEDGE:13,36
RYAN:13,76
RYIONS:58

S
SAMUEL(S):27,43,53,96
SANDERS:72,74,101,110
111,113,176
SANDS:120,123,124
SARPHY:122
SATTERWHITE:161
SAUNDERS:67
SAVAGE:118
SAXON:35
SAYER:80
SAYLE:110
SCANLON:42
SCHLESSINGER:174
SCHMIDT:42
SCOTT:11,13,15,19,27,29,
30,33,38,40,45,47,55,64,
67,93,99,100,111,113,116,
117,131,135,142,148,164,
165,173
SEACOCK:147
SEGAR(SEQUR);110,111
SELLERS:8,59,60,64,83,93
140,160
SELIG:132
SELSER(SULSOR)1,2,10,11,
28,35,40,56,60,70,100,107
118,144
SEMMES:57
SENTOR:56

SERVIER:116
SEWARD:77
SHACKELFORD:90,111,126
SHAIFER:54,125
SHALL:96
SHANKS:3,144,145,147c
SHANNON:76,173
SHARKEY:28,31,41,44,54,110
SHARP:53,108,147c
SHEARER:74,118
SHELBY:1,9,17,21,22,66,76
78,81,88,89,92,93,95,96,
100,127,142,144,146,147c,
151,153,154,177,181
SHELTON:152
SHENACK:147c
SHEPHE(A)RD:4,11,55,106
SHERWOOD(SHAYWOOD):140
SHILLINGS:147c
SHIPP:20,23,62,
SHIRLEY:31,32,45,54,146
SHOAT:13
SHORT:147c,147 d
SHRICKL(SCHRIEF);164
SIBLEY:14
SILL(S):120,173
SIMMONS:159
SIMMS(SIMS):27,28,30,31,
33,37,38,59,88,102,103,
112,113,123,128,130,131
134,139,147c,147d,172,
173,181
SIMPSON:87
SINGLETON:147
SISSON:122
SKINNER:31,37,71,
SKIPWITH:75,112
SLAGEL:144
SLANN:40
SLATER:10,83
SLEMMONS:80,118
SLOCUM:45
SMALL:84,145,146
SMEDES:80,84,91,106,110,
115
SMITH:3,7,14,15,17,21,24,
31,32,35,39,45,53,54,55,
56,57,62,63,64,66,71,72,74
84,86,92,94,96,98,99,100,
103,104,105,106,107,115,
116,118,122,126,128,129,
130,131,137,141,147a,147c
147d,161,165,168,174,177,
180
SMITHERST:168
SMOCK:99
SMYLIE:101,131
SNODGRASS:61

SNOW:5,144,147c
SOJOURNER:140,141
SPARROW:39,64
SPELL:31,55
SPENCER:39,45,111
SPICER:37
SPIELMAN:58
SPIKES:31,33
SPRAGUE:107,116,174
STACKER:85
STAFFORD:68,71,156,175
STALYON:147c,147d
STAMPLEY:11
STAMPS:24,25,32,39,54,87
STANDEFER:42
STANFORD:36
STANTON:48
STARN:87
STARK:93
STEADMAN:24,79
STEEL(E):20,23,84,87,155
STEEN:31,54
STEENBERGER:176
STEER:146
STEEVER:40
STENLINGER:114
STEPHENS:2,10,22,31,43,89
142,144,147a,147c
STEPHENSON:5,7,34,35,51,
54
STEVENS:68,114,152,176,180
STEVENSON:101
STEWART:4,11,55,125,129,
147,147c,159
STILES:172
STINSON:175
STIRLING:125,157
STOATS:169
STOCKTON:6
STOKES:52
STONE:18,46,52,62,63,147,
147c,157,161,162,171,175,
180,147d
STORY:50
STOVALL:117
STOW:69
STOWERS:25
STRATTON:83
STRINGER:4,10,21
STRONG:42
STROTHERS:171
STUART:31,90
SUGGETT:45,55
SULLIVAN(E):35,59,64,113
SUMERALL:29,83,122
SUMMERS:24,36,61,79,113
SURGET:55

SUTTON:25,126,133,137,138
157,171
SWAINE:115
SWAN:19,112,143
SWANSON:15,16,69,71
SWARTZ:152
SWITZER:159,179

T
TACKETT:109
TALBIT:161
TALBOTT:168
TALLEY:4
TAMPLEY:168
TANNER:142
TAPPAN:59
TARPLEY:90,106
TATUM:25
TAYLOR:4,7,14,15,16,18,25
27,30,34,37,38,39,42,43,
45,46,51,54,55,57,58,60,
68,75,88,90,92,103,113,
119,124,130,142,147c,164
167,171,181
TEAGARDEN:31
TEIDEMAN:23,178
TEMPLE:65
TEMPLETON:37,39,56
TERHUIME:8
TERRELL:64
TERRY:1,30,52,94,101,102,
143,167
THACK:46
THEOBALD:33,76,81,83,85,
88,90,91,127,129,131a,131b
131c,131d,132,136,177
THOMAS:2,135,138,140,141,
142,146,177
THOMASON:43
THOMBY:23
THOMLEY:37,48,
THOMPSON:29,83,84,113,125
151,163
THOMSON:15,52,74,76,81,87
91
THORNHILL:148
THORN(S)BURY:2,147c
THORNTON:41,132
THRAICKELL:144
THRASHER:54,65,97
THRE(L)KLED:104,106
THROCKMORTON:147c
TICKBOHOMA:17
TIDWELL:6,
TILFORD:158
TINNIE:57
TODD:83

TOMPKINS:103
TOOMER:75
TORR(E)Y:115,117,121,129
TOUCHSTONE:31,52
TOWNEY:54
TOWSEY:60,84
TRABUL:75
TRADWELL:52
TRAHERN(FRAHERN):24,
TRALHORNE:147c,147d
TRASEMAN:31
TRICE:31
TRIGG:135,136,152,156,
177
TRIMBLE:5,141,147c,147d
TUCKER:11,102,111,147
TUGLER:74
TUNLOW:31
TUNSTALL(E):4,5,8,9,16,
31,141,145,147c,147d
TUPPER:124
TURNBULL:1,2,4,8,9,10,
14,19,22,24,31,35,37,40
41,43,44,50,51,52,59,63
68,76,78,79,80,86,98,106
112,124,127,140,141,142
143,145,146,147,147c,
147d,111
TURNER:vi,vii,viii,30,
139,168
TURNEY:149
TUSSELL:55
TUTTLE:85
TYLER:68,75

U
UPSERY:76
UPTON:96
URQUHART:90

V
VALLIANT:100,155,158
VANCE:126
VANCLEAVE;31,147c
VAN CLINE:31
VAN COCKELBERGHE:127,
131,133
VAN NORMAN(VANORMAN):25
126,171
VANTINE:22,23
VAUGH(A)N:49,122,138,172
VENABLE:101
VERTNER:1,2,35,61,
VICK:2,16,28,29,31,33,
34,46,58,61,69,73,89,101
112,113,114,120,152,153
154,169,

VICKERS:25,147c
VILEY:162
VINSON:79
VOGEL:104

W
WADE:10,14,54,86,147c,
147d
WAILLS:38
WAKEFIELD:173
WALBERT:30
WALCOTT:49,132,181
WALDEN:109
WALKER:9,15,19,24,28,35,
37,39,44,46,47,58,63,84,
124,146,155,170,175
WALL:36,66
WALLACE:2,9,15,18,19,70,
74,83,112,140,141,143,
144,147c
WALLER:116
WALLIS:151,156,163,164
WALTON:2,75
WALU:169
WALWORTH:59
WARD:3,5,7,9,10,16,17,19,
22,37,43,69,74,78,79,83,
85,90,101,102,103,104,106
119,120,143,149,162
WARE:20,25,27,31,33,38,48
77,81,84,117
WARFIELD:4,7,10,12,14,48,
69,70,77,92,98,99,158,159
167,168
WARREN:19,49,74,101,109,
118,122,132,149,171,181
WA(R)TERMAN:119
WASH:91
WASHINGTON:42,61,
WATSON:42,79,99,114,118
119
WATT(S):9,24,129
WAYLAND:96
WEATHERS:143
WEBB:36,147c,147d
WEISS:137
WEISINGER:93
WELC(S)H:7,10
WELLS:8,11,14,19,38,42,48
147,179
WELLES:132
WEST:8,10,33,84,106,114,
124,134,172,178
WESTON:121
WETHERBEE:177
WHEATLEY:132,133

WHEELER:139
WHICLIN:31
WHIPPLE:144
WHITE:47,49,52,63,67,68,
70,72,99,147c
WHITEHEAD:46,120
WHITFIELD:61,103,107,
WHITLOCK:97
WHITMAN:29,31,39,63,144
WHITTEN:35
WHITTINGTON:102
WICKLIFFE:84,135,147,178
WILDER:102
WILKENS(WILKINS):28,29,40
41,49,56,65,90,93,99,165
WILKERSON:2,4,7,10,11,14,
26,33,34,77,86,
WILKINSON:31,49,61,101,
125,142,147c.147d
WILLCOX:83
WILLIAMS:vi,vii,4,8,9,31,
36,54,65,66,69,71,72,73,
74,76,102,104,128,140,173
174,175,179
WILLIAMSON:vi,49
WILLIS:13,16,38,101,107,108
112,115,118,119,122,126,
152,154,171,176
WILLOUGHBY:76,99
WILMOT:132,165,179
WILSON:24,27,31,32,42,49,
59,73,77,84,134,150,154
169,175
WILTSHIRE:47
WINCHESTER:107
WING:173
WINGFIELD:117,134,179,181
WINN:122
WINPEGLER:175
WINTER(S):42,83
WITHERS:110
WITMIN:49
WITMIRE:31
WO(O)LFE:55,57,65,143
WOLFORTH:7
WOOD(S):51,72,76,84,85,108
114,115,117,140,163
WOODBURN:99,139
WOODFORK:66
WOODHOUSE:95
WOODWARD:147c,147d
WOOLFOLK:54,61,66,67,68,
70,
WORTHINGTON:2,3,4,5,6,8,
11,29,31,39,40,72,82,84,
91,94,103,117,118,119,129
130,131,137,140,141,144,

147,147c,149,158,161,164,
165,166,168,174,178,180
WREN:73,146
WRIGHT:128,137
WROTEN:52
WYCHE:14
WYNENS:1,2,10,18,20,85,89
141,143,144,145,147a

Y
YAGER:28
YARBROUGH:27
YEARGAIN:144
YEATMAN:85
YERGER:21,58,61,62,72,73,
75,87,93,95,96,97,98,100,
101,103,104,106,118,123,
124,126,131a,132,139,150,
159,160,165,166,
YOIST:3
YORK:50
YOUNG:30,95,146

www.ingramcontent.com/pod-product-compliance
Lightning Source LLC
Chambersburg PA
CBHW030550080526
44585CB00012B/331